The Finishing Touch

Publications by Charles R. Swindoll

Books:

Active Spirituality

Come Before Winter

Compassion: Showing We Care in a
Careless World

Dropping Your Guard

Encourage Me

Flying Closer to the Flame

For Those Who Hurt

The Grace Awakening

Growing Deep in the Christian Life

Growing Strong in the Seasons of Life

Growing Wise in Family Life

Hand Me Another Brick

Improving Your Serve

Killing Giants, Pulling Thorns

Laugh Again

Leadership: Influence That Inspires

Living Above the Level of Mediocrity

Living Beyond the Daily Grind,
Books 1 and 2

Living on the Ragged Edge

Make Up Your Mind

The Quest for Character

Recovery: When Healing Takes Time

Rise and Shine

Sanctity of Life

Simple Faith

Standing Out

Starting Over

Strengthening Your Grip

Stress Fractures

Strike the Original Match

The Strong Family

Three Steps Forward, Two Steps Back

Victory: A Winning Game Plan for Life

You and Your Child

Minibooks:

Abraham: A Model of Pioneer Faith

David: A Model of Pioneer Courage

Esther: A Model of Pioneer
Independence

Moses: A Model of Pioneer Vision

Nehemiah: A Model of Pioneer
Determination

Booklets:

Anger

Attitudes

Commitment

Dealing with Defiance

Demonism

Destiny

Divorce

Eternal Security

Fun Is Contagious

God's Will

Hope

Impossibilities

Integrity

Leisure

The Lonely Whine of the Top Dog

Moral Purity

Our Mediator

Peace . . . in Spite of Panic

Prayer

Sensuality

Singleness

Stress

Tongues

When Your Comfort Zone Gets the
Squeeze

Woman

The Finishing Touch

A DAILY DEVOTIONAL

Becoming God's Masterpiece

Charles R. Swindoll

WORD PUBLISHING
Dallas • London • Vancouver • Melbourne

THE FINISHING TOUCH

Copyright © 1994 by Charles R. Swindoll

Unless otherwise indicated, Scripture quotations used in this book are from the New American Standard Bible (NASB) © 1960, 1962, 1963, 1968, 1971, 1972, 1973, 1975, 1977 by The Lockman Foundation. Used by permission.

Library of Congress Cataloging-in-Publication Data

Swindoll, Charles R.
     The finishing touch : becoming God's masterpiece : a daily devo-
   tional / Charles R. Swindoll
        p. cm.
     ISBN 0-8499-0981-3 (hard) :
     ISBN 0-8499-1177-X (leather ed.)
     1. Devotional calendars. 2. Christian life—Meditations. I. Title.
   BV4911.S97   1994
   242'.2—dc20

94-28876
CIP

4 5 6 7 8 9 0 1   RRD 9 8 7 6 5 4 3 2 1

Printed in the United States of America

Contents

INTRODUCTION

We hear a great deal today about motivation, goal-setting, and developing a game plan. Much of what we read and hear is insightful and needed. And we all know that getting off the dime is often a Herculean task. Starting well is Plan A, no doubt about it.

But what we don't hear much about is finishing well. About sticking with something until it is done. About hanging tough when the excitement wanes and the crowd goes home and the fun fades. About being just as determined eight minutes into the fourth quarter as at the kickoff—when all that keeps us going is discipline and guts. As Eugene Peterson has remarked, our attention spans have been conditioned by thirty-second commercials. Our sense of reality has been flattened by thirty-page abridgements.

In our culture anything, even news about God, can be sold if it is packaged freshly; but when it loses its novelty, it goes on the garbage heap. There is a great market for religious experience in our world; there is little enthusiasm for the patient acquisition of virtue, little inclination to sign up for a long apprenticeship In what earlier generations of Christians called holiness.

Our generation toys dangerously with an "I'm getting tired, so let's just quit" mentality. And this is not limited to the spiritual realm. Dieting is a discipline, so we stay fat. Finishing school is a hassle, so we bail out. Cultivating a close relationship is painful, so we back off. Working through conflicts in a marriage is a tiring struggle, so we walk away. Sticking with an occupation is tough, so we change jobs.

The let's-just-quit mentality is upon us.

Ignace Jan Paderewski, the famous Polish pianist and statesman, was once scheduled to perform at a great concert hall in America. It was a black-tie affair—a high-society extravaganza.

Present in the audience that evening was a woman who had brought her nine-year-old son, hoping that he would be encouraged to practice the piano if he could just hear the great Paderewski at the keyboard. Weary of waiting for the concert to begin—and being there against his wishes anyway—the lad squirmed restlessly in his seat. Then, as his mother turned to talk with friends, the boy slipped out of his seat and down the aisle, strangely drawn by the ebony concert grand sitting majestic and alone at the center of the huge stage. He sat down on the tufted leather stool, placed his small hands on the black and white keys, and began to play "Chop Sticks."

Suddenly the crowd hushed, and hundreds of frowning faces turned in his direction. Irritated and embarrassed, some began to shout: "Hey, get that boy away from there!" "Where's his mother?" "Somebody stop him!"

Backstage, Paderewski heard the uproar and the sound of the simple tune. When he saw what was happening, he hurried onto the stage. Without a word to the audience, he walked up behind the lad, reached his arms around either side of him, and began to improvise a countermelody. As the two made music together, the master pianist kept whispering in the boy's ear: "Keep going. Don't quit, son. Keep on playing . . . don't stop . . . don't quit."

So it is with us. We hammer away at life, and sometimes it seems about as significant as "Chop Sticks." Then, about the time we are ready to give up, along comes the Master, who leans over and whispers: "Don't quit. Keep going," as He provides His finishing touch of grace, love, and joy at just the right moment.

Are you one of those weary pilgrims? Is the road getting long? Is hope wearing a little thin?

Don't quit. Keep on. Finish the course.

Are you discouraged? Do you wonder if you'll ever get this parenting business right? Will your hopes and dreams ever be realized? Does it seem too long a wait?

Don't give up.

Listen to the Master whispering: "He who began a good work in you will finish it until the day of Jesus Christ" (Phil. 1:6).

The
Touch
of Grace

His touch defines our lives in
every way, from the cradle to
the grave, from morning to
night, from year to year.
Whether we yield to that
touch, of course, is our
choice. But, oh, the
difference . . . .

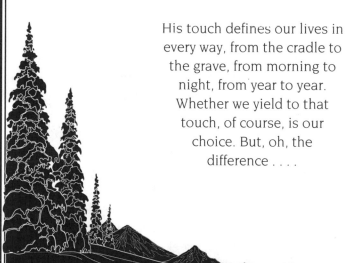

DON'T JUST SIT THERE!

An old year has completed its course. A new year is smiling at us, full to the brim with twelve months of the unknown. I feel like we're sitting on wet sand down at Laguna Beach looking west. An entire ocean of possibilities, including both sun-drenched days and a few storms with howling winds and giant waves, stretch out across the uncharted waters. If we let ourselves, we could become so afraid of the potential dangers, so safety conscious, we would miss the adventure.

That's one option, of course—becoming a beach-dwelling couch potato, someone who looks toward the horizon, entertains a few thoughts that start with "Someday . . . " or "Well, maybe . . . " and "In a year or two I'm gonna . . . " but then leans back and just keeps looking. Australia and those lovely Pacific islands would never have been discovered had everyone chosen to sit tight and stay with a sure thing. Or, what if Christopher Columbus had been content to build sand castles along the shores of Spain?

Sandwiched between January 1 and December 31 are twelve exciting, unlived months of opportunities. Challenges brought on by changes await us. We will be shoved out of our comfort zones and required to respond. We can do so positively or negatively, with hope and optimism or with resentment and pessimism. Even the familiar beach we have gotten used to is in for some changes, forcing us to leave our "spot" and accept new surroundings. If you're not careful, you'll be so preoccupied with complaining, you'll miss your golden moment to grow a little . . . to make some new discoveries.

Now, admittedly, some go a little nuts when they decide a change is needed. Larry Walters did. The 33-year-old truck driver had been sitting around doing zilch week in, week out, until boredom got the best of him. That was back in the summer of '82. He decided enough was enough; what he needed was an adventure. So, on July 2 of that year he rigged 42 helium-filled weather balloons to a Sears lawn chair in San Pedro and lifted off. Armed with a pellet gun to shoot out a few balloons should he fly too high, Walters was shocked to reach 16,000 feet rather rapidly. He wasn't the only one. Surprised pilots reported seeing "some guy in a lawn chair floating in the sky" to perplexed air-traffic controllers.

Finally, Walters had enough sense to start shooting a few balloons, which allowed him to land safely in Long Beach some 45 minutes later. The bizarre stunt got him a Timex ad as well as a guest spot on *The Tonight Show*. Ultimately, he quit his job to deliver motivational speeches. When asked why he did such a weird thing, Walters usually gave the same answer: "People ask me if I had a death wish. I tell them no, it was something I had to do . . . I couldn't just sit there."

Between doing nothing and trying something *that* ridiculous, there's a wide expanse worth probing. Whatever we choose to do, "just sitting there" isn't an option.

Think of the dozens of things God is going to teach us and the many ways we are going to see Him work in the coming year! Frankly, I have found that "my youth is renewed like an eagle" when I'm willing to change and go through needed adjustments.

Let's do it! By the end of this year we will discover that God had several wondrous things for us which we would never have known or experienced had we not accepted the challenge changes inevitably bring.

So then . . . it's up off that sand and time to take on whatever these new weeks and months will bring. The main thing to remember: Don't just sit there! But I should warn you, you will have to change . . . and that won't come easily. Mark Twain was correct when he said, "The only one who likes change is a wet baby."

A Finishing Touch: Breaking out of old, tired routines is one of the secrets of staying young and energetic.

A Daily Reading: Psalm 103

We're off! Ready or not, 364 days stretch out in front of us, full of nothing but seconds, minutes, and hours waiting to be invested with all our high hopes and new motivation.

Tops on the list for a lot of folks is attacking the age-old battle of the bulge. If you question that, just check the magazine rack and your local newspaper. They are filled with ads, fads, before-and-after pictures, and high-powered promises.

Let's face it, though: a diet that works isn't fad or fun; it's tough! I have found no way on earth to get (and stay) trim and fit without being tough on myself. In the final analysis, it isn't all that complicated: the head must rule the bod.

As concerned as I may be about our physical fitness as we enter this new year, I'm even more concerned about our spiritual fitness. I know of no Scripture that teaches we'll be weighed in before entering heaven. There'll be no angelic aerobic classes in glory (which thrills me no end). And so far as I can tell, no lo-cal celestial diet will be handed to those who pass the pearly gates (surely there'll at least be Hagen Daz strawberry). But I am forever bumping into verses that mention our appearing before the Lord for some type of spiritual accountability. That's what the "wood, hay, and straw" stuff is all about in the 1 Corinthians 3 passage.

With a new year sprawled out in front of you, what's your spiritual game plan? A good guide is Psalm 119:1–16.

You'll notice that the first eight verses affirm three absolutes: the reality of God's blessing ("How blessed . . . how blessed . . ."), the authority of God's Word ("thy precepts . . . statutes . . . commandments . . . judgments"), and the necessity of God's presence ("Do not forsake me . . . "). With that, the psalmist asks the same question all of us ask on the edge of twelve new months: How can I keep my life pure (v. 9)? What's the secret? The answer is found in the next seven verses. If you're looking for a diet that really works, you've found it!

Seek the Lord on a regular basis (v. 10). Pursue Him daily. Keep Him involved in the everyday stuff of life. Include Him in your decisions, plans, your fun times, your struggles. The key is consistency.

Treasure His truth in your heart (v. 11). Commit verses of Scripture to memory. A heart full of treasure leaves little room for trash.

Openly tell others of Him (v. 13). Something wonderful happens when we open our own lips and speak to others about how our God has changed our lives. Make this the year you make your faith known.

Rejoice and delight in God's workings (vv. 14, 16). Smile more. Let your delight shine. Laughter has numerous therapeutic benefits.

Spend more of your free moments meditating on His principles (v. 15). Think about them. Weave them into your driving time, your workouts, while waiting for an appointment, before going to sleep.

Give God your full respect (vv. 15–16). Don't hold back. Trust completely. Make this the year you dare to live by faith. When uncertain, hold His precepts in highest regard.

Forget the superficial ads and fads. Follow the Psalm 119 diet. You may not lose twenty pounds of fat, but you'll develop spiritual muscles that will make a difference. When you stand before Him at the end of the race, He won't frown and ask, "How much did you lose?" He will smile and say, "Well done! You have finished well!"

A Finishing Touch: If you don't already keep a daily journal, begin doing so now. Get yourself a notebook—any size that's comfortable for you—and start by writing down that which has spoken to your heart today. Be painfully specific.

A Daily Reading: Psalm 119:1–16

Have you noticed how many day-planners are available these days? Leatherbound, pocket-size, purse-size, briefcase-size. And then there are the time-management self-help books: how to get the most out of your year, how to increase your efficiency, how to make every moment count, how to invest your time wisely and productively.

While all those voices and handy products scream for your attention, I'd like to play devil's advocate and tell you how to waste your time. Five proven ideas come immediately to mind:

First, *worry a lot.* Start worrying early in the morning and intensify your anxiety as the day passes. Short on a supply of things to worry about? Check the newspaper or the network news. You will have enough bad news, doomsday reports, human tragedies, and late-breaking calamities to send your heart and mind churning for at least the rest of the night. Worry about your own failures and mistakes—about what you should or could have done but didn't. To add variety, worry about things you should not have done but did. Regret fuels worry in many creative ways. Worry about your weight, your marriage, your job, and the inescapable reality of aging.

Three o'clock in the morning is a great time to sweat about any of these. Hanging around negative people is another secret you won't want to forget. Remember: potential ulcers need fresh acid.

Second, make hard-and-fast predictions. Why not? Of course, you'll need to ignore that little throwaway line in the fourth chapter of James: ". . . you do not know what your life will be like tomorrow." But forget that comment and set your expectations in motion. Like so many others, be as specific as you can. For example, one month before his July 1975 disappearance, Jimmy Hoffa announced: "I don't need bodyguards."

So, go ahead . . . let those hard-and-fast predictions roll

Third, fix your attention on getting rich. You'll get a lot of innovative ideas from the secular bookshelves (I counted fourteen books on the subject last time I was in a bookstore), plus you'll fit right in with most of the hype that's pouring out of entrepreneurial seminars and high-pressure sales meetings.

Fourth, compare yourself with others. Now, here's another real time-waster. Not only will you ricochet between the extremes of arrogance and discouragement, you will also spend the time not knowing who you are.

If it's physical fitness you're into, comparing yourself with Arnold Schwarzenegger or Jane Fonda ought to keep you busy. If external beauty happens to be your thing, Tom Cruise or Mel Gibson ought to help you men, and those models they plaster on the covers of *Vogue* will do nicely for you women.

Fifth, lengthen your list of enemies. If there's one thing above all others that will keep your wheels spinning, it's perfecting your skill at the Blame Game. With a full arsenal of suspicion, paranoia, and resentment, you can waste endless evenings reveling in your feelings of hate and bitterness, stewing over those folks who have made your life miserable.

Put these five surefire suggestions in motion and you will set new records in wasting valuable time. And you can forget about all the hassles connected with being happy, efficient, productive, and contented. Within a couple months, those things won't even be on your agenda.

A Finishing Touch: All this sounds like foolish exaggeration, doesn't it? But just stop and think: How much time are you already wasting on some of these things?

A Daily Reading: James 4:13–17

A few winters ago in Stockholm, Sweden, an 84-year-old woman sat for two months on her balcony before a neighbor discovered she was dead. The woman was found sitting in a chair on her balcony, dressed in a coat and hat, her forehead leaning against the railing.

A neighbor realized something was wrong when she saw the woman sitting on her balcony around the clock, despite freezing temperatures. "I accused myself for not having seen her earlier," she said later. "I hope this dreadful story makes us better at keeping in touch with our old neighbors."

What happened in Stockholm could just as easily have happened in our town, in our neighborhood, or next door to our church, for that matter. Isolationism is not a Scandinavian phenomenon; it is a human tragedy. For fear of poking our nose in someone else's business or getting involved in something that could backfire on us, we have trained ourselves not to stop, look, or listen.

Like fast-moving cars on the freeway, we dare not concern ourselves with people in need—"Gotta keep the traffic moving." Furthermore, who hasn't read about all those crazies out there? You pull over to help and—boom! You get blown away. Yes, that can and does happen. But somewhere between prudent caution and total isolation there is some sort of measured space worth the risk. Human dignity demands it, if nothing else. People matter!

In a fast-paced world where only the fit survive, it sure is easy to feel dehumanized. Our technological age has made us more aware of our insignificance. Our suspicion that we are not loved for who we are is confirmed daily by the impersonal nature of twentieth-century living. We make a phone call and "voice mail" takes over, shuttling us from the front office to six separate secretaries, to some order clerk, to another electronic voice that spits out times and locations and schedules . . . and if you punch "#," it will start all over again! If folks are not home, you can talk to an answering machine. If you need money at 2:00 A.M., you can drop by the local ATM machine, say nothing, and receive fifty bucks. When you check out of a hotel or return a rental car, just punch in the right stuff, wait for your receipt, and split. No human contact necessary.

Machines write for us, answer phones for us, get money for us, shop for us, think for us, rent cars for us. They can even sign our letters. And the result is scary. A subtle erosion of individuality, followed by a no-touch, don't-bother-me-I'm-too-busy coldness, leading to a total absence of eyeball-to-eyeball interaction, resulting in the ultimate: more loss of human dignity. This is excused because it saves time and allows us to be more efficient and keeps us from getting hung up on knotty things like relationships and people-related concerns. They say that's healthier? NOT!

What's so healthy about becoming completely untouchable? What's so healthy about high-tech efficiency? What's so healthy about computer-generated letters from one friend to another? What's so healthy about spending the day talking to machines?

Machines can't hug you when you're grieving. Machines don't care and won't even listen when you need a sounding board. Machines never affirm you when you are low or confront you when you are wrong. When you need reassurance and hope and strength to go on, you cannot replace the essential presence of another human being.

Christ came to save *people*. Human beings with names and personalities and fingerprints and faces. Upholding human dignity is worth the effort every time.

A Finishing Touch: There's no substitute for the personal touch.
A Daily Reading: Psalm 139

Standing on the front edge of a new year is invigorating for some and a little boring for others. All those months stretching out before us hold many of the answers to today's questions. From this perspective they seem mysterious and intriguing, maybe a little frightening.

But as the winds of winter diminish and the blossoms of spring bring fragrance and fresh color to the land, we'll begin to see that most of the things that characterized our lives last year have come back this year: the good to cheer us and, unfortunately, the bad to haunt us. Funny, isn't it? We can change years, but we don't change ourselves. Annually, we encounter the same unwholesome struggles. Sure gets tiring.

> All things are wearisome . . . . That which has been is that which
> will be, and that which has been done is that which will be
> done. So, there is nothing new under the sun . . . . I have seen
> all the works which have been done under the sun, and behold,
> all is vanity (futility) and striving after wind (Eccl. 1:8–9, 14).

Sounds pretty boring to me. And terribly empty. It's supposed to, frankly. It's a description of the samey-same cycle of existence without God. Remove Him and life is reduced to a monotonous repetition of weeks, months, seasons, years, decades, and generations.

So? So what do most folks do to make all this bearable? Well, to quote a few songs of yesteryear, they "wish upon a star," they look for bluebirds flying "somewhere over the rainbow" . . . most of all, they "dream, dream, dream."

I saw this clearer than ever when I read the results of a poll commissioned by *Money* magazine to find "the American Dream." Here is a quick survey of what a sampling of fairly affluent American couples consider "the good life": 97.8% dream of having a happy home life, 72% want to live well in retirement, 71.3% want to be free of debt. 68% want to have children, 26.7% would like to retire early, and 10.7% dream of owning a late-model car.

Dreams though they may be, most are pretty commendable. Were you as surprised as I was that almost 98% longed for a happy home life? Or that over 70% would love to be debt free? What troubles me a little is that some of the dreams are simply unattainable for many, causing a list like this to discourage rather than encourage. As impressive as the stats may be, reality stares at a lot of folks and sneers, "Lot's o' luck, pal."

Invariably, a new year prompts us to make our own list of things deserving our diligent attention and pursuit. Instead of using the wish-list stats as a kick-starter into the new year, let me suggest that we work off the lists of a few men who have gone before us. Happily, there is not a discouraging or dreamy thought in any of them. And, best of all, they are attainable. And 100% wholesome.

Moses' List (Exodus 19:3–17)

Don't ever place substitute gods before the Lord your God.
Don't make an idol out of anyone or anything.
Don't take the Lord's name in vain. It is holy.
Remember to observe a Sabbath rest every week.
Honor and respect your dad and mom.
Don't murder anyone for any reason.
Never, ever commit adultery.
Don't take things that aren't yours.
Never lie or give a false impression.
Don't covet another person's mate, benefits, or belongings.

Paul's List (Galatians 5:19–23)

Stay away from the things which flesh produce, such as immorality, impurity, sensuality, idolatry, sorcery, arguments, jealousy, angry outbursts, heresies, envyings, drunkenness, and running around with the wrong crowd.

Emulate the things which the Holy Spirit produces, such as love, joy, peace, patience, kindness, goodness, faithfulness, gentleness, and self-control.

Peter's List (2 Peter 1:5–8)

Be a diligent person.
Don't waver in your faith.
Be known for uncompromising moral excellence.
Enlarge your reservoir of knowledge; keep learning.
Stay balanced; guard against extremes.
Persevere.
Make sure your godliness is free of hypocrisy.
Treat others tactfully, graciously.
Let your Christian love flow, let it flow, let it flow.

Been looking for a few hints to stimulate some New Year's resolutions? Need a little invigorating oomph? I suggest you focus more on these biblical lists rather than those earlier-mentioned temporal stats.

If you take these lists seriously, two things are certain for this year: 1) You won't be the same person you were last year, and 2) You certainly won't get bored.

A Finishing Touch: Without God, life is a monotonous repetition of weeks, months, seasons, years, decades, and generations.
A Daily Reading: Exodus 19:3–17

With prayer and thoughtfulness, spend some time thinking about the year ahead and where God may be leading you.

You may want to write down some of your conclusions below so that you can prayer about them and refer back to them from time to time in the coming year.

My List:

_____

_____

_____

_____

_____

_____

_____

_____

_____

_____

_____

_____

A New Week
of
Finishing Touches

2

MONDAY

MEMORIES ARE MADE OF THIS

During the Thanksgiving holiday a few years ago, I experienced a moving moment as I watched our younger daughter, Colleen, with her baby, Ashley Alissa, who at that time was a newborn. Colleen had nursed her back to sleep and was holding Ashley ever so tenderly, as only a mother can do. Colleen didn't see me as I stood in the shadows, thinking . . . remembering . . . reflecting.

Waves of nostalgia swept over me as I recalled another time, another place, two and a half decades earlier. It was as vivid as if it had happened last week.

In my flashback, it was I who held our darling Colleen nestled in my arms. She had been born only a month or so earlier, and her arrival had brought a fresh ray of hope and happiness to our lives. In her tiny eyes, which danced with delight, I found a reason to smile. Her chubby little hands gripped my fingers, as if saying, "I love you, Daddy . . . you're special to me."

As these reflections passed through my mind, I realized anew the profound importance of caring for the young and being sensitive to their needs. I also realized again that both require sacrifice and commitment.

There stood the young mother, who was once our little baby, in the glow of a night light . . . exhausted from too little sleep, yet committed to her baby's comfort, whispering, "I love yous" and determined to do whatever was necessary through the silent, unseen hours before dawn.

Funny, isn't it? Over the passing of time as our hair turns gray and our step slows a bit, so much more of the puzzle called "Life" quietly falls into place.

Some of that happened to me over that Thanksgiving holiday, thanks to that misty moment in the hallway when time stood still. And a baby cried. And a mother sighed. And a father-grandfather wept. And our Father-God smiled.

For many, I realize, such pleasant, nostalgic scenes of home are foreign, even nonexistent. Home was a battleground where only the fittest survived. Some of you who read this may not recall even a handful of pleasant memories springing from your original family. Perhaps you hardly knew your dad. Maybe your mom was anything but committed and sacrificial. Not until Christ found you, won you over, and entered your life, did you begin to discover what love is all about.

To you, the *church*—those folks who people the place, who reach out in compassion, who provide you a healthy and a safe environment in which to grow—has become "home" and "family" as well.

Which is a needed reminder to us that the people of faith are the only models many have to look to, to learn from, to count on. Even Jesus found a closer bond with His friends than He did with His immediate family. He went so far as to call these friends "My mother and My brothers" (Mark 3:34).

It is easy for those who have strong family ties and healthy, happy homes to forget that we are in the minority. Just think of the number of teenagers today who live in broken homes.

What can we in the church do? We can be there to help those who have no memories of parental commitment and sacrifice build new memories.

This requires commitment and sacrifice from us, no doubt about it. But, oh, isn't it worth it all?

A Finishing Touch: Think of some young person(s) in your church who has a need for a family touch. Take the opportunity to build a memory that impressionable individual will never forget.

A Daily Reading: Mark 3

Back when the world's exploding population became such a concern, we began reading prophetic warnings about a coming "identity crisis." Too many people in too little space would turn us into meaningless blips on a computer screen. Before long, all of us would be lost in the no-name jungle of credit cards, digital readouts, phone-answering machines, and the worst of all electronic curses known to humanity . . . *voice mail*!

Now, please understand . . . nobody hates impersonal service more than yours truly. But I'm beginning to question whether an "identity crisis" is really our top concern. It may be on a Top 20 list, but much higher on such a list (certainly within the top 5) is an "authenticity crisis."

I don't know whether this is in some way connected with the population explosion or whether it's high-tech fallout. All I know is that there is more sinful stuff being tolerated or covered up than ever before in my lifetime. Consider . . .

In 1991 James Patterson and Peter Kim released *The Day America Told the Truth*, a study based on an extensive opinion survey which guaranteed the anonymity of its participants. And the truth was shocking! Let me give you a brief sampling of their findings: only 13% of Americans see all Ten Commandments as binding and relevant; 91% lie regularly, both at work and in their homes; most American workers admit to goofing off for an average of seven hours—almost one whole day—per week, and half of our work force admits that they regularly call in sick when they feel perfectly well.

One particular question on the survey really grabbed me: "What are you willing to do for $10 million?" (Are you sitting down?) 25% would abandon their families; 23% would become a prostitute for a week; 7% would murder a stranger!

Now, a word of caution here. Sometimes it's easy for Christians to feel a little smug—to look down our pious noses and sigh in pharisaical tones, "I'm a Christian. I would never do that." Not so fast, my friend. You don't want to hear this, but there's not all that much difference between "us" and "them."

Two other authors, both Christians, did their own sampling of the populace and built their own embarrassing case based on hard evidence. According to their book, *Keeping Your Ethical Edge Sharp*, Doug Sherman and William Hendricks concluded that "the general ethical conduct of Christians varies only slightly from non-Christians" (with some grand exceptions, of course). Believers, they said, are almost as likely as unbelievers to do such things as falsify their income tax returns, steal from the workplace, and selectively obey the laws.

No question about it, depravity is alive and well. Non-Christians and Christians alike lie, cheat, and steal. They break their marriage vows. Hideous sins like gossip and prejudice, incest and idolatry, greed and sloth, deception and manipulation abound. And to make matters worse, they are practiced under a hypocritical cloak of secrecy. Why? Because "inauthenticity" has become the art form of the 1990s.

Want a challenge? Start modeling the truth . . . the whole truth and nothing but the truth, so help you God. Think truth. Confess truth. Face truth. Love truth. Pursue truth. Walk truth. Talk truth. Ah, that last one! That's a good place to begin. From this day forward, deliberately, consciously, and conscientiously speak the truth. Start practicing gut-level authenticity.

A Finishing Touch: Do your own honest soul search. What would you do for $10 million?

A Daily Reading: 1 Kings 2:1–4

"What is your favorite feeling?" When my sister, Luci, asked me that question recently, my brain began to click through a dozen or more possibilities. Being a person to whom feelings are extremely important, I had a tough time selecting one. Finally, I landed on "accomplishment."

She listened patiently as I told her that there is nothing quite as satisfying as crossing off the last item on my to-do list at the end of a busy day and thinking, "All done! Mission accomplished!"

Whether it's finishing my preparation for a message or completing a book or bringing needed reconciliation between two people following a conflict, the feeling of accomplishment is probably my favorite.

I have often thought of Jesus' words when He was only hours removed from the cross. He was praying, actually. And in His prayer to the Father, after doing a quick mental pass-in review, He said, "I glorified Thee on the earth, *having accomplished* the work which Thou hast given Me to do " (John 17:4).

A little over thirty-three years after His arrival in Bethlehem, there He stood in Jerusalem saying, in effect, "It's a wrap." He had done everything the Father sent Him to do . . . and in the final analysis, that's what mattered.

Oh, the satisfaction that comes from the accomplishment . . . *the accomplishment.*

Since my conversation with Luci was a dialogue, I naturally was curious about her favorite feeling. Actually, her answer was somewhat akin to mine. "My favorite feeling is relief," she said.

Now, there's another great feeling that each of us has felt wash over us like a wave of warm oil. So refreshing. So needed, especially if it has been a long time in coming.

The relief from pain by finding the right medication. The relief from financial pressure by an unexpected gift or raise or bonus. The relief from panic by finding the lost wallet. The relief from loneliness by seeing the face of a loved one. The relief from despair by hearing your once-rebellious son or daughter say, "I love you." The relief from guilt and shame by God's promise of forgiveness.

Who hasn't swallowed a big knot when entering through imagination's gate to witness the return of the prodigal son? What relief that father must have felt when he caught his first glimpse of his boy on the horizon. After such a long wait . . . through who knows how many restless nights . . . without announcement, there he stood. Stooped. Dirty. Guilty. Needy. Hungry. Broke. Ashamed. Undeserving. And what relief that son must have felt!

When wayward lad and waiting dad embraced, time stood still. Eyes that once burned in anger were soothed in tears as relief on both sides erased all fear. Ah, the relief . . . *the relief.*

Which is better, accomplishment or relief? Perhaps they belong together, like teeth in matching gears: one follows the other. After years of thinking, praying, planning, and dreaming, working to accomplish that goal, we then bask in the magnificent relief such accomplishment brings. Both feelings are heightened.

Think of the years of God's faithfulness. He saw us through one nagging obstacle after another until the objective was accomplished . . . and the relief experienced.

A Finishing Touch: We don't need more strength than the strength God gives us. We don't need more knowledge than we already have. All we need is the will to do what needs to be done.

A Daily Reading: John 17:1–8

Lists are everywhere. The sports page is full of them: lists of current teams and their standings, lists of former championships and their scores, lists of Hall of Famers, highest and lowest records, even lists of salaries of the highest-paid athletes.

Elsewhere we find lists of Academy Award winners, Pulitzer Prize winners, and beauty contest winners. The publishing world has its best-seller list, the music world its gold and platinum album lists, the financial world its Fortune 500 list. Even the religious world has its list of super churches, largest Sunday schools, biggest worship centers, or those giving most to missions.

Usually after looking over such lists, I have the same thought: Who really cares? It is doubtful that God has ever been impressed with the size of anything. His Book invariably ranks quality above quantity. As a matter of fact, He seems to delight in reminding us that His best work has always been accomplished by a remnant. That greater glory to Him takes place when victory occurs in spite of the odds. As in David vs. Goliath in the valley of Elah. Or the Hebrews vs. the Egyptians at the Red Sea. Or Gideon's few. Or Jesus' small band of disciples.

But about the time I'm ready to suggest that we ignore all lists and get back to the business of faithfulness, I come across a list in the Scriptures! Dozens of them, in fact!

For example, God not only lists the Ten Commandments that depict His holy character, He lists the things He hates to find among His creatures. Remember them? Haughty eyes, a lying tongue, hands that shed innocent blood, a heart that devises wicked plans, feet that run rapidly to evil, a false witness who utters lies, one who spreads strife among brothers (Prov. 6:16–19).

The apostle Paul helps us out by listing "the fruit of the Spirit" (Gal. 5:22–23). Elsewhere, Paul lists the gifts of the Spirit in several of his letters (Rom. 12:6–8; 1 Cor. 12:28; Eph. 4:11), Peter lists the qualities of a maturing Christian (2 Peter 1:5–8), and John lists the first-century churches that represented examples worth noting

(Rev. 2:1–3, 22). There are lists of qualifications for being an elder and also for being a deacon. There are autobiographical lists of personal sufferings and practical lists of spiritual strengths.

Lists, lists, and more lists! And since they are authored by the living Lord, we'd be wise to read and heed each one.

Believers throughout church history—the early church Fathers, the Reformers, the Puritans—have been inspired by these lists to reduce spirituality to two lists known as "the seven sins and the seven virtues" of saintliness. The former includes pride, envy, anger, sloth, avarice, gluttony, and lust. The latter includes wisdom, justice, courage, temperance, faith, love, and hope.

Even though it finds its origin in one whose life was not centered on Christ our Lord, Mahatma Gandhi's own list of "seven deadly sins" in the form of contrasts deserves our attention: Wealth without work, pleasure without conscience, knowledge without character, commerce without morality, science without humanity, worship without sacrifice, politics without principle.

Now, there's a list deserving of more than thinking over. Try carrying them out.

I dare you!

A Finishing Touch: The prophet Micah names the absolute basics "required" by the Lord. The next time you're feeling that living for God is getting too complicated, blow the dust off Micah's list: to do justice, to love kindness, to walk humbly with God.

A Daily Reading: Micah 6:8

I blew the dust off Nehemiah's journal last week. It had been a while since I had taken time to get reacquainted with the man. So, I sat down and looked over his shoulder for a couple of hours, refreshing my mind on the things he recorded during a critical segment of his life.

Jerusalem's protective wall had been destroyed when the Babylonians sacked the city and defeated the Jews. Because of this, Zion lay in ruins and there seemed to be no possibility of recovery. As decades slowly passed, a tiny glimmer of hope appeared on the horizon: someday—some glorious day—those homesick Jews would indeed be able to return.

Before they could enjoy living securely in their beloved Jerusalem, however, that wall would have to be rebuilt. That's where Nehemiah enters the picture. Even though he lived in Persia and worked in the king's palace, he became increasingly convinced that he should lead that wall-rebuilding project.

The rest is history. Once the fellow got to Jerusalem, he rallied, informed, motivated, and organized the people; then he rolled up his sleeves and dived in. Fifty-two days later, they washed off their trowels, stowed their gear, and walked away from a newly finished stone wall, including new gates hanging on iron hinges. They left all their enemies silenced and locked out . . . finally!

As I reread this account, it began to dawn on me that this book is a veritable storehouse of insights on leadership. The first six chapters, if not the entire book, qualify as Leadership 101 in God's curriculum and should be required reading for all who are in leadership or wish to be. I have found no less than seven qualities Nehemiah emulated as a leader.

First, *he had a passion for the project.* Whatever the project may be— rebuilding a wall or providing leadership for a school, chairing a board or pastoring a church, organizing a ministry or putting together a musical—passion, vision, enthusiasm, drive, and determination are absolutely essential. Nehemiah could hardly sleep as he pictured the need and imagined himself involved in the process of accomplishing the objective.

Second, he had the ability to motivate others. Without people, who needs leaders? And what good is leadership if it cannot move people to action? Leaders like Nehemiah inspire others to do their best.

Third, he had an unswerving confidence in God. Leaders who are genuinely Christian in their philosophy or style are people of prayer. While they may occasionally doubt their own ability, they do not doubt God's invincible commitment to His work. Nehemiah's journal is filled with prayers—silent ones, short ones, specific ones. He constantly reminded the people of the Lord's presence and protection.

Fourth, he was resilient and patient through opposition. From the first day when they started to mix the mortar, until the final day when the last gate was hung, critics stayed near . . . and vocal. Nehemiah endured it all—sarcasm, suspicion, gossip, mockery, threats, false accusations—you name it. None of these things moved him. He heard what was said but refused to let it sidetrack him. The best leaders have broad shoulders and have no trouble shrugging off petty offenses.

Fifth, he had a practical, balanced grip on reality. Nehemiah was no airheaded cheerleader: "You see the bad situation we are in," he said in his opening speech to the people (2:17). He had the workers stay at the job with diligence, but he also stationed others, in shifts, to guard the wall from attack. He acted without overreacting; he was gracious but unbendingly firm. Good leaders maintain that needed balance between being positive and being aware of the negative. Their heads may soar in the heavenlies, but their feet stay firmly fixed on earth's dirt.

Sixth, he had a willingness to work hard and remain unselfish. All strong Christian leaders have at least one thing in common: diligence. They know the time, but they don't watch the clock. Diligence mixed with excellence pays off, as it did with Nehemiah who was "appointed to be their governor in the land of Judah" even before the wall was done (5:14). The balance of that fifth chapter also reveals that he accepted the promotion humbly and willingly sacrificed for the good of the people. Nehemiah is a pattern of servant-hearted leadership.

Seventh, he had the discipline to finish the job. Good leaders are finishers. When the task loses its luster, they don't rush elsewhere. They stay at it "in season and out." As Nehemiah recorded, "So the wall was completed . . . in fifty-two days" (6:15). Mission accomplished!

Good leaders see things through with dispatch. And when the task is finished, they celebrate! Nehemiah and his co-workers marched and danced, they shouted and sang until their "songs of praise and hymns of thanksgiving to God" could be heard afar. What a grand party! I love it!

Good, solid Christian leaders are as much in demand today as in Nehemiah's time. Perhaps more so. The problem is not a decline in opportunities but a dearth of candidates.

A Finishing Touch: Are you in a position of leadership or being called to such a position? Think long and hard about God's requirements. If you are not in such a position, you certainly know those who are. Pray for them.

A Daily Reading: Nehemiah 1–6

And all the people gathered as one man at the square which was in front of the Water Gate, and they asked Ezra the scribe to bring the book of the law of Moses which the Lord had given to Israel. Then Ezra the priest brought the law before the assembly of men, women, and all who could listen with understanding, on the first day of the seventh month.

And he read from it before the square which was in front of the Water Gate from early morning until midday, in the presence of men and women, those who could understand; and all the people were attentive to the book of the law. . . . And Ezra opened the book in the sight of all the people for he was standing above all the people; and when he opened it, all the people stood up.

Then Ezra blessed the Lord the great God. And all the people answered, "Amen, Amen! while lifting up their hands; then they bowed low and worshiped the Lord with their faces to the ground. . . . Then Nehemiah, who was the governor, and Ezra the priest and scribe, and the Levites who taught the people said to all the people, "This day is holy to the Lord your God; do not mourn or weep." For all the people were weeping when they heard the words of the law.

Then he said to them, "Go, eat of the fat, drink of the sweet, and send portions to him who has nothing prepared; for this day is holy to our Lord. Do not be grieved, for the joy of the Lord is your strength." So the Levites calmed all the people, saying, "Be still, for the day is holy; do not be grieved" . . . . And there was great rejoicing.

And he read from the book of the law of God daily . . . .

—from *Nehemiah* 8

A FULL EMPTY NEST

As the bride and groom roared off on their shiny black-and-purple Harley-Davidson Heritage Classic, my heart skipped a beat. I waved, put my arm around Cynthia, and found myself drifting back thirty-seven years to our own wedding.

The Place: First Baptist Church in Galena Park, Texas. The Date: June 18, 1955. The Time: 8:00 P.M.

Within a matter of hours we, too, had been on our way to a lifetime of learning and growing, delights and disappointments, heartaches and laughter, and ultimately rearing a houseful of four busy kids.

Now, here we stood, watching our last child ride off into the sunset. I looked Cynthia in the eyes, wrapped her in my arms, whispered the three greatest words in the English language in her ear, and added, "Well, Hon . . . we're back where we started."

And so we are.

We started at ground zero, having never before known what it was like to be a husband or a wife. By God's grace, we discovered—and are still discovering—what that means. We started without knowing what the future held. We still don't. We started in simple faith, excited about God's leading. We're there again. If our God does not lead, we're still not interested in going. We started with hearts in tune to each other. Though young, we had no disagreement over who would have the final word. Our Lord, who had called us to become one, would remain preeminent. We started with a mutual desire to have a family and love each one with equal affection. We were determined not to let anything decrease the priority of our home— not school, not church, not the teenage years, not our own careers. We made it, all praise to His name. And we're still friends . . . still close . . . still committed.

I looked down at Cynthia and smiled. Thirty-seven years rushed between us. Our primary job of parenting was done. Our roles of hands-on mom and dad were changing. Instead of telling our four what to do or how to do it, we would be available, keep our mouths shut, be willing to wait, happy to help, quick to affirm—but definitely would not get in their way. Or control. Or preach. Or manipulate. Their lives are theirs to live, free of our presence or counsel, unless requested. For Chuck and Cynthia, it's back to where we started.

According to the book, *Passages of Marriage*, we have reached the fifth and final stage, "Transcendent Love"—"a profound and peaceful perspective toward your partner and toward life."

That sounds pretty good to me. Frankly, my wife still looks so great to me, has such depth of character, and fulfills my life so thoroughly, I get excited just thinking about cultivating this "transcendent perspective."

Our long-standing love, our museum of memories, and our track record of toughing it out through the hard times are all we need to rekindle the fires of intimacy.

A Finishing Touch: Cultivate your own transcendent perspective with the one you love. Find one way this week to rekindle the fires of intimacy.

A Daily Reading: 2 Corinthians 5:17–21

Let me be the first to tell you: Cynthia and I have a new baby. Yep, nice 'n healthy, strong body, a loud cry. Lots of fun, this kid. We haven't chosen a name yet, but we're workin' on it. Oh, did I mention that it weighs in at 750 pounds?

In case you haven't guessed it, baby is a Harley Heritage Softail Classic, black and blue, with big, bold, white sidewall tires (Harley-Davidson calls them "gangster whitewalls"!) and enough chrome to sink a small boat.

Okay, okay . . . maybe all this "motorcycle nonsense" needs a little background—especially for those of you who seldom take risks, who play your cards real close to your vest, who think people ought to "act their age," who can't wait to mail me the latest scary statistics on the dangers of riding a motorcycle, who think something like this is "beneath the dignity" of a man of the cloth (or better still, the wife of a man of the cloth).

As I watched my son and his new wife roar off after their wedding on their black-and-purple Harley, it occurred to me that this grandfather and his sweetheart of thirty-seven years could enjoy one of those too.

When I first visited the showroom and sat on one of those big machines, Cynthia didn't know whether to laugh out loud or witness to me. She compromised and hopped on behind after I winked at her (she couldn't resist). And suddenly, it was 1952 and we were cruising the back streets of Houston, roaring our way to a Milby Hill School football game. She was wearing my letterman sweater with a ballerina skirt and her red and white saddle oxfords . . . and I had a flattop with a ducktail and a black leather jacket with fringe and chrome studs.

She leaned up and whispered, "You know, I could get used to this, but do you think we ought to be here?" You must understand that our surroundings did not resemble some super-spiritual banquet or fellowship gathering. Guys and gals were hanging out, wearing T-shirts, torn jeans, black boots, and bandannas. Some had tough-looking tattoos on each arm and several sported the Marine Corps eagle, globe, and anchor. That's all I needed to see.

"Of course, honey. I'm a Marine. All I need is a pair of black jeans, leather chaps—and all you need is a tattoo, and we'll blend right in." Cynthia with a tattoo? I'm kidding, right? Yes. But not about the Harley.

What's happening, you may be asking? What on earth would possess a man of my age to start messing around with a motorcycle? What is all this about?

What's it about? It's about forgetting the ridiculous idea that every single moment in life must be grim and sober. It's about breaking another thick and brittle mold of predictability. It's about enjoying a completely different slice of life. It's about being with one of our kids in a world that is totally his turf (for a change), not mine.

It's about breaking the bondage of tunnel vision. It's about refusing to live the rest of my years playing one note on one instrument in one room; instead, I'm finding pleasure in a symphony of sounds and sights and smells. It's about stepping into a tension-free, anxiety-free world where I feel the wind and smell the wildflowers and hug my wife and laugh until I'm hoarse.

It's about freedom. That's it, plain and simple. And, bottom line . . . it's about grace.

A Finishing Touch: Have you laughed yourself hoarse recently? Have you appropriated God's grace and freedom? Listened to any jazz or full-length symphonies lately? Smelled any wildflowers? Maybe you should give yourself permission instead of worrying about who might say what.

A Daily Reading: Galatians 5:13

When the Ritz-Carlton Hotels won the Malcolm Baldrige National Quality Award, I had the opportunity to congratulate the owner of that outstanding organization, Mr. William Johnson, my good friend who lives in Atlanta, Georgia. In typical humility and his wonderful "Southern drawl," Bill gave others the credit. He added that now that they had won this prestigious honor, they would need to work even harder to earn the respect that came with it. "Quality," he said, "is a race with no finish line."

He is correct. Competitive excellence requires 100% all of the time. If you doubt that, try maintaining excellence by setting your standards at 92%. Or even 95%. People figure they're doing fine so long as they get somewhere near it. Excellence gets reduced to acceptable, and before long, acceptable doesn't seem worth the sweat if you can get by with adequate. After that, mediocrity is only a breath away.

Ever tracked the consequences of "almost but not quite"? Thanks to some fine research by Natalie Gabal, I awoke to a whole new awareness of what would happen if 99.9% were considered good enough. If that were true, then this year alone . . . 2,000,000 documents would be lost by the IRS; 12 babies would be given to the wrong parents each day; 291 pacemaker operations would be performed incorrectly; 20,000 incorrect drug prescriptions would be written; 114,500 mismatched pairs of shoes would be shipped (to cite just a few examples).

Instead of applying this negatively to the practical side of life, I'd much rather compare it positively to the theological.

Remember that forgotten word *justification*? Remember what it means? Justification is the sovereign act of God whereby He declares righteous the believing sinner while that person is still in a sinning state. He doesn't suddenly make us righteous (we still sin). He *declares* us righteous. How righteous does God declare us? He declares us 100% righteous.

When you consider how sinful, how totally depraved humanity

really is, that fact is all the more remarkable. Stop and think: Upon believing in Jesus Christ's substitutionary death and bodily resurrection, the once-lost sinner is instantly, unconditionally, and permanently "declared 100% righteous." Anything less and we are not righteous . . . we're *almost* righteous.

If we were declared 99.9% righteous, some verses would have to be rewritten. Like Isaiah 1:18, which might then read: "'Come now, and let us reason together,' says the Lord, 'Though your sins are as scarlet, they will be light pink.'"

Nonsense! The promise of sins forgiven is all or nothing. Eighty percent won't cut it . . . or 90% . . . or 99 and 44/100% . . . or 99.9%. Let's face it, 0.1% is still sinful. I mean, would you drink a gallon of water with only one tiny drop of strychnine in it? Would you feel comfortable having a surgeon cut on you who was wearing almost-sterile gloves?

When our Lord said, "It is finished," He meant "finished." The colossal ransom for sin was fully paid. He satisfied the Father's demand.

Unlike the earthly race for excellence, the universal race against sin had a finish line. Otherwise, when Jesus breathed His last breath, He would've said, "It is *almost* finished." And we would have to keep working at it, adding to something Christ didn't finish at the cross.

Let's never, ever forget that God is into "white as snow," not light pink.

A Finishing Touch: If Christ had paid 99.9% of the debt of sin, not one of us would have a chance at heaven.

A Daily Reading: Romans 4:4–5; Psalm 103

Years ago my older son, then a teenager, and I dropped by the local Hallmark gift shop to find Cynthia a card for Mother's Day. Somewhat bored with the process, Curt wandered back to the posters and soon called me to come look at one he liked. It was a picture of a boat on a very still lake at dawn. A father was sitting at one end, his son at the other, fishing. Both were smiling, obviously enjoying those leisure hours together. Two words were neatly printed at the bottom of that exquisite scene of solitude:

TAKE TIME

It got me thinking about how seldom we really take time to be with our children. Some time later, I saw a column in *Newsweek* entitled "Dear Dads, Save Your Sons," by Christopher Bacorn, a psychologist living in Boerne, Texas. I still can't shake myself free from his words.

He told about an anxious mother in her mid-thirties who came to his office with her fifteen-year-old son. His dad had left four years before, and since then the teenager had descended into alcohol, gang membership, and violence. The boy obviously hated being there, but his mother knew nowhere else to go. After attempting for thirty minutes to open the adolescent clam, Dr. Bacorn realized it was futile. In his column he wrote:

> I have come to believe that most adolescent boys can't make use of professional counseling. . . . What a boy can use, and all too often doesn't have, is the fellowship of men—at least one man who pays attention to him, who spends time with him, who admires him. A boy needs a man he can look up to. What he doesn't need is a shrink. . . . As a nation, we are racked by youth violence, overrun by gangs, guns and drugs. The great majority of youthful offenders are male, most without fathers involved in their lives in any useful way. Many have never even met their fathers.

What's become of the fathers of these boys? Where are they? Well, I can tell you where they're not. They're not at PTA meetings or piano recitals. They're not teaching Sunday school. You won't find them in the pediatrician's office, holding a sick child. . . .

Where are the fathers? They are in diners and taverns, drinking, conversing, playing pool with other men. They are on golf courses, tennis courts, in bowling alleys, fishing on lakes and rivers. They are working in their jobs, many from early morning to late at night. Some are home watching television, out mowing the lawn or tuning up the car. In short, they are everywhere except in the company of their children.

Convicting words, huh? But true. Happily there are exceptions, and maybe you're one of those dads (or moms) doing a bang-up job. But maybe you're not.

What do you do when you have a free day, a holiday, or even a few available hours? Are you tempted to fill this time with "necessary" work projects or a whole day on the links with a few of your buddies? Stop before saying yes to any of the above. Stop and ask yourself, "Why not spend some quiet time with one of my kids?" Go ahead. Circle a few dates on your Daytimer.

Before it's too late . . . take time.

A Finishing Touch: When was the last time you really spent time—real time—with your child? Make time right now to do it. Take time to rebuild a relationship.

A Daily Reading: Psalm 31

John Steinbeck's delightful little volume *Travels with Charley* fascinates me each time I read it. It tells how the author and his dog took to the highways, traveling hundreds of miles, encountering all sorts of interesting people and intriguing situations. William Least Heat Moon, of American Indian stock, wrote a similar work many years later which he titled *Blue Highways*, another casual travelogue worth reading. Fed up with shallow relationships and fast freeways, Moon was curious about life being lived beside the slow lanes across the heartland of America. He deliberately chose the back roads for his journey, the gravel-and-asphalt two-laners off the beaten path. Mixing a few black and white photos with his diarylike text, the man enables you to feel what it was like to mingle with authentic folks in places that will never make the headlines. For years Charles Kuralt did the same thing with his on-the-road camera crew as he stopped and interviewed people whom time seemed to have left behind.

I find myself charmed by that sort of thing. I like back roads, old bridges, service stations still run by mechanics in greasy overalls, banjo-pickin' bluegrass tunes, stores heated by potbelly stoves with a handful of folks sitting on stubby stools, playing dominoes . . . folks who look you in the eye as they answer slowly, smiling warmly. I even like mom-and-pop cafes where the heavyset waitress calls you "darlin'" and serves you a steaming bowl of chili, hot coffee in a thick white mug, and a slice of cornbread big enough for two; and where you can listen to a couple guys at the next table talking about bass fishin' or squirrel huntin' early that morning, or last Friday night's high school football game. Just good, country people who wouldn't have a clue about floppy disks or networking, but who wouldn't hesitate to crawl under you hood and help you find out why your battery isn't charging. To them, that's what user friendly really means.

I got a quick taste of this a few years ago when I drove our youngest son across eight states to get him settled in an apartment near a school he would be attending. We swapped turns driving his pickup, spent several nights in motels, and by the time we rolled into the last driveway, we'd covered 2569 miles. I suppose you could say it was my own "travels with Chuck" . . . and I loved every minute of it.

We had variety aplenty—sandy desert, dry cactus, mountains in the distance, snow, sleet, ice, rolling hills, cattle-covered ranch land, cypress-lined swampland, rain, wind, clear skies, and dark nights. We drove through towns we'd never heard of, over rivers we couldn't pronounce, ate at a few spots we wouldn't recommend, and stayed at a couple of places you can bet AAA doesn't include in their listing . . . and it was great.

Small talk and silence. Deep discussions and laughter. Hamburgers and Cokes, jokes and snoozes. Snow-covered prairies and hill-top vistas offered visual feasts not found in smoggy southern California or the busy streets of the Metroplex. But the best part of all? Being with my twenty-year-old son. Sharing feelings we hadn't talked about for much too long. With a 5 x 8 U-Haul behind us and nothing but miles of highway in front of us, life was distilled to stuff that mattered.

Why did I love the trip? Because I love my son. I cannot tell you the number of times I found myself overcome with nostalgia as I thought about the inescapable reality of six simple words: He is now on his own. He no longer needs his mother or me to make his decisions, to remind him to keep an obligation, to be on time, to study hard, to take this or that when he feels sick, to clean up his place. We are separated not only by 2500-plus miles, but also by a wholesome and very necessary rite of passage.

As the two of us walked together toward the airline terminal where I was to catch a return flight home, we arrived at a small sign: "Only ticketed passengers beyond this point." We stopped. He cocked his head and smiled, "Well, Dad, I guess this is it." Swallowing a knot in my throat, I answered, "Yep . . . I suppose this is it."

Suddenly he wrapped his long arms around me and whispered the words every father longs to hear from his own: "I love you, Dad." I held him tightly and recalled two decades of hugs from this boy who is now a man. I replayed childhood scenes of that little towhead and forced myself not to cling.

As my plane lifted high above the blue highways, I asked the Lord for four things: the unselfishness to release him, the vision to encourage him, the faithfulness to pray for him, and the wisdom to be there for him whenever or wherever that may be. God knows I'm willing to do whatever.

I was even willing to crawl back into that pickup when school was over and take on those same 2569 miles in the opposite direction. Only next time there'd be one spot where we definitely would not stop. The place might be quaint and the waitress might call me "darlin'" but the chili was terrible.

A Finishing Touch: Get off the freeway and travel some blue highways. You'll love the scenery. And, more importantly, you need the break.

A Daily Reading: Psalm 24

Almost always, the answer was the same. "How did your game go?" I'd ask. "Good," he would reply. "How did you do?" . . . "Good."

The response wasn't a curt put-off, nor was it a rote reaction. It was offered honestly, and almost always with enthusiasm. . . . It didn't matter if the final score was 1-0 or 100-0. It didn't matter if he had knocked home the winning run or if he had struck out every time at bat. It didn't matter if the subject was sports, or school, or family or something else.

"How were things?" . . . "Good."

He had so much perspective for a little boy. . . . Sports were like the rest of life. Taking part was what made it worthwhile. . . . Gus found happiness just in taking part.

It wasn't just sports. It was choir and student council at school. It was violin lessons. It was a birthday party at a friend's house. . . . Every day was a new day, a time for a new experience. Life was good.

But life ended for a positive and uncomplaining and involved little boy last Sunday in a fire in Silver Plume, Colorado.

There were so many things undone. We hadn't gone to get Junior Zephyrs cards for this year yet. We hadn't made our trek north to watch the dirt-track races at Erie, Colorado. . . . What we had done, though, was communicate through ten short years. And we had ended every night we were together with the same words: "I love you."

Please let me say it one more time. "Gus, I love you."

—Todd Phipers, *The Denver Post*

Three little words. Because they are often hard to say, because we so easily forget, we need to stay in practice. Todd would give everything he owns to be able to say them to Gus tonight.

A New Week
of
Finishing Touches

4

MONDAY

OUR ULTIMATE HOORAY

What gives a widow courage as she stands beside a fresh grave?

What is the ultimate hope of the handicapped, the abused, the burn victim?

How can the parents of a brain-damaged child keep from living their entire lives exhausted and demoralized?

Why would anyone who is blind or deaf or paralyzed be encouraged when they think of life beyond the grave?

How can we see past the martyrdom of some helpless hostage or devoted missionary?

Where do the thoughts of a young couple go when they finally recover from the grief of losing their baby?

When a family receives the tragic news that a little daughter was found dead or a dad was killed in a plane crash or a son overdosed on drugs, what single truth becomes their whole focus?

What is the final answer to pain, mourning, senility, insanity, terminal diseases, sudden calamities, and fatal accidents?

The answer to each of these questions is the same: *the hope of bodily resurrection.*

We draw strength from this single truth almost every day of our lives—more than we realize. It becomes the mental glue that holds our otherwise shattered thoughts together. Impossible though it may be for us to understand the details of how God is going to pull it off, we hang our hopes on fragile, threadlike thoughts that say, "Someday, He will make it right," and "Thank God, all this will change," and "When we're with Him, we shall be like Him."

More than a few times a year I look into red, swollen eyes and remind the despairing and the grieving that "There's a land that is fairer than day" where, as John promised in the Revelation, "He shall wipe away every tear . . . there shall no longer be any death . . . any mourning or crying or pain . . . there shall no longer be any curse . . . any night . . . because the Lord God shall illumine them; and they shall reign forever and ever" (21:4; 22:3, 5). Hooray for such wondrous hope!

Just imagine . . . those who are physically disabled today will one day leap in ecstatic joy. Those who spend their lives absorbed in total darkness will see every color in the spectrum of light. In fact, the very first face they will see will be the One who gives them sight!

There's nothing like the hope of resurrection to lift the agonizing spirits of the heavy-hearted. Unless, of course, it's all a cruel hoax.

That's Paul's whole point in 1 Corinthians 15. Remember how he put it? If bodily resurrection is only an empty dream, all our preaching has a hollow ring to it, our faith is worthless, the dead have perished, we are still under the condemnation of our sins, and "we are of all men most to be pitied" (vv. 14, 16, 18, 19).

But wait! That hypothetical argument hinges on a conditional presupposition . . . *if.* "If there is no resurrection of the dead. . . ." But there is! We can count on it.

But how can we know for sure, some may ask. What gives us such assurance, such unshakable confidence? All those questions have the same answer: *the fact of Christ's resurrection.*

Because He has been raised, we too shall rise! No wonder we get so excited every Easter! No wonder we hold nothing back as we smile and sing and celebrate His miraculous resurrection from the grave!

Jesus Himself promised: "I am the resurrection and the life; he who believes in Me shall live even if he dies" (John 11:25).

A Finishing Touch: Easter is a double-barreled celebration: His triumphant hurrah over agony and our ultimate hooray of ecstasy.

A Daily Reading: John 11

I must be missing something. Maybe my recent vacation has left me "a little off kilter," as my folks used to say. I don't know; perhaps I would be smart not to pick up this hot potato. But I can't seem to reconcile the conflict, and time isn't helping. It's the voodoo logic that is driving me nuts.

For the life of me, I cannot understand why Magic Johnson has suddenly been elevated from superstar to superhero. I blink, shake my head, look around for others who might be frowning in disbelief along with me, but all I hear is applause. To say that the man is living with a serious problem is certainly true; but to preset him as some sort of model for the world to respect and listen to—I'm sorry. If anything, he has lost much of the respect he once had.

Let me clarify, lest someone misunderstand me. I have been a Magic Johnson basketball fan ever since he made All-American at Michigan State. Not only was he skilled on the court, he dripped with charisma. And, boy, could he win! In a world of prima donnas, Magic was a champion without arrogance, an MVP without a peer.

And then, in one day, that love affair turned sour for some of us. We sat stunned. We couldn't believe our ears. Magic had the HIV virus! No way. It smacked of another ridiculous headline on a grocery store tabloid. But this time it was real. And to make the unbelievable hurt even more, he openly admitted that he had been promiscuous with numerous women ever since he had arrived in Los Angles. As he told *Sports Illustrated*: "The problem is that I can't pinpoint the time, the place or the woman. It's a matter of numbers. . . . I confess that after I arrived in L.A., in 1979, I did my best to accommodate as many women as I could—most of them through unprotected sex."

Will someone please point out to me how those words resulted in such an avalanche of praise and approval, admiration and sympathy? While all the world seems impressed, I am both saddened and angry. Another national hero has been caught with his pants down . . . and now suffers the consequences.

At the risk of sounding terribly severe and perhaps unsympathetic, I must remind you that God's warning came over nineteen hundred years ago and has been true ever since mankind has inhabited this old planet: "Do not be deceived, God is not mocked; for whatever a man sows, this he will also reap. For the one who sows to his own flesh shall from the flesh reap corruption" (Gal. 6:7–8).

Am I concerned over the AIDS epidemic? You bet your life I am. Do we need to warn the public and use every means possible to find ways to combat the disease? Absolutely. But let's choose a plan that makes sense. And let's address the truth rather than accommodate a lifestyle by lowering the standard.

And if we're looking for individuals who have the right to speak publicly, let's choose those who really have been victimized, like innocent folks who were given contaminated blood transfusions or the innocent children who were born with it or brokenhearted parents whose homes have been ripped apart as they helplessly watch their son or daughter die. These and others like them are the real victims of the AIDS virus. Their words will carry far more weight than some athletic fox who spent too much time in the henhouse.

A Finishing Touch: "And oftentimes, to win us to our harm, / The instruments of darkness tell us truths, / Win us with honest trifles, to betray us / In deepest consequence" (William Shakespeare).

A Daily Reading: Galatians 6:7–8

Quick now, who just won the prestigious "Woman of the World" award? She's the same one who has been the winner of the "Most Admired Woman" in the world for three consecutive years. Mother Teresa? Nope. How about former First Lady Barbara Bush or perhaps Supreme Court Justice Sandra Day O'Conner? Maybe you guessed Mrs. Thatcher of Great Britain? All wrong.

Need a few hints? Well, she is the author of six best-selling books. She is the head of a Washington D.C. based realtor's firm. She writes a syndicated column that appears in 450 daily newspapers worldwide. She consistently speaks to "standing room only" audiences. And she has been a personal confidante to presidents and heads of state for years.

She is the world's leading astrologer and "voice of prophesy," none other than Jeanne Dixon.

Among other unsolicited mailing lists, I'm also on the list of The Franklin Mint, and the latest mailing was timed perfectly—immediately after the dawning of this century's final decade. When all of us were thinking about what else? The future.

The offer? Jeanne Dixon's "Crystal Ball" . . . "intricately sculptured and crafted in a dazzling combination of pure 24-karat gold electroplate and brilliant crystal."

That's it, folks. "An heirloom work of art to enhance your home . . . and your future." In Ms. Dixon's own words, "Behold the revelation of your destiny."

What was once practiced behind closed doors and considered part hoax and part superstitious hocus-pocus is now big-time business.

But if you really desire to "behold the revelation of your destiny," stay away from "exquisite" crystal balls and sophisticated "astrological" software. Getting involved with all that will not only empty your purse, it will mess up your head.

Remember, the enemy of our souls has a field day when we take the restraints off our curiosity and plunge full-bore into the so-called mystical world. Substitute the word "demonic" for "mystical" and you won't be nearly so tempted.

If our God had wanted us to gaze into our own crystal ball or invest in computer programs offering intriguing predictions and omens, He would never have prompted James to write:

> Come now, you who say, "Today or tomorrow, we shall go to such and such a city, and spend a year there and engage in business and make a profit." Yet you do not know what your life will be like tomorrow. You are just a vapor that appears for a little while and then vanishes away. Instead you ought to say, "If the Lord wills, we shall live and also do this or that" (James 4:13–15).

I don't care if one of our former First Ladies used a seer. I don't care if some guy on Wall Street guessed right because a few planets formed a "grand trine" with Jupiter. I don't care how elegant looking a crystal ball might be in our living room. And I really don't care that Jeanne Dixon won all those awards. What I do care about is walking with God by faith now and leaving the future completely in His capable hands.

A Finishing Touch: Our problem is not needing to know the truth about tomorrow; it's needing to live the truth we know today.

A Daily Reading: James 4

Paul certainly proved himself a prophet when he wrote: "But the Spirit explicitly says that in later times some will fall away from the faith, paying attention to deceitful spirits and doctrines of demons" (1 Tim. 4:1).

And when he predicted: "But realize this, that in the last days difficult times will come. For men will be lovers of self, lovers of money, boastful, arrogant, revilers, disobedient to parents, ungrateful, unholy, unloving, irreconcilable, malicious gossips, without self-control, brutal, haters of good, treacherous, reckless, conceited, lovers of pleasure rather than lovers of God; holding to a form of godliness, although they have denied its power; and avoid such men as these" (2 Tim. 3:1–5), he foresaw exactly what would transpire.

Could he have really lived in the first century? Sounds like the twentieth to me. You would think he was walking the streets of Oakland or Cincinnati, peering out of a second-story flat in East Los Angeles, or maybe visiting a public high school in Queens, New York.

Abortions. Carjacking. Kidnapping. Robberies. Graffiti. Rape. Senseless murders. Child molestation. Wife battering. Preachers and priests who deceive . . . for years. Financial experts who secretly rip people off and never lose sleep. Deadbeat dads. Homosexuals on parade, shamelessly demonstrating their perverted life-styles. Racial slurs and multicultural prejudices. Construction workers who cut corners. Insurance frauds. Porno shops. Crack cocaine. Greedy athletes. The ugly list doesn't end.

Cynthia and I have a long-time friend who is fighting colon cancer. Following major surgery she is now undergoing extensive chemotherapy. The other day she and another woman went shopping at a mall in Fort Lauderdale. As they got out of the car, our friend was mugged. The attacker slammed her against the car, then brutally flung her to the pavement and began kicking her mercilessly— all in broad daylight. A stranger stepped in to rescue her and the attacker punched him repeatedly, breaking several of his teeth. The motive? Rape? No. Robbery? No. Carjacking? No. The police said it's a new fad . . . randomly assaulting strangers for the sadistic excitement of bringing blood and causing another human being pain.

Paul was right; "difficult times" have indeed come. In a world like ours, it is easy to get twisted. Bitter. Suspicious. To start thinking that everyone is a stalker and everything stinks. Ours is a bad, bad, world, but does that mean nothing's good? Does it mean we have run out of things for which to be grateful? No, no, a thousand times, no! Fragrant wildflowers still pop up above cesspools. Lovely art is still being created.

Bob Green, a newspaper columnist, invited his readers to look on the bright side for a change and send him some of the good things about life in America. So far, more than 50,000 things have come pouring across his desk. Things like a newborn baby's cry of life, Mr. Rogers, literacy volunteers, Special Olympics, sweet corn in August, town meetings, state fairs, and fresh blackberry cobbler.

There are thousands more. But in a cesspool society like ours, it is easy to overlook the lovely blossoms or angrily step on all the flowers. Let's do neither. Let's deliberately take time to smell the fragrance as we call to mind all the good things in a bad, bad world.

A Finishing Touch: Make you own list of "good things."
A Daily Reading: Psalm 1

Well, Colleen, my now grown-up daughter, Saturday is the big day. *The Big Day*. It's the one we have talked about, planned on, and pictured in our minds since you were just a tot, playing make-believe. Remember? I sure do. Those moments of imaginary ecstasy have spilled over into our conversation dozens (maybe even *hundreds*) of times during your twenty-three years under our roof. Wonderful dreamlike moments, which today seem terribly significant to this proud father of the bride. They are moments your mother and I will forever cherish. But come Saturday, you will trade the make-believe for the real thing. And knowing your love for reality, I have the feeling you'll never look back and wish for the way you were. The Big Day will begin, for you and Mark, the best there is.

And why not? You entered our world bubbling over with excitement and enthusiasm. With a healthy set of lungs and a little round face we couldn't help but cover with kisses, you reminded us that you wouldn't be ignored and that life was to be enjoyed, not endured. Your tiny, warm frame in our arms took the chill out of our New England existence and didn't stop doing its magic through Texas and on out to California. That voice, those eyes, the touch of your hand, your burst of laughter . . . .

Forgive me, sweetheart, but memories of yesteryear flood my mind. Take camping, for example. Listening to the rain from inside our tent, sitting around the campfire roasting marshmallows, and shooting the rapids on inner tubes. Wow! I even remember that dreadful day up at Jedediah Smith State Park when you got lost and the Swindoll search party went to work to find you. I acted cool, but deep inside I was dangerously near panic . . . couldn't bear the thought of losing you. Suddenly, after about an hour's time, you came rumbling toward us, riding shotgun in the state park pickup, sitting next to some bewildered park ranger who had been listening to you ramble and jabber. He seemed more relieved than I when he deposited you in our arms! I never told you, but that night I asked God to keep a safety net about you and never let you lose your way again. How good of Him to answer my request.

Then there were your famous parties: birthday parties, slumber parties, swimming-pool parties, school parties, cheerleader parties, graduation parties, New Year parties, all of which were incomplete without the same strange ritual: our entire front yard being covered with toilet paper. I'll never forget the time I slipped out the front door early in the morning to get the paper, following one of your crazy parties. Standing on the front porch without my glasses, I really thought it had snowed. No such luck . . . just another T.P. job.

Hasn't it been fun washing cars together? And picking out Mother's Day cards together? And getting yogurt together? And jogging together? And doing dishes together? And speaking of together, your mom and I will long remember our early-morning, coffee-sipping times where the three of us laughed and cried, probed and prayed, read to each other, listened to each other, struggled through issues, and sort of hammered out life together back on the sun porch.

Such meaningful memories. Twenty-three years of them. Seems only last week that seasoned nurse at Boston Lying-In Hospital handed you to me and I welcomed you to our family. It's hard to believe that you are now a mature woman, excited about life, hopelessly in love, and deeply committed to this man who has stolen your heart. His life, his love, his ministry, his future are now your most-cherished hopes and plans . . . and that is as it should be. The one I once held ever so closely I willingly release to him to enjoy and nurture and adore.

You're ready, he's ready . . . it's right.

You are a spiritually sensitive young woman. By bringing that quality to your marriage, your presence can only enhance your husband's devotion to Christ. You are also an encourager. Mark's years in seminary will take on new dimensions and those tough days of study won't seem nearly so hard, thanks to your affirmation and confidence. Your sense of humor will give light to otherwise dark and dismal tunnels through which the two of you must travel . . . so, whatever else you do, laugh often and prompt your man to do the same.

Both of you have a lifetime together before you, by God's grace. Enjoy every bit of it. As your Aunt Luci would say, "Savor each moment."

In only a matter of hours, *The Big Day* will arrive. We shall celebrate and sing. We shall embrace one another. The Swindolls and the Danes will become one . . . and I don't think it's an exaggeration to say the angels of heaven will sing, smile, and celebrate with us.

When the two of you slip away on Saturday evening your mother and I will step aside, arm-in-arm, and smile through tears of joy as we happily let you go to enjoy the best years of your life. At long last, your make-believe dream will be transformed from the distant sunset of childhood fantasy to the delightful sunrise of husband and wife reality.

It's okay if I miss you from time to time, isn't it?

With all my love,
Dad

A Finishing Touch: Have you ever written a letter to your son or daughter or to a special friend upon a special occasion? How about doing it now.

A Daily Reading: Psalm 45

Like apples of gold in settings of silver
Is a word spoken in right circumstances.
—Proverbs 25:11

The days, weeks, months, and years fly by so quickly. Before you know it, it's too late. Don't let those words go unspoken, unwritten, unsaid.

Like cold water to a weary soul
So is good news from a distant land.
—Proverbs 25:25

How long has it been since you have written to your parents, to your best friend, to old friends long unseen but not forgotten?

Have you ever written to your favorite teachers (school or Sunday school) and told them how much their influence has meant in your life? Can you imagine what news like that might mean to them?

A MONTH FOR LOVE

It is February. Overcast, chilly, bleak-and-barren February. If you're not into skiing the slopes, skating on ice, or singin' in the rain, there's not a lot outside to excite you. Sure was gracious of God to make it last only twenty-eight days . . . well, sometimes twenty-nine. No wonder bears hibernate at this time of year—there's not even Monday Night Football!

But wait. There is something extra special about February. Valentine's Day. Hearts 'n' flowers. Sweetheart banquets. A fresh and needed reminder that there is still a heart-shaped vacuum in the human breast that only the three most wonderful words in the English language can fill.

Don't think for a moment that such stuff is mere sentimentality. As a fellow named Smiley Blanton put it in his book many years ago, life really does boil down to Love or Perish:

Without love, hopes perish.

Without love, dreams and creativity perish.

Without love, families and churches perish.

Without love, friendships perish.

Without love, the intimacies of romance perish.

Without love, the desire to go on living can perish.

To love and to be loved is the bedrock of our existence.

But love must also flex and adapt. Rigid love is not true love. It is veiled manipulation, a conditional time bomb that explodes when frustrated. Genuine love willingly waits! It isn't pushy or demanding. While it has its limits, its boundaries are far-reaching. It neither clutches nor clings. Real love is not short-sighted, selfish, or insensitive. It detects needs and does what is best for the other person without being told.

As we read in that greatest treatise ever written on the subject: "Love is patient, love is kind, and is not jealous; love does not brag and is not arrogant, does not act unbecomingly; it does not seek its own, is not provoked, does not take into account a wrong suffered, does not rejoice in unrighteousness, but rejoices with the truth; bears . . . believes . . . hopes . . . endures all things "(1 Cor. 13:4–7).

Do I write today to a friend? Is love a dominant force in your friendship . . . or has jealousy, arrogance, or perhaps a subtle competitive spirit driven a wedge between the two of you? Love, remember, doesn't seek its own way.

Are my words being read by a husband or a wife? Does your mate know how greatly you treasure her/him? Do you tell her . . . show her? Left him a love note lately? How about a candlelight dinner? Remember when you said "I do"? This is the month to add two more words : "I *do* love you."

Those simple little words—we so easily forget to say them. We assume others know how we feel, so we hold back. Strangely, as we grow older and realize more than ever the value of those three powerful words, we say them even less!

"I LOVE YOU." Simple, single-syllable words, yet they cannot be improved upon. Nothing even comes close. They are better than "You're great." Much better than "Happy birthday!" or "Congratulations!" or "You're special." And because we don't have any guarantee we'll have each other forever, it's a good idea to say them as often as possible.

It is February. Overcast, chilly, bleak-and-barren February. But when you add love, the whole month gathers a glow about it. So— love!

———————————————————————

A Finishing Touch: Tell each one of your kids you love 'em. Don't just say, "Love ya." Say, "I love you." There's a difference. If you don't have any kids, tell your mate. If you're single, call up a close friend and say those three powerful words with feeling.

A Daily Reading: 1 Corinthians 13

We are a success-saturated society. The tell-tale signs are every-where. Each year dozens of books and magazines, scores of audio and video tapes, and hundreds of seminars offer ideas, motivation, techniques, and promises of prosperity.

Curiously, however, few ever address what it is most folks want (but seldom find) in their pursuit of success: contentment, fulfill-ment, satisfaction, and relief. On the contrary, the roads that are supposed to lead to success are not only rocky, they're maddening. As the *Executives' Digest* once reported, "The trouble with success is that the formula is the same as the one for a nervous breakdown."

And what is that? Work longer hours, push ahead, let nothing hinder your quest—not your marriage or family, not your convic-tions or conscience, not your health or friends. Be aggressive, if nec-essary mean, as you press toward the top. You gotta be smart, slick, and sly if success is the bottom line of your agenda. It's the same old fortune-fame-power-pleasure line we've been fed for decades.

At the risk of sounding ultra-simplistic, I'd like to offer some counsel that stands 180 degrees in contrast to all the above. My sug-gestions will never appear in the *Wall Street Journal* or as part of the Harvard Business School curriculum, but they do represent a phi-losophy supported in Scripture:

"You younger men, likewise, be subject to your elders; and all of you, clothe yourselves with humility toward one another, for God is opposed to the proud, but gives grace to the humble. Humble yourselves, therefore, under the mighty hand of God, that He may exalt you at the proper time, casting all your anxiety upon Him, be-cause He cares for you" (1 Peter 5:5–7).

These verses address three crucial realms related to true success: authority, attitude, and anxiety. And the best part of all is this: Fol-lowing God's directives will bring the one benefit not found in the worlds' empty promises: a deep sense of lasting satisfaction. It's what we could call the forgotten side of success.

First, submit yourself to those who are wise. Listen to their counsel, be accountable and open to their reproofs, accept their suggestions, respect their seasoned years, follow their model.

Second, humble yourself under God's mighty hand. In the Old Testament, God's hand symbolizes two things: His discipline and His deliverance. When we humble ourselves under His hand, wanting Him to grant us His kind of success in His own time and way, we willingly accept His discipline as being for our good and His glory, and we gratefully acknowledge His deliverance by whatever means He chooses. In other words, we refuse to manipulate circumstances or maneuver people or massage our own image by some promotional scheme. We let God be God.

Third, throw yourself on the mercy and care of God. Anxieties will come, count on it. Troubles and disappointments, fears and worries, leaving you weary and depressed. So, throw them back on the Lord! Cast your burdens—your anxieties—on God.

This scriptural game-plan cuts cross-grain with today's promote-yourself propaganda. But when God is in charge, both the timing and the extent of whatever success He may have in mind for you will be surprising. This does not mean there is no place for planning or goal-setting or diligence, it just means we refuse to make success our private shrine. When God is in it, we're surprised at it rather than smug about it.

Instead of spending all those hours pushing and promoting, you'll wind up with more time for friends and family. And the Lord will even grant you some time for yourself, plus a few extra hours to go fishing! Seems almost too good to be true, doesn't it? It isn't.

A Finishing Touch: Submission + Humility - Worry = God-Honoring Success with Satisfaction.

A Daily Reading: Matthew 6:24–34

There is nothing quite like the charm and personal touch conveyed by a handwritten note. Since our penmanship, like our fingerprint, is altogether unique, each curve of the letter or stroke of the pen bears its own originality. There is personality and warmth and, yes, special effort too; for, after all, it's much more efficient to click on the PC, bang out a few lines on the keyboard, and print it. But, occasionally, it's nice to think some still care enough to throw efficiency to the winds and look you right in the eye with the harmonious movement of their thoughts and fingers.

I realize that getting a big job done—I mean really big—simply isn't possible by hand. But my concern has nothing to do with mass mailings or duplicated memos in the office. I'm referring to notes and cards and handwritten letters.

To this day I remember receiving such notes and letters from my father. His handwriting came in strong rhythmic swirls, a heavy pen that at times drove the point through the paper, exaggerated commas and slashes above each "i," a determined manner in which he slammed a period at the end of each sentence. His letters revealed much more than words; there was passion mixed with beauty, not to mention color and true concern. His choice of terms yielded clear reasoning, a dash of humor, and always logical thought, but the handwriting (with a broad, bold stylus on his fountain pen) added a depth and elegance mere words typed on paper would have lacked.

While thumbing through some papers last month, I happened upon a note he had written many years ago. I ran my fingers across the back of the sheet and could still feel the indentations he had pressed into the paper. I sat alone and silent, embracing the memory of his life, thanks to the touch he permanently etched into that treasured piece of paper.

I never fail to pause over those rare occasions in Scripture when the writer mentions some facet of the actual writing of the book or letter. My imagination explodes with ideas as I picture Paul, for example, pen in hand, sitting beneath the flicker of a candle as a chilly draft blows through the room, the flow of ink, and such moving words as these being formed by his fingers: "I, Paul, write this greeting with my own hand" (Col. 4:18). "See with what large letters I am writing to you with my own hand" (Gal. 6:11). Have you forgotten that God etched into stone the original Ten Commandments with His finger (Exod. 31:18)?

To have such words typeset in a carefully preserved text is indeed a treasure. But to gaze at the actual manuscript scripted by Paul would be far better. Why? Because his handwriting would communicate a host of valuable things that can't be duplicated or detected in type.

Remember that when your child struggles and fusses while learning penmanship and you're tempted to shrug, "Why sweat it? The future won't leave much room for handwriting." Remember that when you open your stack of impersonal, computer-generated mail this week. Remember that when you go through a time of celebration or pain or loss . . . and someone takes the time to send a handwritten note that means more to you than words could describe.

Let's not allow the speed and efficiency of our high-tech society to crowd out the personal touch. The meaning and expression your fingers add to your words is worth all the effort, regardless of how poor your penmanship may be. If you care enough to write out your thoughts, others will care enough to decipher your handwriting.

A Finishing Touch: Take the time to write out in longhand your words to a friend.

A Daily Reading: Read through the greetings and closings of the apostle Paul's letters to the churches in the New Testament, noting his tone of warmth and concern.

A few things in life are absolutely tragic. Some things are mysteriously strange. Many things, however, are just plain funny.

Maybe I'm weird or something, but there are few days that pass in which I fail to see or hear or perhaps read something that makes me smile. And since laughter is such a needed and effective therapy, I'm grateful that God dispenses this divine medication so frequently. It's also a balm, taking some of the sting out of the painful stuff we wade through on a daily basis. Thus, I find myself looking for things to lighten my load.

Rules, regulations, and statutes aren't meant to be amusing, but sometimes they are. Maybe it's because they are supposed to be so all-fired serious that I find some of them downright hilarious. Some examples?

A San Francisco ordinance forbids the reuse of confetti. In Danville, Pennsylvania, "fire hydrants must be checked one hour before all fires." In Seattle, it is illegal to carry a concealed weapon of more than six feet in length. An Oklahoma law states that a driver of "any vehicle involved in an accident resulting in death shall immediately stop . . . and give his name and address to the person struck." A piece of noise-abatement legislation was passed in the village of Lakefield, Ontario, which permits birds to sing for thirty minutes during the day and fifteen minutes at night.

Religious stuff can also bring a few laughs to the surface. I freely admit, I find some church architecture funny. Correction, I find a lot of it funny. The same could be said for the "business" side of things. I occasionally have to bite my lip when I'm in an ultra-somber meeting and begin to look at the faces in the room. Some of them—and some of the remarks being made—are borderline hilarious. It's not that I make light of those things; I simply find humor in them.

Furthermore, we preachers are an incredibly funny lot. And when I study the faces and read of the lives and lifestyles of the pulpiteers of yesteryear, I confess, I often chuckle. Many of them—deep down—were wild 'n' crazy characters. And it was that which freed them to minster so effectively.

Such humor is not making jokes out of life, it's recognizing the ones that are there.

Now, I'm not suggesting that everybody start reading the comics or watch all those mindless sitcoms (frankly, most of them aren't even amusing) or tell a lot of silly jokes to each other. That's external, superficial, and shallow. I'm suggesting a project far more significant: developing a lighter heart that comes from a confidence in the living God, the loving Creator, the sovereign Lord who gave us humor and smiles every time we enjoy His gift.

In the insightful words of Elton Trueblood:

> The Christian is joyful, not because he is blind to injustice and suffering, but because he is convinced that these, in the light of the divine sovereignty, are never ultimate . . . the humor of the Christian is not a way of denying the tears, but rather a way of affirming something which is deeper than tears.

Yes, a few things in life are absolutely tragic, no question about it. First among them, a joyless Christian.

A Finishing Touch: A truly cheerful face comes from a joyful heart, not from a lack of concern for life's tragedies.

A Daily Reading: Proverbs 15:13,15; 17:22

Back when I was in grade school, it was always a special treat when the teacher gave the class permission to do something unusual.

I remember one hot and humid Houston afternoon when she gave everyone permission to go barefoot after lunch. We got to pull off our socks, stick 'em in our sneakers, and wiggle our toes all we wanted to. During the afternoon recess that extra freedom added great speed to our softball game on the playground.

During my years in the Corps, there were a few times when memos read "Permission Granted" and everybody cheered. Like the time when our Third Division band on Okinawa played late into the night at General Shoup's dress-blues ball . . . and Captain Birch gave us the next two full days off. Nice surprise!

As I look back on the times in my life when someone in authority gave permission to do the unexpected, I cannot recall even once when it wasn't accepted unanimously and enjoyed to the fullest. Nobody in our fifth-grade class even thought of keeping their shoes on during that 90-plus-degree afternoon. Guys and gals alike were barefoot in thirty seconds. And not a single Marine asked the captain if he could go ahead and work those two days. We're talking instant acceptance and total enjoyment. All it took were those two wonderful words, "Permission granted."

Isn't it strange then, now that you and I are grown and have become Christians, how reluctant we are to give ourselves permission to do . . . to think . . . to say . . . to buy and enjoy . . . or to be different and not worry about who may say what?

Even though our God has graciously granted us permission to be free, to have liberty, to break the chains of rigidity, and to enjoy so much of this life, many in His family seldom give themselves permission.

So many use such strange reasoning: "I mean, after all, what would people say?" or "Well, I wasn't raised to enjoy life; I was taught to be more conservative, more responsible and serious than that."

So goes the persuasion of an oversensitive conscience trained in the school of negativism.

Tragic. No, worse than that, it is downright unbiblical.

Have we forgotten the promise, " . . . where the Spirit of the Lord is, there is liberty" (2 Cor. 3:17)? Let that sink in.

Paul jumped all over the Galatians for allowing a handful of legalistic Judaizers to invade their lives and clip their wings. Remember his rebuke?

> You foolish Galatians, who has bewitched you. . . ? Having begun by the Spirit, are you now being perfected by the flesh? . . . It was for freedom that Christ set us free; therefore keep standing firm and do not be subject again to a yoke of slavery. . . . For you were called to freedom, brethren . . . (Gal. 3:1, 3; 5:1, 13).

In other words, "Permission granted." Enjoy! Be who you are. Give yourself the O.K. to break the mold and exercise your God-given freedom.

It may take awhile. And you will have to train yourself to care less and less about what a few may say. It will help if you'll remind yourself when they criticize you that they simply want you to be as miserable as they are. Since they cannot give themselves permission, who do you think you are to get away with that? If you keep that maverick thought in mind, it'll help you soar like an eagle instead of standing around with all the turkeys.

Do you know your biggest hurdle? You. It's giving yourself permission, plain and simple. If you fail to press on while the light is green, you will spend so much of your life in the amber zone waiting for "just the right moment" or "a time when most people will understand" that you will find yourself on your death bed surrounded by regrets.

God, in grace, has purchased you from bondage. Christ has literally set you free. The Spirit of the Lord has provided long-awaited liberty.

Give yourself permission to lift those wings and feel the exhilaration of a soaring life-style.

A Finishing Touch: Allow the green light of grace to shine brighter than the amber light of caution or the red light of don't.

A Daily Reading: Galatians 1:6–10

A bazaar was held in a village in northern India. Everyone brought his wares to trade and sell. One old farmer brought in a whole covey of quail. He had tied a string around one leg of each bird. The other ends of all the strings were tied to a ring which fit loosely over a central stick. He had taught the quail to walk dolefully in a circle, around and around, like mules at a sugarcane mill. Nobody seemed interested in buying the birds until a devout Brahman came along. He believed in the Hindu idea of respect for all life, so his heart of compassion went out to those poor little creatures walking in their monotonous circles.

"I want to buy them all," he told the merchant, who was elated. After receiving the money, he was surprised to hear the buyer say, "Now, I want you to set them all free."

"What's that, sir?"

"You heard me. Cut the strings from their legs and turn them loose. Set them all free!"

With a shrug, the old farmer bent down and snipped the strings off the quail. They were freed, at last. What happened? The birds simply continued marching around and around in a circle. Finally, the man had to shoo them off. But even when they landed some distance away, they resumed their predictable march. Free, unfettered, released . . . yet they kept going around in circles as if still tied.

Until you give yourself permission to be the unique person God made you to be . . . and to do the unpredictable things grace allows you to do . . . you will be like that covey of quail, marching around in vicious circles of fear, timidity, and boredom.

Since the strings have been cut, it's time to stop marching and start flying.

A New Week
of
Finishing Touches

6

MONDAY

A NECESSARY CHANGE

There is a sign along an Alaskan highway that has brought a smile to many a motorist:

CHOOSE YOUR RUT CAREFULLY . . .

YOU'LL BE IN IT FOR THE NEXT 150 MILES

Author Henri Nouwen, in his book *In the Name of Jesus*, admits to being in one for well over twenty years. Judging from externals, he had it made; the University of Notre Dame, Yale, and Harvard were on his resume . . . not too shabby. And his field of study was equally impressive: theology mixed with courses in pastoral psychology and Christian spirituality. Nothing wrong with that, but the rut got so deep he began to churn internally. Listen to his honest admission:

> As I entered into my fifties and was able to realize the unlikelihood of doubling my years, I came face to face with the simple question, "Did becoming older bring me closer to Jesus?" After twenty-five years of priesthood, I found myself praying poorly, living somewhat isolated from other people, and very much preoccupied with burning issues. . . . something inside was telling me that my success was putting my own soul in danger. . . . I woke up one day with the realization that I was living in a very dark place and that the term "burnout" was a convenient psychological translation for a spiritual death.

Nouwen asked the Lord to show him where He wanted him to go and he would follow, "but please be clear and unambiguous about it!" Well, God was. The Lord made it clear to him that he should leave his prestigious role as a distinguished professor at an Ivy League university and join the L'Arche communities for mentally handicapped people.

In Nouwen's own words: "God said, 'Go and live among the poor in spirit, and they will heal you.'" So he did.

70

The lessons awaiting Nouwen were numerous: some painful, a few humiliating, but all of them necessary. Slowly, almost imperceptibly, he experienced a change deep within his own being. The master teacher learned to be the humble servant . . . the self-confident, proud individualist became a compassionate, caring friend.

Most of us have no idea how deeply entrenched we are in the rut of routine. Externally, everything looks fine. Our activities often revolve around the church and Christian friends we love. We have meetings to attend, lessons to prepare, rehearsals to make, and songs to sing. Who can criticize any of that? After all, there is a big job to get done "and the laborers are few." Faithfulness is a big part of Christian maturity, no question.

Unfortunately, this rut of religious activity can numb our souls, until we find ourselves in need of spiritual refreshment—a fresh touch from God, who works to create His masterpiece within us. Frequently we feel this during the waning weeks of winter.

It's then that we need to slow down, pull out of that rut, and take a different path. Sometimes this means just getting away from it all—literally—to a place where there are no demands on your time, where you can find spiritual renewal. Perhaps a weekend retreat sponsored by your church or a week by the lake where you can take long walks, spend time with a close-knit group of family or friends—and, most importantly, with the Lord. Slow down, be quiet, watch the squirrels, gaze at a sunset, and think through your life.

GET OUT OF YOUR RUT;

IT'LL MAKE A DIFFERENCE FOR THE REST OF YOUR LIFE

A Finishing Touch: Filter out the essentials from the incidentals and reestablish your walk with Christ.

A Daily Reading: Psalm 121

Duffy Daugherty, the colorful Michigan State football coach in years past, used to say that you needed only three bones to journey successfully through life: a wish bone, to dream on . . . a back bone, for strength and courage to get through the tough times . . . and a funny bone, to laugh at life along the way. Not bad advice.

When I think of these three bones, the Apostle Paul immediately springs to mind. Though under arrest and facing an uncertain tomorrow, his wish bone was in healthy shape. His dream of spreading the Gospel far and wide was being realized.

> Now I want you to know, brethren, that my circumstances have turned out for the greater progress of the gospel, so that my imprisonment in the cause of Christ has become well known throughout the whole praetorian guard and to everyone else, and that most of the brethren, trusting in the Lord because of my imprisonment, have far more courage to speak the word of God without fear (Phil. 1:12–14).

The man was shackled, but not the message! Instead of throwing a pity party and whining about his unfair circumstances, he tracked his dream and realized God was making another of His famous backdoor deliveries.

How about Paul's backbone? Need I repeat the dark side of his resumé?

> Five times I received from the Jews thirty-nine lashes. Three times I was beaten with rods, once I was stoned, three times I was shipwrecked, a night and a day I have spent in the deep. I have been on frequent journeys, in dangers from rivers, dangers from robbers, dangers from my countrymen, dangers from the Gentiles, dangers in the city, dangers in the wilderness, dangers on the sea, dangers among false brethren; I have been in labor and hardship, through many sleepless nights, in hunger

and thirst, often without food, in cold and exposure. Apart from such external things, there is the daily pressure upon me of concern for all the churches (2 Cor. 11:24–28).

Curiously, though, all this did not embitter or sour the Apostle of Grace. His funny bone stayed intact. In fact, it was well exercised. No other writer of Scripture mentions joy or rejoicing more often. Remember when he and Silas were seized by a hostile mob, dragged into a public marketplace, beaten mercilessly, then dumped into a dungeon with their feet fastened in stocks? As you may recall, it was around midnight at the end of that same day, while their sores were oozing and their bruises throbbing, that he and Silas were praying and singing a few duets of praise (Acts 16:19–25).

What exceptional dreams . . . what relentless courage . . . what contagious joy!

The church—the universal body of Christ—is still being built. The ranks of the faithful are still being filled. History is still being written. And we're still on the journey from here to eternity. The destination's sure for the Christian, but the trip isn't easy.

Dream big . . . don't let anybody or anything break your *wish bone*. Stay strong, full of faith, and courageous . . . keep that *back bone* straight. And along the way, don't forget to laugh and enjoy the journey.

A Finishing Touch: Your *funny bone* isn't merely a nice option; it's part of your survival gear for the trip to glory.

A Daily Reading: Acts 16:19–25

Storm clouds gather. Problem is, they're the wrong kind. We need rain desperately, but these clouds hold no rain. We need refreshment and renewal, a kind of inner relief. Like you feel when a sudden cloud cover blocks the burning rays of the sun and blows a cool breeze across the back of your neck. But the storm clouds I refer to bring no such relief.

These clouds are depressing, not unlike the kind Winston Churchill described in his first (of six) volumes on World War II, which he published in March of 1948 on the heels of that awful conflict. Interestingly, he titled that initial volume, *The Gathering Storm*. I cannot forget his terse, apt description of those months prior to the Nazi blitzkrieg which ultimately leveled much of London: "the future was heavy with foreboding." Then, in eloquent brevity, the Prime Minister remembered the Fuhrer's coming into power: " . . . mighty forces were adrift; the void was open, and into that void after a pause there strode a maniac of ferocious genius, the repository and expression of the most virulent hatreds that have ever corroded the human breast—Corporal Hitler. "

Around the world today, men with similar traits direct their power-hungry dictatorships or uprisings with the same illogical sadism and cruel determination. What will happen next is anybody's guess, which only darkens the harsh clouds about us.

Storm clouds without rain. War clouds without relief.

Then there's the ever-present gloom-and-doom economy. News of vast industry cutbacks, rising unemployment rates, and all the exaggerated gossip that swirls around business lunches and nightly telecasts spread an atmosphere of grim pessimism as we focus on our own "foreboding future."

Such clouds not only cast ominous shadows of uneasiness, they breed pessimism. And unless I miss my guess, many of you are paying more attention to the bad news according to CNN than you are to the Good News according to Christ Jesus, our Lord. You're better students of world geography, public polls, and the *Wall Street*

Journal's analysis of our times than you are of God's sovereign hand in world affairs and His prophetic plan.

Lest you forget, He is still in charge. As the prophet Nahum stated so confidently: "The Lord is slow to anger and great in power; the Lord will not leave the guilty unpunished. His way is in the whirlwind and the storm, and clouds are the dust of his feet" (Nah. 1:3 NIV).

Stop. Read that again, only more slowly this time.

When God is in clear focus, His powerful presence eclipses our fears. The clouds become nothing more than "the dust of His feet."

Seeing above the clouds won't just happen, however. Not as long as we keep feeding our minds on daily doses of media madness and political pessimism. We need to release our fears and refresh our souls as we spend time in the quiet presence of the living Lord.

When we do, we are then able to get on with life with a lighter heart, better sight, and calmer spirit. We discover again how beautifully the truth sets us free.

I can't promise that the clouds will be gone, but I can assure you, you won't be the same. Gathering storm clouds don't change overnight . . . but by learning to see above them, you'll change. And in the final analysis, that's what counts, isn't it? Not removing the clouds, but seeing above them.

A Finishing Touch: When we have God in clear focus, His powerful presence eclipses our fears.

A Daily Reading: Nahum 1

While cleaning out my study at home last Monday, I came across a book I had read about five or six years ago. It's one of those volumes that stays with you—resourceful, insightful, and timeless. The sections I had underscored brought back memories. One particular line about halfway through the book jumped off the page. Somehow I had forgotten the statement, even though it was highlighted in red:

> A time to be careful is when one reaches his goals. The easiest period in a crisis situation is actually the battle itself. The most difficult period is the period of indecision—whether to fight or run away. And the most dangerous period is the aftermath. It is then, with all his resources spent and his guard down, that an individual must watch out for dulled reactions and faulty judgment.

It was that opening line that spoke with fresh realism: "A time to be careful is when one reaches his goals." In other words, vulnerability accompanies achievement. After the long haul, energy drained, dreams realized, enthusiasm peaked, desire accomplished—watch out!

Maybe that is the best explanation for the rarity of repeating champions. Back in the mid-1980s, the Chicago Bears cleaned everyone's plow. They had the goods—a maverick quarterback, an unstoppable all-pro defensive end, a crew of head-hunting linebackers, a straight-thinking, tough-minded coach, a fleet running back who had gained more yardage in his career than any other player in the history of the game. They won it all. The Windy City had waited so long, many were sure their team had what it took to do a repeat performance. How wrong they were! Before the taste of victory became stale, the erosion of self-destruction was underway.

What happens in sports can happen as readily in a ministry. During the difficult years, the watchword is survival and the battle cry is sacrifice. Hard times bind people together. Goals are set. Prayers are offered. Every week is a new adventure in faith. By and by, the pieces fall into place and the goals are finally reached. It is there—on the perilous pinnacle of accomplishment—that the adversary lurks with his corrupting influence.

The same can happen to an individual. My thoughts return to the man whose heart followed hard after God. Though as a boy he never sought the limelight, God began early to shape him into a king. Jesse's youngest son preferred the rugged solitude of the wilderness . . . but Jehovah's plan was that he occupy the throne of Israel. Years of hardship and humiliation under Saul's incessant assault preceded his promotion. Even when he became the king, the thirty-year-old monarch conducted himself with unselfish, untarnished integrity. The nation flourished because David's magnificent obsession was the glory of God—nothing more, nothing less, nothing else.

Then came that infamous day in early spring—the morning David chose to sleep in rather than accompany his men to battle. Who knows why? Could it be that his impressive record of successes made him soft? Only a brief spell of passionate indulgence, yet it changed everything. His peace vanished. His character blasted irretrievably. His family life destroyed.

Alas, he was not the last to fall prey to the peril of past victories. The paths of history are strewn with the litter of heroes who forgot to walk carefully along the narrow ledges of the heights. How are the mighty fallen!

A Finishing Touch: Are you dwelling in the comfortable land of accomplished dreams? If so, *beware*! Resting on your laurels is a synonym for flirting with disaster. Write that reminder down where you can see it frequently.

A Daily Reading: 1 Corinthians 10:31

God's Book is a veritable storehouse of promises—over seven thousand of them. Not empty hopes and dreams, not just nice-sounding, eloquently worded thoughts that make you feel warm all over, but promises. Verbal guarantees in writing, signed by the Creator Himself, in which He declares He will do or will refrain from doing specific things.

In a world of liars, cheats, deceivers, and con artists, isn't it a relief to know there is Someone you can trust? If He said it, you can count on it. Unlike the rhetoric of politicians who promise anybody anything they want to hear to get elected, what God says, God does.

But, are all seven thousand-plus promises ours to claim? I mean, am I free to choose any one of them and believe it's for me—here in my situation—today? Is "every promise in the Book" really mine, like that little chorus you and I were taught in Sunday school?

Much as I hate to disappoint you, I must tell you that even though those words were written with great sincerity, they lack veracity. Think, before you pick up stones to stone me. Many—dare I say most?—of the scriptural promises are ours to claim. But all? Hardly. To claim "every promise in the Book" could be disillusioning at best, disastrous at worst.

To begin with, some promises are uniquely historical in nature. They were made to specific individuals in a particular era and fit only that unique combination. Take Genesis 6, for example: "'My Spirit shall not strive with man forever, because he also is flesh; nevertheless his days shall be one hundred and twenty years.' . . . 'The end of all flesh has come before Me; for the earth is filled with violence . . . and behold, I am about to destroy them with the earth'" (6:3, 13).

Frightening words. True words. Words an evangelist could use to get any number of people scared into the Kingdom. Could . . . but shouldn't. Why? Because that doomsday promise was given specifically to Noah, having to do with the flood that was to cover the earth—and, in fact, did. The context of that promise was altogether unique. God not only warned the people, He fulfilled His word. The deluge finally came, exactly 120 years after the Lord's promise.

Another example? Well, how about this one? ". . . your wife shall have a son." I can just see some well-meaning husband "claiming the promise" of Genesis 18:10. After all, "It's in the Book!" He and his wife could get so excited, they'd be tempted to paint the nursery blue and throw a "we're pregnant" party. Could . . . but shouldn't.

At the risk of being a party pooper, I recommend a closer look at that promise. It was given specifically to Abraham. In fact, the complete promise reads, "Sarah your wife shall have a son." And it came as a direct fulfillment of God's earlier covenant with Abraham (Gen. 12:1–3) in which He promised to make of him "a great nation." That promise of a son was uniquely Abraham's and Sarah's to claim.

Why do I make such a big deal of all this? Because there are numerous sincere, pure-hearted, trusting people in the Body who latch onto such promises, build there hopes high, only to suffer great pain months later in the backwash of disillusionment.

God's special promise of a son was to aging Abraham and Sarah in a tent by the oaks of Mamre, not young Bob and Betty in their apartment in Minneapolis. It was a specific guarantee to a unique couple for a particular era. It wasn't a universal declaration to be claimed by all childless couples throughout the ages. That's like expecting the Ford Motor Company to apply its 50,000 mile warranty to every Model A owner. It ain't gonna happen.

Historically unique promises are delightful to study, but inappropriate if we are try to push those round pegs into our square holes.

There are also conditional promises . . . words of assurance offered to those who first fulfill their part of the arrangement. God promises that He will do such-and-such if (the condition) we will first do so-and-so. The promise is absolutely reliable, but it is linked to a condition. An example? You claim God's promise to direct your steps . . . to lead you clearly into His will. After all, Proverbs 3:6 says, "He will make your paths straight," plain and simple. "If it's in the Book, it's mine to claim!"

Wait a minute. Not so fast. Check out the whole statement, which starts at the beginning of the previous verse (3:5–6): "Trust in the Lord with all your heart . . . do not lean on your own understanding . . . in all your ways acknowledge Him (*our part*), and He will make your paths straight" (*God's promise*).

In case all this is making you feel a little shaky, I need to reaffirm that most of those wonderful promises are still ours to count on. Need a few classic examples? Isaiah 26:3–4; Romans 8:32, 38–39; Galatians 6:9; Psalm 37:7,23,28; 2 Corinthians 4:16–18; Hebrews 6:10. Look 'em up.

Take your stand on the promises of God. Thousands of 'em are right there, waiting to be used . . . like perfectly shaped square pegs ready for our square holes.

A Finishing Touch: Make sure you're standing on the promises and not outside the premises.

A Daily Reading: Look up the promises listed above.

Here's another promise many try to claim . . . without the condition.

"God has offered me His peace, and I'm claiming it now. After all, Philippians 4:7 promises, 'And the peace of God, which surpasses all comprehension, shall guard your hearts and your minds in Christ Jesus.'" But such peace escapes you as you continue to be besieged by worry and fear.

Why?

Because peace isn't dropped in a bundle from heaven by parachute. Peace is a by-product—the promised result following our fulfilling our part of the process. And what is that?

When answering such questions, always go back to the context in which you found the promise, in this case Philippians 4. Notice that just before the promise of peace is the condition on which that promise is based:

"*Be anxious for nothing* (in other words, stop worrying about anything), *but in everything by prayer and supplication* (in addition, start praying about everything) *with thanksgiving* (and don't forget to be thankful in all things) *let your requests be made known to God. And . . . .*"

The equation would look like this:

Absence of worry + Prevalence of prayer + Spirit of gratitude = Peace of God.

Don't be afraid of God's not keeping His promises. He has and He will continue to do so. But make an intelligent and careful study of the one(s) you choose to claim. Be certain they are rightfully yours.

ADMITTING NEED

A prayer to be said
When the world has gotten you down,
And you feel rotten,
And you're too doggone tired to pray,
And you're in a big hurry,
And besides, you're mad at everybody . . .
Help!

There it was . . . one of those posters. Some are funny. Some are clever. A few, thought-provoking. This one? Convicting. God really wanted me to get the message. He nudged me when I first read it in an administrator's office at Mount Hermon Christian Conference Center in northern California. He slapped me hard when I ran into it again in a shop at Newport Beach. While moving faster than a speeding bullet through a publishing firm in Portland, I came face to face with it again, silent as light but twice as bright . . . smashing me down and pinning me to the mat for the full count. It was almost as if I could hear His celestial voice saying: "My son, slow down. Cool it. Admit your needs."

Such good counsel. But tough to carry out.

Asking for help is smart. So why don't we? You want to know why? Pride. Which is nothing more than stubborn unwillingness to admit need. It's been bred into us by that inner voice urging us on, "Prove it to 'em, you can do it . . . you don't need anybody's help."

The result? Impatience. Irritation. Anger. Longer hours. Less and less laughter. No vacations. Inflexibility. Longer and longer gaps between meaningful times in God's Word. Precious few (if any) moments in prayer and prolonged meditation.

My friend, It's time to declare it: No way can you keep going at this pace and stay effective year after year! You are H-U-M-A N— nothing more. So, slow down! Give yourself a break! Stop trying to cover all the bases! Relax!

Once you've put it into neutral, crack open your Bible to Exodus 18:18–27, the account of a visit Jethro made to his son-in-law Moses. Old Jethro frowned as he watched Moses dash from one person to another, one need to another. From morning until night Moses was neck deep in decisions and activities. He must have looked very impressive—eating on the run, moving fast, meeting deadlines, solving people's problems.

But Jethro wasn't impressed. "What is this thing that you are doing for the people?" he asked. Moses was somewhat defensive (most too-busy people are) as he attempted to justify his schedule. Jethro didn't buy it. He advised Moses against trying to do everything alone and reproved him with strong words: "The thing that you are doing is not good. You will surely wear out . . . " (vv. 17–18).

In other words, He told Moses: CALL FOR HELP.

The benefits of shifting and sharing the load? Read verses 22–23: "It will be easier for you. . . . You will be able to endure." Isn't that interesting? We seem to think it's better to have that tired-blood, overworked-underpaid, I've-really-got-it-rough look. Among Christians, it's what I call the martyr complex that announces, "I'm working so hard for Jesus!"

The truth of the matter is, that hurried, harried, appearance usually means, "I'm too stubborn to slow down" or "I'm too insecure to say no" or "I'm too proud to ask for help." Since when is a bleeding ulcer a sign of spirituality . . . or a 70-hour week a mark of efficiency?

The world beginning to get you down? Too tired to pray? Ticked off at a lot of folks? Let me suggest one of the few four-letter words God loves to hear us use: HELP!

A Finishing Touch: Efficiency is enhanced not by what we accomplish but by what we relinquish.

A Daily Reading: Exodus 18

We preachers get asked a lot of funny questions. We also receive some hilarious stuff in the mail, which helps compensate for the periodic blasts that come our way (usually unsigned), most of which we discard without a second thought. I'm particularly grateful for a friend of mine who never fails to lift my spirits by passing on something he has read or heard that I might be able to use.

One item I found especially fascinating was a series of statistics from a book by Daniel Weiss titled *One Hundred Percent American*, in which the author sets forth a sequential series of percentages (from 1% to 100%) that tells us some interesting facts about Americans. For example:

1% of Americans read the Bible more than once a day;

15% of American married men say they do most of the cooking in the household;

30% of Americans smoke cigarettes;

42% of Americans cannot name a country near the Pacific Ocean;

60% of Americans do not spend a lot of time on their personal appearance;

67% of Americans believe files are being kept on them for unknown reasons;

70% of Americans own running shoes but don't run;

74% of Americans say if they had their life to live over, they'd continue with their formal education;

76% of American owners of small businesses do not have a college degree;

83% of American companies have fewer than 20 employees;

84% of Americans believe heaven exists;

94% of American men would change something about their looks if they could;

96% of American school children can identify Ronald McDonald (who is second only to Santa Claus);

99% of American women would change something about their looks if they could.

I remember the old saying that "statistics usually lie and liars use statistics," so I'll not press the point on any of Mr. Weiss's figures. Instead, I'll refer to another item from my friend: a Frank and Ernest cartoon where the two characters are standing before a priest and Frank asks, "How come opportunity knocks once, but temptation beats at my door every day?"

Few would argue that the percentage of occasions when we face life's temptations is terribly high . . . dare I say 98%? Or how about 100%? And I have yet to meet anyone who denies ever being tempted.

Frank is right: Temptation beats at our door every day. But when it comes to opportunity, who can say how rare it is? Less than 10%? Less than 5%? Probably so.

Looking back over your shoulder, I bet you cannot name one opportunity that lingered, gathering dust. The age-old aphorism remains true: "Four things come not back: the spoken word; the speeding arrow; time past; the neglected opportunity."

A Finishing Touch: Time is short. Opportunity is knocking. Please answer it. One hundred percent of those who do find themselves blessed.

A Daily Reading: Luke 21

Stress: That confusion created when one's mind overrides the body's desire to choke the living daylights out of some jerk who desperately needs it.

No, you won't find that definition in the dictionary, but right now, I think it should be. It's been one of those weeks. They have come before . . . they will come again. Know what I mean?

Overcommitment. Deadlines. Unrealized expectations. People problems. A stack of phone calls to return. A couple of major interruptions. Not to mention an enormous bill from the vet after he treated our dog, telling us she has some profound, exotic, inner itch or something. Choked traffic lanes on the freeway—every freeway . . . eating too much, too fast . . . a sprinkler system that went on the blink and sprayed water all over my freshly washed car (in the hot sunshine) . . . the water heater leaking all over the garage. My in-box resembles the Leaning Tower . . . and then one of my grandsons asks innocently, "Bubba, how come you yell when you talk?" On top of all that I receive a six-page letter from a pious soul who feels "led of God" to correct my position on the day Christ died, my too-liberal view of eschatology, my extravagance for owning two cars, and how I ought to be doing this and not that. Page after page. From a guy who doesn't even know me.

I know, I know. I should "turn the other cheek." I really ought to "see the good in it." If I practiced what I preached, I need to thank him for "caring enough to confront." Well, not today. Today, I think he's a jerk. I suppose it's the timing of it all. On some other day I'd probably not give his words a second thought. But when you suffer from stress fractures, the soft cushion of tolerance gets deflated, leaving nerves raw and feelings bloody.

A recent *Sports Illustrated* article painted a vivid picture:

> A stress fracture begins when the shocks and strains of playing game after game create microscopic cracks in the outer layers of bone—usually in the legs and feet. If the pounding continues

and those tiny crevices, which often go undetected, aren't allowed to heal, they can enlarge. When the cracks become large enough to cause pain, they are stress fractures.

Stress fractures aren't limited to athletes. Microscopic cracks in bones are painful, but can they match the hurt of a stress-fractured spirit . . . an aching heart? That's a pain like none other, isn't it? It's deep. It throbs. It lingers in the day and haunts you through the night.

Some folks treat their stress fractures with booze and drugs, extramarital affairs, and hyperactive lifestyles. That's no treatment . . . it's more like pouring a jug of gasoline on a match. There has to be a better way.

So, what do we do to stop the pounding? Ah, that's the question. "Lighten up" is a start. Try not to make a federal case out of everything that happens. Then, laugh more. Admit those imperfections. Let some stuff go. Don't try to be Wonder Woman or the all-powerful Mr. Fix-it. Talk to a friend. Get away for a fun weekend. Go see a good movie. Get absorbed in a fine, relaxing book. You might even spend the night out under the stars. Cancel a few not-that-important meetings.

Above all, turn it over to God. Tell Him everything. He has no problem hearing about our hurts. Furthermore, He can keep any secret you tell Him. He can even handle it when you yell.

As the pounding lessens, so will the pain.

A Finishing Touch: Don't let stress fracture you.
A Daily Reading: Psalm 23

Sleep came hard for me last night, which for me is a rarity. I'm usually out in less than ten seconds. Last night I must have been awake for an hour and a half . . . thinking, musing, and praying.

Earlier that evening, Cynthia and I had read together a letter from our long-time friend Wally Norling, who had just returned from the bedside of Betty, his "loving partner in life for 42 years." Betty is dying of cancer of the liver, and Wally's letter, written in the midst of that, was a gracious, understated masterpiece of faith.

His words left us both pensive. In silence, we dressed for bed, and I'm sure we were thinking the same thing: it could happen to us. If it does, I know this . . . I would not be nearly so brave as my friend, certainly not as eloquent in expressing such feelings.

And so I lay there wide awake, reviewing our almost-forty years together. I thought about those innocent early years, which seemed so tough back then. Years of enforced separation (thanks to the military), of a career change, of the first years in graduate school, of financially lean times, of learning and growing closer together.

Then came our child-bearing years—wonderful years, so incredibly surprising to both of us. The loss of two precious children by miscarriage, the healthy births of four. Yes, four! (And to think I felt one was enough, certainly not more than two.) The simple joys of tent camping, of early schooling, of struggling with "finding myself" in pulpit style, philosophy of ministry, confronting criticism for the first time, and discovering much of what "being a pastor" meant. And all the while, Cynthia was right there . . . understanding, affirming, being mother to our four children and partner with me, assuring me that it was worth all the effort. Though she never bragged about it, I know she prayed me through many a sermon. As I improved, I got the credit, but she deserved the applause. As the song goes, she was the wind beneath my wings . . . and boy, did I need healthy gusts at times! Still do.

Before dropping off to sleep, I did a quick recap of the balance of our years together. Wow! Giant steps through big-time changes. A surprising move to California . . . the teenaged years (among our favorite!), an endless number of high school football games . . . dating, four unforgettable weddings, the birth of new dimensions of ministry, wild 'n' crazy family times, eight grandchildren, summer vacations, backyard barbecues, gaining weight and dieting together, jogging and laughing together, feeling loved, blending strengths with weaknesses, refusing to quit no matter what. Two people so different, yet so close. And now, a whole new direction in training men and women for ministry.

As I remembered all this, I realized anew the enormity of Wally's loss, and that reminds me of what John Donne wrote in 1624:

> No man is an island, entire of itself; every man [or woman] is a piece of the continent, a part of the main . . . any man's [or woman's] death diminishes me, because I am involved in mankind; and therefore never send to know for whom the bell tolls; it tolls for thee.

Last night, in the arms of my wife, I couldn't help but imagine the night that ominous final bell might toll on our marriage. I tried to picture life without my loving partner . . . that dark era when the other side of my bed will be empty and lonely memories will replace the warmth of reality. And, sadly, I fell asleep.

A Finishing Touch: "In the hour of need, the grace of God is more than adequate" (Wally Norling).

A Daily Reading: Romans 14:7–9

Survival requires change. The more intense the need for survival, the more drastic the change.

On October 12, 1972, an amateur rugby team from Uruguay were scheduled to travel from Montevideo, Uruguay, to Santiago, Chile, which meant flying over the Andes. At 3:21 P.M. the pilot reported to air traffic control in Santiago that he was over the Pass of Planchon. At 3:24 he reported being over a small town in Chile. Santiago ground control gave him authorization to turn north and begin his descent. At 3:30 he reported his elevation—15,000 feet. When ground control responded, there was no reply. There would be none for the next ten weeks.

Every attempt to find the plane proved futile, and snow was beginning to fall in the Andes. Finally, as winter's blast intensified, the entire rescue operation had to be stopped. The families and friends slowly released the final threads of hope.

One day while a Chilean peasant was tending his cattle along a long, deep gorge in a remote area, he saw two gaunt, bearded figures across the chasm. Thinking they were terrorists, he ran and hid. The next day he returned and saw they were still there. He quickly gathered a pencil, some paper, and a stone, wrapped them in a handkerchief, and heaved them across to the strangers.

When the package came back, thirteen hand-scribbled words said it all: "We came from a plane that fell in the mountains. We are Uruguayan."

Out of forty-five, sixteen had survived the indescribable ordeal. They did so because they were willing to do the unthinkable. They committed cannibalism, eating from the dead bodies of their companions. Critics came out of the woodwork, especially from their church. Roman Catholic priests and bishops leveled strong words against them . . . but the fact is, because they were willing to take such drastic measures, sixteen survived.

If you and I hope to survive these transitional years into the twenty-first century, it will require some drastic measures on our part, too. It will require a willingness to change. That statement may have a heroic sound to it, but the fact is, some of those changes may be so drastic we cannot even imagine them. Who, among those forty-five passengers, would have ever dreamed they would do what they ultimately did as they took off that cloudy day in October?

To describe our times as intense is to state the obvious. And to complicate matters, the intensity is on the increase. We thought times were wicked when we were growing up; but compared to today, the situation forty or fifty years ago now seems idyllic. I remember when the use of a four-letter word in the movie *Gone with the Wind* made front-page news. When I entered the ministry, certain terms were not mentioned from the pulpit—words like rape, incest, abortion, molestation, homosexuality, condom, and sexual intercourse. Today, those words no longer raise eyebrows among most congregations. "War zones" were once military battlegrounds thousands of miles from our shores. Now, those two words describe urban territories inhabited by hostile, vicious street gangs.

The ancient psalmist asks a question extremely relevant to our day: "If the foundations are destroyed, what can the righteous do?"

Don't just shrug and skate on by . . . answer him! What should we do . . . what *can* we do? Nothing? Run and hide? Worry? Scream? Crusade? Lead a campaign? March on city hall? Escape to Tibet?

While struggling with all that recently, I found encouragement from a statement in Paul's final letter: "Nevertheless, the firm foundation of God stands, having this seal, 'The Lord knows those who are His,' and, 'Let everyone who names the name of the Lord abstain from wickedness'" (2 Tim. 2:19).

Isn't that great! The foundations God has laid won't be destroyed. No matter how bad it gets, no matter how intense the wickedness, God's standard is not subject to change. In other words, He won't say that something is okay today when it was wrong back in the 1930s. He remains consistent. The theological word for it is *immutable*. What's wrong has always been wrong.

So, then, what's all this I've been writing about regarding change? If God's foundations are not shaken but our times are getting decidedly worse, then where do all these drastic changes take place?

Within you and me, of course! Remember, that last part of 2 Timothy 2:19 is a command. It calls for obedience: "Let every one who names the name of the Lord abstain from wickedness." As I see it, He is telling us to make whatever changes are necessary so that we might "abstain from wickedness." Yes, *abstain*.

Surviving times as intense as ours will not occur easily or automatically. Furthermore, it is not something we do corporately or, for that matter, publicly. It's an "inside job," this business of abstaining from wickedness. And it calls for increased discipline in the private realms of our lives. It's a survival secret being overlooked by many.

Whatever changes you need to make . . . spiritually . . . morally . . . ethically . . . start today. Don't hesitate because of the pain it may cause or the problems it may create. Survival requires change. Sometimes, drastic change. Like *abstaining* from wickedness.

A Finishing Touch: Drastic times call for drastic measures.
A Daily Reading: 1 Thessalonians 4:1–8

Here are several very personal questions to help you know how severe we need to be with ourselves in order to "abstain from wickedness." Answer each one honestly.

- ✔ Are you regularly with a person of the opposite sex in inappropriate situations?
- ✔ Are you completely above reproach in all your financial dealings, including your taxes?
- ✔ Do you expose yourself to explicit sexual material?
- ✔ If you have a family, do you invest sufficient time with them?
- ✔ Do you tell the truth? How often do you lie (don't forget to count the little white ones)?
- ✔ How quickly do you say "I am wrong . . . I am genuinely sorry" when you have said or done something that hurts another?
- ✔ Do you hold grudges?
- ✔ Are you knowingly compromising in some area of your life, refusing to acknowledge the consequences that you will surely have to face?
- ✔ Have you formed a habit that is detrimental to your health or your job or your walk with Christ?
- ✔ Are you proud . . . selfish . . . arrogant?
- ✔ Have you taken credit for something that someone else did and should have been rewarded for?
- ✔ Do you return things you borrow?
- ✔ Have you failed to confess something to someone who should know of your wrongdoing?
- ✔ Are you abusing your mate or your children—physically or emotionally?
- ✔ Do you allow abuse to happen without seeking help?
- ✔ Do you regularly spend time in prayer and in the Scriptures?

Various methods are employed to communicate the good news of Christ to the lost. Some of the approaches appear to be successful and effective on the surface, but underneath they leave much to be desired.

Take the Eager-beaver Approach, for example: "The more scalps, the better." This numerical approach is decision-centered, and little (if any) effort is directed toward follow-up or discipleship or cultivating a relationship. These anxious hunters are not difficult to identify. They can usually be overheard counting (out loud) the scalps on their belts or can be seen shooting their flaming arrows into every wagon train they spot. Tact is not their long suit.

The Harvard Approach is quite different: "Let's all discuss the world's religions." This reason-centered approach attracts both genuine and pseudo-intellectuals, and while it is educational and occasionally quite stimulating, it suffers from one mild drawback—*no one ever gets saved!* Being sophisticated is more important than telling the truth about sin or heaven or hell. Discussion is in . . . decisions are out.

Perhaps the most popular is the Mute Approach: "I'm just a silent witness for God." The best you can say about this method is that *no one is ever offended.* That's for sure! The secret-service saint who settles for this self-centered approach could be tagged a Clairol Christian: no one knows for sure but God. Somewhere along the line this person has swallowed one of Satan's tastiest tidbits: "Just live a good Christian life. Others will ask you about Christ if they are really interested, so relax." Frankly, I can count on one hand (and have fingers left over) the number of people who have suddenly come to me and asked me how they might know Jesus Christ. "Faith," please remember, "comes from hearing" (Rom. 10:17).

What we need, I submit to you, is the Philip Approach. This Christ-centered method is set forth in a series of seven principles drawn from Acts 8:26–40.

Philip was engaged in an evangelistic crusade in Samaria when the Lord instructed him to go south to the desert road that ran from Jerusalem to Gaza. Faithful Philip "arose and went". He was *available* (Principle 1). On the road he encountered an Ethiopian statesman traveling home from Jerusalem. The man was sitting in his chariot reading Isaiah! And the Spirit of God prompted Philip to approach the traveler. Philip was *led by the Spirit* (Principle 2). In other words, he sensed that God was clearly opening the door.

Philip cooperated, for *obedience* (Principle 3) is essential. He heard the man reading aloud and asked, "Do you understand what you are reading?" What an excellent start! A *proper opening* (Principle 4) is so important. Philip didn't barge in and start preaching, nor did he corner the guy with a loaded question.

The man invited Philip to sit with him and assist him in his quest for understanding. Philip responded with great *tactfulness* (Principle 5). Even though he had his foot in the door, he remained gracious, courteous, and sensitive to when he should speak of salvation. When that moment came, he "opened his mouth" and became *specific* (Principle 6). No vague dialogue about religion. He spoke only of the Savior, the main issue. The last few verses then describe the brief but memorable *follow-up* (Principle 7) Philip employed.

As you rub shoulders with hungry, thirsty humanity and sense their inner ache for help and hope, keep the Philip Approach in mind. I can't think of a place I'd rather be at the moment Christ returns than riding shotgun in a twentieth-century chariot, speaking openly about faith in the Savior.

A Finishing Touch: As we become alert to those empty chariot seats God wants us to occupy, we may even begin to feel comfortable in them.

A Daily Reading: Acts 8

Floundering with my father is among my most cherished childhood memories.

Armed with a beat-up Coleman lantern, two gigs, a stringer . . . and clothed in old sneakers, faded jeans, torn shirts, and funny hats, we'd head to the water. When the sky got nice 'n' dark, we'd wade in about knee-deep and stumble off into the night, ready to stab a few flat, brown creatures who had chosen our shoreline as the place for a shrimp supper.

Actually, my dad was more addicted to floundering than I. He went to get the fish. I went to be with him . . . which was fine for a while. By and by we'd round the point about a mile away from the bay cottage where the other members of the Swindoll tribe were. If we stopped and listened, we could hear them either singing together or laughing like crazy. And here we were—knee-deep in muddy, cold salt water, with nothing but thick darkness in front of us. To this day I remember looking back wistfully over my shoulder toward that ever-so-tiny light in the distance. A few steps further and it was out of sight.

Soon I began asking myself why. Why in the world had I agreed to come? Why hadn't I stayed back with the family? And if I asked him once, I must have asked a dozen times, "How much longer, Daddy? When are we gonna turn around?" In tones mellow and quiet, he comforted me. I asked, "What if the mantle burns out?" He had a flashlight. "What if the batteries are dead?" He knew the path that would get us back.

While he was searching for flounder, I was listening for those marvelous words, "Well, Son, this is far enough. Let's turn around." Instantly, I found myself wading on tiptoes, caring nothing about finding some poor flounder—only that light, that tiny signal in the distance that assured me my dad really knew the way. Once spotted, my entire personality changed. My anxieties were relieved. My questions were answered. Hope lit the darkness like a thousand lanterns . . . thanks to one tiny light at the end of my childhood tunnel of fears.

Decades have passed since I trudged through the darkness with my father, but they have not erased from my mind the incredible importance of hope. Its significance seems larger than life to me today. How powerful is its presence!

Take from us our wealth and we are hindered. Take our health and we are handicapped. Take our purpose and we are slowed, temporarily confused. But take away our hope and we are plunged into deepest darkness . . . stopped dead in our tracks, paralyzed. Wondering, "Why?" Asking, "How much longer? Will this darkness ever end? Does He know where I am?"

Then the Father says, "That's far enough," and how sweet it is! Like blossoms in the snow, long-awaited color returns to our life. The stream, once frozen, starts to thaw. Hope revives and washes over us.

Inevitably, spring follows winter. Every year. Yes, including this one. Barren days, like naked limbs, will soon be clothed with fresh life. Do you need that reminder today? Are you ready for some sunshine on your shoulders . . . a few green sprouts poking up through all that white? A light at the end of your tunnel?

Look! There it is in the distance. It may be tiny, but it's there. You made it! Your Father knew exactly where He was going. And why. And for how long. That cottage in the distance? Let's name it New Hope. You'll soon be there, laughing and singing again with the family.

Believe it or not, you may live to see the day when your journey into darkness is among your most cherished memories.

A Finishing Touch: There is nothing like light, however small and distant, to put us on tiptoes in the darkness.

A Daily Reading: Psalm 13

The smoky tones of Peggy Lee's voice occasionally blow across my mind: "Is that all . . . is that all there is . . . ?" With no bitterness intended, I ask that haunting question in the backwash of certain situations.

How much like the tide we are! When our spirits are high, we are flooded with optimism, hope, and expectation. But when low, our jagged barnacles of disappointment, discouragement, and disillusionment are exposed. We usually hide such melancholy from others beneath a thick coat of public image shined to a high gloss finish with the wax of superficiality and embellished with a religious cliché or two. But all the while, at low tide within, we struggle to maintain an even keel as the rough winds jerk our sails.

Like the pull of the sea, some of our low tides are almost predictable. There are, for example, peculiar low tides that often follow a great victory.

Is that all . . . is that all there is to victory?

Elijah asked that. Under the gnarled limbs of that twisted juniper tree, he cried out to God—not in spontaneous praise but overwhelmed with self-pity. And he was fresh off a great victory at Carmel! It's hard to believe 1 Kings 18 and 19 are connected. Vulnerable and frightened, he suffered the low tide that often follows victory, perhaps the cruelest dart in the devil's quiver.

Then there are special low tides that accompany great vision.

Is that all . . . is that all there is to vision?

Paul asked that. Having taken gigantic strides into the vast regions of Asia, and having forged out an impeccable theology that was to serve the church for centuries, he was caught at low tide. He freely admits this in his second letter to his friends at Corinth: "For we do not want you to be unaware, brethren, of our affliction which came to us in Asia, that we were burdened excessively, beyond our strength, so that we despaired even of life" (2 Cor. 1:8).

While in the heights of accomplishing the vision, he fell into the depths of sudden despair. No doubt lonely, weary, and emotionally drained, the seasoned apostle hit bottom. Low tide is a malady not limited to century-one saints.

And there are those low tides that attach themselves to great valor.

Is that all . . . is that all there is to valor?

David asked that when, after proving himself a dedicated warrior, unmatched for bravery in Israel's ranks, he was forced to flee from Saul. Reeling in fear and despair, David even disguised himself as insane before the king of Gath. The once-exalted warrior now "scribbled on the doors of the gate, and let his saliva run down into his beard" (1 Sam. 21:13). David was at low tide, and all his valor seemed an empty dream.

Low tide . . . how painful yet how essential. Without it, we cannot have high tide. Without it, there would be no need for Elisha to minister to victoryless Elijahs . . . no need for visionaries to fall in dependence on their faces before God . . . no need for the valiant to be reminded of their Source of strength.

Is that all . . . is that all there is to low tides?

No, there is more, much more, most of which can never be described . . . only discovered.

A Finishing Touch: When it seems like that's all there is, remember all you have in Him.

A Daily Reading: Psalm 55

Thoughts disentangle themselves . . . over the lips and through the fingertips.

I learned that saying over thirty years ago, and just about every time I put it to the test, it works! Whenever I have difficulty comprehending the complicated or clarifying the complex, I talk it out or write it out. This is especially helpful when it comes to scriptural truth. For some strange reason the human brain seems reluctant to retain divine information simply by hearing it.

Take the importance of joy, for example—or, more specifically, giving joyfully to God. Second Corinthians 9:7 says: "Let each one do just as he has purposed in his heart; not grudgingly or under compulsion; for God loves a cheerful giver."

Look again at those final five words: "God loves a cheerful giver." The original meaning of the word translated here as "cheerful" is *hilarious*, and this is the only time it's found in the New Testament. It's the hilarious giver God prizes.

I can think of a couple more examples of hilarious givers in the New Testament: a man named Onesiphorus who "often refreshed" Paul (2 Tim. 1:16–18); and a church—the Philippians—who contributed generously to Paul's needs (Phil. 4:14–16).

Now, how does all this translate into daily life? How do these thoughts disentangle themselves to become meaningful parts of our lives? I'd like to make the following four suggestions for ways we can bring joy into our giving.

Reflect on God's gifts to you.

Hasn't He been good? He certainly has to me. Better than I deserve! My list includes good health, harmonious family, sufficient food, clothing, and shelter. Friends. Great job. In light of God's magnificent grace, a cheerful heart and openhanded generosity seem the most natural responses.

Remind yourself of His promises regarding generosity.

Call to mind a few biblical principles that promise a bountiful harvest to those who sow bountifully. Jesus himself spoke of how much more blessed it is to give than to receive. Bumper crops are

God's specialties, so we have nothing to restrain us from dropping maximum seed. He's honored by such faith.

Examine your heart.

This is something no one else can do for you. Nobody knows the combination to your private vault. Only you can probe its contents by asking the hard questions: Do I really believe God's promises on giving generously? Am I responding as I do because I care or because I feel guilty? Is my giving proportionate to my income. Have I prayed, or is my giving impulsive? Am I a consistent giver or more hot 'n' cold?

Glorify God by becoming generous.

He prizes generosity, especially joyful generosity. Perhaps we need to break the habit of being so conservative, so careful. Maybe we even need to "scare" ourselves with acts of generosity . . . going out on a limb, as it were, and genuinely trusting God to honor our financial faith.

Well, that's it. Just a little lips-and-fingertips clarification. It has helped me to review this. I hope it's helped you, too. Goodness knows, all of us would be wise to address our reluctance to sacrifice financially for the cause of Christ. After all, our goal is joyful generosity, isn't it?

A Finishing Touch: Do you qualify as a "hilarious giver"? If not, why not?

A Daily Reading: 2 Corinthians 9

I can't seem to get past the subject I wrote about recently. When issues like this don't leave my mind, there's a reason. Perhaps it's the Lord prompting me to go back and dig deeper. Or there may be someone dancing dangerously near an inappropriate or illicit relationship and something I write may prompt him or her to call a halt to further involvement. I'm referring to an adulterous or impure sexual liaison which, if not stopped, will spell the ruin of another precious soul. You may be that "someone." If so, read the following very carefully.

To begin with, from all those I have confronted, dealt with, or heard about who have fallen into sexual impurity, two paths led them astray. The first is *subtle deception*. This is an almost passive series of thoughts which include rationalization, ignoring the warnings of a sensitive conscience, the consistent erosion of one's walk with Christ, and tolerating things that were once intolerable. Webster says that "deceive" means "to make (a person) believe what is not true: delude, mislead." It implies "deliberate misrepresentation of facts by words or actions . . . to further one's ends." Pause a moment and think that over.

The Scriptures include direct warnings against deception. In fact, we are frequently commanded not to be deceived. For just a few examples, see 1 Corinthians 6:9–10, 15:33; Galatians 6:7–8; and 1 John 1:8.

Interestingly, nearly all these warnings about being deceived are found in a context of sexual and/or moral impurity. The beast within us feeds on deception. As long as we can convince ourselves that what we are doing is not all that wrong, we have no difficulty proceeding into further perilous territory. Infidelity occurs in the head long before it happens in the bed.

Second, there is the path of *deliberate action*. Once the mental roadblocks are cleared away, the excitement of "stolen waters" becomes sweet to the transgressor's taste. Make no mistake about it, the pleasures of sin—those erotic excursions into secret experiments with forbidden escapades—are both enjoyable and stimulating. The flesh loves such encounters. They may yield only temporary delights, but they are enough to make one's carnal appetites crave more. This, then, calls for more aggressive action as that built-in curiosity pleads for further involvement, which, in turn, pushes the person to become increasingly bolder and usually more bizarre.

Again, God's Word addresses the issue head on: "Flee immorality. Every other sin that a man commits is outside the body, but the immoral man sins against his own body. Or do you not know that your body is a temple of the Holy Spirit who is in you, whom you have from God, and that you are not your own? For you have been bought with a price: therefore glorify God in your body" (1 Cor. 6:18–20).

Flee means just that. Get out! Keep a safe distance. Stop all movement toward lust. Like Joseph, turn away and run like mad in the opposite direction. Don't let yourself get cornered. Counteract those weak and vulnerable places in your psyche by taking practical steps of resistance. That includes being tough on yourself by not allowing "even the appearance of evil" to occur. Too strict? Not according to Paul, who once testified "I buffet my body and make it my slave" (1 Cor. 9:27).

There may still be a few who remain unconvinced. If you are one of them, you may be in a compromising situation and, to be frank, are not ready to call a halt to something that seems tantalizingly appealing. To you, especially, I dedicate the balance of my comments. They have to do with the consequences you probably haven't thought through sufficiently. Sexual temptations are usually softened by emotional narcotics that numb the harsh reality of pain awaiting the sinner at the end of the road.

Before listing several of the inevitable consequences you'll have to face and endure as soon as your secret sins are exposed, let's return to a few pertinent scriptures. They are to the point, therefore they will sting. But hopefully that will help get your attention. Whatever you do, don't excuse sinful behavior by claiming you are "addicted" or "victimized." Those terms only help you escape responsibility.

"Can a man take fire in his bosom, and his clothes not be burned? Or can a man walk on hot coals, and his feet not be scorched? So is the one who goes in to his neighbor's wife; whoever touches her will not go unpunished. . . . The one who commits adultery with a woman is lacking sense; he who would destroy himself does it. Wounds and disgrace he will find, and his reproach will not be blotted out" (Prov. 6:27–29, 32–33).

Burned. Scorched. Punishment. Wounds and disgrace. Reproach. Solomon was right: "The way of the transgressor is hard." Forgiveness may come. The affair(s) may end. Restoration may occur. But the consequences will not go away.

In closing, a few words of encouragement to those who have not fallen. What can be done—what must be done—to keep us from slipping into secret sins? Admittedly, anyone can fall . . . but no one has to. The following guidelines will help only if you put them into action.

Keep reassuring your life's partner. Be willingly accountable and open. Express your commitment . . . say so!

Cultivate the intimacies of your marriage. Work on being creative and sensitive. Keep up those hugs, kisses, and other private, sincere demonstrations of affection. Save your very best for the one you promised to love and honor.

Intensify purity in your private world. Don't play around with sexual things. Keep no secrets. Guard yourself from hidden lusts.

Be absolutely honest. Refuse to allow yourself to live behind a mask. Tell the truth. If you're weakening, call for help.

Know the truth, love the truth, obey the truth, live the truth, speak the truth. The alternative? You suffer the consequences.

A Finishing Touch: God's simple formula is: truth or consequences.

A Daily Reading: Galatians 6:1–10

Following is an incomplete list of what you have in store after your immorality is found out.

Your mate will experience the anguish of betrayal, shame, rejection, heartache and loneliness. No amount of repentance will soften those blows.

Your mate can never again say that you are a model of fidelity Suspicion will rob her or him of trust.

Your escapade(s) will introduce to your life and your mate's life the very real probability of a sexually transmitted disease.

The total devastation your sinful actions will bring to your children is immeasurable. Their growth, innocence, trust, and healthy outlook on life will be severely and permanently damaged.

The heartache you will cause your parents, your family, and your peers is indescribable.

The embarrassment of facing other Christians, who once appreciated you, respected you, and trusted you, will be overwhelming.

If you are engaged in the Lord's work, you will suffer the immediate loss of your job and the support of those with whom you worked. The dark shadow will accompany you everywhere . . . and forever. Forgiveness won't erase it.

Your fall will give others license to do the same.

The inner peace you enjoyed will be gone.

You will never be able to erase the fall from your (or others') mind. This will remain indelibly etched on your life's record, regardless of your later return to your senses.

The name of Jesus Christ, whom you once honored, will be tarnished, giving the enemies of faith further reason to sneer and jeer.

INTIMATE COMMUNICATION

Some frightening facts have been released by the Planned Parenthood Federation. Their growing concern? It is a new trend: increasing sexual activity among preteen girls.

"Agency counselors throughout the country are overwhelmed by these kids," states Dr. Gerry Oliva, medical director for the federation in San Francisco. Consequently, the agency is developing a special program just for girls nine to twelve who are "sexually active and need advice." The problem is complicated when these young girls come into that agency for advice or contraceptives. Says one counselor, "It is hard not to call the parents when the girls are only nine or ten." The simple fact is this: telling a girl the facts of life when she's ten or eleven may be too late!

I am fully aware of the delicate and intimate nature of my subject. I do not wish to linger here unduly nor develop the matter unwisely. I only wish to have you who are parents to think it over . . . to come to terms with this business of communicating openly, tactfully, and intelligently with your children in the areas of intimacy. This is not a job for the school or for the church, though both may occasionally touch on it and, hopefully, reinforce your words. Primarily, it's a parental task that must be handled with great care and wisdom—but it must be handled.

Obviously, it is not to be directed only toward the girls, but boys as well. Nor should it be communicated only by mothers, but by both parents. God's beautiful plan regarding conception and birth needs to be shared from a balanced perspective.

Allow me to put the reluctant parent at ease. Questions from your children regarding sex are as normal as questions regarding science, or sports, or God for that matter. Questions are invitations to step carefully into your child's private thought world—directly, naturally, clearly, tenderly.

Dr. Howard Hendricks is right: "Parents often conduct sex education like preoccupied motorists drive. They sail right past the stop signs and sit like stalled cars in front of the green light."

God has provided you, parents, with the very best teaching model your child needs: affectionate love between you and your mate. A child's deepest and most vivid memories in the areas of intimacy are directly related to what they see in their own home between mom and dad. No greater influence can mark your child than an honest, affectionate, warm relationship between you and your spouse that often expresses itself in kisses, embraces, and tenderness.

But that merely prepares the way. Words must accompany actions. Practical, meaningful, accurate information at appropriate times during your child's growing years is absolutely essential if you want him or her to be intimately healthy, confident, and godly.

Believe me, your youngster *will* learn about sex. Society offers raw, profane, distorted classes every day. If you ignore it long enough, you won't have to bother with it at all. In bits and pieces, it will take its own shape . . . the wrong shape, possibly resulting in marital misunderstanding or personal tragedy (dare I say perversion) that could have been prevented.

So before you cop out, it might be wise to blow the dust off that old adage. Something about "an ounce of prevention . . . ."

A Finishing Touch: Sometimes silence can be deadly.
A Daily Reading: Deuteronomy 6

Elevators are weird places. You're crammed in with folks you've never met, so you try really hard not to touch them. And nobody talks, except for an occasional "Out, please" or "Oh, I'm sorry" as somebody clumsily steps on someone's toe. You don't look at anyone; in fact, you don't look anywhere but up, watching those dumb floor numbers go on and off.

It's almost as if there's an official sign that reads: NO TALKING, NO SMILING, NO TOUCHING, AND NO EYE CONTACT ALLOWED WITHOUT CONSENT OF THE MANAGEMENT, NO EXCEPTIONS!!

In a strange sort of way, an elevator is a microcosm of our world today: a crowded impersonal place where anonymity, isolation, and independence are the norm. In fact, our lives are being diluted, distorted, and demeaned by this "elevator mentality."

A recently published report by sociologist Ralph Larkin on the crises facing suburban youth underscores several aspects of this new malaise of the spirit. Many children of affluence are depicted as passively accepting a way of life they view as empty and meaningless, resulting in a syndrome that includes "a low threshold of boredom, a constricted expression of emotions, and an apparent absence of joy in anything that is not immediately consumable." Makes sense when you observe the significant role now played by music, drugs, booze, sex, and status-symbol possessions. Take away rock concerts and sports events and you seldom witness much display of strong emotion.

Exit: involvement and motivation.

Enter: indifference, non-commitment, disengagement, no sharing or caring, meals eaten with headsets turned up loud, even separate bedrooms, each with a personal telephone, TV, and private bath, and an it's-none-of-your-business attitude. No hassle . . . no conflicts . . . no accountability. No need to share. Or reach out. Or give a rip. Just watch the numbers and look at nobody.

Dr. Philip Zimbardo, author of one of the most widely used psychology textbooks, addressed this issue in a *Psychology Today* article entitled "The Age of Indifference."

I know of no more potent killer than isolation. There is no more destructive influence on physical and mental health than the isolation of you from me and of us from them. It has been shown to be a central agent in the etiology of depression, paranoia, schizophrenia, rape, suicide, mass murder. . . . The Devil's strategy for our times is to trivialize human existence in a number of ways: by isolating from one another while creating the delusion that the reasons are time pressures, work demands, or anxieties created by economic uncertainty; by fostering narcissi and the fierce competition to be No. 1 . . . .

We must come to terms with all this. The need is urgent! Our Savior modeled the answer perfectly. He cared. He listened. He served. He reached out. He supported. He affirmed and encouraged. He touched as well as stayed in touch. He walked with people . . . never took the elevator.

The only escape from indifference is to think of people as our most cherished resource. We need to work hard at reestablishing family fun, meaningful mealtimes, people involvement, evenings without the television blaring, times when we genuinely get involved with folks in need—not just pray for them.

Stop the elevator. I want to get off.

A Finishing Touch: "Speech is civilization itself. The word, even the most contradictory word, preserves contact—it is silence which isolates" (Thomas Mann).

A Daily Reading: John 11:1–44

Doing all things "decently and in order" applies to a lot more areas than theology. It's remarkable how many guys who have the ability to articulate the most exacting details and nuances of their area of expertise never get their desks cleared off or their workrooms organized. The last time a lot of them picked up their socks was when they were finishing a week at summer camp. They're brainy enough to understand Einstein's law of relativity or figure out the answer to that Big Bertha computer foul-up or rebuild some complex engine, but the trash under the kitchen sink can overflow until it's ankle deep and they aren't even aware of it. Isn't it amazing how many men have quiz-kid heads and pig-pen habits?

And it's not limited to the male species. Some women have the toughest time just keeping a path clear from the front door to the den. I heard last week about a gal who was such a lousy housekeeper that *Good Housekeeping* canceled her subscription! She must have been a friend of Erma Bombeck. Erma's the one who says that her idea of being organized is hauling in the garden hose before winter. She's the one who admits that her cupboard shelves are lined with newspapers that read "MALARIA STOPS WORK ON THE CANAL." Of course, it's possible to become a "neatness neurotic." Like the fastidious wife of that poor fella who got hungry and got out of bed for a midnight snack. When he came back to bed, she had it made.

Certainly there are ridiculous extremes. The answer to disorder is not vacuuming four times a day or running around the house nervously clicking off lights and tightening faucets or setting up your monthly bills according to the Dewey Decimal System. Furthermore, who wants to be around such super-structured individuals. Once again, the secret is balance.

Truthfully, however, most of us don't struggle with being *too* orderly. Our problem is the other side of the coin. And the result is predictable: We burn up valuable energy and lose precious time.

Stop and think that over. Maybe a few questions will help prime the pump of self-analysis:

Do you often lose things?

Are you usually late for appointments and meetings?

Do you put off doing your homework until late?

Are you a time waster . . . like on the phone or with TV?

Are you prompt in paying bills and answering mail?

Does your clothing match? Is it clean and pressed? Are your shoes shined?

How many unfinished projects do you have lying around?

Does your desk stay cluttered? How about the tops of tables and counters?

Can you put your hands on important documents right away?

Do you have a will? Is it in a safe place?

Can you concentrate and think through decisions in a logical manner?

We'll talk some more about this tomorrow. For now, think about this: Spending what it takes to become a little more efficient is an investment that pays rich dividends. When we are reluctant to do so, our lives are marked by mediocrity, haphazardness, and disorder.

A Finishing Touch: Time spent on the right things is never wasted.

A Daily Reading: Proverbs 1:1–7

Stab, stab. Twist, twist. Did yesterday's questions hit below the belt?

Maybe so. But they are the kind of questions that reveal the pulse of your efficiency heartbeat.

Now, before you get all hot and bothered, fearing that you're going to be given some gigantic plan only an efficiency expert with a master's degree in minutiae could pull off, relax! If you're like I am, life is too busy to add some unrealistic, humongous, impossible-to-achieve-anyway program.

Instead, let's deal with the problem in a straightforward and simplified manner. First off, admit to yourself that you could stand a change here and there. Try to be specific enough to pinpoint a couple of particular areas that keep bugging you. Don't bite off too much, just one or two trouble spots you plan to deal with first.

Now then, write down the problem. Maybe it would be: "I am usually late to a meeting. More often than not, I have to hurry . . . and even then, I am five to ten minutes late."

Once this is done, think about several practical ways you can conquer the habit or pattern you've fallen into.

Again, write down the plan for correction.

One final suggestion: Work on only one or two projects at a time. If you try to shoot at too many targets at once, you won't hit any. This will frustrate you and may cause you to give up.

And, by the way, don't forget to pray and read a brief portion of God's Word. You'll certainly find help there.

For example, the book of Proverbs puts a high priority on orderliness. You can't read it without getting motivated . . . and convicted! Take 24:30–34, where inefficiency is personified as a "sluggard."

> I passed by the field of the sluggard, and by the vineyard of the
> man lacking sense; and behold, it was completely overgrown
> with thistles, its surface was covered with nettles, and its stone

wall was broken down. When I saw, I reflected upon it; I looked, and received instruction. "A little sleep, a little slumber, a little folding of the hands to rest," then your poverty will come as a robber, and your want like an armed man.

How can this happen to us? The answer is given a couple of chapters later:

The sluggard says, "There is a lion in the road! A lion is in the open square!" As the door turns on its hinges, so does the sluggard on his bed. The sluggard buries his hand in the dish; he is weary of bringing it to his mouth again. The sluggard is wiser in his own eyes than seven men who can give a discreet answer (26:13–16).

The syndrome is painfully clear:
We see danger . . . but we don't care (the lion).
We are concerned . . . but are too lazy to change (the bed).
We become victims of habit (the dish).
We rationalize our failures.
"Decently and in order." That's our goal, remember. Most of us are a lot more decent than we are orderly. Which means we qualify as highly moral, well-behaved sluggards.

A Finishing Touch: An orderly life is like an orderly closet; it looks good and it serves its intended purpose.
A Daily Reading: Proverbs 24–27

A curious phenomenon has plagued families for as long as there have been families. Go back as far as time will take you, and there it is in all its mystery and misery. It's that age-old problem of second-generation fallout that breaks the hearts of godly moms and dads.

The scenario goes something like this. A man and woman fall in love and get married. They also love Christ and desire to serve Him with all their hearts. Their faith is tempered in the furnace of affliction and hammered out on the anvil of hardship. They press on in their spiritual growth by becoming involved in a local church, giving generously and consistently, and serving in various capacities. As their children come along, they teach and train and pray that God will get hold of their little lives and use them for His glory.

Childhood runs its course, leading to the teen years with all the inevitable adjustments and struggles. The family gets busier than ever, walking gingerly through the minefield of financial pressures, school activities, and relational skirmishes. Nothing blows apart, thank goodness . . . and before they know it, the kids are out of high school and on to college, vocations, the military, marriage, whatever.

Mom and dad breathe big sighs of relief ("We made it!"), still stable and strong in their Christian walk.

But what about the now-grown kids? Ah, there's the rub. Somewhere along the way God got pushed way down on their list of priorities. Disciplines like prayer, church attendance, tithing, serving, and serious Bible study got lost in the shuffle.

Is this some kind of twentieth-century malady? Has some giant spiritual eraser somehow wiped out recent generations, leaving us to accept reality and pick up the pieces? You know better. Even a cursory reading of the Scriptures reveals that generational fallout has always been with us. More parents' hearts have been broken than we could number.

Adam and Eve surely wept over Cain's murderous act. Noah was grieved because of Ham's shamelessness. Isaac and Rebekah must have spent countless sleepless nights, worrying about their twin boys. Eli, the priest, was embarrassed more than once because of his two immoral sons. David, who loved the Lord dearly, found himself at a loss to understand Absalom.

The list continues to the present day, and some of you who read these words could add your own name to it. The dilemma is not new.

While messing around recently on one of those obscure backroads of the Old Testament, I stumbled upon a similar family scene. It's one of those father-son stories that still speaks volumes. The dad was Hezekiah, a king who took the throne when he was 25 and reigned until he was 54. He was a good man—not perfect, but "he did right" and led his nation into a courageous reformation (2 Kings 18:3). Idols were destroyed, prophets were honored, enemy attacks were defeated, and the name of Israel's Lord was upheld.

At age 39, Hezekiah was healed from a terminal illness and granted 15 more years to live (2 Kings 20:1–7). During those years he became intensely involved in several impressive projects, including the re-establishment of temple worship (2 Chron. 32:27–31). On top of all this, he accumulated "immense riches and honor" and collected "silver, gold, precious stones, spices, shields, and all kinds of valuable articles."

All the while, his heart remained warm toward his God, and God prospered him. What a man!

When Hezekiah was 42, he and his wife, Hephzibah, had a son, Manasseh. The boy lived 12 years in the shadow of his famous father, the man God had immensely blessed. The young prince heard about and saw his father's great accomplishments. Then, suddenly, Hezekiah died . . . and his son (at age 12!) "became king, and reigned fifty-five years" (2 Kings 21:1).

But you'd never know he came from Hezekiah stock. Talk about second-generation fallout! Manasseh broke all the records. According to the inspired historian's account: He did evil in the sight of the Lord like none other. He rebuilt the idol altars his dad had destroyed. He erected idol altars in the house of the Lord. He practiced the occult. He seduced the people of Judah "to do evil more than the nations whom the LORD destroyed" (2 Kings 21:9).

The famous Jewish historian Josephus affirms that Manasseh not only slew the righteous men of Judah, but daily slew the prophets until Jerusalem was "overflowing with blood". Tradition has it that he had the prophet Isaiah sawn in two.

What went wrong? Why didn't Hezekiah's righteousness and passion pass to his son? I believe there are at least three reasons:

First, Manasseh had a will of his own—as we all do—and with that will he stubbornly and deliberately refused to respond to the Lord (2 Chron. 33:10).

Second, he was weak-willed and overly influenced by ungodly and wicked associations (2 Kings 21:3, 6). How else would he have learned of idolatry, witchcraft, and child sacrifices?

And third, he was neglected by his preoccupied, busy father. The king was at the zenith of his reign when Manasseh was born, and there is every indication that the prince saw little of his father during the formative years of his life. Hezekiah simply never took the time.

Sound familiar at all? Tune in tomorrow, and we'll talk about what might have prevented (or, in your case, might still prevent) this generational fallout.

A Finishing Touch: It is amazing how powerful first-generation presence can be when it comes to curing the second-generation plague.

A Daily Reading: 2 Kings 18–21

Those three reasons we discussed yesterday cause me to reserve my concluding thoughts for you parents who still have your children under your roof. Let me be painfully and firmly honest with you as I offer three suggestions:

First, *teach personal responsibility.* "Son, even though you are the only one, do what's right. Don't be afraid to stand alone." Then explain how it can be done. Or, "Sweetheart, even though others may be involved, take responsibility for your part in any wrongdoing." Ours is an era where passing the buck is an art form, where seeing oneself as an "innocent victim" is in vogue. Help your child face up to the hard facts . . . to tell the truth, regardless.

Second, *emphasize the erosion principle.* Evil is getting increasingly worse but also more cleverly disguised. Point that out. Explain how easy it is to get used to it . . . to shrug it off, rather than identify it and confront it.

Gary Bauer tells the shocking yet true story of a teacher who, twenty-five years ago, used to walk into her fourth grade class and greet them. "Good morning, children," to which they would respond, "Good morning, Miss Jones." She left teaching for many years to have her own family and rear them. She returned recently to the classroom and began the day in her usual way, "Good morning, children." To which a young thug on the front row responded, "Shut up, b—!" That's what I mean by the "erosion principle." If your youngster isn't alert, he or she will get swept up in it.

Third, *take time.* Not just to eat together, or work together around the house, or do homework together or go to the athletic games together, although those are important, too. Take time to talk together and walk together. To play together. To relax together. To do fun stuff together . . . just to be together.

Want a tip? Start today.

GOD'S DELIVERY SERVICE

I don't know where all this finds you today, but I have a sneaky suspicion that you, too, might have a few intruders crowding into your life and could use some divine reinforcements. If so, say so. Don't hesitate to call for help. Tell your Father that you are running out of hope and energy and ideas . . . that your mind is getting foggy and you need ". . . not . . . words taught by human wisdom, but . . . those taught by the Spirit, combining spiritual thoughts with spiritual words. . . . For who has known the mind of the Lord, that he should instruct him? But we have the mind of Christ" (1 Cor. 2:13, 16).

Since I cannot name all the possible tests being endured by everyone who reads my words, I will pick only one. You may have cancer. Damnable disease! The very word has a hiss in it. When the doctor uses it (or one of its nicer-sounding synonyms), it's devastating. Your heart is chilled, your head swims, you think you might have misunderstood, but you know you didn't. Words like "incurable" and "terminal" and "treatments" and "therapy" crowd out all other thoughts as you lay awake at night. For the first time in your earthly existence you feel mortal. Prayer is no longer a theological theory. Your life passes in review.

You fear a long and painful process after which you may recover . . . or you may not. Your body is carrying a disease . . . but you are determined not to let it conquer your mind. Good for you! Your physical appearance may change and your health may go through some severe ups and downs, but your spirit can remain triumphant. You want that more than anything else this side of a miraculous healing.

So what can you do? You dial Heaven 911 and you tell God you have an emergency need: "I have cancer, Lord, and I need wisdom." And at that very moment He will begin to make His deliveries.

Each morning from then on you ask for, and accept, the gift of His wisdom and you count on His strength for that day.

Amazingly, you soon discover that your greatest enemy is not the disease but subtle, slippery feelings of despair, the thief of peace. And so you rely on God's daily delivery service to get you through that one day. And then the next. And the next.

When Dan Richardson, an enthusiastic believer in Christ, lost his battle with cancer, the following piece was distributed at his memorial service.

> Cancer is limited . . .
> It cannot cripple love,
> It cannot corrode faith,
> It cannot eat away peace,
> It cannot destroy confidence,
> It cannot kill friendship,
> It cannot shut out memories,
> It cannot silence courage,
> It cannot invade the soul,
> It cannot reduce eternal life,
> It cannot quench the Spirit,
> It cannot lessen the power of the resurrection.

You may ultimately be healed. You may not. Whichever God sovereignly wills will be your lot. It's part of life's puzzle. You cannot deny that you have the disease, but you can deny despair from taking control.

Wherever you are, whatever your circumstances, call for God's daily delivery of wisdom, strength, and grace.

A Finishing Touch: Each morning, slam the door on despair. If you don't, it will slip in and rob you. And you'll soon find a peace missing.

A Daily Reading: 1 Corinthians 2

We Christians have too many meetings! Where did we get the idea that our goal in the family of faith should be seeing who can absorb the most information? Since when do we equate spirituality with a numb posterior?

Now, don't jump to the conclusion that I'm questioning the value of meeting together. Some of the most helpful and meaningful times in my life have taken place in a gathering of believers. But when I review our Lord's style of instruction, I cannot help but see how different it was from ours. He never suggested that the Twelve write anything down or repeat His words verbatim. And when He did exhort them, He used simple words, vivid illustrations, everyday examples, and easily understood applications—prompting them to action.

Words. Words. Words. We have become "too wordy" in our faith, which explains our excessive interest in meetings. When did we get the idea that more information leads to deeper consecration?

Jesus' arch enemies, the Pharisees, were great on loud, dogmatic commands, lengthy requirements, and drawn-out demands. Oh, how they loved the sound of their own words! But when it came to doing, they struck out.

James exhorts us to be "doers of the word, and not merely hearers who delude themselves" (James 1:22). In other words, don't talk compassion, lend a hand. Don't pound a pulpit about generosity, give. Just do it.

We won't be met at the portals of heaven by some angel with a clipboard, who asks, "And how many meetings did you attend in your lifetime on earth?" But while we're on earth, there is a question we do need to answer: "Why call ye Me, 'Lord, Lord,' and do not the things which I say?"

Several years ago I came across an eloquent albeit convicting piece entitled "The Lesson."

> Then Jesus took his disciples up the mountain and gathering them around him, he taught them, saying: Blessed are the poor

in spirit, for theirs is the kingdom of heaven, Blessed are the meek, Blessed are they that mourn, Blessed are the merciful, Blessed are they who thirst for justice, Blessed are you when persecuted, Blessed are you when you suffer, Be glad and rejoice for your reward is great in heaven.

Then Simon Peter said . . .

Do we have to write this down?

And Andrew said . . .

Are we supposed to know this?

And James said . . .

Will we have a test on this?

And Philip said . . .

I don't have any paper.

And Bartholomew said . . .

Do we have to turn this in?

And John said . . .

The other disciples didn't have to learn this.

And Matthew said . . .

Can I go to the boys' room?

And Judas said . . .

What does this have to do with real life?

And Jesus wept.

Sometimes I think I can still hear Him weeping.

A Finishing Touch: What do you think would happen if, instead of going to some meeting or conference, you spent that time alone with the Father?

A Daily Reading: James 1:22–25

There is something grand about old things that are still in good shape. Old furniture, rich with the patina of age and history, is far more intriguing than the uncomfortable, modern stuff. When you sit on it or eat off it or sleep in it, your mind pictures those in previous centuries who did the same in a world of candlelight, oil lamps, buggies, outhouses, and potbelly stoves. Each scrape or dent holds a story you wish you knew.

Old hardback books are far more fascinating than today's slick paperbacks. Classic, leather-bound works with marbled endsheets and gilded edges carry a feel and a smell that defy duplication. I find it therapeutic to hold in my hands pages that have endured the ages, to pore over lines that other eyes have pondered and other fingers have marked. Reading the same words in updated reprints is not the same. It is the authenticity of antiquity that thrills me within.

Old churches affect me the same way. In the English countryside, in the valleys of Virginia, or on the rolling hills of Texas you can still find stained-glass windows, hardwood floors, and wooden pews. As you settle into the creaking oak pew, you can hear the pipe organ filling the sanctuary with one of Bach's masterworks. The thunderous voice of the preacher is in the woodwork, and the altar beckons you to be still and know that God is God. The graveyard adjacent to the church, with its gray slate stones and eloquent etchings, reminds that the sting of death broke other hearts.

Strangely, such sights and sounds and smells equip us to face our own battles with renewed vigor, for it's the old things—things that have outlived fashions and fads, that have endured wars and recessions, presidents and plagues—that remind us to pause and encourage us to strengthen our roots. Old bridges, old walls, old houses, old boats, old bikes, old hymns, old pictures, old memories . . . these do more than prompt nostalgic feelings; they remind us that we are not alone in this adventurous pilgrimage from earth to heaven.

By standing on the shoulders of yesterday, the view into tomorrow is not nearly so frightening. New feelings pulsate within us. New determination to press on. New courage to stand alone. New feelings of gratitude to keep us humble. New joys to take the grind out of today's demands. New strength to endure today's tests.

The Bible is old also—ancient, in fact. Its timeless stories have for centuries shouted, "You can make it! Don't quit . . . don't give up!" Its truths, secure and solid as stone, say, "I'm still here, waiting to be claimed and applied." Whether it's a prophet's warning, a patriarch's prayer, a poet's psalm, or a preacher's challenging reminder, the Book of books lives on, offering us new vistas. It still speaks as it did in the days when reformers heralded hope from strong pulpits, when rough-hewn revivalists pleaded for souls in open-air campaigns, when faithful expositors taught saints of yesteryear and, perhaps more importantly, lived lives of uncompromising integrity, when rugged missionaries left the comforts of home to carry its message to hostile tribes and foreign climes.

The truths of this old Book have endured in spite of the attacks of its critics and the attempts of the Adversary to silence its message—like an ageless anvil wearing away the hammers.

Though ancient, it has never lost its relevance. Though battered, no one has ever improved on its content. Though old, it never fails to offer something pure, something wise, something new.

A Finishing Touch: By touching something old, something new is stirred within us.

A Daily Reading: Isaiah 40

Remember me? I'm the guy who promotes waiting. Refusing to run ahead. Allowing the Lord to open the doors, clear the way, smooth the path, shove you through. You know, all the stuff you expect a preacher to say. "Waiting" is one of my favorite axes to grind. I even tie a ribbon on the ol' ax by quoting verses to support all the above.

But I do think we occasionally need a different emphasis. We can get so good at waiting that we never act . . . cobwebs form, a layer of dust settles, we yawn and passively mutter, "Maybe, someday" as we let opportunities slip away.

Some people are more wait-conscious than a roomful of heavies in an aerobics class. They put everything on hold! Like having friends over for ice cream or going on a picnic. Like using their fine china or celebrating a birthday . . . or slipping away for a weekend of relaxation and romance . . . or taking a cruise or traveling abroad . . . or sailing for a day . . . or spending a week away with the family. "Not this year . . . but maybe, someday. . . ."

Don't wait! If you continue such passivity, someday will never come—and you'll regret it for the rest of your days. I realized this anew when I read the following in the *Los Angeles Times*. If this doesn't get you off the dime, nothing will. Ann Wells writes:

> My brother-in-law opened the bottom drawer of my sister's bureau and lifted out a tissue-wrapped package. . . . He discarded the tissue and handed me the slip. It was exquisite; silk, hand-made and trimmed with a cobweb of lace. The price tag with an astronomical figure on it was still attached.
>
> "Jan bought this the first time we went to New York, at least eight or nine years ago. She never wore it. She was saving it for a special occasion. Well, I guess this is the occasion."
>
> He took the slip from me and put it on the bed with the other clothes we were taking to the mortician. His hands lingered on the soft material for a moment, then he slammed the drawer shut and turned to me.

"Don't ever save anything for a special occasion. Every day you are alive is a special occasion."

I remembered those words through the funeral and the days that followed when I helped him and my niece attend to all the sad chores that follow an unexpected death. . . .

I'm still thinking about his words, and they've changed my life. . . . I'm not "saving" anything; we use our good china and crystal for every special event—such as losing a pound, getting the sink unstopped, the first camellia blossom. . . .

"Someday" and "one of these days" are losing their grip on my vocabulary. If it's worth seeing or hearing or doing, I want to see and hear and do it now. . . . I'm trying very hard not to put off, hold back, or save anything that would add laughter and luster to our lives. And every morning when I open my eyes I tell myself that it is special.

Grabs you, doesn't it? Makes me want to drain every last ounce of joy out of every day. It also breaks me free from the concrete of procrastination that sets up harder every time I'm tempted to whisper to myself, "Later, Chuck . . . just put it off till later."

Remember me? I'm the guy who now says, "Don't wait!"

A Finishing Touch: Every day is that special day you've been waiting for. Don't wait!

A Daily Reading: 2 Corinthians 6:1–10

As a communicator, Jesus was nothing short of remarkable. Without the assistance of a public address system or the comfort of beautiful music, soft seats, and air-conditioning, His audiences listened with rapt attention. And most of His teaching occurred outside, amidst the distractions of nature and/or the noise of busy city streets. But none of that seemed to matter. When He talked, people listened.

While reading through Mark's Gospel recently, I was drawn into the scene of chapter 4. You remember, it's that time He sat down in a little boat by the seashore and talked about a farmer who dropped seeds into the dirt. Simple story. Easy to remember, even if you're a little kid. Same seed, different soil. Same time of sowing, but different results. Four to be exact.

Some seeds fell beside the road . . . the birds gobbled them up.

A few seeds fell on rocky ground . . . the searing rays of the sun scorched the rootless growth and they withered and died.

Other seeds fell among thorns . . . which choked out the growth so severely there was no crop to harvest.

Still other seeds fell into good soil . . . bumper crop.

Interestingly, Jesus closed off His brief talk with that familiar line, "He who has ears to hear, let him hear" (Mark 4:9). Almost as if He assumed, "You're gonna miss what I'm saying if you don't let these things penetrate . . . hear them well . . . absorb their significance . . . don't let anything drown out My voice!"

I kept reading, somewhat preoccupied with my goal of completing the chapter, only to be caught short with that "ears to hear" phrase again and again.

So I returned to the Master's story and reread it. As I did, I was rebuked for my shortsightedness, especially as I began to digest His follow-up explanation. For, unlike most parables He told, Jesus went back over this one point by point, leaving no room for doubt or misunderstanding.

First, He said, the seed represents "the word." I believe we're safe in saying that "the word" refers to truth. God's truth. Truth for living. Life-giving words provided for us by the Lord our God. The Scriptures, yes, but also the insights, the perspective, and the wisdom that grow in us when the seed takes root.

Second, the different soils represent people's varied responses to that "word." All four, please notice, "hear," but not all reap a harvest. That's significant. Hearing guarantees nothing. It simply means the seed fell: "the word" was made available.

Next, the results are directly related to the condition of the soil . . . not the quality of the seed. Same seed, remember, but different soil. In some it is wasted, in others it soon withers, in some it is choked, in others it grows well. If you look closely, you'll see that the first two groups lack roots. Only with the last two groups does Jesus mention fruit.

I think it's obvious that the first two groups of people are without spiritual life. No roots, no fruit, no growth, no change whatsoever. The last two have roots . . . they just differ in the realm of fruit. One "becomes unfruitful," while the others "bear fruit thirty, sixty, and a hundredfold." The third group hears, but only the fourth group "hears the word and accepts it," resulting in strong, healthy growth.

It's the third group that intrigues me. These people hear everything the fourth group hears. But those truths are not really accepted, allowed to take root, and grow. Instead, the thorns "choke the word and it becomes unfruitful."

Thorns that choke? What are they? Jesus, being the excellent communicator that He was, doesn't leave us in the dark. Choking thorns are "the worries of the world, and the deceitfulness of riches, and the desires for other things" (Mark 4:19).

The term "worry" is derived from the old German word *wurgen*, which means "to choke." Somehow, by extension, the word came to denote "mental strangulation," and, finally, to describe the condition of being harassed with anxiety.

It's the thorns that bug us. Always growing, ready to "choke the word" right out of our minds. Take worry (I wish somebody would!). It begins as a thin stream, trickling through our minds. If entertained, it cuts a deeper channel into which other thoughts are drained. The same is true of "the deceitfulness of riches." What a consuming passion . . . yet how empty, how unsatisfying! And yet we rationalize by saying they don't mean that much to us. Like the great heavyweight champ, Joe Louis, who smiled and said, "I don't like money actually, but it quiets my nerves." Yeah, sure, Joe.

But the third species of thorns is the killer: "the desires for other things." Better think that one through. It's the picture of discontentment, the plague of pursuit: pushing, straining, stretching, relentlessly reaching, while our minds become strangled with the lie, "enough just isn't enough," which makes great thorn fertilizer. Ah, when will we learn?

Being the great communicator that He was, the Nazarene left much of the application unsaid. He was careful not to smother His listeners, but to let each person draw his or her own specific conclusions.

"He who has ears to hear, let him hear."

A Finishing Touch: When the thorns of life scratch us, we need the pruning shears of the Word.

A Daily Reading: Mark 4

The bad news is this: Listening won't make the thorns go away, no matter how much we concentrate and welcome Jesus' teachings. Thorns come with the territory called depravity.

But the good news is this: Listening—I mean really giving heed to the seed—results in deeper roots and greater fruit . . . and thorns can't strangle such healthy growth.

Jesus is still communicating, but if we're not careful, we'll let our mental strangulation drown out His voice. Things that strangle us grow well in comfortable surroundings even when we look like we're listening.

In what way might these thorns be encroaching in your life. Go back and reread the meditation and the Scripture and then do some honest assessment.

Worries?

_____

_____

The deceitfulness of riches?

_____

_____

The desires for other things?

_____

_____

EXPECTING THE UNEXPECTED

It had been a long time since Horace Walpole smiled. Too long. Life for him had become as drab as the weather in dreary old England. Then, on a grim winter day in 1754, while reading a Persian fairy tale, his smile returned. He wrote his longtime friend, Horace Mann, telling him of the "thrilling approach to life" he had discovered from the folk tale . . . how it had freed him from his dark prison of gloom.

The ancient tale told of three princes from the island of Ceylon who set out on a pursuit of great treasures. They never found that for which they searched, but en route they were continually surprised by delights they had never anticipated. While looking for one thing, they found another.

The original name of Ceylon was Serendip, which explains the title of this story—"The Three Princes of Serendip." From that, Walpole coined the wonderful word *serendipity*. And from then on, his most significant and valued experiences were those that happened to him while he was least expecting them.

Seren-dip-ity—the *dip* of the *serene* into the common responsibilities of life. Serendipity occurs when something beautiful breaks into the monotonous and the mundane. A serendipitous life is marked by "surprisability" and spontaneity. When we lose our capacity for either, we settle into life's ruts. We expect little and we're seldom disappointed.

Though I have walked with God for several decades, I must confess I still find much about Him incomprehensible and mysterious. But this much I know: He delights in surprising us. He dots our pilgrimage from earth to heaven with amazing serendipities. Several individuals in Scripture immediately come to mind.

Weary Moses, after forty years of tending sheep, stopped and took the time to see why the bush refused to burn up. The serendipity of an exodus was just around the corner.

Troubled Jacob finally confessed, "The Lord is in this place and I knew it not!" Result? A personal transformation.

Confused Paul, having had one Asian door of opportunity after another slammed shut without explanation, was sensitive enough to hear those pleading words in a dream at Troas, "Come over and help us." He did . . . and Europe heard the good news of the Savior.

Legalistic Peter, determined not to eat anything "common or unclean," had an enormous non-kosher banquet spread before him. That serendipity prepared him for ministry to the Gentiles.

Isaiah's words make me smile every time I read them because I have seen their truth come to pass time and again. God still stands behind this promise:

> See, I am doing a new thing!
> Now it springs up; do you not perceive it?
> I am making a way in the desert
> and streams in the wasteland (Isa. 43:19 NIV).

Your situation may be as hot and barren as a desert or as forlorn and meaningless as a wasteland. You may be tempted to think, "There's no way!" when someone suggests things could change. All I ask is that you read that verse one more time and be on the lookout. God may very well be planning a serendipity in your life.

A Finishing Touch: God has been doing "a new thing" in drab deserts and wintry wastelands for centuries.

A Daily Reading: Isaiah 43:15–19

Even though the song was composed before I was born (which makes it a real oldie), I often find myself humming it in the shower at the beginning of a busy day, between appointments and assignments in the middle of a hectic day, and on the road home at the end of a tiring day. Somehow it adds a soothing touch of oil to the grind: "Without a song the day would never end ... without a song. ..."

True, isn't it? The right combination of words and melody seldom fails to work its magic. And given the pressures and demands we are forced to cope with on a daily basis, we could use a little magic. Consider the relentless daily grind of ...

The homemaker with children at her feet who faces fourteen or more hours a day in the grind of meeting deadlines, making decisions, competing with strong wills, and completing an endless list of chores.

The professional who deals with the grind of people, people, people ... especially dissatisfied people who'd rather scream and sue than smile and solve, which only increases expectations and decreases energy.

The truck driver who heads into the grind of traffic snarls, weather hazards, thoughtless drivers, and monotonous miles.

The athlete who lives with the grind of repetition. Unending hours of practice. Fierce competition. Injuries, boredom, exhaustion.

And who can deny the exacting requirements of academic pursuits? Students and faculty who face the cyclical grind of daily preparation and assignments, exams and papers.

Fact is, no matter who you are or what you do, the grind ain't gonna go away! The sales person has quotas. The performer has rehearsals. The therapist can't escape one depressed soul after another. The pilot has to stay strapped in for hours. The preacher is never free of sermon preparation. The broadcaster cannot get away from the clock any more than the military person can escape the hassle of red tape. Days don't end ... roads don't bend ... help!

The question is: How do we live beyond the daily grind? The answer is: A song. But not just any song! Certainly not some mindless, earsplitting tune yelled into a microphones. No, not that. I have in mind some songs that are really old. We're talking ancient here. In fact, they are the ones inspired and composed by our Creator-God—the original Rock music, with a capital "R." They're called psalms.

These are the timeless songs that have yielded delicious fruit in every generation. Not silly ditties, but strong melodious messages specially designed to help us live beyond the grind. That's right, *beyond it.* "We'll get along as long as a *psalm* is strong in our souls."

Those age-old compositions drip with the oil of glory that enables us to live beyond the grind. Songs of victory, affirmation, and encouragement, of confidence-giving strength, of hope, of compassion.

Without God's song in our soul, our long days will never end and those wearisome roads will never bend.

A Finishing Touch: God's Book is full of songs—150 of them. Let's sing them frequently and allow their time-tested lyrics to oil our days.

A Daily Reading: Exodus 15:2

How many people stop because so few say "Go"?!

In his fine little book *Fully Human, Fully Alive*, author John Powell relates an experience which happened to a friend while he was vacationing in the Bahamas. The friend was sightseeing when he noticed a crowd gathered toward the end of a pier. He walked down to investigate the commotion. Powell says:

> . . . he discovered that the object of all the attention was a young man making the last-minute preparations for a solo journey around the world in a homemade boat. Without exception everyone on the pier was pessimistic. All were actively volunteering to tell the ambitious sailor all the things that could possibly go wrong. "The sun will BROIL you!" "You won't have enough food." "That boat of yours won't withstand the waves in a storm." [And, of course, those familiar words] "You'll never make it."
>
> When my friend heard all these discouraging warnings to the adventurous young man, he felt an irresistible desire to offer some optimism and encouragement. As the little craft began drifting away from the pier towards the horizon, my friend went to the end of the pier, waving both arms wildly like semaphores spelling confidence. He kept shouting: "BON VOYAGE! You're really something! We're with you. We're proud of you!"

Had you been there as that homemade boat was leaving, which group would you have joined? C'mon, be honest. No doubt the great majority of us would have thought more of the danger than the adventure. Most of us would have anticipated the rigors and the difficulties and the risk rather than the fun, the discoveries, the incredible opportunities that lay ahead of the man putting out to sea. How few are those who see beyond the danger . . . who say to those on the edge of some venture, "Go for it!"

Funny, isn't it? I suppose it's related to one's inner ability to imagine, to envision, to be enraptured by the unseen, all the hazards and hardships notwithstanding.

I'm convinced that one of the reasons mountain climbers connect themselves to one another with a rope is to keep the one on the end from going home. Guys out front never consider that as an option . . . but those in the rear, well, let's just say they are the last to get a glimpse of the glory.

I've been thinking recently about how glad I am that certain visionaries refused to listen to the crowd on the pier. I'm glad . . .

— that Edison didn't give up on the light bulb
— that Luther refused to back down
— that Michelangelo kept painting
— that Lindbergh kept flying
— that Papa Ten Boom said "Yes" to frightened Jews
— that the Julliard School of Music saw beyond the braces and wheelchair and admitted a violin student named Perlman.

You could add to that list. You may even belong on the list.

Almost every day—certainly every week—we encounter someone who is in his or her own homemade boat, thinking seriously about setting forth. It may be a friend, a mate, a colleague, a neighbor, a family member. The ocean of possibilities is enormously inviting, yet terribly threatening. Urge them on! Shout a rousing "You are really something . . . I'm proud of you!" Dare to say what they need to hear the most, "Go for it!" Then pray like mad.

How much could be accomplished if only there were more brave souls on the end of the pier smiling and affirming.

A Finishing Touch: Most of the time it's not a matter of having the goods, but of hearing the bads.

A Daily Reading: Luke 5:1–10

For over an hour the other day I strolled down Nostalgia Lane with a September 4, 1939, copy of *Time* magazine. What a journey!

A youthful photograph of Sir Winston Churchill graced the cover, while the advertisements woven through the pages made their own statements about the way we were back then.

Top-grade gasoline was called "Ethyl." Florsheim shoes were priced from $8.75 to $10. Pickups sold for $465 and best-selling books cost $2. Big news in the music world was Bing Crosby whose records sold for 35 cents a platter. Glenn Miller was also big time. A one-carat diamond started at $325 and two carats sold for between $900 and $1750.

What was most intriguing, however, was the international scene, as presented by the staff writers. The threat of war was a slumbering giant, and Adolf Hitler's name appeared on almost every page of the Foreign News section. President Franklin Roosevelt was busy calming the troubled waters of our nation's fear of war, speaking openly of his "lovely hope for peace." In spite of the Nazi war machine that had already consumed Italy, Sicily, Albania, and was primed to pounce on Poland, Hungary, Belgium, and France, the talk in America was amazingly casual, a smug business-as-usual attitude.

A Nazi-Soviet Treaty had been signed. Britain had had its jitters quieted by another so-called "treaty," even though portable bomb shelters were being placed in strategic locations across London. British diplomats and ambassadors wore worried looks in all the pictures that appeared in that late-summer issue. Herr Hitler's face was unusually free of those ominous lines of fatigue that appeared later. Even Soviet ruler, Joseph Stalin, appeared cheery. All seemed relatively quiet on the western front.

So much has changed since then—only fifty-some years later. The names and faces that filled the pages are now gone. The words that made such good sense and gave our country a false sense of security and goodwill now seem so foolish and sound so hollow. With the foresight of hindsight, we're able to see right through the false promises and empty dreams. How simple life seemed. How naive we were! Little did we know that within months the insane Fuhrer would unleash a hellish nightmare from which we could not escape. Before his screams were silenced, acres of soil would be covered with small white crosses, and thousands of American homes would have their tranquil plans for peace invaded by the brutal enemy of grief.

Back when Crosby crooned us to sleep and most folks in our country were blushing over a four-letter word in *Gone With the Wind*, who would have imagined the atrocities of Auschwitz and Dachau?

Ever so often when we enter such a relatively calm era, it is easy to forget the prophet's warning to beware of those who superficially heal the brokenness of a nation by announcing "peace, peace" when "there is no peace" (Jer. 6:14; 8:11). And if we feel sufficiently comfortable and relaxed, it's mighty easy to block from our minds the Savior's prediction of "wars and rumors of wars" and His warning that "many false prophets will arise and mislead many" (Matt. 24:6–7, 11).

Who knows? Fifty years from now another preacher could be leafing through a *Time* magazine yellow with age, feeling a nostalgic twinge and smiling at what we consider modern times. He will no doubt notice the business-as-usual look on our faces, only to be seized with the realization that we had no idea what a ragged edge we were living on in our relaxed American culture.

If indeed there is an America fifty years from now.

A Finishing Touch: We need to be alert. Sometimes the best of times may be a breeding ground for the worst of times.

A Daily Reading: Jeremiah 6:14, 8:11; Matthew 24:6–7, 11

I've been giving a lot of thought these days to the subject of God's will. While engaged in a particular study of that issue recently I came across a term we rarely use or read these days. In fact, it is so rare, the word sounds old-fashioned. Archaic, even.

The term is *providence*. And the only time we ever hear it is when someone refers to the capital city of Rhode Island. Read the writings of Christians from earlier centuries, however, and you will find frequent references to God's providence.

Why don't we hear more about it today? Because the spirit of naturalism, which views all events in nature as ruled by independent natural forces, has left its mark on our generation. Too bad. We would do well to reintroduce this grand word to our tongues as well as to our young.

The root meaning of providence is "foresight . . . to see in advance" or "to provide for." But those definitions could leave us with too shallow an understanding. For God is not a fine old gentleman, standing back as a spectator of human events. Providence contains far more than a passive reference to His foreknowledge.

Back in the seventeenth century, the Westminster divines hammered out a much more thorough statement:

> God, the great Creator of all things, doth uphold, direct, dispose, and govern all creatures, actions, and things from the greatest event to the least, by His most wise and holy providence, according to His infallible foreknowledge, and the free and immutable counsel of His own will, to the praise of the glory of His wisdom, power, justice, goodness and mercy.

While Paul was addressing those sophisticated eggheads on Mars Hill, he spoke of providence when he stated "for in Him we live and move and exist: (Acts 17:28). God not only struck the spark that gave you and me life, He continues to prompt each heartbeat in every chest. And what He does for us as individuals, He does for the vast universe about us. Furthermore, what God creates, God sustains. As the Scriptures state so clearly, He upholds all things by His power. Think of it . . . *all things*!

The universe may seem fiercely independent, but it is wholly dependent upon its Creator: " . . . *all things* have been created by Him and for Him. And He is before *all things*, and in Him *all things* hold together" (Col. 1:16b-17, italics added).

Make no mistake about it, "He's got the whole world in His hands." His governing authority is limitless. From the greatest to the least, nothing is beyond the scope of His sovereign power and providential care. He makes the rain fall, the sun shine, the stars twinkle—in this and all other galaxies. He raises up people and kingdoms and He brings down both. He numbers the hairs on our heads and determines the days of our lives. In doing so, He weaves everything together into His design. Ultimately, the tapestry of His handiwork will be something to behold!

This is an ideal moment for me to urge you to remove three words from your vocabulary as you add providence. They are chance, fate and luck. Those humanistic terms suggest that there are blind, impersonal, and spontaneous forces at work in the ranks of humanity. NOT! Only One is at work: "for it is God who is at work in you, both to will and to work for His good pleasure" (Phil. 2:13).

But wait, I hear someone say. Don't you and I possess a will? We're not robots, are we? Aren't we able to act independently of a sovereign God? R.C. Sproul addresses this well in *Essential Truths of the Christian Faith*:

> We are creatures with a will of our own. We make things happen. Yet the casual power we exert is secondary. God's sovereign providence stands over and above our actions. He works out His will through the actions of human wills, without violating the freedom of those human wills.

Theologians have given an appropriate name to this: they call it *concurrence*. One of the clearest examples of concurrence is found in the story of Joseph and his brothers. Though they were guilty of a treacherous plot, cruelty, and deceit, hoping to bring permanent harm to Joseph, God was concurrently working out His perfect and sovereign will even through their sin. Joseph later realized this, which freed him from an unforgiving, bitter spirit. Many years later he told them, "And as for you, you meant evil against me; but God meant it for good in order to bring about this present result . . ." (Gen. 50:20).

All this helps us focus more on the Creator and less on the created . . . to appreciate the Giver instead of idolizing the gifts. Providence enlarges our perspective, and all of us certainly need that, especially when so much of what we can see around us falls into the category of wickedness and wrong.

God's redemptive providence is always at work, even through the most diabolical schemes and actions. Classic illustration? The betrayal of Jesus Christ by Judas. Strange as it may seem, Judas' worst act of wickedness helped to bring about the best thing that ever happened: the Atonement.

So, take heart, my friend. God is in full control. Nothing is happening on earth that brings a surprise to heaven. Nothing is outside the scope of His divine radar screen as He guides us safely home. Things that seem altogether confusing, without reason, unfair, even wrong, do indeed fit into the Father's providential plan.

A Finishing Touch: Nothing touches us that has not first passed through His hands.

A Daily Reading: Genesis 50

After a lengthy bout with despair, severe depression, and suicide attempts, writer and poet William Cowper (1731–1800) discovered comfort in God's providence, which led him to write "Shining out of Darkness":

> God moves in a mysterious way,
> His wonders to perform;
> He plants his footsteps in the sea
> And rides upon the storm.
>
> Deep in unfathomable mines
> Of never failing skill,
> He treasures up his bright designs,
> And works his sovereign will.
>
> . . . .
>
> Judge not the Lord by feeble sense,
> But trust him for his grace;
> Behind a frowning providence,
> He hides a smiling face.

Can you think of instances in your own life, with the advantage of 20-20 hindsight, wherein someone or something "meant evil" against you, "but God meant it for good"? Thank and praise Him for it—and for His continual providence.

A LITTLE COURTESY, PLEASE

Spring has sprung. Longer days are before us. And baseball, that grand old American game, is upon us. One hundred and sixty-two regular-season games, to be specific.

That's a lot of strikeouts and double plays, hot dogs and Cokes, relaxed conversations and fun memories. One of the things I've always enjoyed about the game is the atmosphere that surrounds the fans in the stands. You have time to sit and tell stories together. Families can hang out and spend the whole evening doing really nothing. It's great! While all those men are out there playing a kid's game, nobody has any reason to get uptight. It's baseball, remember . . . nine (or more) innings of laughs and jokes, nachos and peanuts, crowd-watching and scorekeeping. Unlike professional hockey and NBA basketball, you can take your eyes off the field for several minutes and not miss much. Most pitchers have to jerk on their jerseys, scratch, spit, readjust their caps, walk around the mound a time or two, and scratch again (!) before slinging that ball toward home plate.

Funny thing about baseball, though. The guys who have more reason than anyone else to get nervous and uneasy are on the field, but they're not on a team. They're the guys in uniform, affectionately referred to as "the umps" . . . or stuff much worse than that.

We're awfully hard on the umpires, but I'm told that's our right, since we paid to get in. I've never quite figured out that logic. Why would buying a ticket give anyone the right to insult, curse, scream at, or ridicule a person who has the toughest job in baseball? Can you imagine how hopelessly impossible it would be to play the game without them? You'd think they were the bad guys if you didn't know better.

The horror stories they tell never cease to sadden and sometimes shock me. If it wouldn't mean my loss of limb or life, I'd like to take some fans who delight in insults and say, "Hey, let's remember that those fellows are doing a lot better job than we could do. Show a little courtesy, please!" And if you're the type who needs a verse of Scripture to verify an exhortation, how about this one: "Be kind to one another, tender-hearted, forgiving each other . . . " (Eph. 4:32).

I would especially like to see some changes like this at Little League games, where nobody pays to get in. This is supposed to be a pleasant setting where boys have the opportunity to learn more about the game of life than the game of baseball. That was driven home to me recently when I read the words of Donald Jensen, who was struck in the head by a thrown bat while umpiring a Little League game in Terre Haute, Indiana. He continued to work the game, but later that evening was placed in the hospital by a physician. While being kept overnight for observation, Jensen wrote an eloquent letter to folks whose shenanigans make you cringe or bow your head in shame. At one point he says:

> The purpose of Little League is to teach baseball skills to young men. Obviously, a team which does not play well in a given game, yet is given the opportunity to blame that loss on an umpire for one call or two, is being given the chance to take all responsibility for the loss from their shoulders. A parent or adult leader who permits the younger player to blame his failures on an umpire . . . is doing the worst kind of injustice to that youngster. . . . This irresponsibility is bound to carry over to future years.

What Donald Jensen wrote that night in Indiana was absolutely right. Next time you're tempted to insult or mistreat an umpire, remember him—the late Donald Jensen. The following morning he died of a brain concussion.

A Finishing Touch: How we play often reveals how we live.
A Daily Reading: Ephesians 4:29–32

Recently a friend dropped by my study to chat about several items of mutual interest. This man is a true friend, and my life is richer because our paths have crossed. He also speaks the truth in love, which brings me to the most important part of our visit—the last twenty minutes.

As he closed his folder, he had that look of unfinished business. He tilted his head and took a deep breath, obviously gathering courage to say something.

"Go ahead . . . tell me what's eating away at you," I urged.

"Well, I don't know how I should say these things, Chuck, But I can't just ignore them either. The fact is, I'm concerned."

"Concerned about what?" I probed.

He then went on to tell me, his dark eyes fixed squarely on mine, that he was concerned about the number of responsibilities I had been taking on of late. "I don't think you'll fall morally or ethically," he said. "What does worry me is that you could be tempted to let your time with God and your time in the study of the Scriptures become less and less important to you. I want to urge you: *Do not let that happen.*"

He said several other equally important things, which I'll not forget. I told him how much I appreciated his words of warning, the genuineness of his heart, the courage of his reproof. And I assured him that I never wanted to neglect the essentials in my life or my ministry. God deserves my best, not the leftover scraps of a harum-scarum schedule.

His visit was both timely and memorable. He needed to say those things, and I needed to hear them. In them I could also hear the echo of my mother's voice saying, "Do your job, Charles."

Ours is a day of superficiality. If you can fake it, you're often admired as being clever, rather than being criticized for being phony. And mediocrity can mark the ministry just as easily as it can mark those in other callings and vocations. The painful truth is that we ministers can be lazy, indifferent, perfunctory, controlling, and even

144

mean-spirited. We are not above predictability or plagiarism, especially if we've not managed our time well. I know of few professions where envy can be more prominent and where pride can be more manipulative. It is easy to learn how to hide those ugly faces behind pious masks. We're all depraved. The difference is that some of us are better at cover-up.

So, after my friend left, I made a few promises. Maybe these are promises you should make, too, adapting them to your own situation.

I promise to keep doing original and hard work in my study. Those to whom I am called deserve my best efforts.

I promise to maintain a heart for God. That means I will pray frequently and fervently, and stay devoted to Him and to my calling.

I promise to remain accountable. Living the life of a religious Lone Ranger is not only unbiblical, it's dangerous.

I promise to stay faithful to my family. My wife deserves my time, affection, and undivided attention. Our now-grown children deserve the same.

I promise to be who I am. Just me. I plan to keep laughing, saying things a little off the wall, being a friend, and making a few mistakes each month.

I have my friend to thank for this recommitment. He deserves the credit. He's the guy with guts enough to tell me, in so many words, "Do your job, Charles."

We all need more friends like that.

A Finishing Touch: Do you need to "tell the truth in love" to someone? Do you need to make a few promises yourself?

A Daily Reading: 1 Kings 3:5–15

Every time you pick up a daily paper or watch the news you see that someone is protesting something. When I think of "protest," however, my thoughts often turn to that small band of men who had the guts to protest a religious system of beliefs and practices that had become corrupt to the core.

Godless church prelates paraded their carnality, indulging in shameless acts of the flesh. Bibles, banned from the common people, were chained to ornate pulpits and printed only in Latin, the "secret language" of the clergy. Instead of demonstrating compassion, unselfishness, grace, and other servant-like characteristics, those who led were anything but models of Christ.

"Enough!" thought a few straight-thinking souls. Men like Wycliffe, Tyndale, Zwingli, Knox, Calvin, and Luther refused to sit back, smile, and stay quiet. Their zeal became contagious, and they led thousands of others who joined their band of "protestants." And protest they did!

Lest you think these men were paragons of perfection, however, let me introduce you to the real Dr. Luther. Few religious leaders were more eccentric . . . more extreme. By his own admission he struggled vigorously with sins of the flesh. Especially outrageous anger. Sarcasm dripped from his pen. Once he admitted: "I never work better than when I am inspired of anger; when I am angry I can write, pray and preach well."

As is true of most larger-than-life characters, exaggeration and extravagance swarm around his story, making it difficult to filter out myth from truth. But one thing is certain: Martin Luther was not irrelevant. Irreverent, yes; irrelevant, no. Out of step, yes; out of touch, no. Off base, yes; off target, no. Insulting and offensive, yes; impertinent and tedious, no.

His philosophy could be summed up in his own timely words: "If you preach the gospel in all aspects with the exception of the issues which deal specifically with your time—you are not preaching the gospel at all."

In other words, the Gospel isn't to be changed. But it is to cut into each generation, like a flashing sword sharpened on the stone of Scripture, tempered in the furnace of reality, relevance, and need. Of all the reactions a person may have to the Gospel, I can think of none worse than a yawn . . . a sleepy "So what?" . . . a bored "Who cares?"

Jesus Christ met people where they were. His words touched nerves. There was a lot more here-and-now than then-and-there in His talks. His attack on the hypocrisy and prejudice of religious phonies came through loud and clear. He met people as they were, not as they "ought to" be. Angry young men, blind beggars, proud politicians, loose-living streetwalkers, ignorant fishermen, naked victims of demonism, and grieving parents were as clearly in His focus as the Twelve who sometimes hung on His every word.

His enemies misunderstood Him, but they couldn't ignore Him. They hated Him, but were never bored around Him. Jesus was the epitome of relevance. Still is.

It is we who have hauled the cross back out of sight. It is we who have left the impression that it belongs beneath the soft shadows of stained glass and marble statues.

And so . . . let's never lose relevance as we continue on in our work of reforming. Let's never bore people with the Gospel. Let's never think that Christianity is something we must keep to ourselves and fearfully protect. Let's stay in the trenches of real-world involvements.

A Finishing Touch: "Jesus was not crucified in a cathedral between two candles, but on a cross between two thieves" (George MacLeod).

A Daily Reading: 1 Corinthians 15:58; 1 Peter 5:8–11

Tucked away in the folds of Hebrews 11 is a two-word biography worth a second glance: ". . . he endured" (11:27).

The *Living Bible* says, ". . . he kept right on going."

The *New International Version*: ". . . he persevered."

The *New English Bible*: ". . . he was resolute."

The *Amplified*: ". . . he held staunchly to his purpose."

And *Moffatt's* quaint rendering: ". . . he never flinched."

The "he" refers to Moses. Moses was the one who hung tough, who refused to give in or give up, who decided that no amount of odds against him would cause him to surrender. He had staying power. Once Moses made up his mind, nothing would deter the man. He possessed the disciplines of durability.

He endured, despite the contempt of Pharaoh, the mightiest monarch of that era. No amount of resistance from Egypt's throne dimmed his determination. He endured, despite the stubbornness of the Hebrews who grumbled, blamed, complained, and rebelled. Nothing they said or did made Moses retreat. He endured, despite the criticism of Miriam and Aaron, his own sister and brother. Their words cut deeply, but he refused to back off. Misunderstood, maligned, murmured against, and misrepresented, Moses "never flinched." He endured, despite the disappointments he encountered. When ten out of twelve spies came back with their nay-sayings, Moses stood fast. When Korah and Dathan and Abiram led a cold, cunning conspiracy against him, Moses remained "resolute."

Maybe the great apostle of grace had such things in mind when he introduced his classic essay on the armor of God by saying, ". . . and having done everything . . . stand firm" (Eph. 6:13).

Stand firm when conspirators seem to prosper. Stand firm when the wicked appear to be winning. Stand firm in times of crisis. Stand firm even when no one will know if you compromised. Stand firm when big people act contemptibly small. Stand firm when petty people demand authority they don't deserve. Stand firm . . . keep your head . . . stay true . . . endure!

I have no idea where this finds you. For all I know, you are stronger than ever, determined not to shrink back, pressing on with a full tank of resolve. That's great. However, you may be getting shaky. Your normally thick hide of moral purity and ethical integrity may be wearing thin. It's possible you've begun to listen too closely to your critics or need others' approval too much. You may have led with decisiveness in the past when you stood alone against the tide . . . but today you're feeling yourself weakening. Maybe you've started giving in to the kids in little areas you once resisted because you're tired, sort of shrugging off your better judgment. Others' opinions may have begun to carry too much weight.

Among the disciplines of durability is loneliness; never forget that. An aching, inescapable loneliness.

Moses endured—even in his eighties. How? The same verse tells us: by focusing his attention on "Him who is invisible." He fixed his heart and soul on the One who, alone, judges righteously. He continually reminded himself that his sole purpose in life was to please the Lord . . . to obey Him . . . to glorify Him . . . to gain His approval at all cost.

Whatever it is you're facing, stand strong. Walk in quiet confidence, not veiled pride. Be sure without being stubborn . . . firm without being unteachable . . . enduring but not discourteous . . . full of truth balanced with grace.

Exacting indeed are the disciplines of durability.

A Finishing Touch: "To be torn unmercifully by external forces, and still to preserve one's . . . inward integrity, is to know the discipline that endures" (V. Raymond Edman).

A Daily Reading: Hebrews 11

In our overpopulated, impersonal world, it is easy to underestimate the significance of one.

With so many people, most of whom seem so much more capable, more gifted, more prosperous, more important than I, who am I to think my part amounts to much?

That's the way most folks think. They really do!

Aren't you glad Patrick Henry didn't? And Henry Ford? And Martin Luther King, Jr? And Walt Disney? And Martin Luther? And Winston Churchill? And Jackie Robinson? And Irving Berlin? And Abraham Lincoln? And Charles Wesley? And Marian Anderson?

"But it's a different world today, man. Back then, there was room for an individual to emerge and stand out in a crowd, but now, No way!"

Wrong.

God has always underscored individual involvement . . . still does.

How many did it take to help the victim who got mugged on the Jericho Road? One Good Samaritan.

How many were chosen by God to confront Pharaoh and lead the Exodus? One.

How many sheep got lost and became the object of concern to the shepherd? One.

How many were needed to confront adulterous David and bring him to his knees in full repentance? One.

How many prophets were called to stand before wicked King Ahab and predict a drought? One.

How many did the Lord use to get the attention of the land of Palestine and prepare the way for Messiah? One.

Never underestimate the power of one!

Many centuries ago a woman almost did. She thought things were too far gone. And she certainly didn't think there was anything *she* could do. It was only a matter of time before all the Jews would be exterminated.

Her name was Esther. She was the Jewish wife of a Persian king, the man who was about to be tricked into making an irrevocable, disastrous decision. All Jews would be exterminated.

But the tide could be turned by . . . guess how many? You're right, one.

Esther's adoptive father, realizing that she, alone, held the key to her husband's heart, appealed to her conscience. "If you remain silent at this time . . . you and your father's house will perish . . . " (Est. 4:14).

She listened to his impassioned plea. What got her attention was his final line, "And who knows whether you have not attained royalty for such a time as this?" (4:14).

That did it. She broke long-standing protocol, marched into the king's throne room, spoke her mind . . . and rescued the Jews from holocaust.

One woman—only one voice—saved an entire nation.

As is true of every person who stands in the gap, she was willing to get personally involved, to the point of great sacrifice. Or, as she said, "If I perish, I perish" (4:16).

She didn't think, *Someone else should be doing this, not me* . . . nor did she ignore the need because of the risk. Sacrifice! It's the stuff of which people who make a difference are made.

And before you allow yourself to toss this aside, thinking, "Aw, that's for somebody else—how much difference can I make?" go back and review the value of one.

> I am only one.
> But still I am one.
> I cannot do everything,
> But still I can do something;
> And because I cannot do everything
> I will not refuse to do the something that I can do.
> —Edward Everett Hale

Having done that, please put aside all excuses and ask yourself, "What should I be doing?"

Yes, you alone can make a difference.
The question is, will you?

A Finishing Touch: If you don't do your part, who will?
A Daily Reading: Esther 1–10

Aren't we glad somebody has always believed in the significance of one?

Like back in—

1645 . . . when one vote gave Oliver Cromwell control of England.

1776 . . . when one vote gave America the English language instead of German.

1845 . . . when one vote brought the state of Texas into the union.

1868 . . . when one vote saved President Andrew Johnson from impeachment.

1875 . . . when one vote changed France from a monarchy to a republic.

1941 . . . when one vote saved the Selective Service System just twelve weeks before Pearl Harbor was attacked.

And did you know that in 1923, one vote gave Adolph Hitler control of the Nazi Party?

Ah, the power of one! Never underestimate it.

You, alone, can make a difference!

APPLAUSE

If a modern Rip van Winkle were to awaken from twenty years' slumber and stumble back into today's world, I suspect he'd be amazed. Some of the changes would make the old gentleman wonder about us.

Picture him as he strolls through the local shopping mall and stopping in front of the video arcade where he sees wall to wall bodies staring into black boxes, punching in quarters like they were going out of style. When he steps outside to catch his breath, he picks up the classified section somebody left on a bench. Imagine his face when he sees the average cost of a little three-bedroom bungalow! Throw in all the profanity he'd hear on television, supermarkets with high-pitched beeps instead of cash register clicks, plus a couple of people at the bank around midnight "talking to" an electronic teller . . . and our old friend is ready for church on Sunday morning. Or is he?

Here he finds more cars, more lines, more feeling like a number. Inside, however, he's relieved to find a semblance of order and quietness. Except for a number of wristwatches that chime on the hour, he's able to forget that he's surrounded by computer-age people. There are pews to sit in, hymnals to sing from; there are Bibles and prayers and music that bring tears to his eyes as he begins to connect with his God in worship.

And then something happens that causes him to sit up with a start. To his amazement, he hears folks clapping! He looks around. Frowning, he feels suddenly and strangely interrupted. Why are these people applauding? Wasn't that music an offering of praise to the One they have gathered together to worship? Isn't silence—just the awesome sound of silence—sufficient? Continuing to observe, he finds inconsistency in it all.

Why don't these people applaud everything? How come a singer receives applause and the one who reads Scripture never does? And why don't they applaud the sermon?

Besides, he concludes, he prefers to do his applauding in his mind and heart.

But, then, doesn't the Bible talk about God's people clapping their hands? Yeah, it does. Several times in the psalms. But it also mentions shouting and dancing and groaning and playing on instruments we don't even have today. Obviously, God doesn't want us to be stoic and grim all the time. There have to be occasions when such spontaneous bursts are prompted by the Spirit within us. To cap off all such expressions would not only be unfair, it would be unbiblical.

Maybe, then, what these people need is to be sure that their responses in corporate worship are prompted by the Spirit and not by a small group of people who are ready to clap at anything . . . for any reason. But the opposite extreme is equally inappropriate: "I will never clap at anything . . . for any reason."

What I would tell our visitor is that it all has to do with the spirit of God's truth rather than the letter of the Law. If anyone can show me *from Scripture* the up-tight, air-tight guideline for putting a stop to all spontaneous applause, I'm ready to listen. But let's also remember that when we come together to worship we're not an audience watching a show where entertainers expect applause.

And no offense, but I tend to agree with old Rip. I've never seen a group of people applaud a snow-capped mountain range or an exquisite, priceless painting or a breathtaking sunset.

Silence befits the profound, the awesome.

A Finishing Touch: Think before you applaud. Is it the best way to give God your praise? Is it appropriate? Is it necessary? Would silence be better?

A Daily Reading: Matthew 6:1–18

Sometimes fundamentalists can be the ugly ducklings of Christendom. Historically, we have felt that beauty and elegance are suspect, "too much like the liberals," unimportant to God, and unnecessarily extravagant. Because of this, we have come to the erroneous conclusion that our concern should never be with aesthetic values but always and only with the message we proclaim. So what do we do? We sometimes clothe the infinite riches of Christ in unattractive rags! As a result, the treasure of Truth is tainted and cheapened by the way it is presented to the public.

Pick most any town and drive to the church which announces that it preaches Christ and embraces the fundamentals of the faith. Chances are (with, thankfully, some exceptions) you will find an unattractive structure surrounded by pathetic landscaping. The sign is either out of date, obscure, unattractive, or big as a battleship.

Inside, you will find that the cheapest possible grade of lumber, paint, carpet, musical instruments, and furnishings were used. The piano is out of tune. The hymnals are worn out and dog-eared, some of them literally held together with Scotch tape. Seven light bulbs are burnt out. The faucet in the baptistry drips. A dusty window is broken and doesn't quite close all the way. The nursery has dark paneling (it was given to the church and had to be used). The floor creaks behind the pulpit. The bulletin has several misspelled words, strikeovers, and an unattractive cover.

And please don't think I'm nit-picking or being unduly critical. These are just a few examples I've seen with my own two eyes.

I'll tell you, it takes all the forces of heaven and the prevailing prayers of the saints just to get a visitor into a place like that, much less get him or her saved or spiritually turned on. That's why Satan dances with glee when churches cut every financial corner and emphasize only their so-called "stand for truth."

Several years ago a man told me that his first contact with a Christian was so offensive he "never wanted to hear about Jesus again." He said the person who witnessed to him had bad breath and body odor, never once smiled, was dressed in clothing completely out of date, and angrily closed his remarks with, "Don't blame Jesus if you go to hell."

Meanwhile, I've just finished reading the account in First Kings where God worked through Solomon in the building of the temple. What quality! What attention to details! What exacting requirements! What fabulous beauty! The same was true of the tabernacle in Moses' day. No one could ever say that God didn't care about how attractive His workmanship was. Beauty was not an optional thing with Him. It still isn't. All you have to do is look at the beauty and intricacy of the world He created.

As Christians, we represent the magnificent King of kings. So does our church. We may not have a fortune, but whatever we do or build or sing or print or teach or type or promote or present certainly ought to be attractive and appealing. The same is true for us individually. Our wardrobe may be limited, and it certainly doesn't have to be the most expensive, but it can always be neat and clean. Shoe polish, soap, and toothpaste are still pretty inexpensive. We Christians have enough barriers to overcome in this society without increasing the friction by sloppy dress, poor workmanship, and offensive habits that repel rather than attract.

Let's not change our message. But it will be worth it to change our appearance from the ugly duckling to the swan. We are His workmanship, and all we do should reflect that beauty and grace.

A Finishing Touch: Sometimes people can't see past us to hear our message. We never have a second chance to leave a first impression.

A Daily Reading: 1 Kings 5–6

I don't know anyone who would build a summer home at the base of Mt. Vesuvius, and it would be tough trying to get campers to pitch their tents where Big Foot had been spotted. No family I know is interested in vacationing in a houseboat up the Suez Canal. Or swimming in the Amazon near a school of piranhas. Or building a new home on property that straddles the San Andreas fault.

I mean, some things make no sense at all. Like lighting a match to see if your gas tank is empty. Or stroking a rhino to see if he's tame. They've got a name for nuts who try such stunts. Victims. Or, if they live to tell the story, just plain stupid.

And yet there are Christians running loose today who flirt with risks far greater than any of the above. And they do so with such calm faces you'd swear they had ice water in their veins. You'd never guess they are balancing on the tightwire of disaster. Without a net.

Who are they? They are the ones who rewrite the Bible to accommodate their life-style. We've all met them. Outwardly they appear to be your basic believer, but down inside, operation rationalization transpires daily. They are experts at rephrasing or explaining away the painful truth of the text.

Whenever they run across Scripture verses or principles that attack their position, they alter them to accommodate their practice. That way, two things occur: 1) All desires (no matter how wrong) are fulfilled. 2) All guilt (no matter how justified) is erased.

That way everybody can do his own thing and nobody has any reason to question another's actions. If he does, call him a legalist and plow right on.

Here is a sampling of accommodating theology:

God wants me to be happy. I can't be happy married to her. So I'm leaving . . . and I know He will understand.

There was a time when this might have been considered immoral. But not today. The Lord gave me this desire and wants me to enjoy it.

Look, nobody's perfect. So I got in deeper than I planned. Sure, it's a little shady, but what's grace all about, anyway?

Hey, life's too short to sweat the small stuff. We're not under law, you know.

If that's true . . . if that's right, then what in the world does it mean to be *holy*?

"As obedient children, do not be conformed to the former lusts which were yours in your ignorance, but like the Holy One who called you, be holy yourselves also in all your behavior; because it is written, 'You shall be holy, for I am holy'" (1 Peter 1:14–16).

Or *pure*?

"For this is the will of God, your sanctification; that is, that you abstain from sexual immorality . . . abstain from every form of evil" (1 Thess. 4:3; 5:22).

Or under *grace*?

"When then? Shall we sin because we are not under law but under grace? May it never be!" (Rom. 6:15).

The simple fact is this: We reap precisely what we sow. If we sow a life-style that is in direct disobedience to God's revealed Word, we ultimately reap disaster.

"Do not be deceived, God is not mocked; for whatever a man sows, this he will also reap" (Gal. 6:7).

The consequences of sin may not come immediately . . . but they will come eventually. And when they do, there will be no excuses, no rationalization, no accommodation. God doesn't compromise with consequences.

A Finishing Touch: When the bill comes due, the wages of willful sin must be paid in full.

A Daily Reading: 1 Peter 1:13–2:3

Whoever is soft on depravity should go see *Schindler's List*.

It's not for the fainthearted, I warn you. It is a raw, harsh, shocking exposé of unbridled prejudice, the kind of anti-Semitic prejudice spawned in hellish hate among the Nazis prior to and during World War II.

Many of the scenes were absolutely chilling: Trainloads and truckloads of horrified men, women, and precious children being hauled like helpless cattle to their deaths. The inhuman condition of the work camps, the "showers," the ovens, the smokestacks belching human ashes. Worst of all, the ability of human beings to carry all that out with hardly a shrug.

This is not meant to excite your morbid curiosity—in no way. Neither is it my attempt to applaud the film. Frankly, I was appalled by it. Emotionally bruised. Stunned. Saddened. Silenced.

As everyone filed out, including my oldest son and one of my sons-in-law, we noticed that nobody said a word. You could have heard the proverbial pin fall to the carpet. We drove home, all caught in the grip of the same question: *How?*

How could such hatred, such extreme, vicious hatred fill the minds of those wearing swastikas? How could they sleep at night or eat during the day? How could they walk back into their barracks or offices or homes and smile or carry on their duties or forget what they had just done?

I believe I know. Really, the answer is simple. One word will do. *Depravity.*

It's not a sickness. It's death. Living death. It's ugly, unashamed, uncovered, unrefined, unrepentant depravity. It's the filthy cesspool of the unregenerate heart.

And let's not feel so smug about it. Because you and I carry around within us just such killer natures. Born spiritually dead and diseased by sin from our mother's womb, we have the roots of wickedness deep within us. You do. I do. Every human does, including children.

The psalmist admits: "Behold, I was brought forth in iniquity, and in sin my mother conceived me" (51:5).

Gripping words, those.

Hitler had no corner on depravity. The same nature that was in him is in us. Yes, us! Raw depravity is there in all its ugliness.

Need a little biblical proof before you're willing to tolerate such an indictment? Read these words from the pen of the apostle Paul:

> What then? Are we better than they? Not at all; for we have already charged that both Jews and Gentiles are all under sin; as it is written, "There is none righteous, not even one; there is none who understands, there is none who seeks for God. All have turned aside . . . there is none who does good, There is not even one" (Rom. 3:9–12).

That's us . . . in the raw. Were the Great Physician to do a universal autopsy of humanity, that would be His report.

And only after we read such a report can we truly appreciate the words that have become so familiar: "But God demonstrates His own love toward us, in that while we were yet sinners, Christ died for us" (Rom. 5:8).

Which brings us back to the same question we asked in the car that night: How? How could God possibly give His Son for such hopelessly lost sinners? How could He look past the hate and horror of our depravity? How could you and I have found our name on the Savior's List?

Again, the answer is simple. One word will do. Grace.

A Finishing Touch: "There is no man so good that if he placed all his actions and thoughts under the scrutiny of the laws, he would not deserve hanging ten times in his life" (Montaigne).

A Daily Reading: Isaiah 64:6–7

The book of Job drips with mystery. The sobs of the man and the silence of his God form a strange combination.

From the start, there are surprises and anomalies. Job is portrayed for us as "blameless, upright, fearing God, and turning away from evil" (1:1) . . . and yet the bottom drops out of his world. He loses everything except his life and his wife. How strange of God to permit one of His own to become the victim of a devil-inspired plot to reduce him to putty.

The man's misery knew no bounds, but his integrity remained intact, which amazed his wife—not one of the most helpful of mates. In a gush of grief-stricken anxiety, she asked: "Do you still hold fast your integrity? Curse God and die!" (2:9).

To top things off, a handful of frowning fellows gathered around Job to "preach at him," as if the man needed sermons . . . condemning ones at that. Oh, they looked like caring friends who had "come to sympathize with him and comfort him" (2:11), but the truth is, they came to condemn. One after another, time after time, Job's "counselors" pointed long fingers of accusation and cut him down.

Finally . . . there was no place to look but up; however, even then he felt shut out. He longed to approach God and pour out his woes, but he couldn't. At least he couldn't do so on his own. Why? Listen to Job's answer to that question: "He is not a man as I am that I may answer Him, that we may go to court together. There is no umpire between us, who may lay his hand upon us both" (9:32–33).

What did he need? What was it Job longed for? An advocate. Job called him "an umpire," someone who could stand in his stead and represent him, a suffering sinner, before God, the holy One. The Hebrew term from which "umpire" is translated is YAH-KAAK, which in verb form means "to decide, to prove, convince, reason, to argue." Those are the things an advocate does for the one being defended. Job wished for someone who would understand his predicament, take up his cause, and argue his case. Because he had no advocate, he felt hopeless and helpless, defenseless and depressed.

Victims need advocates. Often, those who are objects of abuse lack the courage or the ability to protect themselves. How important it is for others to come alongside and be their mouth—to actually speak for them. If you have ever been falsely accused of a crime, you know better than most the value of an advocate in court—to represent you, to take up your cause, to help convince the jury of your innocence.

An advocate is someone who has authority, someone who will be heard and respected, where we would be ignored. The more passionate and complicated the issue, the more vital is our need for a qualified go-between. Someone to carry our torch. Someone who understands the issues and is able to articulate the salient points of the argument.

Yet there is one Advocate we all need—one who represents sinners like us in the highest of all places—the presence of God: "And if anyone sins, we have an Advocate with the Father, Jesus Christ the righteous" (1 John 2:1).

What a great promise! "We have an advocate." He is there and, like a good "umpire," He is not silent.

A Finishing Touch: The next time you start feeling like Job—alone, accused, deserted by friends, misunderstood, ripped off—turn to Him, your own "Advocate with the Father."

A Daily Reading: 1 John 2

Grace frees us to fly. So, fly!

Dare I give a few illustrations? Aw, why not?

You've had your eye on that sailboat or catamaran or sports car for some time. Why not?

You've thought a lot about a cruise or a trip to Europe but never permitted yourself to do more than think. Why not?

Your hairdo has looked the same for three decades. You've wondered about trying something really chic. Why not?

You long to get your degree, but everybody tells you to give up that dream; it's too late. Should you press on? Why not?

You were raised to play it safe, never risk, to think of all the missionaries who have it so tough . . . so you've never given yourself permission to skydive or bungee jump or hop into a pair of roller blades or let your hair blow in the breeze with the convertible top down. Why not? (If it helps, most missionaries I know wouldn't hesitate to do any of those things at a second's notice. So don't use them as your excuse!)

Your kids are still around and you realize it won't be many more years and they will all be gone . . . so why not build some great memories? Take them out of school for the day and go to Disneyland. Or how about a fishing trip or a drive up into the mountains for an overnight out under the stars? Or plan a big family reunion this summer? Why not?

You're an adult. But your mom or dad still maintains too much control over you. You long to be strictly on your own, free of those manipulative "hints" and guilt trips. It's time to break away and get unstuck. Why not?

You'd love to throw a big, crazy party with a few happy-go-lucky folks who know how to have fun. Why in the world not?

Grace frees us to fly. So, fly!

The
Touch
of Joy

When His joy invades our
lives, it spills over into
everything we do and onto
everyone we touch.

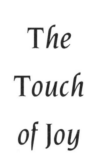

A New Week
of
Finishing Touches

14

MONDAY

Flying ace Chuck Yeager has written a book with an inviting title: *Press On!* A guy with his adventurous background, plus a chest full of medals to prove it, probably has a lot to say about "pressing on." Few will ever know the thrill of breaking sound barriers, but all of us live with the daily challenge of pressing on. The question is how?

How does the widow or widower go on after the flowers wilt and the grass begins to grow over the grave? How does the athlete go on after age or injury takes its toll and someone younger takes his or her place? How does the mother go on after the children grow up and no longer need her? How does the victim move beyond the abuse or injustice without turning bitter?

How does the patient go on after the physician breaks the news about the dreaded biopsy? How does the divorcee go on after the divorce is final? How does anyone press on when the bottom drops out? What's the secret?

Well, I'm not sure I would call it a secret, but I have recently discovered some principles from Scripture that have certainly come to my rescue. They emerge from the life of David when he found himself unable to escape tough times.

It happened when David and his fellow warriors were returning from battle. Exhausted, dirty, and anxious to get home, they came upon a scene that took their breath away. What was once their own quiet village was now smoldering ruins; and their wives and children had been kidnapped by the same enemy forces that had burned their homes to the ground. Their initial reactions?

"Then David and the people who were with him lifted their voices and wept until there was no strength in them to weep" (1 Sam. 30:3–4).

As if that were not bad enough, David's own men turned against him, and talk of mutiny swirled among the soldiers.

"Moreover David was greatly distressed because the people spoke of stoning him, for all the people were embittered, each one because of his sons and his daughters" (30:6).

Those descriptive words, "greatly distressed," represent deep anguish and intense depression. If ever a man felt like hanging it up, David must have at that moment. But he didn't.

What did he do instead? Read this very carefully: "But David strengthened himself in the LORD his God" (30:6).

He got alone and "gave himself a good talking to," as my mother used to say. He poured his heart before the Lord . . . got things squared away vertically, which helped clear away the fog horizontally. He did not surrender to hard times.

Why not? How did he go on?

By refusing to focus on the present situation only.

What happens when we stay riveted to the present misery? One of two things: either we blame someone (which can easily make us bitter) or we submerge in self-pity (which paralyzes us). Going on with our lives will never occur as long as we concentrate all our attention on our present pain.

Instead of retaliating or curling up in a corner and licking his wounds, he called to mind that this event was no mistake. The Lord wasn't absent. On the contrary, He was in full control. Bruised and bloody, David faced the test head-on and refused to throw in the sponge.

A Finishing Touch: When we get things squared away vertically, it helps clear away the fog horizontally.

A Daily Reading: 1 Samuel 30:1–6

Having just held a memorial service for a friend several years younger than I who had died with liver cancer, I have been thinking about how to respond when struck by an arrow of affliction. Not a little irritating dart, but an arrow plunged deeply.

My friend chose not to curl up in a corner with a calendar and put X's on days. On the contrary, the news of his malignancy only spurred him on to drain every ounce out of every day. His physician had told him he would probably be gone before last Thanksgiving. "Says who?" he mused. Not only did he live through Thanksgiving, at Christmas he threw a party, the following Easter was delightful, a fun picnic on the Fourth of July was a gas . . . and he had a special celebration in the planning stage for this Thanksgiving! A close friend of his told me that the last time they talked he had made an appointment to have his teeth fixed.

I love that kind of spunk! It underscores one of my unspoken philosophies of life: when struck by an arrow, don't seek more days in your life but more life in your days. Forget quantity; pursue quality. Look beyond the pain and you'll find incredible perspective.

When the thorn punctured Paul's balloon, he refused to wallow in self-pity and whine away the balance of his days. He learned to glory in his weaknesses. He discovered a contentment, even a joy, in the midst of "distresses . . . persecutions . . . difficulties" (2 Cor. 12:10). In weakness he found inner strength.

In spite of his brothers' cruel mistreatment, subsequent slavery in Egypt, false accusations from Mrs. Potiphar (resulting in being dumped into a dungeon for years), Joseph steered clear of bitterness. As a matter of fact, he ultimately told his brothers, "God turned into good what you meant for evil" (Gen. 50:20 TLB). Talk about incredible perspective regarding life's arrows!

During his darkest days following the Bathsheba affair, David had arrows in his front and back. Broken in spirit, he fled the throne rather than fight with his rebel son Absalom, who had deceived his way to the top. While retreating, a man named Shimei threw stones at David and shouted curses and ugly accusations—more arrows. David's response? He refused to answer back; instead, he took it on the chin. The king had matured, thanks to pain, and therefore entertained no thought of retaliation.

Arrows don't change a person's direction. They merely deepen his or her character; they help the afflicted rediscover certain values before achieving even greater things—if we let them.

Back in the mid-1980s, Bill Marriott, Jr. had hit the big time. His hotels and service were the talk of the industry. He had acquired new properties in New York city, Washington, and Atlanta. Financially, he was fixed—even had a fine family resort on a beautiful lake in New Hampshire. Then, while starting the engine of his boat one morning, Bill was literally blown out of the water—an accident that would scar him for the rest of his days. Did he give up? Did he surrender to the arrow that stung him so deeply? No, he accelerated! He determined to press on stronger than ever.

So, which arrow has struck you recently? News of an alleged "terminal" illness? Physical pain? Unfair treatment? False accusations? Struggles at home? Somebody throwing rocks? An accident that's left you scarred? Don't waste time licking your wounds or wondering why. Make a decision to do what you were doing even better than ever. Life's arrows are nothing more than momentary setbacks that help us regroup, renew, and reload—so, what are you waiting for?

A Finishing Touch: Don't seek more days in your life but more life in your days.

A Daily Reading: 2 Samuel 16:10–12

The sound was deafening. Although no one was near enough to hear it, ultimately it echoed around the world. None of the passengers in the DC-4 ever knew what happened—they died instantly. That was February 15, 1947, when the Avianca Airline flight bound for Quito, Ecuador, crashed into the 14,000-foot-high peak of El Tablazo not far from Bogota, then dropped—a flaming mass of metal—into a ravine far below.

One of the victims was a young New Yorker named Glenn Chambers, who had planned to begin a ministry with the "Voice of the Andes."

Before leaving the Miami airport earlier that day, Chambers had written a note to his mother on a piece of paper he picked up in the terminal. The paper was a piece of an advertisement with the single word WHY? sprawled across the center. In a hurry and preoccupied, he scribbled his note around that word, folded it, and stuffed it into an envelope addressed to his mother.

The note arrived after the news of his death. When his mother received it, there, staring up at her, was that haunting question: WHY?

Of all questions, this is the most searching, the most tormenting. It accompanies every tragedy. It falls from the lips of the mother who delivers a stillborn . . . the wife who learns of her husband's tragic death . . . the child who is told, "Daddy won't be coming home any more" . . . the struggling father of five who loses his job . . . the close friend of one who commits suicide.

Why? Why me? Why now? Why this? Nothing can fully prepare us for such moments. Few thoughts can steady us afterward . . . perhaps only one.

Consider Job . . . imagine his feelings!

"You've lost your livestock, they've been stolen. Your sheep and camels were also destroyed. Your employees were murdered, Job. Oh, one more thing—your children were crushed in a freak windstorm . . . they are dead, my friend, all ten of them."

That actually happened. Job got all this news in one brief period of panic. Shortly thereafter he broke out in boils—from head to toe. Grief-stricken. Stunned. Bankrupt. In excruciating pain, both in body and spirit. At a total loss to explain even one tragedy, to say nothing of five! It was naked, raw agony, and the heavens were mute. No explanation thundered across the celestial chasm. Not one reason . . . not a single one. And then his wife advised: "Curse God and die!"

Boldly Job snapped, "You sound like a fool, woman!" Wisely he stated, "Shall we accept only good from God and never adversity?"

Notice very carefully what Job claimed that day. Don't miss the thing that carried him through. Unlike the stance of the stoic—"Grin and bear it . . . or at least grit your teeth and endure it"—Job grabbed one great principle and held on. It formed the knot at the end of his rope . . . it steadied his step . . . it kept him from cursing. No other single truth removes the need to ask "Why?" like this one:

GOD IS TOO KIND TO DO ANYTHING CRUEL . . . TOO WISE TO MAKE A MISTAKE . . . TOO DEEP TO EXPLAIN HIMSELF.

That's it! Job rested his case there.

It's remarkable how believing that one profound statement erases the "Why?" from earth's inequities.

It was the same knot a brokenhearted mother in New York tied in the winter of 1947. Mrs. Chambers stopped asking *Why?* when she saw the *Who?* behind the scene.

All other sounds are muffled when we claim His absolute sovereignty. Even the deafening sound of a crashing DC-4.

A Finishing Touch: When we know Who, we can stop asking "Why?"

A Daily Reading: Job 2:9-10

Who would've ever guessed it?

Out of the blue came this nobody. He had spent his youth away from the crowded streets of the city, working for his dad in the quiet, rugged outdoors. Now, suddenly, he was the most famous man in the country. His name was on everyone's lips. They even wrote a song about him, which everybody knew by heart within a matter of hours. The original skyrocket-success story. It must have swept the kid off his feet. But if it did, nobody knew it. He couldn't wait to retreat to the hills where life was simple and uncluttered.

That first night back under the stars must have been a restless one as he recalled the frightening scene of battle . . . the intimidating sound of the giant's voice as it echoed across the chasm . . . the rush of patriotic zeal through his veins . . . the feel of those five smooth stones . . . the deadening thud as rock struck forehead . . . the shout of triumph . . . the admiring look of dismay from the tall Israeli king. Now, silence. He was back where he belonged.

Little did the lad know that God would lead him to more valleys—deeper than he could have dreamed possible. The events that followed the giant-killing defied logic.

Even though David conducted himself with humility, loyalty, and grace, the man whose face—and life!—he had saved turned against him. Displeased by the boy's popularity, insecure over his own eclipsed public image, possessed by demonic thoughts that ranged between rage and murder, King Saul became a human savage, driven mad by suspicion and jealousy.

In spite of this tragic twist in their relationship, David prospered. Three times in the biographical account we read that fact (1 Sam. 18:5, 14, 15). In addition, "he behaved himself more wisely than all the servants of Saul" (18:30). This led to growing popularity, increased favor in the eyes of Saul's inner circle, military victories, and enormous praise from the public. It came in such a flood, he could not escape it. David found himself sandwiched between public applause and private horror. Saul's sharp spear was never far away, and for more than a dozen years the young hero was forced to run for his life.

Adversity became David's constant companion. He must have wondered if he would ever be relieved of the savage's shadow.

It is easy to forget that two magnificent, lasting benefits were born out of that womb of woe: first, the deepening of much of David's character; and second, the composing of many of David's psalms. The traits we remember and admire as being worthy of emulation were shaped, honed, and polished while he lived like a fugitive in the wilderness. Great character, like massive roots, grows deep when water is sparse and winds are strong, and the psalms we turn to most often emerged from a broken heart while tears wouldn't stop and questions remained unanswered. Great music, like massive rivers, must come from torrential rains in order to keep flowing, leading to the splendor and vastness of oceanlike depths.

And where are you today? Has there been a recent breakdown? A trust no longer there? A friend no longer near? A dream no longer clear? A future no longer bright? Tears now where there was once laughter? Loneliness now instead of companionship? Misunderstanding now instead of support, affirmation, and loyalty? Maybe a Saul dogging your steps, sharpening his spear, waiting for just the right moment to lunge?

Take heart! It is in that precise crucible that God can (and often does) do His best work!

A Finishing Touch: Some of your best traits and some of your finest works will grow out of the incredibly painful periods in your life.

A Daily Reading: 1 Samuel 18

You would think we were on the edge of the Alps. Fresh-fallen snow had blanketed the range of mountains on the northeast rim of the Los Angeles basin. When I caught my first glimpse of it in the distance, I found myself smiling and saying aloud, "Beautiful!" Usually the smog blocks that view, but the previous day's rain had washed the skies crystal clear, giving us a rare day to enjoy the white-capped range, with snow now down to the 2,000-foot level. Seventy-five miles away, it was beautiful. Up close, well, that was an entirely different matter.

Early in the morning, Cynthia and I decided to enjoy a few hours together up near Lake Arrowhead, a quiet hamlet nested in a crevice of those mountains at about 6,000 feet. The clouds looked a little threatening before we left, but a brisk walk a mile high would be refreshing and invigorating—and long overdue. So we bundled up and took off. What we encountered could easily make one of those you'll-never-believe-it *Reader's Digest* articles.

About the time we reached 4,500 feet, narrow Highway 18 began to gather white dust. The temperature was right at freezing, the clouds were thick, and the wind had picked up considerably. I could have turned back then—and should have—but we were only fifteen or so minutes from our destination. So we pressed on.

The "freak storm," as some in the village called it, was surprising to those at Arrowhead and, I must admit, frightening to us. It became increasingly more obvious that things weren't going to get better, so we decided to cut short our visit. By now the wind was howling and the snow was swirling across the asphalt. Disappointed, we piled back into the car and began a journey we shall never forget. And for the next several miles a brief conversation haunted me. It occurred before we left:

"Shouldn't we buy tire chains?" she asked

"Naw, this won't be any problem," he answered.

"Are you sure? It's downhill all the way back," she reminded him.

"Don't worry, hon. We'll be outa this in no time," he said.

An hour and a half—which seemed more like a decade—later, we reached San Bernardino. Between 6,000 feet and sea level, only the Lord knows for sure what happened.

I have driven since I was fourteen. I have been in just about every conceivable situation—alone or with a car full of kids, in desert and mountains, the dead of night and blistering sun, sports car and 38-foot motor home, across town and across the continent, in fog and downpour and sleet—but never have I spent a more hair-raising ninety minutes in my life.

There was no sin—mortal or venial, thought, word, or deed—I didn't confess. No prayer I didn't use. No verse I didn't claim. You know how folks say that when you are drowning your entire life passes before your eyes? Well, I can assure you the same is true as you fishtail your way down a glazed, winding, narrow, two-lane mountain highway, trying every maneuver known to man just to keep from colliding with an oncoming car or crashing into the mountainside . . . or toppling over the precipice.

Tony Bennett may have left his heart in San Francisco, but I left my stomach, kidney, liver, and bladder all the way down Highway 18. And if anyone has the gall to ask me if I plan to purchase tire chains, I need to warn you ahead of time, I'll punch you in the mouth. Trust me—this stubborn guy learned his lesson—permanently. Everyone with Swindoll blood will own snow chains. I'm even going to see if they make them for bikes and trikes!

There's another lesson, one I will think of every time I see any beautiful snowcapped mountain range. It may seem beautiful from a distance, but when you get real close the scene is entirely different. It's a lot like life.

Behind that beauty are bitter cold, screaming winds, blinding snow, icy roads, raw fear, and indescribable dangers. Distance feeds fantasy. Any mountain range seems more beautiful when viewed from a sunlit street seventy-five miles away. Small wonder artists paint those high-priced scenes of such breathtaking grandeur; most of them do so in warm, safe studios in the city! Put them in the back seat of a four-wheel vehicle where everything is a blur and survival is one's only goal and I guarantee the canvas will look different.

But the comforting fact is that as we journey through life, we have a Guide who knows all about those places. He knows our way, and He will get us through.

A Finishing Touch: The Lord is our spiritual road atlas. When we rely on Him, we'll never get lost.

A Daily Reading: Isaiah 29:13–16

From a distance we in the church often look like beautiful people. We're well-dressed. We have nice smiles. We look friendly. We appear cultured, under control . . . at peace.

But what a different picture comes in view when someone gets up close and in touch!

What appeared so placid is really a mixture of winding roads of insecurity and uncertainty . . . maddening gusts of lust, greed, and self-indulgence . . . and pathways of pride glazed over with a slick layer of hypocrisy. All this is shrouded in a cloud of fear of being found out.

From a distance, we dazzle; up close, we're tarnished. Put enough of us together and we may resemble an impressive mountain range. But when you get down into the shadowy crevices . . . the Alps we ain't.

That's why our Lord means so much to us. He is intimately acquainted with all our ways. Darkness and light are alike to Him. Not one of us is hidden from His sight. All things are open and laid bare before Him: our darkest secret, our deepest shame, our stormy past, our worst thought, our hidden motive, our vilest imagination . . . even our vain attempts to cover the ugly with snow-white beauty.

He comes up so close. He sees it all. He knows our frame. He remembers we are dust.

Best of all, He loves us still.

WE HOPE . . . WE WAIT

"Rome wasn't built in a day." If I heard that once, I heard it a hundred times while I was growing up. I was young and impatient, anxious to reach the goals I felt were important. But there was always this irksome reminder that good things take time and great things take even longer.

Now, however, at long last, I am discovering that stuff about Rome is true. And Paul's words to the century-one Christians who lived there are also truer than ever: "But if we hope for what we do not see, with perseverance we wait eagerly for it" (Rom. 8:25).

Four words jump out at me as I chew on that thought—"we hope . . . we wait." And sandwiched between—"what we do not see"—are the things that take so long. Several examples flash across my mind.

Rearing children. Few processes require more patience. Time and again we parents repeat cautions or instructions until we are blue in the face. We wonder if our words will ever sink in. Months turn into years and we're still going back to the basics. Many a night we drop into bed exhausted, sometimes even mildly depressed. "Lord! What's wrong? I don't see much change."

So "We hope . . . we wait." Take it by faith—one day you'll find that it sank in . . . and you'll be so glad you persevered.

Standing alone. Here's another tough one, especially if you're the dependent type. Your tendency to lean on another person has eroded into *needing* that individual in order to make it. You need his or her approval. You need the strength of that person's character. Instead of enjoying his or her company, you cling.

So you decide to break if off. "I need to do this . . . I must stop finding my identity in someone else's life." But all that self-talk keeps getting submerged beneath your habit of overdependence. And so, again, "We hope . . . we wait." We count on God to make it happen. And happily, after awhile a glimmer of light appears.

Accepting defeats. Ours is a winner-oriented world. Whether it's sports or politics, education or sales, winning is essential for survival. Sounds so right. Seems so logical. But isn't it strange that the best lessons are invariably learned from defeat? Pain remains a strict but faithful teacher, and the crucible produces much more character than waving the winner's flag. We know that theoretically. But let some defeat hit us squarely in the chops, and we drop like a two-ton anchor. Job's question—"Shall we indeed accept good from God and not accept adversity?"—continues to get "No" for an answer (Job 2:10). It seems like it will take a lifetime to say "Yes"!

And so—"We hope . . . we wait."

Looking young. I am amused at the extent to which some folks will go to hide or deny the presence of age. Face-lifts, weird corsets, hairpieces, and no mention—ever—of age are only a few of the things announcing, "I'm staying young." Uh . . . sure.

Now, I'm all for keeping one's mind young and body strong and perceptions keen, but I cannot understand this frantic drive to pretend we're not getting older. The last time I checked, the Scriptures honored age and spoke of gray hair with respect. Besides, it means we are all that much nearer seeing our Lord face to face . . . a truth for which "We hope . . . we wait."

The good news is that in the process we're gaining wisdom.

And so, fellow Romans, we're in it together . . . we keep hoping and we keep waiting.

A Finishing Touch: Whether you're rearing children or learning to stand alone or accepting defeat or simply facing the truth that you're getting older, take heart! Better still, relax! You, like ancient Rome, are still being built.

A Daily Reading: Romans 8:18–27

Ever felt weird because you were "normal"? I remember the first time I had that feeling. I was a teenager surrounded by other teenagers in a testimony meeting. One girl, with tears running down her face, told of an alcoholic father who beat her mother almost every weekend. She described how she would hide in the closet lest she become a target of his drunken rage. Then she told how her friend at school had led her to Christ.

I sat very still. My dad didn't drink nor had I ever hidden from him or seen him hit my mother. And the only time I'd ever heard him swear was when we had a flat on the way to our two-week vacation at my granddad's cottage. It was pouring rain and he had to unload the trunk to get to the jack and spare tire, which was also flat. Since that was enough to make St. Francis of Assisi utter an oath, I never though much of it.

After the girl sat down, a guy stood up and talked about how he had spent a couple days in jail the past summer. He had been caught shoplifting for the third time and had been carted off to the Houston Youth Facility. He said it was the worst place he'd ever seen. While he was waiting for his stepmother to scrape up enough money to bail him out, a chaplain had told him about Jesus. That's when he became a Christian.

I didn't know what the inside of a "Youth Facility" looked like. The worst place I had ever seen was the men's room at the old baseball stadium off the Gulf Freeway. And since my mom was my real mom, I could only imagine getting used to a stepmom. I felt strangely "normal," which meant I didn't have much of a testimony. So I kept my trap shut and looked cool.

And then another girl stood up. She looked "fast" (my mother's term)—too much makeup, teased hair, big earrings. In between two dozen "uh's" she struggled to admit that she had gotten pregnant and her folks had kicked her out. A nice couple from our church (her aunt and uncle, I believe) had taken her in. She didn't say she'd had an abortion, but that was the impression she left.

Once again, I could only imagine, I hadn't even had a date yet . . . and the thought of being kicked out of my home was as foreign to me as having a stepmother. Compared to that girl, I was Cub Scout material. Thankfully, she had been led to the Lord by her aunt, and she spoke of the peace that had replaced all the trash she once knew.

Me? Peace was my everyday partner. I thought everyone had good meals, a comfortable bed, and a happy, harmonious family. Not until I joined the Marines several years later did I realize my life was the exception rather than the rule.

Today, however, the "abnormal" is considered the norm. You're a freak unless you've got a ton of trash to unload. If you are not recovering from something, addicted to something, or a victim of something, you feel like I felt sitting in that testimony meeting.

Question: Is there a place where you can feel normal being "normal"? Or, if you're still struggling with something, still trying to come to terms with some heartrending problem, is there a place where you won't feel "weird"?

Well, there should be, and it should be the local church—the body of Christ. The church is a place for young and old, single and married, broken or healing, happy or sad, truck driver or brain surgeon, student or retiree, saint or seeker, you name it.

Whether we are normal or nearly normal or hoping someday to be normal, we belong. Whatever our situation, our status, our struggle, or our style, we are all looking for the magnificent truths of God, for genuine Christian fellowship and togetherness.

A Finishing Touch: In the body of Christ we are all the same: forgiven, but not perfect. Except for One.

A Daily Reading: Ephesians 4:1–7

I remember the year NBA stars Michael "Air" Jordan and Earvin "Magic" Johnson were vying for the Most Valuable Player award. Each year the MVP is given to the athlete who represents the qualities considered "most valuable" not only to his team but also among those in the league. In previous years, the winners had been such standout players that nobody could disagree with the final selection. Guys like Kareem Abdul-Jabbar, Wilt Chamberlain, and Larry Bird deserved it and won it, hands down.

That year, however, it was incredibly close, and the final tally resulted in Johnson's winning the award by the narrowest of margins. The choice boiled down to an understanding of the definition of "valuable" as opposed to the definition of "outstanding."

As one sportswriter correctly stated, few people would disagree that Jordan was the single most "outstanding" professional basketball player that year. The leading scorer in the NBA, the man was virtually unstoppable. No one would argue that he alone was the reason the Bulls gave the Pistons a run for their money. Jordan was a wizard in sneakers. He seemed to defy gravity as he lifted off, spun, twisted, ducked, turned, pumped, then finally slam dunked the ball as defensive players watched in helpless disbelief. Magic himself admitted that the Bulls' whirling dervish could do more in the air than anyone else could do on his feet. The title "superstar" was no exaggeration.

In spite of all this, however, Jordan wasn't voted MVP. Why? Because that award is reserved for the man who exemplifies the best all-around qualities of a basketball player. The MVP not only takes into consideration superb individual performance but also the ability to inspire and involve one's teammates, encouraging and enabling them to excel.

And when that dimension was added, there was no question that Magic was more deserving.

Most outstanding? That would've been Jordan. But "most valuable"? That was Magic.

In thinking about this, it occurs to me that the ranks of Christianity include a few "superstars"—extremely capable women and men who have been appointed and anointed by God to occupy significant roles of responsibility. Such people have emerged in every generation, from the first century through the twentieth. The solo work they accomplish is beautiful to behold, and we thank God for giving us these pacesetting models, each one seeming to have no peer.

As significant as these outstanding folks may be, however, the greater award goes to the most valuable—those individuals who may not be as impressive or as popular or even as capable on their own, but who can inspire and involve others on the team. Whenever they are engaged in the action, good things happen.

The qualities needed to be valuable? Let me suggest at least eight:

Initiative—being a self-starter with contagious energy.
Vision—seeing beyond the obvious, claiming new objectives.
Unselfishness—releasing the controls and the glory.
Teamwork—involving, encouraging, and supporting others.
Faithfulness—hanging in there in season and out.
Enthusiasm—providing affirmation, excitement to a task.
Discipline—modeling great character regardless of the odds.
Confidence—representing security, faith, and determination.

Are you ready for a challenge? Stop worrying about not being more outstanding as a soloist and start focusing on being more valuable as a team player. It's not nearly as much pressure, and it's a whole lot more fun. Furthermore, who would pass up the MVP for the MOP award?

A Finishing Touch: What qualities do you value and why?
A Daily Reading: Philippians 1:1–11

In his November 11, 1942, report on the war to the British House of Commons, Winston Churchill referred to "the soft underbelly of the Axis." While half the world was intimidated by the powerful blitzkrieg style of Nazi warfare, the perceptive prime minister focused on the other side—the hidden side: the insecurity, the lack of character, the insanity behind the public image of the German dictator. Adolf Hitler may have seemed strong to his adoring public and the goose-stepping soldiers who proudly wore their Fuhrer's swastika. But the pudgy, cigar-smoking resident of 10 Downing Street was neither impressed nor frightened. He knew it was only a matter of time before the corruption lurking within exposed the soft underbelly of "Corporal Hitler."

Mark Twain used another word picture to convey a similar thought: "Everyone is a moon, and has a dark side which he never shows to anybody."

This dark side can exist for years behind carefully guarded masks.

Most of us remember the Watergate scandal. Like me, many firmly resisted the thought of corruption in the Oval Office till the very end. Such compromise and corruption was unthinkable. As time passed and the truth emerged, however, the soft underbelly of Richard Nixon came to light. Conversations with those who were there at the time, participating in the cover-up, and books documenting those events, forced me to accept what I once denied.

Sammy Davis Jr. died in mid-May 1990. He was only 64, a victim of throat cancer. For years he drew the applause of packed houses as he sang and danced and cracked his jokes. Who will ever know how many aspiring young men and women watched with envying eyes as he laughed and charmed his way into America's heart? But behind all the glitter and gold, we now know, was a man at war with himself.

According to a May 17, 1990, *Los Angeles Times* article: "He buried his pain in alcohol and cocaine—chasing the delusion that his 'swinging' lifestyle somehow compensated for his two divorces, his estrangement from his children, and his futile efforts to become what he thought others expected him to be."

Death exposed the other side of "Mr. Entertainer," bringing to light what had been hidden for years. The same thing happened at the death of film star Rock Hudson, whose hidden world was quite the opposite of his public image. Soft underbellies refuse to stay hidden. The next time you're tempted to think otherwise, remember Chappaquiddick.

Life magazine's feature article on Elvis Presley in June 1990 was yet another reminder of how much difference there can be between image and reality. Appropriately titled "Down at the End of Lonely Street," the documented account of how the man existed in private toward the end of his life was nothing short of shocking. The handsome, seemingly happy-go-lucky performer, whose smile and wink melted hearts the world over, existed in a nightmare world of depression, despair, and massive doses of drugs.

The lesson in all this is obvious: The safest route to follow is Authenticity Avenue, walled on either side by Accountability and Vulnerability. The alternate route dead-ends at Lonely Street, whose bleak scenery is best stated in a verse from the ancient book of Numbers: ". . . be sure your sin will find you out" (32:23). Haunting thought, but oh, so true. I cannot explain how or why, I only know that rattling skeletons don't stay in closets . . . lies don't remain private . . . affairs don't stay secret—it's only a matter of time.

A Finishing Touch: Hidden works of darkness always come to light.

A Daily Reading: Romans 7:14–25

Overwhelming odds can make cowards of us all.

Because there is so much to be done, we can easily lose heart and do nothing. Because there are so many to reach, it is easy to forget that God wants to use us to touch those few within our sphere of responsibility.

I remember the first time I felt overwhelmed regarding ministry in a vast arena. My life had been quiet and manageable. From my birthplace in a south Texas country town I moved with my family to Houston, where we lived through my high school years. Our home was small and secure. After marriage, a hitch in the Corps, and seminary, Cynthia and I became involved in ministries that were like our past . . . small, pleasant, and fulfilling. Our children were small, our lives were relaxed and rather simple, and our scope of God's work was quite comfortable.

The call to Fullerton, California, in 1971 changed all that. In fact, it was as the plane descended over Los Angeles when we were coming to candidate that I got this overwhelming feeling. I looked out the little window and watched as mile after mile of houses and freeways and buildings passed beneath us. I tried to imagine ministering to this sprawling metropolis of never-ending humanity. I thought, How can I possibly get my arms around this monstrous task? What can I do to reach the multiple millions in Southern California?

Suddenly, God gently reminded me, as He does to this day: I *will never reach them all—that is humanly impossible. But I am responsible for those I come in contact with, and with God's help, I will make a difference in their lives.*

I stopped paying attention to the enormity of the impossible and started pouring my time and energy into the possible—the people and the place God had called me and my family. Call my vision limited if you will, but it has made all the difference in my peace of mind. I cannot do it all . . . I cannot get my arms around the vast boundaries of our region (no one can!), but I am able to touch those who come into the scope of my "radar screen." Peace of mind comes in knowing that in at least their lives, my touch can make a difference, even if it is only one here and another there.

That kind of thinking is illustrated vividly in a story I read recently. A businessman and his wife were busy to the point of exhaustion. They were committed to each other, their family, their church, their work, their friends.

Needing a break, they escaped for a few days of relaxation at an oceanfront hotel. One night a violent storm lashed the beach and sent massive breakers thundering against the shore. The man lay in bed listening and thinking about his own stormy life of never-ending demands and pressures.

The wind finally died down and shortly before daybreak the man slipped out of bed and took a walk along the beach to see what damage had been done. As he strolled, he saw that the beach was covered with starfish that had been thrown ashore and helplessly stranded by the great waves. Once the morning sun burned through the clouds, the starfish would dry out and die.

Suddenly the man saw an interesting sight. A young boy who had also noticed the plight of the starfish was picking them up, one at a time, and flinging them back into the ocean.

"Why are you doing that?" the man asked the lad as he got close enough to be heard. "Can't you see that one person will never make a difference—you'll never be able to get all those starfish back into the water. There are just too many."

"Yes, that's true," the boy sighed as he bent over and picked up another and tossed it into the water. Then as he watched it sink, he looked at the man, smiled, and said, "But I sure made a difference to that one."

One person cannot beat the odds. There will always be more to reach than time or energy or commitment can provide. But the truth is that each one of us can touch a few. How wrong we would be to stop helping anyone because we cannot help everyone.

Don't panic. Count on the Lord to honor and multiply even your smallest efforts. Last time I checked, He was still rewarding faithfulness.

A Finishing Touch: Ignore the odds. Even though you cannot do everything, you can do something. You may be only one, but you can still make a difference. So, make a difference!

A Daily Reading: Mark 6

Centuries ago a little boy found himself in the midst of a vast crowd of people—larger than any group he'd ever seen. He had come out of curiosity, having heard that a man named Jesus was nearby.

Not knowing how far he would have to travel or how long he would be gone, the boy had packed a small lunch for himself, a couple of small fish and some bread.

Suddenly a man tapped the lad on the shoulder and asked what he had in his hand. And the next thing the boy knew, his lunch was feeding over five thousand people!

Once Jesus got hold of the boy's simple meal there was no limit to what He could make of it.

Feeling a little overwhelmed? Starting to get the idea that you're surrounded by folks getting giant things done while it's all you can do to make it through the week? Maybe you've fallen into a well of comparison and you're drowning in discouragement because "Compared to ____" you're not making nearly the difference he or she is.

To all who feel overwhelmed or who are tempted to take a much too critical look at their lives and feel insignificant . . . take heart! Do what you can!

A HOPE TRANSFUSION

Easter and hope are synonymous. That special day never arrives without its refreshing reminder that there is life beyond this one. True life. Eternal life. Glorious life. Those who live on what we might call "The outskirts of hope" need a transfusion. Easter gives it.

I think of all those who are living with the dread disease of cancer. Talk about people living on "the outskirts." They fight the gallant battle, endure the horrible reactions of chemotherapy, and anxiously await the results of the next checkup. Men and women, boys and girls for whom a hope of transfusion is essential. Easter provides it.

And then there are those who still grieve over the loss of a mate, a child, a parent, or a friend. Death has come like a ruthless thief, snatching away a treasured presence, leaving only memories. The sadness of those who mourn casts a spell of loneliness too powerful for spoken words or shallow songs to break. What is missing?

Hope.

Hope has died.

There is nothing like Easter to bring hope back to life. Easter has its own anthems. Easter has its own Scriptures. And Easter has its own proclamation: "'He is not here, for He has risen, just as He said . . .'" (Matt. 28:6).

I cannot explain what happens on this day, nor do I need to try. The simple fact is this. There is something altogether magnificent, therapeutic, and reassuring about Easter morning.

When Christians gather in houses of worship and lift their voices in praise to the risen Redeemer, the demonic hosts of hell and their damnable prince of darkness are temporarily paralyzed.

When pastors stand and declare the unshakable, undeniable facts of Jesus' bodily resurrection and the assurance of ours as well, the empty message of skeptics and cynics is momentarily silenced.

As the thrill of standing shoulder to shoulder with those of "like precious faith" flows through the people of God, an almost mysterious surge of power floods over us.

The benefits are innumerable. To list only a few:

Our illnesses don't seem nearly so final.

Our fears fade and lose their grip.

Our grief over those who have gone on is diminished.

Our desire to press on in spite of the obstacles is rejuvenated.

Our differences of opinion are eclipsed by our similar faith.

Our identity as Christians is strengthened as we stand in the lengthening shadows of saints down through the centuries, who have always answered back in antiphonal voice: "He is risen, indeed!"

A hope transfusion awaits us. It happens every year on Easter Sunday.

Alleluia!

A Finishing Touch: Jesus lives and so shall we! Death, where is your victory?!

A Daily Reading: Job 19:25–26

The clothing industry makes a killing every spring when people come out from under rocks to wrap themselves in new Easter threads, shoes, and hats. It won't be any different this year, I'm sure. Kids will be dragged from store to store as their little frames are fitted with Sunday stuff. The boys won't want to, but they will have to wear stiff shoes, dinky caps, bow ties, and (ugh!) long-sleeved shirts with cuffs that go halfway over their hands.

Now the girls—that's different. With glee they will waltz from shop to shop, picking up new frills, white gloves, patent leather purses, and little round hats with long ribbons. To them heel blisters and hair clips to hold on wayward bonnets will hardly be noticed.

Not so with the guys! What the fellas will hate most will be any discomfort, posing for camera shots, nutty-looking vests, pants that haven't been "broken in," and Mom's adamant refusal, "No, you can't wear your sneakers!"

I've been through the Easter-apparel torture chamber too many years to ignore the obvious: most boys never outgrow their shrug-of-the-shoulder attitude toward new clothes . . . and most girls will forever maintain their ecstatic delight for such. Why? Now that's a question worth some thought.

I'm of the opinion that most men buy their clothes for purely functional purposes. A suit of clothes hides your underwear, keeps you warm (or cool), and provides pockets for cash, keys, and a handkerchief. But when a woman buys a garment, she is usually looking for something that will change or enhance her.

Now wait! Before you reject that, listen to what Sydney J. Harris, the syndicated newspaper columnist, says: "What a woman wants in a new dress, or suit, or coat is another facet to her personality."

Frankly, this helps explain three mysteries men often wrestle with: (1) How can a woman stand before a closet full of garments and say, "I don't have a thing to wear!"? (2) Why do women's clothes seem to be made in such a flimsy fashion with loosely held snaps and hooks? (As planned, they are not supposed to last eight to ten years!) (3) Why is a woman so distraught when she sees another woman wearing the same garment?

Well, so much for my philosophizing. Maybe it will help some husbands to be more tolerant . . . and perhaps it will help some wives not to feel guilty about having fun in the department store this week. Relax! We men love the difference between us. If clothing helps express another facet of the real you, have at it!

Simon Peter was married, too. So he knew what he was talking about when he wrote a reminder to the ladies:

> Your beauty should not come from outward adornment. . . . Instead, it should be that of your inner self, the unfading beauty of a gentle and quiet spirit, which is of great worth in God's sight (1 Peter 3:3–4).

A Finishing Touch: We cannot substitute outer garb for inner godliness.

A Daily Reading: 1 Samuel 16:7; Matthew 5:5

I love music! Choral music, instrumental music, popular music, classical music . . . folk tunes, ballads, country western and bluegrass . . . the patriotic and romantic. For me, music is a must.

This has resulted in my becoming a student of the hymns of the church . . . those that have endured the test of time. Those we sing on Sunday linger in my mind for most of the week. I hum them on my way home and find myself singing them in the shower the next day or two.

Like you, I also have my favorites—the ones that hold some special meaning for me or evoke grand and vivid memories of significant events connected to them. Invariably, those things pass in mental review as I become "lost in wonder, love, and praise" in my worship.

While thinking of the glorious message of the Resurrection recently, I found myself suddenly overwhelmed with the music that has accompanied the celebration of the empty tomb for centuries. Various scenes crossed my mind. I saw myself as a lad holding my mother's hand in a little Baptist church in South Texas. I remembered a sunrise service on the island of Okinawa when I fought back tears of loneliness. Another Easter hymn took me to Chafer Chapel on the campus of Dallas Seminary, where 350 young men preparing for ministry stood side by side and sang heartily of the Savior we'd soon be proclaiming.

During my nostalgic pilgrimage, at each geographical spot revisited, I gave God thanks that Job's words were mine as well: "I know that my Redeemer liveth." (Job 19:25).

Gaither's familiar lyrics then brought me into the seventies: "And because He lives, I can face tomorrow. Because He lives, all fear is gone."

What a grand heritage is ours! We dare not allow the season of the Resurrection to pass without sufficiently rejoicing in and declaring our hope. It is Jesus Christ—the miraculously resurrected Son of God—who remains the Object of our worship, the Subject of our praise. Samuel Stennett was absolutely correct, way back in 1787, when he wrote:

> To Him I owe my life and breath,
> And all the joys I have;
> He makes me triumph over death,
> And saves me from the grave.

That hope has kept believers strong in the darkest places.
Easter is great-music time.
Easter is revival-of-hope time.
Easter is Christ-exalting time.
That should come as a surprise to no one . . . but it will.
To most folks, Easter is nothing more than church-going time. Are they in for a surprise!
So while you and I are singing and reflecting, let's also be praying that on Easter Sunday some will discover that Easter is sin-dropping time.

A Finishing Touch: "Thus far did I come, burdened with my sin. Nor could ought ease the grief that I was in 'til I came hither. What a place is this! Must here be the beginning of my bliss? Must here the burden fall from off my back? Must here the chains that bound it to me crack? Blest cross! Blest sepulchre! Blest rather be, the Man who was put to shame for me" (John Bunyan).

A Daily Reading: Isaiah 53

No need to prolong the story. Or complicate it. Or embellish it. Or try to explain it. Or defend it. Just declare it.

The facts speak for themselves.

Jesus of Nazareth said He would be "in the heart of the earth" three days and nights (Matt. 12:40).

Later, He said that He would "suffer . . . be killed, and be raised up on the third day" (Matt. 16:21).

Betrayed by Judas, He was seized, placed under arrest, pushed hurriedly through several trials (all of them illegal), and declared guilty . . . first of "blasphemy," next of "treason" (Luke 22:70–23:24).

Finally, "all the disciples left Him and fled" (Matt. 26:56).

Alone and forsaken, He endured the torture of scourging, the humiliation of insults and mockery, and the agony of that walk to Golgotha (Mark 15:15–22).

The horrors of crucifixion followed, leaving Him suspended for six excruciating hours . . . the last three of which were spent in eerie darkness that "fell over the whole land" (Mark 15:33).

By three o'clock that afternoon He uttered His final words. "Father, into Thy hands I commit My spirit" (Luke 23:46).

Then . . . He died (Matt. 27:50; Mark 15:37; Luke 23:46; John 19:30).

Two men, Joseph of Arimathea and Nicodemus, took Him down from the cross, prepared the body for burial, and placed it "in the garden in a new tomb" (John 19:38–41).

Because He had predicted, "After three days I am to rise again," the chief priests and the Pharisees had the tomb secured by a large stone, a seal set on the stone, and a body of men sent to guard the site (Matt. 27:62–66).

Guarded and sealed, the tomb was silent as He remained lifeless, untouched, and unseen until the early hours of the morning on the first day of the week (Luke 24:1–2).

Before dawn a miracle occurred. Bodily, silently, victoriously, He arose from death. In resurrected form, He passed through the stone, leaving the mummy-like wrappings still intact (John 20:1–8).

When astonished people visited the site that morning, they found the stone rolled away and the body gone. Then they were asked by angels, "Why do you seek the living One among the dead? He is not here, but He has risen" (Luke 24:5–6).

There are many who still seek for Him among the dead. But they will never find Him there. Why? Because just as Jesus promised, He arose.

If you are among those who believe in miracles . . . if you find hope in Christ's resurrection . . . if you thrill at the sounds of "Christ the Lord is risen today! Hallelujah!" then say so.

He is risen!

Christ is risen, indeed!

A Finishing Touch: "And when I saw Him, I fell at His feet as a dead man. And He laid His right hand upon me, saying, 'Do not be afraid; I am the first and the last, and the living One; and I was dead, and behold, I am alive forevermore'" (Rev. 1:17–18).

A Daily Reading: Luke 24; John 20

Edith, a mother of eight, came home from a neighbor's house one afternoon and noticed that things seemed a little too quiet. Curious, she peered through the screen door and saw five of her children huddled together. As she crept closer, trying to discover the center of their attention, she could not believe her eyes. Smack dab in the middle of the circle were five baby skunks!

Edith screamed at the top of her voice, "Quick, children . . . run!"

Each kid grabbed a skunk and ran.

Some days are like that, aren't they? Even when we try to solve them, pressures and problems tend to multiply.

Jesus, the Son of God, was not immune from pressures when He was among us. He was teaching on a regular basis in the synagogue, answering people's questions, facing their criticisms, dodging the Pharisees' and Sadducees' bullets, casting out demons, healing the sick, confronting the forces of evil. . . .

In the midst of all this, at one point, He sought a place of rest and solitude. Spotting a fishing boat at the water's edge, He stepped in and sat down.

Once He caught His breath, however, He "began teaching the multitudes from the boat." Though His emotions were spent and His body was weary, He stayed at it.

When He had finished speaking, he told Simon Peter, "Put out into the deep water and let down your nets for a catch."

Simon said, "Master, we worked hard all night and caught nothing, but at Your bidding I will let down the nets" (Luke 5:4–5).

No one can criticize Peter for being reluctant. He'd been fishing all night and caught zilch. But he wisely surrendered.

> And when they had done this, they enclosed a great quantity of fish, and their nets began to break; and they signaled to their partners in the other boat, for them to come and help them. And they came, and filled both of the boats, so that they began to sink (5:6–7).

When the Master of heaven, earth, sea, and sky calls the shots, things happen . . . which explains Peter's explosive reaction:

> But when Simon Peter saw that, he fell down at Jesus' feet, saying, "Depart from me, for I am a sinful man, O Lord!" (v. 8).

Notice anything unusual? Earlier, Peter called Jesus "Master." After the miracle, he calls Him "Lord." Gripped with the realization that he was in the boat with the living God, Peter sounds like Isaiah of old, "Woe is me!"

Then Jesus said to him, "Do not fear, from now on you will be catching men" (v. 10).

There the two of them stood, hip-deep in fish, and Jesus used the opportunity to give them His real message of deep-water faith.

> And when they had brought their boats to land, they left everything and followed Him (v. 11).

Amazing, isn't it? Once they heard His invitation, they literally dropped everything. Their lifelong occupation. Their familiar surroundings. Their own goals. Their nets, boats, business, and future dreams. Everything!

Perhaps it is time for you to take a mental boat trip out into the deeper waters of faith. And when Jesus says "Follow Me," do it. Unlike Edith's kids, drop everything and run.

A Finishing Touch: Is your life full of appointments, activities, hassles, and hurry? Are you finding all your security in your work . . . your own achievements? What is your "everything"?

A Daily Reading: Luke 4 and 5

In the silences I make in the midst of the turmoil of life I have appointments with God. From these silences I come forth with spirit refreshed, and with a renewed sense of power. I hear a Voice in the silences, and become increasingly aware that it is the Voice of God.

O how comfortable is a little glimpse of God!

—*David Brainerd*

Why should we be willing to drop everything and follow Jesus Christ? And what happens when we do? I can think of at least six reasons:

1. *Jesus chooses not to minister to others all alone.* He could, but he deliberately chooses not to. He could have rowed that boat Himself. He could have dropped those nets over the side Himself. He certainly could have pulled up the nets choked with fish. Instead, He had them do it. And He specifically stated, "From now on your will be catching men."

2. *Jesus uses the familiar to do the incredible.* He came to their turf (lake, boat), their place of work (fishing), and had them use their skills (nets). In a familiar setting, He made them aware of incredible possibilities.

3. *Jesus moves us from the safety of the seen to the risks of the unseen.* He led them "out into the deep water" where nobody could touch bottom before He commanded, "Let down your nets." Nothing spectacular occurs in shallow water..

4. *Jesus proves the potential by breaking our nets and filling our boats.* When God's hand is on a situation, nets break, eyes bulge, deck planks groan, and boats almost sink. It's His way of putting the potential on display.

5. *Jesus conceals His surprises until we follow His leading.* Everything was business as usual on the surface. Boats didn't have a halo; nets didn't tingle at their touch; the lake water didn't glow; a chorus of angelic voices didn't thunder from the sky. No. The divinely arranged surprise came only after they dropped the nets. Remember, it wasn't until he followed Jesus' instructions that Peter changed "Master" to "Lord."

6. *Jesus reveals His objective to those who release their security.* He could read their willingness in their faces. Then—and only then—did He tell them they would be engaged in "catching men." And guess what—they jumped at the chance!

WANTED: THINKERS

Entertainment is everything today. So important, in fact, that we have television programs and magazines devoted solely to the subject. All of which makes it real difficult to be committed to substance rather than the superficial. This includes reading widely, probing deeply, seeing with discernment, rejecting the false, learning the facts. In short, thinking!

Television doesn't help at all. To twist Isaac Watt's words to the limit: "Is this wide-screen a friend to grace to help me on to God?" Hardly. Critic Neil Postman, author of *Amusing Ourselves to Death*, correctly argues that television is converting us from a "word-centered culture" to an "image-centered culture." Even the news broadcasts are under increasing pressure to entertain more than inform.

Ted Koppel, the penetrating host of "Nightline," calls this "Vannatizing" (after Vanna White, "Wheel of Fortune's" celebrity hostess, whose role on the highly rated game show is a matter of looking cute and saying "hello" and "bye-bye.") Toddler talk. Don't think, just look. Don't question, relax. "There's not much room on television for complexity," says Koppel. "We now communicate with everyone and say absolutely nothing."

I can handle "Vannatizing" a game show. No problem. I can even tolerate a little of it on the nightly news. By that time of day most of us aren't ready for intellectual lectures and nonstop talking heads. But when it comes to our faith, "Vannatizing" is intolerable.

I'm about up to here with our "image-centered culture" invading the ranks of religion. When will we ever learn that sacred things cannot be staged and remain sacred? What will it take to finally convince us of what Muggeridge stated so well, "You cannot present an authentic message by means of an inauthentic medium"? Glitz and glamour are nasty flies in the ointment of undefiled religion.

My hope rests in the remnant of believers who still believe in thinking . . . who have an insatiable hunger for learning . . . who appreciate the hard work that goes into knowing where they stand theologically and yet knowing where they need to bend practically.

Understand, I don't get excited about Christians who are so hung up on learning they forget to use deodorant or say "please" and "thank you." We don't need more fanatics who will argue until they turn blue against the consubstantiation theory of the Eucharist but can't match their socks when it comes to relationships. We have more than enough of those scary folks already.

What I'm pushing for is more who know what they believe, and why. Folks who can spot phony baloney before it hits the headlines . . . who know some guru is spouting heresy even though his promises sound inviting. Folks who don't wait to be told every move to make, who are challenged within to grow, to study, to learn.

Such discernment never comes automatically. Thinking is hard work, but, oh, so rewarding. And so essential for survival.

Furthermore, you won't feel quite so intimidated the next time some guy who just heard you're a Christian leans over and asks why. Your defense will make better sense.

A Finishing Touch: If you have the opportunity, take a course at a nearby Bible school, Christian college, or seminary. Or perhaps your church offers some in-depth study electives. You will gain a broader base of knowledge, a wider scope of awareness, and a deeper commitment to truth.

A Daily Reading: 2 Peter 3

Most folks I know like things to stay as they are. You've heard all
the sayings that reveal our preference for the familiar:

Leave well enough alone.

I don't like surprises.

If it ain't broke, don't fix it.

Stay with a sure thing.

What's wrong with the way things are?

Being creatures of habit, we resist change, we protect our comfort
zone, we are uneasy with the unexpected.

We admire pioneers . . . so long as we can just read about them,
not finance their journeys. We applaud explorers . . . but not if it
means we have to load up and travel with them. Creative ideas are
fine . . . but "don't get carried away," we warn. Plans that involve
risks prompt worse-case scenarios from the lips of most who wait
in the wings.

Don't misunderstand. Innovative ideas do include the very real
probability of something going wrong. Just because the plan is creative is no guarantee that stuff won't backfire. On the contrary, surprises and disappointments await anyone who ventures into the
unknown.

We've all been there, at one time or another, when those "best-
laid plans" have blown up in our faces, leaving us wondering why
we ever said yes in the first place.

But the fact is, the alternative is worse. Can anything be worse
than boredom? Is there an existence less challenging and more
draining than the predictable? I don't think so.

More importantly, God doesn't seem to think so either. As I read
through the biblical accounts of His working in the lives of His
people, the single thread that ties most of the stories together is the
unexpected. Need some examples? Here are just a few.

After aging Abraham finally got the son God had promised to
him, after he cultivated a father-son bond closer than words could
describe, after fixing his hopes on all that God had said He would

do through that boy to whom Sarah gave birth, God told Abraham to sacrifice Isaac on the mountain.

Once Elijah had done the hard thing by standing toe to toe with King Ahab, God told the prophet to hide out by the brook Cherith, where he would drink from the brook and thereby be sustained. Shortly thereafter, the brook dried up.

Though David had been faithful to his father by keeping his sheep, courageous in killing Goliath, loyal to King Saul, and humble in the midst of national fame, God stepped back and allowed the jealous king to dog his steps and threaten his life for well over a decade.

Even though the prophet Hosea had lived righteously before his Lord and had been faithful to his wife, Gomer, she left their home and family and became a harlot in the streets of Israel. God's instructions? Go find her and remarry her.

When it came time for God to send His Son to earth, He did not send Him to the palace of some mighty king. He was conceived in the womb of an unwed mother—a virgin!—who lived in the lowly village of Nazareth.

In choosing those who would represent Christ and establish His church, God picked some of the most unusual individuals imaginable: unschooled fishermen, a tax collector(!), a mystic, a doubter, and a former Pharisee who had persecuted Christians. He continued to pick some very unusual persons down through the ages. In fact, He seems to delight in such surprising choices to this very day.

So, let God be God. Expect the unexpected.

A Finishing Touch: God likes surprises. Breaking molds is His specialty.

A Daily Reading: Psalm 8

Satan is the greatest rip-off artist of all time.

As Jesus illustrated so vividly, the seed—the Word of God—is carefully sown (Mark 4). Yet shortly after we hear God's Word, the enemy of our souls, Satan himself, comes and takes away the biblical insights that have been deposited in our hearts.

Before the freshly baked cake is cool, he comes and licks off all the frosting. Before the new bike is ridden, he sneaks up and lets all the air out of the tires. Before the dress is worn, he slips up and jerks out the hem and jams the zipper. Before we crank up the car at 12:20, he's stolen the stuff we heard at 11:45.

Amazing! But you gotta remember, he's been at it since he winked at Eve and ripped her off in the Garden. He's a master at the art of the rip-off.

There are others who follow in his trail. Like the basketball fan at the Portland airport awaiting the arrival of the Trailblazers following a victory over the Lakers and attempting to scalp a couple of tickets to the next game. As the shyster wormed through the crowd, he located a well-dressed man who listened to his offer.

"How much?" asked the gentleman.

"One hundred fifty bucks," the scalper replied under his breath.

"Do you realize you're talking to a plainclothes officer of the law?" the man asked. "I'm going to turn you in, fella."

Suddenly the seller began to backpedal. He talked about how large a family he had . . . how much they needed him . . . how he'd never do it again.

"Just hand over the tickets and we'll call it even," said the well-dressed man. "And I'd better never catch you here again!"

But the worse was yet to come. The man was no officer at all. Just a quick-thinking guy who used a little ingenuity to rip off two choice seats to the next playoff game (as he anonymously admitted in the local newspaper several days later).

Satan's strategy is just as ingenious and effective. For example, he hears what we hear from the pulpit on Sunday morning, and in the process he plans his approach. He baits the rip-off trap, then sets it up with just the right hair trigger:

- ✔ An argument in the car after church over where to go for dinner.
- ✔ Lots of activity, talking, and needless noise Sunday afternoon.
- ✔ Preoccupation with some worrisome problem during the message.
- ✔ A personality conflict with another church member.
- ✔ Irritation over how far away you had to park.
- ✔ Pride, that says, "I'm so glad Doo Dad is here. He really needs to get straightened out."

All these (and more) are satanic rip-offs. Silently he prowls around, camouflaged in the garb of our physical habits and our mental laziness, seeking to devour. Then, at the precise moment when it will have its greatest impact, he snatches away the very truth we need the most, leaving us with hardly a memory of what God said earlier. It occurs every Lord's Day at every local church where the Scripture is declared.

Remember that next Sunday morning. Prepare your heart and mind before the service, girding yourself with the armor of God.

Don't let Satan rip you off.

A Finishing Touch: In case you question the effectiveness of Satan's strategy, think back just two or three weeks. Maybe even one will do. Do you remember the sermon title? How about the outline? Do you recall a couple applicable principles? You see, his plan is working brilliantly.

A Daily Reading: 1 Peter 5:8–9

Morale and vision fade fast. This is especially true when the battle is raging. Or when the pace is blistering. Or when the task is boring.

Many war veterans tell spine-tingling stories pulsating with heroism and enthusiasm. Without exception, such remarkable acts of bravery were accomplished because the troops felt fresh surges of determination which caused the odds against them to pale into insignificance. Those same veterans can tell of other occasions when the battle was lost due to low morale and fuzzy vision.

Optimism, courage, and faithfulness feed on high morale. The ability to push on, alone if necessary, requires clear vision. In order for goals to be reached, there has to be a stirring up from within . . . a spark that lights the fire of hope, telling us to "Get at it" when our minds are just about to convince us with "Aw, what's the use?" It's called motivation.

Coaches are great at this. (They'd better be . . . there's a name for those who aren't—unemployed). We've all seen it happen. The team is getting stomped. They can't get anything going during the entire first half. It's like they're playing with boxing gloves on. Rather than taking charge, they're being charged.

But then . . . magic!

Back in the locker room, away from the fans, the coach and team meet head-on. What results is nothing short of phenomenal. You'd swear that another bunch of athletes put on the same uniforms and played the victorious second half as they took charge and blew away their opponents. But these really are the same guys . . . or are they? They were transformed through the inspiration of a few minutes with one who is a master at building morale and clearing vision.

Christians should have no difficulty identifying with soldiers in the field or athletes in a game. Our ability to accomplish what is expected of us is directly linked to our morale and vision. Lose those two things and it isn't long before we begin to descend into the Slough of Despond. Life gets dreary. Ministry gets tedious. Obstacles loom larger and larger in our heads. Imagination, the fuel pump of our inner drive, gets clogged with pessimistic trash and depressing debris. Finally, our battery is drained, and we lose our charge.

What we need is a charge of renewal. God understands that. His people have been that way since the beginning.

For Abraham, the place of renewal was Bethel, where he "built an altar to the Lord and called upon the name of the Lord" (Gen. 12:8). He returned there frequently for a transfusion of courage.

For Moses and the Israelites, it was the tabernacle in the wilderness. Think of the strength they gained simply by meeting at the place where God's glory rested.

For the Twelve, it was their frequent meetings with Jesus. For His followers, it was the upper room at Pentecost. For early believers it was Paul's visits and return visits.

All of us need such times and places of renewal, when our morale and vision are reignited and our spiritual batteries are recharged . . . when the Spirit of God can do His masterful work of motivation. When that occurs, a burst of new energy returns and we're back on our feet, winning a second-half victory on the same turf that had earlier spelled defeat.

Morale starting to fade a little? Vision getting a tad blurry? What you need is your very own tabernacle in the wilderness where your imagination can get unclogged and your inner battery can get recharged.

A Finishing Touch: We cannot deliver the goods if our heart is heavier than the load.

A Daily Reading: Acts 1

I just returned from our nation's capital where I was privileged to spend time with many of the highest ranking officers in the military, stationed at the Pentagon. If you have ever wondered if there is anyone in the upper echelon of the military who loves Christ and desires to walk with Him, wonder no longer. Many of these men and women are magnificent models of strong Christian commitment who frequently put their faith on the line. I have returned home thanking God for these genuine disciples of Christ, modern-day "saints in Caesar's household."

While sitting around a table one morning, discussing some of the things I had spoken on, the subject of moral purity surfaced. I'd talked about personal integrity earlier that day, challenging them to be men and women whose private lives were free of carnal escapades. I warned of secret sensuality and cautioned them about hypocritical lifestyles that would compromise their testimony and give unbelievers a reason to sneer. This led us deeper into the all-important realm of character.

They spoke of the importance of an officer's having a clean record and maintaining strong character traits if he or she hoped to be trusted in larger realms and promoted to higher ranks. Impressed by their commitment to personal integrity, expressed so spontaneously and sincerely, I told them they would make great pastors.

Suddenly, several of them looked at each other and the group became quiet. Detecting the change in mood, I probed, "What's everybody thinking? Why the silence?" Finally, one of the men told me that our conversation had touched a nerve. Most of them attended the same church, he said, "a fine church with a rich history of strong biblical preaching, wonderful fellowship, and a healthy testimony in the community, until—"

My stomach churned. I looked down and shook my head. I didn't want to guess what he was leading up to, even though I could have.

". . . until our pastor had an affair with a woman and both of them left their mates and children. They are now living together and we're left to pick up the pieces." His voice trailed off. Tears and embarrassed looks and slowly shaking heads spoke eloquently of their bewilderment, their anger and deep disappointment. This pastor had been at that church for almost twenty years, and during that time the congregation had become one of the leading evangelical witnesses in the greater D.C. area—"until . . . ."

As I listened to them, I was humiliated to think that a standard of high moral character was still of paramount importance among military officers while within the ranks of the clergy an epidemic of impurity rages. Oh, the details may differ, but the disaster is painfully similar. Families are destroyed. A body of God's people is scandalized. A staff is ripped apart. The world sneers. And the church whose message was once clear and powerful in the community now bows its head and wonders why. What happened? All attempts to understand the pastor's Jekyll and Hyde lifestyle fail. His ability to betray and deceive defies logic—this man they trusted, respected, and looked to as spiritual leader and guide.

As Christian leaders, we need to reaffirm our commitment to moral purity and to private lives that are absolutely free of secret sins. While forgiveness continues to be the pulse-beat of a grace-oriented ministry, a firm commitment to holiness remains vital. Those who adopt a deceptive, compromising life of hypocrisy are responsible for the damage that occurs when they are found out. Nor are the consequences erased, even though they may repent and seek the Lord's and others' forgiveness.

Often, we are too quick to breeze past the damage that has been done, attempting to hurry the process of forgiveness at the expense of the restoration process. The guilty are often the more judgmental, screaming, "You need to forgive me!" which means, "You need to allow me all the rights and privileges I once enjoyed. I've changed! Remember God's grace!"

Not so fast. Not only does a contrite heart have no expectations and make no demands, it acknowledges that the deception and the extent of continued sin result in the continued forfeiture of many of the privileges that were once enjoyed. Please read that again. If you've gotten soft on this issue, stop and read the daily reading suggested below. Don't try to explain these verses away. They mean exactly what they say.

Physicians and lawyers found guilty of malpractice may certainly be forgiven, but they don't keep on practicing their professions. Murderers may certainly be forgiven, but they cannot escape the consequences of prison bars . . . and in some cases the loss of their own lives by capital punishment. Liars and thieves may certainly be forgiven, but they quickly discover that winning the public's trust is a long and painful process. Felons may serve their time and be forgiven, but they never again have the privilege of voting like other citizens. The consequences of wrongdoing don't magically go away.

This has nothing to do with forgiveness. Get that straight. The issue here is not a lack of forgiveness; it's the faulty thinking that forgiveness is synonymous with the returning of all rights and privileges.

Too strong? Ask that victimized flock in the D.C. area or any of a multitude of other congregations who have had to pick up the pieces left by a sweet-sounding shepherd who yielded to wolf-like lust. Or ask the betrayed mate who must endure the humiliating ordeal alone.

Never has the truth of Peter's words resounded more clearly: "It is time for judgment to begin with the household of God" (1 Peter 4:17).

A Finishing Touch: As believers, we need to reaffirm our commitment to moral purity and to private lives that are absolutely free of secret sins.

A Daily Reading: Proverbs 6:27–29, 32–33

Nathan then said to David, "You are the man! Thus says the Lord God of Israel, 'It is I who anointed you king over Israel and it is I who delivered you from the hand of Saul. I also gave you your master's house and your master's wives into your care, and I gave you the house of Israel and Judah; and if that had been too little, I would have added to you many more things like these!

"'Why have you despised the word of the Lord by doing evil in His sight? You have struck down Uriah the Hittite with the sword, have taken his wife to be your wife, and have killed him with the sword of the sons of Ammon.

"'Now therefore, the sword shall never depart from your house, because you have despised Me and have taken the wife of Uriah the Hittite to be your wife. . . . Indeed you did it secretly, but I will do this thing before all Israel, and under the sun.'"

Then David said to Nathan, "I have sinned against the Lord," And Nathan said to David, "The Lord also has taken away your sin; you shall not die. However, because by this deed you have given occasion to the enemics of the Lord to blaspheme, the child also that is born to you shall surely die" (2 Sam. 12:7–14).

David was "a man after God's own heart." Yet, once he crawled into bed with Uriah's wife on that moonlit spring night, never again did he know all the former joys of close family ties, public trust, or military invincibility.

This wasn't his family's fault or the public's fault or the Philistines' fault or the prophet Nathan's fault. It was David's fault, full-on.

COMPASSION IN SLOW MOTION

The timing is as critical as the involvement. You don't just force your way in. Even if you've got the stuff that's needed . . . even if you hold the piece perfectly shaped to fit the other person's missing part of the puzzle . . . you can't push it into place. You must not try.

You must do the most difficult thing for compassion to do.

You must wait.

Yes, that's correct. W*ait*.

Even if there is rebellion? Even if there's rebellion.

Even if sin is occurring? Yes, often even then.

Even if others are suffering and disillusioned and going through the misery of misunderstanding, heartache, and sleepless nights?

Believe it or not, yes.

There are times (not always, but often) when the better part of wisdom restrains us from barging in and trying to make someone accept our help. The time isn't right, so we wait.

Like Isaiah reported to the nation whom the Lord called "rebellious children" (Isa. 30:1). These people were rife with shame, reproach, unfaithful alliances, oppression, and a ruthless rejection of God's holy Word. Their unwillingness to repent added insult to injury.

But what was Jehovah's response? Hidden away in the first part of verse 18 is the incredible statement:

> Therefore the Lord longs to be gracious to you,
> And therefore He waits on high to have compassion on you.

Instead of storming into the dark alleys of Judah, screaming "Repent!" and shining bright lights to expose the filthy litter of their disobedience, the Lord tapped His foot, folded His arms . . . and waited. Not even the Lord pushed His way in. He waited until the time was right.

O people in Zion, inhabitant in Jerusalem, you will weep no longer. He will surely be gracious to you at the sound of your cry; when He hears it, He will answer you (Isa. 30:19).

Our Lord would love to piece together the shattered fragments of your life. But He is waiting . . . graciously waiting until the time is right.

Until you are tired of the life you are living . . . until you see it for what it really is.

Until you are weary of coping . . . of taking charge of your own life . . . until you realize the mess you are making of it.

Until you recognize your need for Him.

He's waiting . . . .

A Finishing Touch: God's timing is always on time.
A Daily Reading: Isaiah 30:1–26

THE OPERA AIN'T OVER . . . 'TIL THE FAT LADY SINGS.

It was a banner hung over the wall near the 40-yard line of Texas Stadium. The guys in silver and blue were struggling to stay in the race for the playoffs. So some Cowboy fan, to offer down-home encouragement, had splashed those words on a king-size bedsheet for all America to read. It was his way of saying, "We're hangin' in there, baby. Don't count us out. We have three games left before anybody can say for sure . . . so we're not givin' up! The opera ain't over."

Sure is easy to jump to conclusions, isn't it? People who study trends make it their business to manufacture out of their imaginations the proposed (and "inevitable") end result. Pollsters do that too. After sampling 3 percent of our country (or at least they say that's what it equates to), vast and stunning statistics are announced: "So-and-so will, for sure, wind up doing such-and-such." At times it's downright scary.

Every once in a while it's helpful to remember times when those preening prognosticators wound up with egg on their faces.

Like when Wellington whipped Napoleon

And when Truman beat Dewey

Like that time the earthquake didn't hit

And England didn't surrender

And Hitler wasn't the Antichrist

And the Communists didn't take over America by 1975

And Muhammad Ali could get beaten

And a nation could survive assassinations, political scandals, and energy crises.

Yes, at many a turn we have all been tempted to jump to "obvious" conclusions, only to be surprised by a strange curve thrown our way. God is good at that.

Can you recall a few biblical examples?

Like when a young boy, armed with only a sling and a stone, whipped a giant over nine feet tall.

Or the time an Egyptian army approaching fast left the Israelites with no possible way to escape. Suddenly, against all the laws of nature, the sea opened up and allowed the Hebrews to walk across.

And how about the vast "indestructible" wall around Jericho? Who would've ever imagined?

Or that dead-end street at Golgotha miraculously opening up at an empty tomb three days later?

Anybody—and I mean anybody—who would have been near enough to have witnessed any one of those predicaments would certainly have said, "Curtains . . . the opera is over!"

Unless I miss my guess, a lot of you who are reading this page are yourselves backed up against circumstances that seem to spell THE END. Pretty well finished. Apparently over.

Your adversary would love for you to assume the worst, to heave a sigh and resign yourself to the depressed feelings that accompany defeat, failure, maximum resentment, and minimum faith.

But take heart. When God is involved, anything can happen. The One who directed that stone and opened that sea and leveled that wall and brought His Son back from the dead takes delight in the incredible.

The blind songwriter, Fanny Crosby, put it another way: "Chords that were broken will vibrate once more."

In other words, don't manufacture conclusions. Don't even think in terms of "this is the way things will turn out." God has a beautiful way of bringing good vibes out of broken chords. There are dozens of fat ladies waiting in the wings. And believe me, the opera ain't over!

━━━━━━━━━━━━━━━━━━━━━━━━━━━━━━━━━━━━━━━

A Finishing Touch: God delights in mixing up the odds as He alters the obvious and bypasses the inevitable.

A Daily Reading: Exodus 14–15

Remember comedian Flip Wilson's old line, "Da debil made me do it"? Whether the guy believed in an actual Satan was immaterial. All he was interested in was getting a laugh. But the thing that made it so effective was the scenario the guy was acting out.

Here was this character who had obviously done something bad. But instead of taking the blame, he pointed an accusing finger at "da debil." Why did we laugh? We weren't just laughing at his hilarious routines; we were laughing at ourselves—at one of our favorite indoor games: The Blame Game. And since he is altogether wicked and invisible and unable to challenge our accusation in audible tones, there's no better scapegoat than old Lucifer himself.

But when this practice becomes a daily habit, it stops being funny and starts being phony. It's when we become escape artists, dodging the responsibility of our own disobedience, that we carry the thing too far. Not just blaming Satan for every evil action, but finding him in every nook and cranny . . . thinking he is the subtle force behind all wicked events and encounters. It's the age-old conspiracy mentality.

There are those, for example, who see and hear the devil in certain types of music. They tell us to play the tapes backwards and we can hear the subliminal satanic message . . . which seems a lot like reading a book in a mirror to detect its evil connotation. Strange.

They warn us against Proctor and Gamble because the beard of a face in the tiny logo includes 666. Don't laugh. So many believed this that the company was forced to spend a fortune trying to combat fears of a satanic connection. A Christian woman in Kansas City went to court to get her license plate changed from CPG666 (note the P and G) on the grounds that her fellow church members were shunning her.

While I'm on the subject, the 666 scare stuff is getting downright ridiculous. The fact is that those three digits can be uncovered in almost anybody's name, if you're willing to work at it hard enough. Using the code A=100, B=101, and so on, Hitler adds up to 666. With a simpler code of A=1, B=2, and multiplying each letter-value by 6 (whew!), Sun Moon adds up to 666. The same technique works on Kissinger, as well as the word "computer" (that I can believe).

Talk about nuts! I've even had a well-meaning believer claim he had the demon of nail-biting and another the demon of overeating. Next thing I know, I'll hear I have the demon of preaching too long!

You and I know there is a devil and a host of demons. There is an authentic "prince of the power of the air," whose sole goal is to infect and influence with evil. He is on the prowl (1 Peter 5:8), diabolical in nature and deceptive in method (2 Cor. 11:3). He is responsible for much wickedness, but not all of it—there's also the world and the flesh, remember (1 John 2:15–16). If he cannot get us entrapped in one extreme, where he's an imaginary prankster with horns, pitchfork, and red longjohns . . . then it's the other, where he's everywhere, in everything, embodying everyone, and we start listening to music backwards and sniffing out signs of 666 in labels, license plates, and leaders.

C'mon, Christian, let's wise up. We look foolish enough in the eyes of the lost without giving them fuel for the fire. Leave the funny stuff for the comedians and the phony stuff for fanatics. We've got our hands full maintaining a sensible balance on the tightrope of truth. For if there's one thing "da debil" can't stand, it's the truth.

A Finishing Touch: Some people spend so much time looking for what isn't there that they fail to see what is.

A Daily Reading: 1 John 1

Earthquakes! Prison riots! Economic pressures! Divorce! No jobs! Drugs! Disease! Death! Pretty serious scene, isn't it? Yet that is the emotional environment in which we live. No wonder someone has dubbed this the "aspirin age." Small wonder more of us are not throwing in the towel.

In spite of these bleak surroundings—or perhaps because of—I firmly believe we need a good dose of Solomon's counsel. Listen to David's wisest son:

> A joyful heart makes a cheerful face, but when the heart is sad, the spirit is broken. . . . All the days of the afflicted are bad, but a cheerful heart has a continual feast. . . . A joyful heart is good medicine [the Hebrew says, "causes good healing"], but a broken spirit dries up the bones (Prov. 15:13, 15; 17:22).

How is your sense of humor? Are the times in which we live beginning to be reflected in your attitude, your face, your outlook? Solomon talks straight, friend. He (under the Holy Spirit's direction) says three things will occur when we have lost our sense of humor: a broken spirit, a lack of inner healing, and dried-up bones. What a barren portrait!

Have you begun to shrivel into a bitter, impatient, critical Christian? The Lord tells us that the solution is simple: "A joyful heart" is what we need . . . and if ever we needed it, it is now.

By a sense of humor I am not referring to distasteful or vulgar jesting, nor to foolish and silly talk that is ill-timed, offensive, and tactless. I mean that necessary ingredient of wit: those humorous, enjoyable, and delightful expressions or thoughts that lift our spirits and lighten our day. When we lose our ability to laugh—I mean *really* laugh—life's oppressive assaults confine us to the dark dungeon of defeat.

Humor is not a sin. It is a God-given escape hatch . . . a safety valve. Being able to see the lighter side of life is a rare, vital virtue.

Humor is a great asset in missionary life, believe it or not. Indeed, if a missionary lacks a good sense of humor, it is a serious deficiency.

I read recently of a missionary from Sweden who was urged by friends to give up the idea of returning to India because it was so hot there. "Man," he was urged, "it's 120 degrees in the shade!" "Vell," said the Swede in noble contempt, "ve don't always have to stay in the shade, do ve?"

Personally, I think a healthy sense of humor is determined by at least four abilities:

The ability to laugh at our own mistakes.

The ability to accept justified criticism—and get over it!

The ability to interject (or at least enjoy) wholesome humor when surrounded by a tense, heated situation.

The ability to control those statements that would be unfit—even though they may be funny.

James M. Gray and William Houghton were two great, godly men of the Word. Dr. Houghton writes of an occasion when he and Dr. Gray were praying together. Dr. Gray, though getting up in years, was still interested in being an effective witness and expositor. He concluded his prayer by saying: "And, Lord, keep me cheerful. Keep me from becoming a cranky, old man!"

You and I should pray the same prayer.

A Finishing Touch: Let's ask our understanding Father to remind us frequently of the necessity of a cheerful spirit and to give us an appreciation for laughter.

A Daily Reading: Ecclesiastes 3:1–13

Remember when men were men?

Remember when you could tell by looking?

Remember when men knew who they were, liked how they were, and didn't want to be anything but what they were?

Remember when it was the men who boxed and wrestled and bragged about how much they could bench press?

Remember when it was the women who wore the makeup, the earrings, and the bikinis?

Remember when it was the men who initiated the contact and took the lead in a relationship, made lifelong commitments, and modeled a masculinity grounded in security and stability?

I'm not talking about Rambo types who suffer from macho mania . . . those who always look for a fight, walk with a swagger, never apologize, and give off that make-my-day stare. Those guys may be able to destroy half of North Vietnam singlehandedly, but they make terrible neighbors, horrible business colleagues, and brutal husbands and fathers. Being a man is not the same as living like an animal ready to pounce.

Neither do I have in mind the Archie Bunker-type loudmouth who slouches in his chair, barks out orders, and thinks the world revolves around him. Dogmatism, prejudice, and selfishness do not masculinity make. That fellow is living in a fantasy world, imagining that he's running the show. In actuality, he's a frightened child inside a man's body.

True manhood calls for discipline of character, strong determination to set a course of action, and courage to stay at a task.

Brutality? Vulgarity? Lack of courtesy? Hardly. Authentic men aren't afraid to show affection, to release their feelings, to hug their children, to cry when they're sad, to admit when they're wrong, to ask for help when they need it. Vulnerability fits beautifully into mature manhood. So does integrity.

What I am concerned about is a vanishing masculinity that was once in abundance.

I'm talking about men who are discerning, decisive, strong-hearted, who know where they are going and are confident enough in themselves (and their God) to get there. Men who aren't afraid to take the lead, to stand tall, firm in their principles, even when the going gets rough.

Such qualities not only inspire the respect of women, they also engender healthy admiration among younger men and boys who hunger for heroes. We need clear-thinking, hard-working, straight-talking men who, while tender, thoughtful, and loving, don't feel the need to ask permission for taking charge. Such men are fast becoming an endangered species.

Over the last three decades we have seen a major assault on masculinity. The results are well represented in the arts, the media, the world of fashion, and among those who have become the heroes of our young people. Androgynous individuals prance to and fro on rock concert stages across America. Poster-size portraits of male celebrities paper the walls in thousands of boys' bedrooms. The most shocking part of all is that many of these performers no longer even pretend to be masculine. Sex roles are deliberately blended. Female impersonations are now the hot ticket in show places around the world, performing mainly before male audiences. Weird? Kinky? In my opinion, *disgusting*.

Several years ago a *People* magazine article, "Invasion of the Gender Blenders," included a dialogue between a psychologist and his seven-year-old nephew. The professional asked the boy, "Is Michael Jackson a boy or a girl?" The boy thought for a moment, then answered, "Both."

Gender blending is no longer a fad on society's bizarre edge. It's here, and it is neither subtle nor silent.

On the heels of a bloody Civil War, Josiah Holland wrote a passionate prayer on behalf of our country. It begins, "God, give us men . . . ."

But the truth is, God doesn't give a nation men; He gives us *boys*. Baby boys, adolescent boys, impressionable boys who need to know what becoming a man is all about. God's plan is still as He designed it at creation. And it starts in the home.

Moms and Dads, we must seize our responsibility firmly and seriously. We owe our sons this debt: to rear them to be authentically masculine—Christian gentlemen, yes, but distinctly and unquestionably masculine—so that when they are grown they think like, look like, and act like men.

A Finishing Touch: Men, are you modeling manhood according to God's Word? Moms and Dads, are you raising your sons to be authentically masculine? If not, why not? Think it over!

A Daily Reading: Psalm 78

Future Shock author Alvin Toffler saw all this happening in his 1980 book, *The Third Wave*, where he announced:

> . . . the role system that held industrial civilization together is in crisis. This we see most dramatically in the struggle to redefine sex roles. In the women's movement, in the demands for the legalization of homosexuality, in the spread of unisex fashions, we see a continual blurring of traditional expectations for the sexes.

Toffler is on target but too soft. The separate distinction of male and female is not merely a "traditional expectation"; it's a biblical precept.

"Male and female He created them" (Gen. 1:27).

And it isn't simply a "role system that held industrial civilization together." It is a major foundational block upon which any healthy civilization rests.

When male and female roles get sufficiently blurred, confusion and chaos replace decency and order. When effeminate men begin to flood the landscape, God's long-suffering reaches the length of its tether, ushering in the severest judgment imaginable . . . a la Sodom and Gomorrah.

Romans 1:24–27 is still in the Book.

A New Week
of
Finishing Touches

19

MONDAY

God's sharp sword stabbed me deeply this week as I was on a scriptural hunt in the Ephesian letter. I was searching for a verse totally unrelated to the one that sliced its way into me. It was another of those verses I feel sorry for (like John 3:17 and 1 John 1:10—look 'em up). This was Ephesians 5:19: "speaking to one another in psalms and hymns and spiritual songs, singing and making melody with your heart to the Lord."

Everybody knows 5:18, where we are told "be filled with the Spirit." But have you ever noticed that verse 18 ends with a comma, not a period? The next verse describes the very first result of being under the Spirit's control: WE SING! We make melody with our hearts. We communicate His presence within us by presenting our own, individual Concert of Sacred Music to Him.

Now let's go further. Ephesians 5 never once refers to a church building. I mention that because we Christians have so centralized our singing that we seldom engage in it once we walk away from a service. Stop and think. Did you sing on the way home last Sunday night? How about Monday, when you drove to work . . . or around the supper table . . . or Tuesday as you dressed for the day? Chances are, you didn't even sing before or after you had your time with the Lord any day of the week. Why?

The Spirit-filled saint is a song-filled saint! Animals can't sing. Neither can pews or pulpits or Bibles or buildings—only you. And your melody is broadcasted right into heaven, where God's antenna is always receptive . . . where the soothing strains of your song are always appreciated.

If Martin Luther were alive today, he'd be heartsick. That rugged warrior of the faith had two basic objectives when he fired the reformation cannon into the sixteenth-century wall of spiritual ignorance. First, to give the people a Bible they could read on their own, and second, to give them a hymnal from which they could sing on

226

their own. The Bible we have, and its words we read. The hymnal we have—but where, oh, where has the melody gone? We simply do not sing as often as we ought . . . and therein lies the blame and the shame.

Let me offer five corrective suggestions:

Whenever and whatever you sing, concentrate on the words. If it helps, close your eyes.

Make a definite effort to add one or two songs to your day. Remind yourself, periodically, of the words of a chorus or hymn you love and add them to your driving schedule or soap-and-shower time.

Sing often with a friend or members of your family. It helps break down all sorts of invisible barriers. You might even sing before grace at mealtime in the evening. That is so enjoyable, you may get addicted, I warn you.

Blow the dust off your tape or CD player and put on some beautiful music around the house. Just watch what happens to the atmosphere when you do this. And don't forget to sing along and add your own harmony and "special" effects.

Never mind how beautiful or pitiful you may sound. You are not auditioning for the choir; you're making melody with your heart. SING OUT!

If you listen closely when you're through, you may hear the hosts of heaven shouting for joy. Then again, it might be your neighbor . . . screaming for relief.

A Finishing Touch: Sing loud enough to drown out those defeating thoughts that clamor for attention.

A Daily Reading: Psalm 98

ET has gone home. I wonder if he ever sees ST?

Who's ST? Another fantasy figure originated in Stephen Spielberg's fertile mind? Nope, nothing fantasy about this fella. This one's real. Manmade, in fact. And it is a whole lot bigger than the little guy who hid in closets and raided refrigerators several years ago. Weighs in at around twelve tons, in fact, and looks like an extra-terrestrial grain silo.

Let me introduce you to the Hubble Space Telescope (affectionately dubbed "ST"). Now that it has finally been fitted with its corrective lens(!), this massive spy in the sky will expand the volume of the visible universe by showing the farthest galaxies ten times more clearly than earthbound telescopes ever have or ever could. Because of its enormous size, its location in space, and its precision, a window into space will be opened to us that scientists and astronomers never dreamed possible.

Says one authority: "It's not hyperbole to say that ST is as much an improvement over the most powerful existing telescope as Galileo's first spyglass in 1609 was over the human eye . . . it could bring into focus the stars on an American flag at a distance of 3,000 miles. ST will record images . . . via electronic light collectors so sensitive they could detect a flashlight on the Moon. But the telescope's greatest advantage is that the shuttle will lift it above the atmosphere, the thick veil of air that makes stars appear to shimmer."

Thanks to ST, a mind-boggling new dimension will open to us because it will take us back into time. To understand this, think of a bolt of lightning flashing across the sky. Five or six seconds later we hear a thunderclap. In actuality, we are hearing back into time. The sound of the thunder is signaling an event that—thanks to the lightning flash—we know happened five to six seconds earlier.

Astronomer Richard Harms uses this analogy to describe ST's ability to help us view the distant past by virtue of its capacity to see great distances. "Instead of sound waves from thunder," he suggests, "think of light waves traveling from a far galaxy to the space telescope above the earth. Light moves very fast, but the distance is so vast that a certain amount of time has to elapse before the light can get from there to here." A "light year" is the distance light travels in one year, 5.8 trillion miles. Thus, ST should be able to pick up images that have been traveling for as long as twelve billion years.

Are you ready for this? That means we'd be able to see events that transpired when the universe was a dozen billion years younger!

And just think of some of the nagging questions it may answer: Is there really extraterrestrial life out there? What about those mysterious "black holes"? And what about those vast galaxies outside our own?

Just this morning, thinking about all this, I read these familiar words: "And God made the two great lights, the greater light to govern the day, and the lesser light to govern the night; He made the stars also. And God placed them in the expanse of the heavens" (Gen. 1:16–17).

Wouldn't it be something if one of ST's most distant signals revealed evidences of the creative hand of God? That should be sufficient to turn goose-pimple excitement into mouth-opening faith, even for the most cynical of scientists.

A Finishing Touch: "O world invisible, we view thee, O world intangible, we touch thee, O world unknowable, we know thee" (*The Kingdom of God*, Francis Thompson).

A Daily Reading: Psalm 19

My desk was top-heavy with research works on Paul the apostle and his century-one letter to the Philippians. Well-worn volumes, lexicon, dictionary, concordance, Greek New Testament, maps, charts, several versions of the Scriptures, pen, pencils, a couple of stacks of paper needed to be put away. I had just completed a manuscript and my heart was full of joy. Not only because I was through (isn't that a wonderful word?) but because joy, the theme of the inspired letter I had spent weeks studying, had rubbed off. It was as if Paul and I had shared the same room and written at the same desk

I was smiling and humming the little chorus "Rejoice in the Lord always, and again I say, rejoice!" as I inserted the books I had used back onto my library shelves. It was late in the evening. The sun had set and the shadows of dusk outside my study window would soon give way to night.

As I shoved the last volume in place, my eyes fell upon an old work by a British pastor of yesteryear, F. B. Meyer. It was his work on Philippians, but for some reason I had not consulted it throughout my months of study. Thinking there might be something to augment my now-finished manuscript, I decided to leaf through it before calling it a day. I leaned back in my old leather chair, propped my feet up, and opened Meyer's book.

It was not his words that spoke to me that evening, however, but the words of my mother. For as I began looking through it, I realized the book had once been a part of her library; after her death in 1971 it had found its way into mine. Little did she realize that her words would become part of her legacy to me. In her inimitable handwriting, my mother had added her own observations, prayers, and related Scriptures in the margins throughout the book. Inside the back cover she had written: "Finishing reading this, May 8, 1958."

When I saw that date . . . 1958 . . . memory carried me back to a tiny island in the South Pacific where I had spent many lonely months as a Marine. There, in May of '58 I had reached a crossroad in my own spiritual pilgrimage. In fact, I had entered these words in my own journal at the time: "The Lord has convinced me that I am to be in His service. I need to begin my plans to prepare for a lifetime of ministry."

Amazingly, it was the same month of that same year that my mother had finished Meyer's book. As I scanned her words, I found one reference after another to her prayers for me as I was far, far away . . . her concern for my spiritual welfare . . . her desire for God's best in my life.

And in that moment I thanked God anew for the touch of my mother's love and the effectiveness of her prayers. I bowed my head and wept with gratitude.

Suddenly the shrill ring of the phone broke the silence. Our youngest, Chuck, was on the line wanting to tell me something funny that had happened. As we laughed together, he urged me to hurry home. I promised I'd be there in fifteen minutes.

As I slid Meyer's book back on the shelf, I thought of the invaluable role my parents had played during the formative years of my life . . . and how the torch had been passed from them to Cynthia and me to do the same with our sons and daughters—and they, in turn, with theirs.

In the gathering dusk I smiled and said softly, "Thank you, Mother." I could almost hear her voice answering, "Charles. I love you. I'm still praying for you, Son. Keep walking with God. Finish strong!"

A Finishing Touch: What treasured legacy has been passed on to you? What prevailing prayers, lasting love, wise warnings, hearty laughter? What are you passing on to your children?

A Daily Reading: Acts 20:16–24

If there's one attitude families are guilty of more than any other when it comes to mothers, it's presumption . . . taking them for granted . . . being nearly blind on occasion to the load moms carry. This was reinforced in my mind last week as I was thumbing through a row of crazy greeting cards at a local drugstore. Time and again the joke in the card drew its humor from this obvious attitude that pervades a household: *Forget the housework, Mom. It's your day. Besides, you can always do double duty and catch up on Monday!*

Like this one: On the front of the card was a beleaguered mother. Draped over her neck were three unmatched socks and at her feet was an enormous stack of unwashed clothes. On the stove was a hot skillet burning the food. A cold, stained coffee pot needed attention. The refrigerator door was ajar and milk had spilled in it. The dishes, naturally, looked like a homemade Eiffel Tower reaching out of the sink. Inside the card was scribbled: *"Look, lady, nobody said it was gonna be a free ride!"*

But my favorite was a great big card that looked like a third-grader had printed it. On it was a little boy with a dirty face and torn pants pulling a wagonload of toys. On the front it read: *"Mom, I remember the little prayer you used to say for me every day . . . "* and inside, *"God help you if you do that again!"*

Jimmy Dean, the country-western singer, does a number that always leaves me with a big knot in my throat. It's entitled "I Owe You." In the song a man is looking through his wallet and comes across a number of long-standing "I owe yous" to his mother . . . which he names one by one.

Borrowing that idea, I suggest you who have been guilty of presumption unfold some of your own "I owe yous" that are now yellow with age. Consider the priceless value of the one woman who made your life possible—your mother.

Think about her example, her support, her humor, her counsel, her humility, her hospitality, her insight, her patience, her sacrifices. Her faith. Her hope. Her love.

Old "honest Abe" was correct: "He is not poor who has had a godly mother." Indebted, but not poor.

Moms, on Mother's Day Sunday we rise up and call you blessed. But knowing you, you'll feel uneasy in the limelight. You'll probably look for a place to hide. True servants are like that.

If you don't watch it, you'll be planning lunch during the sermon. But that would be a waste of time. Especially since you're going to be taken out to eat (which will add to our indebtedness!). But in all honesty, it won't come anywhere near expressing our gratitude.

So, live it up on Sunday. It's all yours.

My advice? Shake up the family for a change. Order steak and lobster!

A Finishing Touch: Mother's day should not be just one day a year.

A Daily Reading: Proverbs 31:10–31

Several years ago someone interviewed the contemporary artist Marc Chagall for a PBS program. The young, arty interviewer started the session with a question about influences. His question was very long and involved and exhibited his own learning along the way, giving everybody, including Chagall, a lecture on the nature of influences on the artist.

When the young man finally gave the artist a chance to answer for himself, Chagall said, in the simplest way possible, that his greatest influence was his mother. It took the poor young man a bit of time to get his bearings after that.

I know of no more permanent imprint on a life than the one made by mothers. I guess that's why Mother's Day always leaves me a little nostalgic. Not simply because my mother has gone on (and heaven's probably cleaner because of it!), but because that's the one day the real heroines of our world get the credit they deserve. Hats off to every one of you!

More than any statesman or teacher, more than any minister or physician, more than any film star, athlete, business person, author, scientist, civic leader, entertainer, or military hero . . . you are the most influential person in your child's life.

Never doubt that fact!

Not even when the dishes in the sink resemble the Leaning Tower . . . or the washing machine gets choked and dies . . . or the place looks a wreck and nobody at home stops to say, "Thanks, Mom. You're great."

It's still worth it. You are great. This is your time to make the most significant contribution in all of life. Don't sell it short. In only a few years it will all be a memory. Make it a good one. For, as Helen M. Young has so aptly and poignantly written, "Children Won't Wait":

> There will be a time when there will be no slamming of doors,
> no toys on the stairs, no childhood quarrels, no fingerprints on
> the wallpaper.

Then may I look back with joy and not regret.

. . . .

God, give me wisdom to see that today is my day
    with my children.
That there is no unimportant moment in their lives.
May I know that no other career is so precious,
No other work so rewarding,
No other task so urgent.
May I not defer it nor neglect it,
But by the Spirit accept it gladly, joyously,
    and by Thy grace realize
That the time is short and my time is now,
For children won't wait!

There would never have been an Isaac without a Sarah, a Moses without a Jochebed, a Samuel without a Hannah, a John without an Elizabeth, a Timothy without a Eunice, or a John Mark without a Mary.

These men were the men they were, in great part, because of the mothers they had. The hidden secret of that winning combination? Mother with child—just that simple. So, please . . . please, stay at it!

A mother's influence is so great that we model it even when we don't realize it, and we return to it—often to the surprise of others.

As I think of my own mother's influence on me, two words come to mind: class and zest. My mother, being a classy lady, was determined to keep our family from being ignorant of the arts or lacking in social graces. I have her to thank for my love of artistic beauty, fine music, which fork to use, and no gravy on my tie. She also possessed such a zest for life. I am indebted to her for my enthusiasm and relentless drive. Her indomitable spirit got passed on, thank goodness.

And so, mothers, don't ever forget the permanence of your imprint. The kids may seem ungrateful, they may act irresponsible, they may even ignore your reminders and forget your advice these days. But believe this: they cannot erase your influence.

A Finishing Touch: Think about how your own mother has influenced your life. Have you ever thanked her? Have you thanked God for your mother's influence in your life?

A Daily Reading: 2 Timothy 1:1–5

Several years ago I asked the ministry staff at the church I was pastoring to reflect on how their mothers had influenced their lives. Here are a few of the responses I received:

"The interest, concern, and care for older people that my mother modeled in a Christlike manner impacted my life to the extent that today I am involved in a ministry with senior adults" (Dave Jobe).

"Trying to define my mother's influence is like trying to talk definitively about clean air, pure water, warm sunshine, and the law of gravity. She consistently modeled faith, patience, love, hard work, and forgiveness" (Paul Sailhamer).

"It was at my mother's knee that I learned many of the values I hold today. A disciplined life of service for the Lord and to the needy stand out in my mind. No job was too big, no sacrifice too great, no circumstance too difficult to serve the Lord. Total trust in an all-powerful God was her guarantee of success. Her unflinching belief in me gave me motivation and strength" (Doug Haag).

"My mom is the greatest. I will always remember her for taking time to be with me as a child, praying for me as I wandered away from the Lord as an adolescent, and even now caring about me as an adult. It was through her that I learned the compassionate side of life" (Bruce Camp).

"One of the fondest memories of Mother's influence on my life came in the first grade when I was sent to sit outside the class for talking out of turn. My mother worked as an aide at the school, and I was filled with dread as I saw her walking down the breezeway toward me. As she approached she asked, 'Have you been talking aloud in class?' I nodded. She laughed. She never mentioned the incident again. In her own subtle way she was teaching me that I had the responsibility of accepting the consequences for my own actions" (Dean Anderson).

A New Week of Finishing Touches

20

MONDAY

Blow that layer of dust off the book of Nahum in your Bible and catch a glimpse of the last part of verse three, chapter one: "The way of the Lord is in the whirlwind and in the storm" (*Berkeley Version*).

That's good to remember when you're caught in a rip-snortin' Texas frog strangler as I was last week. I reminded myself of God's presence as the rain-heavy, charcoal-colored clouds were split apart by lightning's eerie fingers and the air shook with earth-shattering, ear-deafening reports of thunder. Once again the Lord, the God of the heavens, was having His way in the whirlwind and the storm, I thought, as Nahum and I visited together through Weatherford and Cisco and Abilene and Sweetwater.

But how about those storms of life? What about the whirlwinds of disease, disaster, and death? What about the storms of interruptions, irritations, and ill-treatment? Well, if Nahum's words apply to the heavenly sphere, they also apply to the earthly—to the heart-rending contingencies of daily living.

Ask Nebuchadnezzar, and he would reply: "And all the inhabitants of the earth are accounted as nothing, but He does according to His will in the host of heaven and among the inhabitants of earth; and no one can ward off His hand or say to Him, 'What hast Thou done?'" (Dan. 4:35).

David, if asked, would answer: "But our God is in the heavens; He does whatever He pleases" (Ps. 115:3).

Paul would add: "For it is God who is at work in you, both to will and to work for His good pleasure" (Phil. 2:13).

Moses nailed it down with his comment: "When you are in distress and all these things have come upon you . . . you will return to the Lord your God and listen to His voice" (Deut. 4:30).

Life is filled with God-appointed storms. A sheet of paper ten times this size would be insufficient to list the whirlwinds of our

238

lives. But two things should comfort us in the midst of daily lightning and thunder. First, we all experience them. Second, we all need them. God has no other method more effective. The massive blows and shattering blasts (not to mention the small, constant irritations) smooth us and humble us and force us to submit to the role He has chosen for us.

William Cowper could take the stand in defense of all I have written. He passed through a period of great crisis in his life. Finally one bleak morning he tried to put an end to it all by taking poison. The attempt at suicide failed. He then hired a coach, was driven to the Thames River, intending to throw himself from the bridge . . . but was "strangely restrained." The next morning he fell upon a sharp knife—but the blade broke! He later tried to hang himself, but was found and taken down unconscious . . . still alive. Some time later he took up a Bible, began to read the book of Romans, and was gloriously saved. The God of the storms had pursued him unto the end and won his heart.

After a rich life of Christian experiences—but not without constant whirlwind and storm—Cowper sat down and recorded his summary of the Lord's dealings in the familiar words:

> God moves in a mysterious way
> His wonders to perform;
> He plants His footsteps in the sea,
> And rides upon the storm.

A Finishing Touch: Before the dust settles, why not ask God to have His way in *today's* whirlwind and storm?
A Daily Reading: Nahum 1

The path of the pale horse named Death, mentioned in Revelation 6:8, is littered with bitterness, sorrow, fear, and grief. This ashen stallion started his lengthy journey ages ago and races through time with steady beat and dreadful regularity. As long as we exist in the land of the dying, we shall hear the somber knell of his hoofbeats.

Call me a prophet of doom if you wish—but I must remind you: DEATH IS CERTAIN. Sadly, some people hurry their appointment with it. Painful though it may be to hear and accept, thousands of people will take their own lives during the next twelve months. For in our land, suicide is now almost an epidemic.

Once *every minute* someone in the United States attempts suicide.

Every day, seventy Americans take their own lives . . . that's nearly three each hour.

In this country, there are 24 percent more deaths by suicide than by murder.

In Los Angeles County, more people kill themselves than die in traffic accidents.

Suicide is the No. 9 cause of adult death in the USA. For Americans between fifteen and thirty years of age, it is the No. 3 cause of death. It is the No. 2 cause among teenagers.

The suicide rate for Americans under thirty years of age has increased 300 percent in the past decade.

Until recently, women attempted suicide three times as often as men (but men succeeded three times more often). Statistics now show a drastic increase in successful attempts by women—especially young black women.

Four out of five people who commit suicide have tried it previously. Those who are unsuccessful usually try again.

Contrary to popular opinion, people who threaten suicide often mean it. The old myth "those who talk don't jump" is dangerously false. Threats should be taken seriously.

While man's greatest instinct is to live, there are those among us who are so troubled that they lose this healthy and natural desire.

Feeling alone, worthless, unloved, and unlovely, they have exhausted the alternatives to effect change. When that happens, to them suicide becomes the only way to escape—the ultimate option.

Thankfully, suicidal individuals usually communicate such feelings before acting, thus making this irrevocable act preventable if those who are close are wise and sensitive enough to read the signals.

Some of the warning signals or clues you should be aware of are: (1) talk about suicide, (2) a sudden change in personality, (3) deep depression, (4) physical symptoms—sleeplessness, loss of appetite, decreased sexual drive, drastic weight loss, repeated exhaustion, (5) actual attempts, and (6) crisis situations—death of a loved one, failure at school, loss of job, marital or home problems, and a lengthy or terminal illness. These are certainly not "sure signs," but if any or several persist over a period of time, please step in and offer help. Contact your physician or ask advice from your local Suicide Prevention Center's 24-hour crisis line; you may also want to contact one of the spiritual leaders or officers of your church or a member of the pastoral staff. Such situations are often emergencies. To delay could result in tragic consequences.

Those who are strong need to bear the weaknesses of the weak (Rom. 15:1). That may mean blocking the path of the pale horse!

A Finishing Touch: Sometimes if we are to hear what is being said, we need to listen to what is not being said.
A Daily Reading: Psalm 23

[Reader alert: I wrote this back when Len Dykstra was playing for the Mets. But the truth still applies.]

No offense, but Len Dykstra doesn't look like much of an athlete. He looks more like some team's mascot. Or like the guy who wears that silly chicken suit and does cartwheels around stadiums. The kid can't stand much more than five-seven. Seeing him with the team, you'd swear he was the batboy. But since he chews a big plug, spits, and lets it run down his chin, you figure maybe he's one of those dead-end kids from the Bronx who snuck in a back gate at Shea Stadium and stole a uniform. Tiny Tim wearing No. 4. Mickey Rooney in spikes.

Nope. None of the above. That little Dutch boy is the starting center fielder for the National League New York Mets. Nicknamed Nails—as in "tough as" and "harder than." And if you don't believe that, you haven't been watching the baseball playoffs lately. In a game of intimidating physical powerhouses, with starting lineups that resemble a work detail from the Eastham Prison Farm, Dykstra looks more like a Little League bench warmer with a runny nose . . . until he steps into the batter's box. Somehow, when that occurs, the baby-faced runt becomes a snarling creature out of the swamp. Just stick a bat in his hand, then run for cover. He ain't called "Nails" for nothing.

With game three fairly boring and all but over—bottom of the ninth, Mets losing—veteran Astro reliever Dave Smith must have smiled down inside as the little guy walked up to the plate. Dykstra fouled off Smith's stinging fastball; and then, without hesitation, he slammed the next one over the fence. We're talking Big Apple Explosion!

As L. A. *Times* sportswriter Gordon Edes put it: "His you-gotta-believe-it, two-run home run gave the Mets a 6-5 win and transformed Shea Stadium—as polite as Carnegie Hall for most of the overcast afternoon—into a high-fivin', Astro-defyin', bring-on-the-World-Series-jivin' madhouse."

The Houston players, who had led the entire game, stared in stunned disbelief as the little guy danced his way around the bases.

I loved it! Even though I'm not a Mets fan, or, for that matter, all that big on Len Dykstra, I always sit up and take notice when odds are defied. We all do, don't we? That's why we pull for the underdog. And why we never tire of the David-and-Goliath story. Or the way those walls fell flat at Jericho. Or the crossing of the Red Sea. Or Daniel standing nose-to-nose with a den full of hungry lions. Or a thousand other I-can't-believe-it accounts of heroism with the odds against the little guy.

It's no big deal for huge hunks of humanity to hit homers. But when the little fella smashes one over 400 feet, that's news.

Why? Because that gives all of us hope. If he can do that, surrounded by all those towering odds stacked against him, then there's hope for me, facing all my odds. It's like getting a shot of fresh motivation in both arms.

Want to defy the odds? Aim high. Forget "I can't."

Or, in baseball parlance, get hold of that bat, step up to the plate, and slam that sucker outa the park!

A Finishing Touch: "But the bravest are surely those who have the clearest vision of what is before them, glory and danger alike, and yet notwithstanding go out to meet it" (Thucydides).

A Daily Reading: 1 Samuel 17

Better than any other word I can think of, *change* describes our world. Vast, sweeping changes, especially in the last 150 years. Simply to survive requires adjusting, and to make any kind of significant dent calls for a willingness to shift in style and to modify methods. The old Roman politician, Publilius Syrus, was right when he wrote: "It is a bad plan that admits of no modification."

And I don't mean just slightly. Some things must undergo drastic alterations if we hope to stay on the cutting edge. Consider three of the more pronounced changes in our world.

Population. It was not until 1850 that the number of people on this globe reached one billion. By 1930 (a mere eighty years later) the number had doubled. Only thirty years later—1960—it had shot up to three billion. Demographers project that by the end of this century, seven billion bodies will be moving and eating and talking and struggling on this planet. Ours is a completely different world than it was 130 years ago. Profoundly different.

Speed. Until the early 1800s the fastest any human being could travel was about 20 miles per hour—on the back of a galloping horse. By 1880 the "streamline" passenger train whipped along at 100 miles per hour, an unheard of and fearsome velocity. Then on December 17, 1903, at Kitty Hawk, North Carolina, a strange machine became airborne for 59 seconds. Today, less than a hundred years later, the supersonic Concorde can cruise at well over 1000 miles per hour and manned space rockets jump the speed to 16,000 miles per hour.

Books. Relatively few works were published before the end of the 17th century—and then only a few hundred in the entire world. By the end of the 19th century, about 25,000 books per year were being released. Today? No less than 400,000 titles are produced annually around our globe. Those are not all the books available; those are just the new ones!

No need to keep stacking the facts in front of you. The point is obvious. And I haven't even mentioned the technological advancements in the last century, or the enormous changes made in military armament and defense, agricultural processes, housing, modes of transportation, medicine, music, architecture and engineering, luxury items and personal conveniences, computers, clothing, and cars.

Since God is eternally relevant, since none of this blows Him away (omniscience can't be mind-boggled!), He is still in touch, in control, and fully aware. Why He has caused or allowed this radical reshaping of human history, nobody can say for sure. But we can reasonably surmise that God is up to something.

Some would suddenly shout, "These are signs predicting Christ's soon return." Quite possibly. But what about until then? What is essential? We're back where we started, aren't we? Being adaptable, willing to shift and change.

With changes come new challenges, things our parents and grandparents never faced.

Take communication. The way it was done in the 1800s and early 1900s is "out of it" today. We must hammer out new and fresh styles on the anvil of each generation, always guarding against being dated and institutionalized. This calls for creativity, originality, and sensitivity.

More than anything else, I'm convinced, the thing that attracted people to Jesus was His fresh, authentic, original style in a world of tired phrases, rigid rules, and empty religion. Remember the report made to the Pharisees? "Nobody ever spoke like this man." He was in step with the times without ever stepping out of the Father's will.

A Finishing Touch: Though times may change, the Lord is constant.

A Daily Reading: Matthew 16

For years we Americans have been hung up on records and statistics—particularly in the world of sports. They have become the standards for greatness. For example, in track-and-field you have the 4-minute mile, the 30-foot long jump, the 60-foot triple jump, the 8-foot high jump, and the 20-foot pole vault.

Back when I was a kid growing up in Houston, I watched the papers to see if anybody was getting close to breaking those standards.

No way.

Oh, some guys tried hard . . . like Cornelius Warmerdam, a vaulter back in 1940 who cleared the 15-foot barrier, using a stiff bamboo pole. In fact, if memory serves me correctly, I think he vaulted that height many times before he retired. Fifteen feet! I remember thinking, "That's a story-an'-a-half vault. Any more, and a guy would break his leg when he fell into the sand pit."

Of course, you need to remember that was back when a high school basketball team was grateful to have a couple of players six feet tall. (Our center during my senior year at Milby High School in 1953 was 6' 5", the tallest kid on any team in the city, prompting one of the sportswriters to call him "a freak"). Nowadays, it's not uncommon for 6' 8" guys to start at guard. Makes me wonder how come the kids are all taller now. It's amazing.

But what's really amazing is that all those "unreachable" world records now seem reachable. Some, like breaking the 4-minute mile, are now so commonplace we hardly notice anymore. And Ukrainian-born Sergei Bubka beat all the competition at the 1983 World Championships with a 18' 3/4" pole vault when he was only nineteen. The next summer he set a new world record of 19' 2 1/4". After that he added one inch after another, until finally he broke the magic barrier by clearing 20' 1/4". And since then, he's cleared 20' 1" for another world record. Before long, that 20-foot standard will be as big a yawner as the 4-minute mile.

What I'm looking forward to is the day somebody can clear 1250 feet . . . something over one hundred stories. That's the vault I can't wait to witness. I mean, at the rate today's athletes are going, they'll probably clear that by the end of this decade, right?

"Wrong," you answer. "In fact, impossible." And you are absolutely correct. Warmerdam could vault 15' back in the 1940s. John Uelses cleared 16' in the early 1960s. And a man named John Penner broke the 17' barrier a year after Uelses' record-setting vault. But 1250 feet? The height of the Empire State Building? Get serious. It ain't gonna happen.

Which is exactly the point of a statement that appears in a letter written during the first century: "For all have sinned and fall short of the glory of God" (Rom. 3:23).

The spiritual standard God has set for all who wish to measure up is perfection, nothing less. To clear that level calls for a spotless record, a flawless past, impeccable morality, a complete absence of wrong. In plain and simple English, *no sin*.

Whoever qualifies, please step forward . . . line forms to the right. No one?

Well, okay, let's not limit it to folks living today. How about anyone from the ranks of human history? Check the encyclopedias. Search the pages of *Who's Who?* Examine the long lists of pioneers, entertainment stars, scientists, philosophers, military heroes, artists, musicians, political statesmen and women, and other remarkably gifted folks. Toss in a genius or two, a child prodigy, a brilliant composer. Still no one?

Well, don't stop. Pull up on your computer an exhaustive record of athletes, explorers, inventors, authors, business leaders, physicians, psychologists, financial wizards, presidents, educators, lawyers, and, for sure, religious leaders. Some are impressive, to be sure . . . wonderful examples of human greatness . . . but p-e-r-f-e-c-t? No one. A few could clear twenty feet, spiritually speaking, but none come close to the Empire State Building. Not even one. All "fall short" of the standard.

Oops, wait a second. My mistake. Seems like there was one unusual man who didn't "fall short." As I recall, He claimed to be God, then demonstrated it to perfection. He even promised to draw people to

247

himself, to forgive their sins, to give them a place in heaven if they would believe in Him.

But didn't He wind up just outside Jerusalem on a cross? Wasn't He crucified? He died, didn't He? Too bad. If He were really God, as He claimed, death would not have stopped Him, right? I mean, He would have come back more alive than ever. And when He did, He certainly wouldn't have had any trouble clearing the Empire State Building, would He? In fact, He would still be alive today, still drawing people to Himself, wouldn't He?

Do you wonder whatever happened to Him?

Have I got some good news for you!

A Finishing Touch: The best news is the good news of the Gospel.

A Daily Reading: John 3:11–17

Now if Christ is preached, that He has been raised from the dead, how do some among you say that there is no resurrection of the dead?

But if there is no resurrection of the dead, not even Christ has been raised; and if Christ has not been raised, then our preaching is vain, your faith also is vain.

Moreover we are even found to be false witnesses of God, because we witnessed against God that He raised Christ, whom He did not raise, if in fact the dead are not raised.

For if the dead are not raised, not even Christ has been raised; and if Christ has not been raised, your faith is worthless; you are still in your sins.

Then those also who have fallen asleep in Christ have perished.

If we have hoped in Christ in this life only, we are of all men most to be pitied.

But now Christ has been raised from the dead, the first fruits of those who are asleep. For since by a man came death, by a man also came the resurrection of the dead.

For as in Adam all die, so also in Christ all shall be made alive.

—1 Corinthians 15:12–22

Hallelujah!

Like sticks of dynamite taped together with a short fuse, our times are really threatening. Maybe volatile is a better description. Anger is ready to explode into physical violence at the slightest provocation. This entire globe seems brimming with hair-trigger hostility, ready to flare into full-scale disaster.

It's not just a vast global problem, however. It's personal. It's in your neighborhood. Your school. Where you work. Women don't jog after dark unless they carry a can of mace. Only fools leave their cars unlocked. Home security systems are no longer considered a luxury for the rich. Even teachers are not safe in the classroom. A recent educational journal, after telling about a high school teacher who was hit across the back of her head with a large piece of wood swung by a student filled with rage, offers eight suggestions for other teachers who will surely be victims of such trauma in the future.

But I must confess, the final straw of shock came when I read of the murder of John White in a quiet neighborhood in southwest Cleveland. The killer? A 19-year-old hired by White's two kids. That's right. His 17-year-old son and 14-year-old daughter paid $60 to have their own father killed. The daughter, by the way, waited in another room until the fatal shot was fired.

Then what? Well, the teenagers paid off the murderer, then hid the body in a back room of the house. After that they used their dad's credit cards to go on a 10-day spending spree. They spent some $2,000 on televisions, video games, bicycles, and other amusements and entertainment. While their father's body was decaying in the utility room, they were cooking meals in the kitchen a few feet away and enjoying themselves in the living room.

After being caught, they openly confessed the entire, bizarre event. When asked why, they answered: "He wouldn't let us do anything we wanted." The dad had angered the kids by trying to enforce

250

an evening curfew and by not allowing them to quit school or "smoke pot." So they had him killed.

Centuries ago, slumped over a piece of parchment under the flickering glow of candlelight in a stone dungeon, the apostle Paul wrote his last few sentences. Yet, today, they stab us awake with incredible relevance:

> But realize this, that in the last days difficult times will come. For men will be . . . arrogant, revilers, disobedient to parents, ungrateful, unholy . . . brutal, haters of good, treacherous, reckless . . . (2 Tim. 3:1–4).

The Greek term he chose for "difficult times" means, literally, "fierce, harsh, hard to deal with, savage." It is used only one other time in the New Testament, when it describes two demon-possessed men as "exceedingly violent" (Matt. 8:28).

An apt description of our times. Exceedingly violent. Operation powder keg. Ready to explode.

Yet there is a glimmer of hope amid this flood of violence. It is this: Christ's coming cannot be far away. These "last days" of pain—though they may seem to pass slowly—are daily reminders that our redemption draws near. And "we shall all be changed, in a moment, in the twinkling of an eye . . . " (1 Cor. 15:51–52).

Like, fast. Really fast. Faster than a short fuse on sticks of dynamite.

A Finishing Touch: When everything looks hopeless, we have the comfort of our eternal Hope.

A Daily Reading: 2 Timothy 3:1–5

Remember that time you got ticked off trying to find a verse in the Bible and couldn't? That was almost as bad as the day you decided to read a couple chapters and got hung up on *Nazarite* . . . or scratched your head over *cubit*.

And how about the morning you were leading the family devotions and your five-year-old darling asked, "What's an ephod?" or "Where's Philistia?" With a blank look you tilted your head and gazed at the wall like a calf staring at a new gate.

These are common yet frustrating stop signs . . . outlaws that rob insight. They are like hardened, glazed coverings that suddenly obscure our understanding of God's truth. The pick and shovel of good intentions simply will not cut through. Sharper tools than that are needed, believe me!

Admittedly, many believers shrug their shoulders and think, "Well, that's the preacher's job . . . I'm no theologian anyway," and back on the shelf goes the Bible.

Listen, you don't have to be a theological brain to dig into God's riches . . . but you do need some mining equipment.

These tools are basic to intelligent, meaningful Bible study. They will enable you to find most of the answers you need, and they are as easy to use as your TV guide. There are at least four you should have on hand.

A *Bible concordance*. This is indispensable. It contains an alphabetical index of all the terms found in the Bible, and it comes in handy when you want to put your finger on a particular verse but can only remember a few words in it. It's also invaluable if you want a complete list of all the verses using the same word. For example, if you'd like to study *manna* or *marriage* in Scripture, you'd start with your concordance. The same is true for any other topic . . . from *Aaron* to *Zuzim*!

The best concordances available are Robert Young's *Analytical Concordance to the Bible* and James Strong's *Exhaustive Concordance to the Bible*. I must also add W.E. Vine's *Expository Dictionary of New Testament*

Words for you who are serious students, wanting to learn the shades of meaning and theological implications of different New Testament terms.

A *Bible dictionary*. You cannot do without this tool either. It is more than a list of words and definitions, much more. It's like a one-volume encyclopedia, containing vital information on people, places, doctrines, customs, and cultural matters. It is rich in history and even archaeological information, much of it fascinating! All topics, of course, are arranged alphabetically and include concise summaries for those in a hurry.

I recommend either *Unger's Bible Dictionary* (well illustrated, relevant, carefully documented, scholarly but readable) or *The New Bible Dictionary* (less complete than Unger's but contains longer articles on technical subjects).

A *Bible atlas*. Don't think you can get by without this tool. But it won't be easy to make your selection. Nearly all major publishers have good works on the market. Their very abundance complicates your choice.

The most popular is *Baker's Bible Atlas*. Another reliable one is *Macmillan Bible Atlas*, containing over 250 different maps dealing with virtually every facet of Bible history. If you can't afford an atlas, at lease purchase a good set of biblical maps.

A *Bible commentary*. This is a single-volume book that offers comments and insights on every chapter in the Word of God. Hands down, my favorite is *The Wycliffe Bible Commentary* edited by Pfeiffer and Harrison. It is reliable and well arranged.

Don't delay now. Get those tools you need soon . . . and don't let them rust on you!

A Finishing Touch: It's amazing how a few of the right tools, when used correctly, can open God's treasures.

A Daily Reading: 2 Timothy 2:15

The definition reflects devastation. "Trauma: An injury (as a wound) to living tissue caused by an extrinsic agent . . . a disordered psychic or behavioral state resulting from mental or emotional stress or physical injury."

Like potatoes in a pressure cooker, we century-twenty creatures understand the meaning of stress. A week doesn't pass without a few skirmishes with those "extrinsic agents" that beat upon our fragile frames. They may be as mild as making lunches for our kids before 7:30 in the morning (mild?) or as severe as a collision with another car . . . or another person. Makes no difference. The result is "trauma." You know, the bottom-line reason Valium remains the top seller.

Our emotional wounds are often deep. They don't hemorrhage like the wounds of a stabbing victim, but they are just as real, just as painful . . . sometimes more.

When Dr. Thomas Holmes and his colleagues at the University of Washington carried on extensive research into the world of human stress, they concluded that an accumulation of two hundred or more "life change units" in any year may mean more disruption—more trauma—than an individual can stand. On their scale, death of a spouse equals one hundred units, divorce represents seventy-three units . . . and Christmas equals twelve units! That helps explain why "something snaps" inside certain people when the final straw falls on them. Our capacity for trauma has its limits.

The late Joe Bayly, insightful Christian writer and columnist, certainly understood that. He and his wife lost three of their children: one at eighteen days (after surgery); another at five years (leukemia); a third at eighteen years (sledding accident plus hemophilia). In my wildest imagination, I cannot fathom the depth of their loss. In the backwash of such deep trauma, Joe and his wife stood sometimes strong, sometimes weak, as they watched God place a period before the end of the sentence on three of their children's lives. And their anguish was not relieved when well-meaning people offered shallow, simple answers amidst their grief.

H. L. Mencken must have had such situations in mind when he wrote: "There's always an easy solution to every human problem—neat, plausible, and wrong."

Eyes that read these words might very well be near tears. You are trying to cope without hope. You are stretched dangerously close to the "200-unit" limit . . . and there's no relief on the horizon. You're bleeding and you've run out of bandages. You have moved from mild tension to advanced trauma.

Be careful! You are in the danger zone emotionally. You're a sitting duck, and the adversary is taking aim with both barrels loaded, hoping to open fire while you are vulnerable. Bam! "Run!" Boom! "Think suicide."

Listen carefully! Jesus Christ opens the gate, gently looks at you, and says: "Come to Me, all you who labor and are . . . over burdened, and I will cause you to rest—I will ease and relieve and refresh your souls" (Matt. 11:28 *Amplified*).

Nothing complicated. No big fanfare, no trip to Mecca, no hypnotic trance, no fee, no special password. Just *come*. Meaning? Unload. Unhook the pack and drop it in His lap . . . now. Does He know what trauma is all about? Remember, He's the One whose sweat became like drops of blood in the agony of Gethsemane. If anybody understands trauma, He does. Completely.

He's a Master at turning devastation into restoration. His provision is profound, attainable, and right.

A Finishing Touch: Allow Him to take your stress as you take His rest.

A Daily Reading: Matthew 11:27–30

During the reign of Oliver Cromwell, the British government began to run low on silver for coins. Lord Cromwell sent his men to the local cathedral to see if they could find any precious metal there. After investigating they reported: "The only silver we can find is in the statues of the saints standing in the corners."

To which the radical soldier and statesman of England replied: "Good! We'll melt down the saints and put them in circulation!"

Not bad theology for a proper, stuffed-shirt Lord Protector of the Isles, huh? That brief but direct order states the essence of the practical goal of authentic Christianity. Not rows of silver saints crammed into the corners of cathedrals, but melted saints circulating through the mainstream of humanity. Where life transpires in the raw. Without the aura of stained glass and the familiar comforts of padded pews and dimmed lights. Where bottom-line theology is top priority. You know the places:

On campuses where students carve through the varnish of shallow answers. In the shop where employees test the mettle of everyday Christianity. At home with a houseful of kids, where R&R means run and wrestle. In the concrete battlegrounds of sales competition, seasonal conventions, and sexual temptations, where hard-core assaults are made on internal character. On the hospital bed, where reality never takes a nap. In the office, where diligence and honesty are forever on the scaffold. On the team where patience and self-control are checked out.

It's easy to kid ourselves. So easy. The Christian must constantly guard against self-deception. We can begin to consider ourselves martyrs because we are in church twice on Sunday. Really sacrificing by investing a few hours on the "day of rest."

Listen, my friend, being among the saints is no sacrifice . . . it's a brief, choice privilege. The cost factor occurs on Monday and Tuesday and throughout the week. That's when we're "melted down and put in circulation." That's when they go for the jugular. And it is remarkable how that test discolors many a silver saint. "Sunday religion" may seem sufficient, but it isn't. And pity the person who counts on it to get him through.

It's the acid grind that takes its toll, isn't it? Maybe that explains why Jeremiah, that venerable prophet of God, touched a nerve when he probed: "If you get tired racing against men, how can you race against horses? If you can't even stand up in open country, how will you manage in the jungle by the Jordan?" (Jer. 12:5 *Good News Bible*).

Doing battle in the jungle calls for shock troops in super shape. Sunday-go-to-meetin' silver saints in shining armor are simply out of circulation if that's the limit to their faith. Racing and jungle fighting call for sweat, energy, keen strategy, determination, a good supply of ammunition, willingness to fight, and refusal to surrender. And that is why we must be melted! It's all part of being "in circulation."

Sure, you can opt for an easier path. You can keep your own record and come out smelling like a rose:

Dressed up and drove to church. Check

Walked three blocks in the heat. Check

Got a seat and sat quietly. Check

Sang each verse and smiled appropriately. Check

Gave money . . . listened to the sermon. Check

Closed my Bible, prayed, looked pious. Check

Shook hands, walked out. Check

Still a saint? Yep. A silver one, in fact. Icily regular, cool and casual, consistently present . . . and safely out of circulation . . . until the Lord calls for an investigation of the local cathedral.

A Finishing Touch: Those who successfully wage war with silent heroism under relentless secular pressure—ah, they are the saints who know what it means to be melted.

A Daily Reading: Jeremiah 12

Class Action is a class act. It's a film about two lawyers who go head-to-head, both in court and in life. They are father and daughter . . . on opposite sides of a complicated case charged with the full spectrum of emotions. The father is defending a man who lost both legs when his car exploded after it was hit by another vehicle. The daughter is representing the maker of the automobile, a huge corporation that intends to win, no matter what, since millions are at stake. The father's law firm is a small, unimpressive outfit comprised of a few hard-working folks while the daughter is one step below a partner in a large, slick, legal firm. Without revealing the outcome, let me just tell you that the story finally boils down to an issue of personal integrity, which introduces a dimension rarely found on the screen today.

It is the father-daughter interplay, however, that gives the story its definition. During her early teen years her father was often on the road, busily engaged in various cases and crusades. During that impressionable era of her life, he was not only unfaithful to her mother, he was virtually out of touch with the family. Though he loved them, he was morally weak and failed to demonstrate his affection. His wife chose to stay with him, not allowing his infidelity to destroy their home. But the daughter was not nearly so magnanimous, choosing instead to resent her father's lifestyle. In fact, her resentment festered into full-blown competition, both privately and professionally. Nothing would please her more than winning that class-action suit in the courtroom . . . a perfect place to unleash her rage, to humiliate her father and retaliate on behalf of her mother, whom she idolizes.

Her problem, plain and simple, is an unwillingness to forgive. Behind this brilliant woman's drive and accomplishments lie demons of bitterness. Unknown to the young woman, her soul awaits that moment when she can finally forgive her father . . . and be free.

Free to win or lose. Free to love and live. Free to grow and mature. Truly free. That's what forgiveness can do.

What is true in the make-believe world of film is all the more true in the real world of life. Jesus himself spoke of forgiveness on several occasions. Like the time Peter asked Him if forgiving someone "seven times" was sufficient. After all, that was over twice the going rate according to the Pharisees' teaching. To paraphrase Jesus' terse answer: "Would you believe seventy times seven?" In other words, an infinite number of times . . . no limit.

Jesus then went on to point out that without forgiveness there cannot be freedom, and He told them the story of a man who, after having been forgiven an enormous debt, refused to forgive someone who owed him a measly twenty bucks. The man who would not forgive was called back before the king, who "handed him over to the torturers" (Matt. 18:34). That word means "inquisitors," conveying the idea of personal torment . . . internal torture.

Jesus added: "'So shall My heavenly Father also do to you, if each of you does not forgive his brother from your heart'" (18:35).

You tell me. Does that sound like forgiveness is important?

My concern today is not some lawyer portrayed on film; it's any one of us who is being slowly eaten up by the acid of resentment because of someone who has done us wrong.

Am I suggesting the offender deserves to be forgiven? Not necessarily.

Am I implying that the wrong wasn't all that bad? In no way.

All I'm saying is that we need to forgive.

I cannot explain how it works or why it's so powerful. All I know is that the arduous journey to freedom invariably leads through the door named Forgiveness. Refuse to open that door and you remain locked in your own chamber of horrors.

Forgiving a wrongdoer goes against all the stuff your old nature wants to see happen. Everything within you screams, "Get back . . . get even . . . punish!" As logical as that seems, however, those are the very sounds of misery that fill the torture chamber of an unforgiving heart.

We are most like beasts when we kill. We are most like men when we judge. We are most like God when we forgive.

Why not reach out and unlock the door to freedom? Do it today.

The latch is on the inside. No one else can turn it for you.

Of all the actions you can carry out, that one is the ultimate class act.

A Finishing Touch: Freedom and forgiveness both begin with the same letter.

A Daily Reading: Matthew 18

Do you need to be set free?

Honestly now, is your next step the need to forgive?

Do it.

Don't let anything or anyone talk you out of it.

I know, I know. After all the misery you have had to endure, why should you have to be the one who humbles yourself and forgives?

Christ could have asked the same question at Golgotha. Perhaps He did at Gethsemane. But once He discerned the Father's determination, there was no looking back . . . no turning back.

Remember His cry from the cross? "Father, forgive them . . . " (Luke 23:34).

Look up "forgive" and "forgiveness" in your Bible concordance and read the Scriptures listed. One you will find there is:

> And be kind to one another, tender-hearted, forgiving each other, just as God in Christ also has forgiven you (Eph. 4:32).

A GIFT FOR DAD

In an age of equal rights and equal time, it seems only fair to give dads equal attention.

Sometimes seems the only time that happens is during the big commercial buildup for Father's Day, and then it's all buy, buy, buy! Every store window, newspaper, and magazine in America parades gift ideas before your eyes. Families wonder whether to wrap us in robes, fill us with food, surprise us with skis, tickle us with tools, or just cover us with kisses. If I know dads, most of 'em blush no matter what you do. They are so used to providing, receiving is a little weird. Occasionally, it is downright embarrassing! Most dads are quick to say to their families (with pardonable pride): "Look, just sit back and relax . . . and leave the striving to us!"

For the next several minutes, think about your father, okay? Meditate on what that one individual has contributed. Think about his influence over you, his investment in you, his insights to you. Study his face . . . the lines that are now indelibly etched in your mind. Listen again to the echo of his voice . . . those unique expressions that emerge through the miracle of memory. Feel his hand wrapped around yours . . . his strong, secure arm across your shoulders. Remember his grip that once communicated a balanced mixture of gentleness and determination . . . compassion and masculinity . . . not only his "I understand" but also his "Now, straighten up!" Remember his walk. Those sure steps. That inimitable stride. Arms swinging and back arched . . . head tilted just so.

Best of all, take time to recall his exemplary character. The word is _integrity_. Pause and remind yourself of just one or two choice moments in your past when he stood alone . . . when he stood by you . . . when he stood against insurmountable odds . . . when he provided that shelter in your time of storm. When he protected you from the bitter blast of life's harsh consequences. When he chose to say,

262

"Honey, I forgive you" instead of, "Why, you ought to be ashamed!" Wonderful memory!

In the wake of such a legacy which time can never erase, give God thanks. Thank the Giver of every good and perfect gift for the meaningful marks your dad has branded on the core of your character . . . the wholesome habits he has woven into the fabric of your flesh. While meandering through this forest of nostalgia, stop at the great oak named Proverbs and reflect upon the words the wise man carved into its bark long centuries ago:

"A righteous man walks in his integrity—

How blessed are his sons [and daughters] after him."

How very true! How blessed you are! Our Lord declares that you are the beneficiary in a perpetual, paternal policy. For the balance of your life, you receive the dividends from your father's wise and sacrificial investments in "integrity stock."

Dad is not perfect; he would be the first to admit it. Nor is he infallible, much to his own disappointment. Nor altogether fair . . . nor always right. But there's one thing he is—always—he is your dad . . . the only one you'll ever have. Take it from me, there's only one thing he needs on Father's Day. Plain and simple, he needs to hear you say, "Dad, I love you."

That's the best gift you can give. Nothing you can buy will bring him anywhere near the satisfaction that four-word gift will provide. "Dad, I love you."

A Finishing Touch: Look your dad in the eye or call him on the phone and give him the gift he needs more than anything. Give him your love.

A Daily Reading: Proverbs 13

I feel like starting with the words the nurse says as she approaches your bed with one hand behind her back: "This won't take long, but it may sting a little."

Don't tense up now. Just relax a few minutes and listen.

Are you aware of what waiters and waitresses say about the Christians they serve? Do you have any idea how much they dread waiting on our tables in restaurants after church on Sundays? Or any other day when we go in groups with big Bibles under our arms? We gobble up the chow, asking for this favor and that, seldom pausing long enough to smile or say, "Thank you." That's bad enough, but then we leave a tip that is more of an insult than a generous expression of gratitude.

Think I'm exaggerating? Ask around. Talk to almost any person who faces the Christians and the lions regularly. Ex-waiters and ex-waitresses are also good people to corner and question. They'll tell you straight.

Just last week one informed me that the place where he works has the toughest time getting a full crew to wait tables on Sunday. "We'd all rather work late Friday and Saturday nights week after week than work Sunday afternoons," he said.

When I asked, "Why?" he told me.

"Because Christians are usually loud, they often lack good table manners, and they are stingy with the tips."

Ouch! Like I said, it stings . . . but that is an exact quote. Now before you become defensive, give me one more minute.

The waiter who spoke to me is a Christian. He's on our side. And he's embarrassed. Says he has a tough time talking to the crew about Christ after the place closes at night. They give him this cynical "You gotta be kidding!" response that comes after six or eight of Christ's followers walk away, leaving a tract and a dollar bill. Or maybe just a tract. Sometimes, neither.

Am I saying it's universal . . . that every Christian is guilty? Certainly not. But I will hazard a guess that many are, based on what

I've heard from servers who have unloaded their opinions. We've earned a pretty tacky reputation, and it's high time we face the music.

If you're among the thoughtful, the gracious, the kind who leave a full fifteen percent or more, keep it up. Turn the page and chalk up one for courtesy and generosity. May your tribe increase.

But if you're the type who falls into the tightfisted and less than thoughtful category, how about thinking of your witness as something more than a Bible in your pocket and words out of your mouth. Sometimes it's what comes out of your pocket after something has gone into your mouth . . . and I'm not referring to a tract. Listen:

> It is possible to give away and become richer! It is also possible to hold on too tightly and lose everything. Yes, the liberal man shall be rich! By watering others, he waters himself (Prov. 11:24–25 TLB).

C'mon, Christian, loosen up . . . you can do it. If you can afford to eat out, you can also handle a healthy tip. Maybe all you needed was a shot in the arm.

A Finishing Touch: There's no doubt about. Actions often speak much louder than words. What are your actions saying?

A Daily Reading: Proverbs 22:9

Wisely labeled "the saving virtue," tact graces life like fragrance graces a rose. One whiff erases any memory of the thorns.

Tact is like that. It's remarkable how peaceful and pleasant it can make us. Its major goal is avoiding unnecessary offense, and that alone ought to make us crave it. Its basic function is a keen sense of what to say or do in order to maintain the truth and good relationships, and that alone ought to make us cultivate it. Tact is incessantly appropriate, invariably attractive, incurably appealing, but rare . . . oh, is it rare!

Remember the teacher who lacked tact? Learning was daily sacrificed on the altar of fear. Each morning you wondered if that was the day you'd be singled out and embarrassed by some public putdown. Remember the salesman who lacked tact? Once you found that out (and it usually takes about 60 seconds), you wanted only one thing—to get away! Remember the boss who lacked tact? You never knew if he ever understood you or considered you to be a valuable person. And who could forget that tactless physician? You weren't a human being, you were Case No. 36.

Ah, that's bad . . . but it isn't the worst. The classic example of tactless humanity, I'm ashamed to declare, is the abrasive Christian (so-called) who feels it his or her calling to fight for the truth with little or no regard for the other fella's feelings. Of course, this is supposedly done in the name of the Lord—"to do anything less would be compromise and counterfeit." This individual plows through the feelings of people like a John Deere tractor, leaving them buried in the dirt and, worst of all, deeply offended.

This person's favorite modus operandi is either to overlook or openly demean others, leaving a backwash of broken hearts and bitter souls. Unfortunately, some preachers are the greatest offenders. They seem to delight in developing a devastating pulpit that scourges rather than encourages, that blasts rather than builds. Their murder weapon is that blunt instrument called the tongue.

"The heart of the righteous ponders how to answer," writes

Solomon. "That which turns away wrath is a gentle answer," said he. "The wise person uses his tongue to make knowledge acceptable," he adds. "The tongue of the wise brings healing," and "A man has joy in an apt answer and how delightful is a timely word!"

Let's stop hurting and start healing. Let's be gentle and sensitive when we are touching the tender feelings of others. The fact is that love and acceptance of one another are nurtured in a context of tact.

No facts need be subtracted when tact is added, by the way. Years ago, I used to sell shoes. My seasoned employer, with a twinkle in his eye, instructed me never to say, "Lady, your foot is too big for this shoe!" I was taught to say, instead, "I'm sorry, but this shoe is just a little too small for your foot." Both statements expressed the facts, but one was insult while the other was tactful.

It didn't shrink her foot, but it did save her face . . . and that's what tact is all about.

A Finishing Touch: Let's get aboard the Lord's bus and enjoy each other, as we leave the striving to Him.

A Daily Reading: Proverbs 18:19, 21

Remember the words Marine private Gomer Pyle used to repeat in almost every episode of his television show? *"Surprise, surprise!"*

Surprises come in many forms and guises . . . some good, some borderline amazing, some awful, some tragic, some hilarious. But there's one thing we can usually say—surprises aren't boring.

Surprises are woven through the very fabric of all our lives . . . they await each one of us at unexpected and unpredictable junctures.

Some surprises *refresh* us. We're low. Under the pile. Then, out of the blue, we receive a letter of affirmation. Those lines, though few, lift our spirits. Maybe it's an unexpected phone call or a hug of reassurance that sends us soaring. On the day we need to hear or read those words, we are refreshed by surprise.

Some surprises *relieve* us. This certainly happened to my brother Orville and his family when they were caught in Hurricane Andrew near Miami. As the wind reached 160 miles an hour, he, his wife, and their loved ones took refuge in the master bedroom. They heard windows crash, doors blow off their hinges, and walls break apart. Roof tiles were torn off, and objects from miles away imbedded themselves in the wood like exploding shrapnel.

Only one room sustained no damage to walls, floor, or roof: *the master bedroom*, where Orville and his family had huddled and prayed for six terrifying hours! When angry Andrew moved on, they found themselves relieved by surprise. And, as Orville told our sister Luci, something good came out of the calamity. "When all the fences were blown down, we finally met all our neighbors." Surprise, surprise!

Some surprises *rebuke* us. Like the minister who received a simple pair of gloves for services rendered and felt disappointed—until he discovered a ten dollar bill stuffed into each finger and thumb. What a rebuke!

In a recent "Dear Abby" column I read a poignant story. A young man from a wealthy family was about to graduate from high school. It was a custom in their affluent community for parents to give their graduating children a new car, and the boy and his dad had spent weeks visiting one dealership after another. The week before graduation they found the perfect car. The boy was certain it would be in the driveway on graduation night.

On the eve of his graduation, however, his father handed him a small package wrapped in colorful paper. It was a Bible! The boy was so angry he threw the Bible down and stormed out of the house. He and his father never saw each other again.

Several years later the news of the father's death finally brought the son home again. Following the funeral, he sat alone one evening, going through his father's possessions that he was to inherit when he came across the Bible his dad had given him. Overwhelmed by grief, he brushed away the dust and cracked it open for the first time. When he did, a cashier's check dated the day of his high school graduation fell into his lap—in the exact amount of the car they had chosen together. Rebuked by surprise!

Life is short. God is sovereign. All plans are in His hands, not ours. When God repeats "Surprise, surprise!" through various episodes of our lives, let's not waste valuable time asking "Why *me*?" or "Why *now*?" or "Why *this*?" Just keep in mind, "He does all things well." Yes, *all things* . . . .

A Finishing Touch: Surprises are God's divine plan, designed to remind us that He is still in charge.

A Daily Reading: Exodus 6:1–8

You—or someone you know—may soon be graduating. The time has finally come for the ol' cap-and-gown routine and your last group gathering with your class. I extend my congratulations! Whether you set new academic records or not, you finished. You got it done. You saw it through. I commend you.

I'm sure that at times the course seemed lengthy, at times tedious, and occasionally dull . . . but you made it. And soon you will be so far removed from the disciplines of academia, it will all seem a blur.

Before that happens, however, before you rush off to summer jobs, beach parties, vacation with family, college preparation, or your first job, I want to pass along some thoughts that may help you "continue in the things you have learned" (2 Tim. 3:14).

Let me give you four simple commandments which apply to anyone who is graduating . . . whether you are earning your Ph.D. or getting your high school diploma. My thoughts grow out of the final four verses of 2 Timothy 3.

1. *Don't stop your learning.* Paul urges his friend Timothy to "continue in the things you have learned" (3:14). It is one thing to take a course, to complete one's work, to earn a diploma or a degree; it's another thing to become a student for the rest of your life . . . to remain hungry for knowledge, to stay curious, to read widely, to be adventurous, creative, on a never-ending pursuit of truth.

It is not difficult to spot people who are still learning. There is something exciting about being around them. They are resourceful, interesting, and broad-minded. Learners are continually challenged by life's mysteries, unwilling to stay glued to a television set or to be influenced by majority opinion. They love to think. They are fiercely independent. They read the inscriptions on monuments. They are fascinated by the small print, stimulated by out-of-the-way places. They even like studying maps! No source of information eludes them.

And so, graduate, may this truly be your commencement into a quest for knowledge that is never satisfied.

2. *Don't forget your leaders*. As Paul reminds his friend to continue in what he has learned, he adds, "knowing from whom you have learned them." Timothy needed to remember, to stay near, to thank the teachers who had impacted his life and contributed to his growth.

Graduate, never forget those who played a part in your years of formal learning. Take time, both now and later, to thank them. Take note of what they taught you, directly and indirectly, as instructors and as persons. There is something healthy about keeping in touch with your mentors, calling to mind the things they modeled, remembering the benefits of having been the recipient of their wisdom, their reproofs, their guidance. The inspiration of a great teacher will go with you forever.

3. *Don't discount your legacy*. Timothy didn't just coincidentally pop into Paul's presence. And his heart didn't just happen to be open and sensitive to spiritual things. He was the product of a legacy, a spiritual continuum. His mentor Paul acknowledges it as he reminds Timothy, " . . . from childhood you have known the sacred writings which are able to give you the wisdom that leads to salvation through faith which is in Christ Jesus" (3:15). And earlier in the same letter, Paul affirms, "For I am mindful of the sincere faith within you, which first dwelt in your grandmother Lois, and your mother Eunice . . . " (1:5).

Timothy's "sincere faith" had been cultivated by a mother and a grandmother who taught him "the sacred writings." A love for God and His Word and a strong faith in Christ and His life are like priceless batons passed from parent to child in the legacy relay. Paul's implied admonition was that Timothy never lose sight of the legacy he'd received . . . and must pass on.

And so, graduate, do not discount the legacy of your own life. You are the product of your past, just as Timothy was. Though imperfect, your parents (perhaps grandparents as well) have marked you, shaped you, and provided roots for you that have helped you become the person you are. Do not fail to do the same for your children.

4. *Don't ignore your Lord*. As Paul closes these very personal lines

to his younger friend, he returns to "the sacred writings" and assures Timothy that "All Scripture is inspired by God and profitable . . . that the man [and woman] of God may be adequate, equipped for every good work" (3:16–17). In effect he was saying that God's Word would remain a reliable, profitable source of nutritious food throughout his life and was exhorting him to stay close to the Lord, regardless . . . whether his path would be marked by prosperity or poverty, fame or obscurity, a long fruitful ministry or painful days that abruptly ended in martyrdom.

And so, graduate, keep your inner fireplace warm for God. Watch those future decisions that come with strings attached. Steer clear of the age-old thorns that still choke the Word and make it unfruitful. Remember them? They haven't changed for centuries: "the worries of the world, and the deceitfulness of riches, and the desires for other things" (Mark 4:19).

Stay near the flame of His Spirit—so close you can feel the warmth of His presence.

A Finishing Touch: For those of you for whom graduation is a dim memory, the admonition remains the same: Don't stop your learning. Don't forget your leaders. Don't discount your legacy. Don't ignore your Lord.

A Daily Reading: 2 Timothy 3

This weekend I would challenge you to read through the entire book of 2 Timothy. Then, try to make a list of all Paul's admonitions to his young friend. What examples does Paul give from his own life?

_____

_____

_____

_____

How are you living in the light of these?

_____

_____

_____

_____

Pull a sheet of scratch paper out of your memory bank and see how well you do with the following questions:

Who taught Martin Luther his theology and inspired his translation of the New Testament?

Who visited with Dwight L. Moody at a shoe store and spoke to him about Christ?

Who worked alongside and encouraged Harry Ironside as his associate pastor?

Who was the wife of Charles Haddon Spurgeon?

Who was the elderly woman who prayed faithfully for Billy Graham for over twenty years?

Who financed William Carey's ministry in India?

Who helped Charles Wesley get underway as a composer of hymns?

Who found the Dead Sea Scrolls?

Who taught G. Campbell Morgan, the "peerless expositor," his techniques in the pulpit?

Who followed Hudson Taylor and gave the China Inland Mission its remarkable vision and direction?

Who discipled George Muller and snatched him from a sinful lifestyle?

Who were the parents of the godly and gifted prophet Daniel?

Okay, how'd you do? Before you excuse your inability to answer these questions by calling the quiz "trivia," better stop and think. Had it not been for such unknown persons—such "nobodies"—a huge chunk of church history would be missing. And a lot of lives would have been untouched.

Nobodies. What a necessary band of men and women . . . servants of the King . . . yet nameless in the kingdom! Men and women who, with silent heroism and faithful diligence, relinquish the limelight and live in the shade of public figures.

As Jim Elliot, martyred messenger of the Gospel to the Aucas once remarked: "Missionaries are a bunch of nobodies trying to exalt Somebody."

But don't mistake anonymity for *unnecessary*. Otherwise, the whole Body gets crippled . . . even paralyzed . . . or, at best, terribly dizzy as the majority of the members within the Body become diseased with self-pity.

Face it, friend, the Head of the Body calls the shots. It is His prerogative to publicize some and hide others. If it's His desire to use you as a Melanchthon rather than a Luther . . . or a Kimball rather than a Moody . . . or a Hoste rather than a Taylor, relax!

Better than that, praise God! You're among that elite group mentioned in 1 Corinthians 12: ". . . some of the parts that seem weakest and least important are really the most necessary . . . . So God has put the body together in such a way that extra honor and care are given to those parts that might otherwise seem less important" (vv. 22, 24 TLB).

If it weren't for the heroic "nobodies," we wouldn't have any sound or lights or heat or air-conditioning in our churches next Sunday. We wouldn't have cassette-tape ministries or Bible studies. We wouldn't have homes in which high schoolers can meet on Sunday nights to sing and share. We wouldn't have church staff and officers and teachers working together behind the scenes.

Nobodies . . . exalting Somebody.

A Finishing Touch: Are you playing a behind-the-scenes roles? Thank God for giving you that opportunity.
A Daily Reading: 1 Corinthians 12:19–25

When I was deep in the redwoods some time ago, I laid back and looked up. I mean *really* up. It was one of those clear summer nights when you could see forever. So starry it was scary. The vastness of the heavens eloquently told the glory of God. The expanse silently declared the work of His hands. No words could adequately frame the awesomeness of that moment. One of my mentors used to say, "Wonder is involuntary praise." That night, it happened to me.

What boggled my mind as I curled up in my sleeping bag that night was this: *Everything I have seen belongs to this one galaxy. Perhaps there are a hundred more beyond our own. Maybe a thousand. Or a hundred thousand . . . each one much larger than ours. Who knows?*

But let's limit our thinking just to this one solar system . . . a tiny fraction of the universe above us. Because it is impossible to grasp the astounding distance about us, we need analogies—simple comparisons to assist us. Hold on as we take a quick trip to the regions beyond.

If it were possible to travel the speed of light, you could arrive at the moon in 1 1/3 seconds. But continuing at that same speed, do you know how long it would take you to reach the closest star? Four years. Incredible thought!

New York City's Hayden Planetarium has a miniature replica of our solar system showing the speeds and sizes of our planets. What is interesting is that the three outer planets are not even included. There wasn't room for Uranus, Neptune, and Pluto. Uranus would be in the planetarium's outer corridor, Neptune would be around Eighth Avenue. And Pluto? Another three long avenues away at Fifth Avenue. By the way, no stars are included, for obvious reasons. Can you imagine (on the same scale) where the nearest start would be located? Cleveland, Ohio. Vast! An, remember, that's just our own local galaxy.

A scientist once suggested another interesting analogy. To grasp the scene, imagine a perfectly smooth glass pavement on which the finest speck can be seen. Then shrink our sun from 865,000 miles in diameter to only two feet . . . and place the ball on the pavement to represent the sun.

Step off 82 paces (about two feet per pace), and to represent proportionately the first planet, Mercury, put down a tiny mustard seed. Take 60 steps more and for Venus put down an ordinary BB. Mark 78 more steps . . . put down a green pea representing earth. Step off 108 paces from there, and for Mars, put down a pinhead. Sprinkle around some fine dust for the asteroids, then take 788 steps more and place an orange on the glass for Jupiter. After 934 more steps, put down a golf ball for Saturn.

Now it gets really involved. Mark 2,086 steps more, and for Uranus . . . a marble. Another 2,322 steps from there you arrive at Neptune. Let a cherry represent Neptune. This will take 2 1/2 miles, and we haven't even discussed Pluto!

We have a smooth glass surface 5 miles in diameter, yet just a tiny fraction of the heavens, excluding Pluto. Now, guess how far we'd have to go on the same scale before we could put down another two-foot ball to represent the nearest star. We'd have to go 6,720 miles before we could arrive at that star. Miles, not feet! And that's just the first star among millions. In one galaxy among hundreds, maybe thousands. And all of it in perpetual motion . . . perfectly synchronized . . . the most accurate timepiece known to man. Phenomenal isn't the word for it.

No God? All by chance? Are you kidding? Listen carefully:

"Since the creation of the world God's invisible qualities—His eternal power and divine nature—have been clearly seen, being understood from what has been made, so that men are without excuse" (Rom. 1:20 NIV).

A Finishing Touch: The boggled mind leads to a bended knee.
A Daily Reading: Romans 1:18–20

"Physician. One upon whom we set our hopes when ill and our dogs when well," defines A. Bierce in *The Devil's Dictionary*.

Of all the professions, that of the physician has to be the most paradoxical. Brilliant and quick-thinking . . . yet unable to write so that anybody (except a pharmacist) can decipher the words. It's easier to translate a line of Egyptian hieroglyphics than to make out a simple prescription for Darvon. Decisive and disciplined . . . yet more preoccupied than an overworked inventor on the edge of a discovery. He's the only guy I know who can have both hands in your mouth while asking you three questions back to back as he stares up your nose and has his mind on his golf game. Honest and principled . . . yet lies through his teeth every time he says, "This won't hurt a bit . . . you'll hardly feel it."

Mysterious people of air-tight privacy . . . yet each one knowing the most intimate secrets of a thousand lives. Memory of an elephant when it comes to weight gain and X-rays and surgical techniques . . . yet when it comes to names and anniversaries and where they parked their car—no way! Firm, stable, and fearless . . . yet abruptly shaken at the thought of a courtroom scene or the little old lady who threatens to sue. And why not? The cry "malpractice" can be heard in every locale.

The physician lives with two unique pressures—day and night.

The pressure of life and death. A wrong decision, an unexpected change in a person's body, a drastic reaction to medication, a risk that backfires, a misdiagnosis, a hurried oversight, and a dozen other technical or ethical errors can result in death. Irreversible, irrevocable, irretrievable. What a heavy weight to hang on the thin wire of fallible humanity!

The pressure of success and failure. In a moment of time, years of schooling and decades of a respected practice can crumble and fall. Or, because of "the breaks," the doctor can find himself on the lofty pinnacle of power, prestige, and wealth, dangerously close to the point of idolatry. Two opposite problems to anticipate: tumbling all the way down or soaring high above the clouds. Or, as Sonny Jurgenson once described the life of the professional football quarterback. "He's either in the penthouse or the outhouse every day of his career."

Both pressures are accompanied by the five most destructive companions on earth: pride, humanism, loneliness, greed, and discontentment. Is it any wonder that suicide runs so high among physicians? If any profession on earth calls for a living, vital, incessant relationship with the eternal God, this one does. And yet therein lies the greatest paradox. Most of those dealing with life-and-death issues are themselves neither prepared to live nor ready to die.

In light of all this, it is interesting to ponder how much we owe to one medical doctor of the first century. His name was Dr. Luke, the beloved personal physician of Paul the great apostle.

Through Luke's counsel and treatment, Paul was able to live on, fight hard, finish his course, and reach the Roman Empire with the message of hope. Like all great physicians, Luke realized all he could do was diagnose properly, treat the illness correctly . . . and then wait. Only God can heal.

And so, we thank our Lord for every Dr. Luke today living in the demanding arena of relentless pressures, thankless people, exacting decisions, and growing criticism. Not miracle workers, but mere humans desperately in need of the Divine.

A Finishing Touch: Our Great Physician understands the unique pressures each one of us faces, day and night. Ask for His counsel and diagnosis.

A Daily Reading: Matthew 9:10–12

Snap a telescopic lens on your perspective for the next few minutes. Pull yourself up close . . . close enough to see the real you. Pore over your own pores. Study what you see. Like a physician giving you a physical. Like an artist painting your portrait. Like a biographer writing your story.

From the reflection in your mental mirror, pay close attention to your life. Try your best to examine the inner "you" on the basis of time. Time, that elusive, slippery phantom, that haunting melody. Get a good look at yourself with your arm around time.

The only way we can do this, of course, is to look in two directions . . . backward and forward. In many ways what we see in our past and visualize in our future determines how we view ourselves today . . . in that third dimension we call "the present."

As *we look back*, one overriding thought eclipses all others. It's not new nor very profound, but it's the truth: LIFE IS SHORT. That's not only a valid observation from experience . . . it's biblical.

Psalm 90 is loaded with reminders of the brevity of life. Listen to some of the analogies used by the composer: *Life is short . . . like yesterday when it passes by . . . as a watch in the night . . . like grass, it sprouts and withers . . . like a sigh, soon it is gone.* Standing arm-in-arm with time brings a subtle, perhaps painful, reminder that we aren't getting any younger. Life is indeed short.

As *we look ahead*, we again see one major message. And it's neither new nor profound, but it sure is true: LIFE IS UNCERTAIN. A single adjective could precede most every event in our future: *unexpected*. Unexpected surgery, transfer, change, accomplishment, loss, benefit, sickness, promotion, demotion, gift, death. Life is indeed uncertain.

James 4 verifies both these thoughts. He says that our lives are merely vapors that appear then vanish (life is short), and that we do not know what our lives will be like tomorrow (life is uncertain). Dr. Time teaches us both lessons well.

Well then, since life is so brief and uncertain, how should we view our present? Most philosophers offer advice that is dangerously near despair—or, at best, discontentment. Philosophy will clip even an angel's wings.

I suggest there are three words that adequately and accurately describe the present. They do not contradict either lesson we have learned from time, nor do they require rose-colored glasses. Neither do they agree with philosophy's futile meanderings. For as we look at the present, we discover: LIFE IS CHALLENGING.

Because it is short, life is packed with challenging possibilities. Because it is uncertain, it's filled with challenging adjustments. I'm convinced that's much of what Jesus meant when He promised us an abundant life. Abundant with challenges, running over with possibilities, filled with opportunities to adapt, shift, alter, and change. Come to think of it, that's the secret of staying young. It is also the path that leads to optimism and motivation.

With each new dawn, life delivers a package to your front door, rings your doorbell, and runs. Each package is cleverly wrapped in paper with big print. One package reads: "Watch out. Better worry about this!" Another: "Danger. This will bring fear!" And another: "Impossible. You'll never handle this one!"

When you hear that ring tomorrow morning, try something new. Have Jesus Christ answer the door for you.

A Finishing Touch: Life's most challenging opportunities are often brilliantly disguised as unsolvable problems.

A Daily Reading: James 4:13–15

I don't often recommend a volume without reservation, but I think every man should read *Temptations Men Face* by Tom Eisenman. I'm not saying I agree with everything in it, or that you will, but it's one of those works that deserves being read . . . especially by men. I appreciate Tom's candor and practicality. He pulls no punches; neither does he wrench your gut with guilt. His observations, insights, and suggestions are both penetrating and provocative. In fact, with Father's Day coming up, that book got me thinking about the top temptations fathers face.

First, the temptation to give things instead of giving ourselves— our presence, our personal involvement.

Don't misunderstand. Providing for one's family is biblical. First Timothy 5:8 calls the man who fails to provide for his family's needs "worse than an unbeliever." But the temptation I'm referring to goes far beyond the basic level of need. It's the toys vs. time battle: a dad's desire to make up for his long hours and absence by unloading material stuff on his family rather than being there when he is needed. Like in the bleachers during ball games or in the audience during a band concert, like by your child's side when the homework calls for a father's encouragement or driving the boat when your child is learning to water ski. Nothing takes the place of a father who gets involved. N-O-T-H-I-N-G!

Second, the temptation to save our best for the workplace.

Nobody has an endless supply of emotional energy, creativity, enthusiasm, ideas, humor, leadership drive, and a zest for life. How easy it is for dads to use up all those things at work, leaving virtually nothing for the end of the day. As a result, the wife and kids get only the leftovers. Fathers, our families deserve better! By failing to pace ourselves, by not deliberately saving some of our creative energy for home, we tend to be listless, negative, boring, and predictable around the house. How rare are those unselfish men who think ahead, maintain right priorities, and keep their families surprised by joy.

Third, the temptation to deliver lectures rather than earning respect by listening and learning.

James 1:19 is worth a look, here: "My dear brothers, take note of this: Everyone should be quick to listen, slow to speak and slow to become angry" (NIV). When things get out of hand at home, it's our normal tendency to reverse the order James suggests. First, we get mad. Then, we shout (lecture No. 38 . . . or it is No. 39?). Last, we listen. When that happens, we get tuned out (I've learned that the hard way). Our family members may stop. They may look. But they aren't listening. They go through a slow burn. It's a sobering realization, dads, but our home is not an extension of the office . . . and our wife and children are not employees. Maybe we get respect automatically where we work; but at home we must earn it the old-fashioned way. We must work for it.

Fourth, the temptation to demand perfection from those under our roof.

We fathers can be extremely unrealistic, can't we? It does me good to remember that a .350 batting average is considered tops in the big leagues. That means the professional ball player swings and misses well over half the times he's at the plate. Yet .350 means that he's still considered the batting champ. In fact, if he keeps that up long enough, he's Hall of Fame bound. Sure is easy to set our expectations for the wife and kids out of reach, expecting them to bat a thousand. Fathers are commanded not to exasperate their children (Eph. 6:4), which suggests being an annoyance, an irritation, one who causes grief. An exasperated kid is one who can't jump quite high enough, thanks to a demanding father who mistakenly thinks good coaching means always raising the bar.

Fifth, the temptation to find intimate fulfillment outside the bonds of monogamy.

Thanks to our ability to rationalize, we men can talk ourselves into the most ridiculous predicaments imaginable. I've heard most of them. I've also listened to the children of adulterers after the fact, who never understand, who hurt beyond description, who carry scars indefinitely. The charm of seductive passion is incredibly strong, able to blind even the godly. The enticement can be powerful enough to make a man momentarily forget his family as well as ignore the crippling consequences of his sin. That's why I suggest that dads carry a picture of their brood and look at it often. It's impossible to fantasize sensual lust while looking at the smiling, trusting faces of your family.

Sixth, the temptation to underestimate the importance of your cultivating your family's spiritual appetite.

Yes, *you* cultivate it. Fathers, listen up: Your wife and kids long for you to be their spiritual pacesetter. Children love knowing that their dad loves God, walks with God, and talks about God. Never underestimate your role as the spiritual head. If your wife is running circles around you in this area, that tells me a lot more about you than about her. And don't think the kids don't notice, and wonder.

Ready for a challenge? Begin to spend time with God, become a man of prayer, help your family know how deeply you love Christ and desire to honor Him.

Why not start today? C'mon, men . . . it's one of the greatest gifts any father can give a family.

A Finishing Touch: How about facing the music and then changing the tune? Say a firm "NO" to any of these subtle, sneaky, slippery temptations that have slipped into your life.

A Daily Reading: Ephesians 6:4–8

How have *you* responded to these temptations in your own life?

_____

Do you give things instead of giving yourself, your presence, your personal involvement?

_____

Do you save your best for the workplace?

_____

Do you deliver lectures rather than earning respect by listening and learning?

_____

Do you demand perfection from those under your roof?

_____

Do you try to find intimate fulfillment outside the bonds of monogamy?

_____

Do you cultivate your family's spiritual appetite?

_____

A New Week
of
Finishing Touches

24

MONDAY

A birth is always exciting. Yes, *always*. Whether it is your baby or someone else's, those first cries never fail to make our hearts flutter.

"It's a boy!" will bring smiles to every face. "It's a girl!" will melt even the coldest soul in the place.

Take away new births and tiny-baby smells and soft, warm cuddles and first staggering steps . . . and you've removed from life one of its most priceless treasures. Family ties are strengthened as new life extends the roots. Everybody moves in closer and smiles approvingly . . . even aunts and uncles, nephews and nieces.

What power little babies possess!

What frequently happens in a home occurs all too rarely in a church. Somehow the natural and beautiful drive to reproduce gets lost in the youthful busyness of church life. And if she's not careful, the church begins to grow old, brittle, and inbred, losing interest in giving birth.

The result is tragic: a selfish shell of activity where the *talk* of new life replaces the actual joy of birth. It's a disease, sort of a Laodicean lukewarmness, that causes the once-vibrant, attractive church to turn inward, to become a religious relic, an overweight body lacking vision, passion, and mission. And the terminal verdict (which nobody wants to admit) is ultimately whispered in the hallways of history: *sterility*.

Thankfully, some churches stand in contrast to such a scene, giving birth to new bodies.

Under the watchful eye of a mature church, a young body springs to life. For months the older body gives the baby great prenatal care, resisting the temptation to hurry the birth. They nurture each family member and keep the communication lines open. A teachable spirit coupled with a desire to cultivate its own identity and distinct style of ministry eventually enables the healthy new body to live and breathe on its own.

Then, finally, it's time to cut the cord and detach the new body from the "mother." Smiles brighten faces as the labor is ended . . . and as God witnesses the moment of delight and announces from heaven, "It's a church!"

Being a part of such new life, beginning life anew away from the security and the stability of the parent church, is courageous and, in some ways, sacrificial. But it is right. It is biblical. It is also exciting, as all births are.

When I think of all this, I always think of the journeys of the apostle Paul and the delight he took in the various churches he saw come to life and maturity.

If you have not already witnessed such an event in your own church life, I hope you will have the opportunity sometime in the future. When the time is right, you will know it. 'Cause you know how births are. You just can't delay them, even if you try.

A Finishing Touch: Wouldn't you like to contribute to an event that is a part of Christ's own prediction, "I will build my church"?

A Daily Reading: Acts 20:25–38

"My treat!"

Nice words to hear, huh? They have flowed into my ears from any number of places.

At Thirty-one Flavors on a smoggy, stifling, sweltering August afternoon after I've ordered a double decker "pralines 'n' cream, dark cone" with a buddy. He digs deeper, faster. I start lickin', smilin'. Full of gratitude, I leave wondering why I ordered two scoops. We laugh. I say thanks.

In line for Angel game tickets with another couple, Cynthia and I are looking forward to nine innings of relaxation, when our friends surprise us. "But we said Dutch." "Yeah, well, not this time." Great game. Friendship deepens. Everybody wins (even the Angels!).

After a delightful threesome lunch, as I reach for the check, the man across the table practically rips my hand off as he puts a stop to any idea I may have had. Brief argument. I lose. Three guys walk out arm in arm. Closer.

Treats are neat. Spontaneous. Unexpected. Pleasant moments that communicate: "You are special . . . loved, appreciated, affirmed, deserving," and a half dozen other warm fuzzies we need to hear but seldom hand out.

Treats don't normally come on holidays, birthdays, or anniversaries. Instead, they arrive during the ordinary, run-of-the-mill, no-big-deal times in our lives. Like the old "Candid Camera" line, they arrive "When you least expect it . . . ."

That's one kind of treat—when somebody else picks up the tab. In that case, treat is a verb: "an act of generosity as an expression of regard or friendship."

But treat can also be a noun: "an unexpected source of joy, delight, or amusement." Rather than an *act*, this represents a *fact*. A happy happening.

I'm thinking of something that never fails to enhance, to encourage, to refresh, to renew. Not every so often, but every single time. The kind of treat where you pick up the tab but the expense is virtually forgotten, thanks to the meaningfulness of the event and the memory that will never be erased. Like time spent on a vacation or at a retreat or at a conference center. A full week or two away from the daily grind. Out where birds still sing and squirrels still run free and nights are still cool and skies are still clear. That's the *where*.

But the essential question is *why*? Because you need a place to relax and get your emotional battery recharged. You need a time to rediscover some of the sparkling gems tucked away in God's Book that have gathered dust, thanks to our fast-paced schedule. You need an opportunity to sing your heart out, to relax.

Now that's what I'd call a "source of joy, delight, or amusement."

So, take time out of your too-busy schedule to walk, to play, to nap, to get reacquainted with your loved ones, family, or friends.

Take time to meet with God . . . alone. This is one treat you can't deny yourself.

Tell yourself "my treat," and it will be everybody's treat.

A Finishing Touch: Treat yourself to refreshment for your spirit as well as your body.

A Daily Reading: Philemon

Call me sentimental, but some tunes really send me reeling. "Old Blue Eyes" can usually do it with his ballads. So can Neil Diamond and Kenny Rogers. Roger Williams playing "Autumn Leaves" on the keyboard is another one, and so is John Denver's "Sunshine on My Shoulders." Yep, even the themes from "Gone with the Wind" and "Dr. Zhivago" never fail to push my nostalgia button.

At those times I get real quiet. Sometimes, a little misty.

But nobody—I mean nobody—does it any better than Barbra Streisand. Her rendition of "The Way We Were" is pretty close to the ultimate in my book. Remember the words? "Memories . . . light the corners of my mind . . . ." Take your time . . . .

I don't know what Streisand thinks of when she sings those words, but I know what Swindoll thinks of when he hears them. I think of the lovely teenaged girl I married in '55. I think of the paths we've walked together, the smiles and laughter we've shared, the pain we've endured, the decisions we've made, the places we've lived, the four children we've reared . . . yes, especially them. How brightly they light the corners of my mind!

Memories . . .

Those misty, water-color memories take me back to birthday parties, afternoon picnics, vacation trips, school projects, ball games, graduation excitement, quiet talks, and long walks in the woods. Those scattered pictures are full of smiles we left behind—smiles we gave to one another at places like the trails at Mount Hermon and the lake at Forest Home. Yeah, those are the memories time can never erase.

Sometimes it seems that things were so much simpler then. Yes, in many ways I think they were. Just pack the kids in the ol' station wagon, lock up the house, and head for family camp. We did that year after year after year.

Memories . . .

There are times this bride of mine and I glance back over our shoulders and ask each other some pretty gutsy questions. Like, "If we had the chance to do it all again, would we?" *You bet.* "Could we?" *No doubt.* Fact is, we still do. We're still building . . .

Memories . . .

And we've noticed that our married kids are starting to do the same thing. And why not? Summer isn't summer for a Swindoll unless it includes a week (or more) of time away from the hassle and the heat, investing ourselves in the lives of a few folks who love the same things . . . who realize if you don't take the time, you won't have the stuff which makes life bearable, like—

Memories . . .

Want to have something meaningful to look back on for the rest of your life? Want a scrapbook of scattered pictures filled with smiling faces? Do yourself and your family a favor. Paint some watercolor memories together this summer . . . or fall . . . or winter . . . or spring.

People who do that are not just sentimental . . . they're smart.

A Finishing Touch: Tomorrow's memories come from today's decisions.

A Daily Reading: Malachi 3:16–18

It was Ernest Hemingway who once said, "Time is the least thing we have of." And he was right.

How quickly time passes—and how often we lament this. If only we could tack an extra twenty-five or thirty years on to the usual span. There is so much more we want to see, to celebrate, to do. So many places to go, so much to enjoy, to feel, to read, to talk about, to participate in, to encounter. Yet, for each of us, this thing called time is in such short supply.

Wouldn't it be great to bring back Joshua? The first thing I would do is ask him to put the brakes on the sun . . . or the earth . . . or whatever it was he did back then to make time stand still.

Our frustration is only compounded by the numerous unimportant, dumb things that steal our minutes and siphon the significance out of our hours. You know what I mean. Stuff like getting gas or a haircut, standing in the eternal line at the DMV, doing the laundry, washing all the dishes after every meal, mowing the lawn, and a dozen other time-consuming things that have to be done but keep you from doing the things that make life so invigorating and fulfilling.

We have this wonderful gift of sixteen or eighteen waking hours every day. Yet when all is said and done and some guy finally closes the lid on our coffin, the average American, in a lifetime, will have spent six months waiting at stoplights, eight months opening junk mail (and that's going higher every year), a year and a half looking for lost stuff, and five years standing in lines of various types.

I *knew it*! I was sure that an unbelievable number of hours were going down the drain. And if we tossed in the time we spend gathering dust in doctors' waiting rooms, plus trying to get on the freeway during rush hour, plus enduring all those mindless TV commercials, plus figuring out the IRS tax hieroglyphics year after year after year, we hardly have enough time left in life to get our ducks in a row.

Since "time is the least thing we have of" and since there is no way we're going to escape all the stupid time-traps that accompany our earthly existence, seems to me that we're left with two choices: either we can fuss and whine about six months of stop lights and eighteen months trying to find our keys, or we can take the time we've got left and spend it wisely. I mean *really* wisely, with our priorities in the right order.

Speaking of that, what are you doing with the rest of your life? I'm talking about cultivating relationships, building memories that will help lift the load of future trials, and the deliberate pursuit of activities that will yield eternal dividends.

Do you have a family? Rather than leaving them the leftovers and crumbs and giving your job your best hours and your most creative ideas, how about rethinking the value of strengthening those ties? And while we're at it, let's not leave out necessary time for quietness, for personal reflection and refreshment.

You say you don't have time to add another week to your squirrel-cage lifestyle. Don't kid yourself. You keep blowin' and goin' like you've been doing most of your adult life, and you'll wind up mumbling to yourself in the twilight years, wondering how you could have stayed so busy yet accomplished so little.

Hey, maybe Hemingway wasn't right after all. You and I have more time than we realize . . . once we get our priority ducks in a row.

A Finishing Touch: Have you ever wondered how you can stay so busy yet accomplish so little? Think seriously about how you can reorder those priorities.

A Daily Reading: Revelation 1:1–3; 3:11–12

While traveling across northern California several years ago, I tuned in on a radio talk show where the host had just completed conducting a poll of his listeners regarding job satisfaction. Some sort of questionnaire had been mailed to folks within a broad radius of several cities along the San Francisco peninsula and East Bay region. The show's host had gathered and compiled the answers and was, that day, announcing the results. The project had taken over a month to complete.

To his surprise (and mine) he discovered that well over 80 percent who responded were dissatisfied with their occupations, and when he tabulated the results by cities, some were as high as 84 percent. And the unhappiness he discovered in the workplace was not passive, meek, and mild. Some even responded with intense words like "despise . . . resent . . . dread."

When I later turned the dial to some easy-listening music, I began to imagine the scene. It made me more than a little depressed to think of over 80 percent of all those people in that heavily populated area dragging themselves out of bed every morning, dreading not only the drive but the eight to ten hours of work in front of them. I thought about their nervous systems on the ragged edge, the interpersonal conflicts that would certainly occur, the low level of productivity, the inevitable family fallout, the pressure of feeling trapped, forced to stay (because of the economics or the benefits or the location or the skill level or any number of other reasons) yet craving to escape. Frustration mixed with mediocrity, abounding Monday through Friday!

Work in America isn't what it used to be. Without getting into a lot of heavy historical stuff, let me address today's scene as I analyze it. It is my personal opinion that today's employee expects work to be fulfilling—even "fun." Thirty or forty years ago that whole idea would have been considered foolish, maybe even outrageous. If I had welcomed my dad home from work with the question, "Did you feel fulfilled and have fun today?" he would have stared at me and asked, "What kind of a question is that?" Not because he was a Scrooge—he wasn't—but because work back then had little to do with being fulfilled and enjoying oneself.

Today's work force is a different breed of cat. I found my secret theory verified in a book by John Naisbitt entitled *Re-inventing the Corporation*. While addressing the employee's need to feel fulfilled on the job, he writes:

> The economic demands of the information society together with the new values of the baby boom generation are fostering the "work should be fun" idea . . . . Who put this strange notion into their heads?
>
> Oddly enough, it was probably their own parents, who grew up in the Depression and toiled in the factories of industrial America. For the parents of the baby boom, work was quite possibly not fun. Determined that their children would have more education and more of everything, parents sacrificed for their children's sake. And succeeded in giving them what they lacked.
>
> But the education and affluence changed people's expectations. Result: The "work should be fun" ethic has begun to displace the puritan ethic, which holds that work is honorable and valuable in and of itself, that work must have some drudgery attached.

The average worker in the 1940s and 1950s was a male breadwinner with a wife and a houseful of kids to support. He worked full time and long hours either in an office or a factory—mainly a factory since America was still an industrial society. He was a member of a union, motivated by job security, steady pay, and he looked forward to retirement at age sixty-five. His work was his world.

How things have changed!

Among other changes, today's "average worker" does not belong to a union and would not consider joining one, plans to work past retirement age (many work well into their seventies), and is willing to accept a certain amount of risk of security in exchange for the possibility of being rewarded for superior performance. Maybe that explains why one-third of Americans switch jobs each year

What's true for the "average worker" in the workplace may also be true for the "average worshiper" in the churchplace, where things are also surprisingly different than in the 1940s and 1950s. Perhaps that need to change was one of the things Jesus had in mind when He mentioned the impossibility of "putting new wine into old wineskins" (Matt. 9:17).

I wonder how many churchgoers, if polled, would be honest enough to admit that frustration mixed with mediocrity also abounds on Sunday. If they had a chance to say so, I wonder if some would respond with intense words like "despise . . . resent . . . dread." And if they did, I wonder if many in the church would care enough to listen or to change.

Be honest, now . . . would you?

A Finishing Touch: Not all change is good, but not to change can be bad.

A Daily Reading: Mark 2

A Public Agenda Foundation study, coauthored by Daniel Yankelovich, came up with these top ten qualities that today's workers want in a job:

1. Work with people who treat me with respect
2. Interesting work
3. Recognition for good work
4. Chance to develop skills
5. Work for people who listen if you have ideas about how to do things better
6. A chance to think for myself
7. Seeing the end results of my work
8. Working for efficient managers
9. A job that is not too easy
10. Feeling well-informed about what is going on

Ponder that list. Notice what isn't included in the top ten: job security, benefits, vacation time, and high salary. Yet most companies still operate as though they are the big three—the only ways to motivate and keep their employees.

Ours is a new world. We cannot exist as though it isn't changing.

Now, think about your church. Do you think any of the above might apply? Do any of them apply to you? How is your church meeting the changes and challenges of today?

The old prophet Habakkuk wrote relevant words of truth when he put this down in the first chapter of his prophecy:

Yes, destruction and violence are before me;
Strife exists and contention arises.
Therefore, the law is ignored
And justice is never upheld.
For the wicked surround the righteous;
Therefore, justice comes out perverted (Hab. 1:3-4).

The writer of those words died centuries ago, but oh, how his words live on! If you are even *slightly* aware of everything happening in the world around us, you know how up-to-date his words really are.

Have you ever been amazed at the way laws can be twisted and altered? Have you ever seen such a perversion of justice as in the last decade?

The criminal is now the hero, sadly misunderstood and mistreated. The victim is the selfish sadist who decides to press charges because he is bigoted, rash, or confused. The cold, hard facts are softened and slanted by the semantic footwork of slick political pawns. The courtroom now resembles a stage peopled by actors vying for starring roles, rather than a dignified chamber of law and order. Judges and juries can be bought, bribed, swayed or wooed, given sufficient time in the legal pressure cooker. Jury members, who used to be anonymous and sequestered in the name of fairness and objectivity, now appear on talk shows.

James Russell Lowell was right, way back in 1844, when he described our dilemma so well in his work *The Present Crisis*: "Truth forever on the scaffold, wrong forever on the throne."

And remember that beloved childhood tale of Little Red Riding

298

Hood? Well, if that scenario took place today, here's what would probably happen.

After the heroic woodcutter rescued Little Red Riding Hood by killing the wolf, who had already eaten her grandmother and then tried to kill Little Red, there would be an inquest. At this time, certain "facts" would emerge. First of all, the wolf, prior to his execution, had not been advised of his rights. Then, the ACLU would enter the picture, maintaining that "although the act of killing and eating the old woman may have been in bad taste," actually the hungry and needy wolf was merely "doing his thing" and thus did not deserve death.

On this basis the judge would decide that there was no valid legal basis for charges against the wolf and, therefore, *the woodcutter was guilty* of unaggravated assault with a deadly weapon. He would then be arrested, tried, convicted, and sentenced to 99 years.

A year from the date of the incident at grandmother's, her cottage would be dedicated as a shrine for the wolf who had bled and died there. Wreaths would be placed there in memory of the brave, martyred wolf—even by Little Red Riding Hood, who would explain that while she was grateful for the woodcutter's intervention, in retrospect she realized that he had overreacted. There would not be a dry eye in the whole forest.

If this were not so tragic and true a picture, it would be amusing. But frankly, I'm not laughing. Injustice isn't at all funny.

A Finishing Touch: Sometimes justice truly *is* blind. Shouldn't we be helping to remove the blindfolds.

A Daily Reading: Amos 5:14–15, 24

> You do not have to sit outside in the dark. If, however, you want
> to look at the stars, you will find that darkness is required. The
> stars neither require it nor demand it (Annie Dillard).

A lot of things in life are like that, aren't they? We have to pay a price if we hope to enjoy the benefits, the beauty, the splendor. But the source is there, silently awaiting our discovery. Without shouting at us or shaming us, it patiently waits.

A piano sits in a room, gathering dust. It is full of the music of the masters, but in order for such strains to flow from it, fingers must strike the keys . . . trained fingers, representing endless hours of disciplined dedication. You do not have to practice. The piano neither requires it nor demands it. If, however, you want to draw beautiful music from the piano, that discipline is required.

A child plays at your feet, growing and learning. That little one has incredible potential, a hidden reservoir of capability and creativity, but in order for those possibilities to be developed, parents must take time . . . listen, train, encourage, reprove, challenge, support, and model. Moms and dads do not have to do any of that. The child neither requires nor demands that we do so. If, however, we hope to raise secure and healthy offspring, those things are required.

Time spreads itself before us, directionless and vacant. That time can be filled with meaningful activities and personal accomplishments, but in order for that to occur, you must think through a plan and carry it out. You do not have to plan or follow through. Time neither requires it nor demands it. If, however, you hope to look back over those days, weeks, months, and years and smile at what was achieved, planning is required.

What is true of the stars, a piano, a child, and the days ahead is especially true of your mind. It awaits absorption. It will soak up whatever you feed it: imaginary worries, fears, filthy and seductive thoughts, hours of television, and selfish greed . . . *or* good books, stimulating discussions, exciting risks of faith, the memorization of Scripture, and learning a few new skills. You can even take a course of two that will stretch your mental muscles.

You do not have to pay the price to grow and expand intellectually. The mind neither requires it nor demands it. If, however, you want to experience the joy of discovery and the pleasure of plowing new and fertile soil, effort is required.

Light won't automatically shine upon you nor will truth silently seep into your head by means of rocking-chair osmosis.

It's up to you. It's your move.

A Finishing Touch: If the splendor of the stars is worth sitting outside in the dark, believe me, the joy of fresh discovery is worth sitting inside in the light.

A Daily Reading: 1 John 5–7

What those little Visine drops do for our eyes, *relief* does for our sighs . . . "it gets the red out."

Few feelings bring a greater sense of satisfaction than relief, which Webster defines as "the removal or lightening of something oppressive, painful, or distressing."

When we are relieved of physical pain, we breathe easier. Hope returns as pain departs.

When guilt assaults us, eating like an invisible cancer within, relief brings back a calmness of spirit.

When a relationship is strained and we finally work things out, that sense of relief is better than anything money can buy.

When we finally crawl out from under the load of a heavy financial debt, nothing can compare to that sweet relief.

God calls this divine gift of relief *mercy*. That's right, *mercy*. It's a twin alongside *grace*.

Grace and mercy are usually seen together, but for some strange reason, mercy seems to live in grace's shadow, eclipsed by her popularity and prestige.

Check it for yourself. When the two are named together, grace always comes first. I find the result of that a little unfortunate, because most folks emphasize grace so much that mercy is seldom highlighted.

So, it's time to give mercy her due!

According to Ephesians 2:4, God is "rich in mercy." His is loaded with it! And aren't we glad?

If He were not rich in mercy, we might feel secure in God's love and we might be encouraged by His grace, but our lack of relief would hinder the presence of peace.

The essential link between God's grace and our peace is His mercy . . . that is, God's infinite compassion actively demonstrated toward the miserable. Not just pity. Not simply sorrow or an understanding of our plight, but divine relief that results in peace deep within.

302

Paul, after admitting that he was "formerly a blasphemer and a persecutor and a violent aggressor," was allowed to become not only a follower of the Way, but a participant in the service of the King.

How?

Read 1 Timothy 1:12–13 for yourself:

> I thank Christ Jesus our Lord, who has strengthened me, because He considered me faithful, putting me into service; even though I was formerly a blasphemer and a persecutor and a violent aggressor. And yet I was shown mercy . . . ."

In the simplest of terms, revolutionary changes occur in our lives because we were " shown mercy."

What a relief!

A Finishing Touch: The essential link between God's grace and our peace is His mercy.

A Daily Reading: Ephesians 2:1–9

The words of Psalm 23 are very familiar to all of us. This psalm is, in fact, one of the most well-known and beloved of all passages of Scripture. Yet, unless we read that psalm through the eyes of a sheep, we will miss its magnificent message. Remember how it concludes?

> Surely goodness and mercy shall follow me all the days of my life: and I will dwell in the house of the Lord for ever (KJV).

Think of goodness and mercy as God's sheepdogs. They stay with us, close by our side, "all the days of our lives." And what helpful companions they are!

The ancient Hebrews had one word they used most often for mercy, *chesed*, pronounced "kesed." It is frequently translated kindness and lovingkindness. While grazing through the Old Testament this past week, I was interested to find no less than five different "miseries" to which mercy brings needed relief.

When we're suffering the pain of unfair and unjust consequences. Genesis 39:21-23 informs us that Joseph, when dumped into a dungeon because of a false accusation, was given *chesed*—divine relief. It relieved him of the *misery of bitterness*, the companion of unfair treatment.

When we're enduring the grief of a death. Ruth 1:8-9 records the words of Naomi to her grieving daughters-in-law shortly after the premature deaths of their husbands, in which she asks the Lord to grant them *chesed*. God not only gives "dying grace," He also provides "grieving mercy," which relieves us of the *misery of anger* in the backwash of our accepting the loss of a loved one.

When we're struggling with the limitations of a handicap. Second Samuel 9 is the account of how David extended *chesed* to Mephibosheth, the crippled son of Jonathan, and provided him a place at the king's table for the rest of his days. Mercy relieves the *misery of self-pity* that often accompanies a handicap.

When we are hurting physically. Job 10:12 speaks of the Lord's giving *chesed* to Job, which strengthened him to go on during his days of intense pain. Divine relief removes the *misery of hopelessness* that would otherwise overwhelm us in times of great affliction.

When we are under a cloud of guilt after we have committed a transgression. Psalms 32:10 and 51 both speak of David's gratitude for *chesed* after the Bathsheba affair. His sin was not only forgiven, his guilt was taken away. In His mercy and lovingkindness, God relieves the *misery of guilt* . . . the lingering sting of wrongdoing.

No unfair consequence is too extreme for mercy. No grief too deep. No handicap too debilitating. No pain too excruciating. No sin too shameful.

Sheep are often in need, so mercy, our faithful companion, stays near.

A Finishing Touch: "There's a wideness in God's mercy, like the wideness of the sea" (Frederick W. Faber).

A Daily Reading: Psalm 32

I was raised to believe in the importance of a "quiet time." To the surprise of some, that concept did not originate with the late Dawson Trotman, the founder of The Navigators, but with the Lord Himself.

The Scriptures are replete with references to the value of waiting for the Lord and spending time with Him. When we do, the debris we have gathered during the hurried, busy hours of our day gets filtered out, not unlike the silt that settles where a river widens. With the debris out of the way, we are able to see things more clearly and feel God's nudgings more sensitively.

David frequently underscored the benefits of solitude. I am certain he first became acquainted with this discipline as he kept his father's sheep. Later, during those tumultuous years when King Saul was borderline insane and pursuing him out of jealousy, David found his time with God not only a needed refuge but his means of survival.

When he wrote, "Wait for the Lord; be strong, and let your heart take courage; yes, wait for the Lord" (Ps. 27:14), he was intimately acquainted with what that meant. When he admitted, "I waited patiently for the Lord; and He inclined to me, and heard my cry" (40:1), it was not out of a context of unrealistic theory. The man was hurting, in great pain. And when he wrote: "Vindicate me, O Lord, for I have walked in my integrity; and I have trusted in the Lord without wavering. Examine me, O Lord, and try me; test my mind and my heart" (26:1–2), he wasn't whipping up a few emotional thoughts to wow the reader. Those words splashed from the depths of his troubled soul, like the salty spray that explodes when wave crashes against rock.

Time with God? Who experienced its value more than Job after losing it all? In worship he wrote: "Naked I came from my mother's womb, and naked I shall return there. The Lord gave and the Lord has taken away. Blessed be the name of the Lord" (1:21). And his quiet trust didn't wear thin; the man continued to commune with his God. Remember his confession? What makes it even more remarkable is that he stated it while surrounded by those who accused him:

> But He knows the way I take; when He has tried me, I shall come forth as gold. My foot has held fast to His path; I have kept His way and not turned aside. I have not departed from the command of His lips; I have treasured the words of His mouth more than my necessary food (23:10–12).

That's it! That is exactly what occurs when we remove ourselves from the fast track and keep our appointment with Him who made us. His words take on greater meaning than a good meal. What great thoughts He has for us, what insights, what comfort, what reassurance!

And the best part of all is that such divine breakthroughs come so unexpectedly. Though you and I may have met in solitude with God morning after morning, suddenly there comes that one day, like none other, when He reveals His plan . . . and we're blown away.

It happened to Moses. Alone with Jethro's flock of woollies on the backside of the desert, perhaps after the howling night winds of the wilderness had settled and the searing rays of Sinai's sun began to peek over the awesome slopes of Horeb, God spoke from the midst of a bush that remained strangely ablaze.

And what was it God said? What was it that eighty-year-old, over-the-hill shepherd heard? "Lead the exodus!"

Who would've ever guessed that an otherwise ordinary dawn would find the old man reeling in disbelief? Least of all, Moses, as F. B. Meyer writes with eloquence in *Moses: The Servant of God*:

> There are days in all lives which come unannounced, unheralded; no angel faces look out of heaven; no angel voices put us on our guard: but as we look back on them in after years, we realize that they were the turning points of existence. Perhaps we look longingly back on the uneventful routine of the life that lies beyond them; but the angel, with drawn sword, forbids our return, and compels us forward. It was so with Moses.

Understand, those phenomenal moments are the exception, not the rule. If God spoke to us like that on an everyday basis, burning bushes would be as commonplace as traffic lights and ringing phones. Fact is, never again in all of time has the voice of God been heard from a bush that refused to be consumed with flames. You see, God is into original works, not duplicated recordings.

But never doubt it: He still longs to speak to waiting hearts . . . hearts that are quiet before Him.

A Finishing Touch: Keep your daily appointment with God. It's the one meeting you can't afford to miss. Don't be late!

A Daily Reading: Exodus 3

If you aren't already doing so, I would strongly urge you to begin keeping a personal journal and write in it daily. This will not only help you focus your thoughts during and after your quiet time with God, but will enable you to look back on His footprints in your life.

Make sure this journal includes your prayer diary. Spend time in prayer every day—every single day.

As David, who knew what it meant to be alone with God, wrote:

> Therefore, let everyone who is godly pray to Thee in a time when Thou mayest be found; Surely in a flood of great waters they shall not reach him. Thou art my hiding place; Thou dost preserve me from trouble; Thou dost surround me with songs of deliverance. I will instruct you and teach you in the way which you should go; I will counsel you with My eye upon you (Ps. 32:6–8).

A New Week
of
Finishing Touches

26

MONDAY

It was dear old Vance Havner, that venerable, leathery prophet of God, who once declared: "If you don't come apart . . . you *will* come apart."

Wise counsel based on Mark 1:35, where we read of Jesus:

And in the early morning, while it was still dark, He arose and went out and departed to a lonely place, and was praying there.

Some time later, after His disciples had been slugging it out in the trenches, preaching, counseling, ministering to the needs of others, and skipping meals, our Savior observed their drooping shoulders and said:

"Come away by yourselves to a lonely place and rest a while." (For there were many people coming and going, and they did not even have time to eat.) And they went away in the boat to a lonely place by themselves (Mark 6:31–32).

It wasn't planned. Nor was it requested or expected by the men. It was, however, absolutely essential. So the Master interrupted their activities with a brief parenthesis of time. To come apart. So they wouldn't come apart.

There are times when God has to force us to hear His words . . . when He can no longer allow us to ignore His words . . . for our own good.

I can vividly recall a time when this happened to me. A friend who also happened to be a doctor invited me to lunch. During out time together, he warned me about my stress load. That same week a preacher friend called and asked me directly, "Chuck, are you tired . . . really exhausted?" About the same time, my wife and kids were reminding me of some of the very truths I have proclaimed above—and had often proclaimed to others. And, most important of all, the Lord God tapped me on my inner man's shoulder and told me, "Come apart."

So for the next several days, I did just that. I ignored the phone calls, postponed my correspondence, disregarded previous plans, and stepped aside for several days.

And you know what? The world didn't come to an end.

And you know what else? When I returned from that "quiet place," my perspective was fresher and my mind was clearer.

Feel someone tapping on your shoulder?

A Finishing Touch: The shortest distance between two points is not always a straight line.

A Daily Reading: Mark 1

Many great men and women down through the ages have offered counsel on how to keep our tongues checked and caged. Like Will Noris, the American journalist who specialized in rhymes that packed a wallop. He once wrote:

> If your lips would keep from slips
> Five things observe with care:
> To whom you speak, of whom you speak,
> And how . . . and when . . . and where.

Publius, the Greek sage, put his finger on another technique we tend to forget when he admitted:

> I have often regretted my speech, never my silence.

King David put it even more bluntly in Psalm 39:1:

> I said, "I will guard my ways,
> That I may not sin with my tongue;
> I will guard my mouth as with a muzzle . . . ."

That's what it takes, friends and neighbors. A conscious, tight muzzle on the muscle in your mouth. With emphasis on *conscious*.

To accomplish that disciplined objective, I offer these three suggestions:

Think first. Before your lips start moving, pause ten seconds and mentally preview your words. Are they accurate or exaggerated? Kind or cutting? Necessary or needless? Wholesome or vile? Grateful or complaining?

Talk less. You increase your chances of blowing it if you talk too much. Furthermore, compulsive talkers find it difficult to keep friends. Conserve your verbal energy! Make your words like good shampoo: concentrated and rich.

Start today. You've read enough already on these two pages to help you bring your tongue into submission. Fit that muzzle on your mouth *now*. It's a project you've put off long enough.

Johann Wolfgang von Goethe, the brilliant German poet and playwright, stated a practical guideline worth remembering:

> One ought, every day at least to hear a little song, read a good poem, see a fine picture, and, if it were possible, to speak a few reasonable words.

A Finishing Touch: Think first. Talk less. Start today.
A Daily Reading: Psalm 39

Ever made a mental list of things that irritate you? Here are a few I've got on mine:

- ✔ Traffic jams
- ✔ Long lines
- ✔ Misplaced keys
- ✔ Untrained pets
- ✔ Stuck zippers
- ✔ Cold food
- ✔ Interruptions
- ✔ Late planes
- ✔ Tight clothes
- ✔ Squeaking doors
- ✔ Incompetence
- ✔ Flat tires

Makes me think of a saying I saw one time on a small wooden plaque: "I am planning to have a nervous breakdown. I have earned it . . . I deserve it . . . I have worked hard for it . . . and nobody's going to keep me from having it!"

If it weren't for irritations, we'd be very patient, wouldn't we? But like taxes, they are ever with us. They comprise the major occupational hazard of being a member of the human race.

One of these days it should dawn on us that we'll never be completely free of irritations as long as we are on this planet. Never. Upon coming to this profound conclusion, we would then be wise to consider an alternative to losing our cool. The secret is adjusting.

Sounds simple . . . but it isn't. Several things tend to keep us on the edge of irritability. For one thing, we are creatures of habit. We develop habit reactions, wrong though they may be. Also, we're usually in a hurry—impatient. Add to that the fact that our daily expectations are unrealistic; there's no way we can possibly get it all done anyway. All this increases the level of pressure within us. And when you increase the heat by a fiery irritation or two (or three) to our highly pressurized system . . . BOOM! Off goes the lid and out comes the steam.

When it comes to irritations, I've found that it helps if I remember that I am not in charge of my day . . . God is. And while I'm sure He wants me to use my time wisely, He is more concerned with the development of my character and the cultivation of the qualities that make me Christlike within. One of His preferred methods of training is through adjustments to irritations.

A perfect illustration? The oyster and its pearl.

Pearls are the products of irritation. This irritation occurs when the shell of the oyster is invaded by an alien substance—like a grain of sand. When that happens, all the resources within the tiny, sensitive oyster rush to the irritated spot and begin to release healing fluids that otherwise would have remained dormant. By and by the irritant is covered—by a pearl. Had there been no irritating interruption, there could have been no pearl.

No wonder our heavenly home has pearly gates to welcome the wounded and bruised who have responded correctly to the sting of irritations.

J. B. Philips must have realized this as he paraphrased James 1:2–4: "When all kinds of trials crowd into your lives, my brothers, don't resent them as intruders but welcome them as friends! Realize that they come to test your faith and to produce in you the quality of endurance . . . let the process go on until that endurance is fully developed, and you will find you have become men (and women) of mature character ."

A Finishing Touch: How many pearls have you made this week?
A Daily Reading: James 1

I'll forgive . . . but I'll *never* forget. We say and hear that so much that it's easy to shrug it off as "only natural." That's the problem! It is the most natural response we can expect. Not *supernatural*. It also can result in tragic consequences.

In his book *Great Church Fights*, Leslie B. Flynn tells of two unmarried sisters who lived together, but because of an unresolved disagreement over an insignificant issue, they stopped speaking to each other (one of the inescapable results of refusing to forget). Since they were either unable or unwilling to move out of their small house, they continued to use the same rooms, eat at the same table, use the same appliances, and sleep in the same room . . . all separately . . . without one word. A chalk line divided the sleeping area into two halves, separating doorways as well as the fireplace. Each would come and go, cook and eat, sew and read without ever stepping over into her sister's territory. Through the black of the night, each could hear the deep breathing of the other, but because both were unwilling to take the first step toward forgiving and forgetting the silly offense, they coexisted for years in grinding silence.

Refusing to forgive *and forget* leads to other tragedies, like monuments of spite. How many churches split (often over nitpicking issues), then spin off into another direction, fractured, splintered, and blindly opinionated?

After I spoke at a summer Bible conference meeting one evening, a woman told me she and her family had been camping across America. In their travels they drove through a town and passed a church with a name she said she would never forget—THE ORIGINAL CHURCH OF GOD, NUMBER TWO.

Whether it is a personal or a public matter, we quickly reveal whether we possess a servant's heart in how we respond to those who have offended us.

And it isn't enough simply to say, "Well, okay—you're forgiven, but don't expect me to forget it!" That means we have erected a monument of spite in our mind, and that isn't really forgiveness at all.

Servants must be big people. Big enough to go on, remembering the right and forgetting the wrong

Perhaps Amy Carmichael put it best when she wrote in her book *If*:

> If I say, "Yes, I forgive, but I cannot forget," as though the God, who twice a day washes all the sands on all the shores of all the world, could not wash such memories from my mind, then I know nothing of Calvary love.

A Finishing Touch: Forgetting an offense means being, in the true and noble sense of the term, self-forgetful.

A Daily Reading: Matthew 18:21–35

Maybe I'm weird, but there are times the Bible makes me laugh. I mean really laugh. The older I get and the more comfortable I feel in the Book, the more often it happens. I'd like to think it's because a more relaxed mind-set gives me the freedom to see what I once missed. But, in all honesty, I'm finding more and more times when a smiling response is not only appropriate, it's expected.

Perhaps you find yourself doing the same. It's not that we are getting soft on inerrancy; it's just that some scenes, stories, actions, and reactions strike us funny. Actually, they're supposed to!

Because the Bible is good literature (along with being God-breathed truth), we find in it all the makings of such: color, intrigue, mystery, romance, surprise, subtlety, tragedy, poetry, art, and a dozen other ingredients that make it interesting. So why should anyone be shocked to think that some of the stuff is funny?

There is humor in both Testaments, but the Old Testament seems to have an abundance. Like that time when the main event at Mount Carmel brought out 450 idolatrous prophets on one side and Elijah, all alone, on the other.

You remember the story (1 Kings 18). Baal vs. Jehovah. Big altar, prayer for fire, the classic wait 'n' see plot. The One who "answers by fire" . . . that's the One to follow.

From morning 'til noon those prophets of Baal called on their deity: "O Baal, answer us . . . O Baal, answer us . . . O Baal, answer us . . . O Baal, answer us . . . " with the nauseating monotony of that droning airport voice, "The white zone is for loading and unloading only, no parking!" And just as effective. Those guys got so anxious that they "leaped about the altar which they had made."

If that doesn't bring a smile, the next statement should. Elijah became amused at their antics and started mocking them:

"Call out with a loud voice, for he is a god; either he is occupied or gone aside, or is on a journey, or perhaps he is asleep and needs to be awakened" (18:27).

Jab, jab, twist, twist. And to amplify the humor, some scholars believe that the Hebrew idiom rendered "gone aside" suggests that Baal may have "gone to the bathroom." Come on, smile; it's okay. Frankly, I wouldn't put that past that leathery old prophet.

There are many more incidents that add a touch of humor to God's truth. The way Jehu drove his chariot like a hot rod is enough to make anybody chuckle. And who can restrain a smile when they discover the way King Saul dumped off his losing daughter onto young David? (Well, I doubt that David laughed at that one.) And can't you imagine the early-morning scene when that hungry worm made its way to Jonah's gourd house? I often picture in my mind that pouting prophet trying like mad to stomp the worm.

Years ago, when my preaching was limited to the King James text, I would stumble across archaic words and phrases that inevitably struck me (and others) funny. An unforgettable one emerges from Genesis 26, when Isaac and Rebekah moved down to Gerar. Afraid of being killed because his wife was so beautiful, Isaac lied to King Abimelech, telling the monarch she was his sister. For the longest time the king believed Isaac, until one day he "looked out at a window, and saw, and, behold, Isaac was sporting with Rebekah his wife" (26:8). I guarantee you, they weren't playing Ping-Pong. There are others, but I'd better stop there!

Well, maybe one more. Just the other day while I was digging through the dark days in David's life, I came upon another choice piece of humor. David was beside himself. Saul's jealousy had grown into murderous rage, which forced David to run for his life. Pressure led to paranoia. Suddenly, surrounded by a bunch of strangers from Gath, he didn't know what else to do but fake insanity.

"So he disguised his sanity before them, and acted insanely in their hands, and scribbled on the doors of the gate, and let his saliva run down into his beard" (1 Sam. 21:13).

Now, that was anything but funny. But when you read the next couple of verses, you can't help laughing. Upon witnessing this strange phenomenon, the people of Gath didn't know what to do. So they hauled the stranger up to their king's front door. And it's his response that's so funny:

"'Behold, you see the man behaving as a madman. Why do you

bring him to me? Do I lack madmen, that you have brought this one to act the madman in my presence? Shall this one come into my house?'"

In other words, King Achish was up to his ears with more than enough nuts in his kingdom! All he needed was another madman who scribbled on doors and foamed at the mouth . . . and he's not about to have this one moving in to live with him!

Truth is not only stranger than fiction, it's often funnier. When it is, we don't insult God by laughing; we honor Him. It's our way of expressing appreciation for His desire to touch us where we live and to keep His truth interesting, appealing, and, yes, real . . . for so much of life *is* funny. *Really* funny.

A Finishing Touch: God sets His truth in picture frames of life.
A Daily Reading: 1 Kings 18

Do you teach the Bible? If so, that's great. No other calling is more needed or carries with it greater responsibility.

My advice?

Study hard.

Pray for insight.

Be accurate with facts.

Be clear in your delivery.

Take your time. Relive and imagine those scenes.

Try not to blot out the color.

Guard against running a marathon with only seriousness setting your pace.

When you happen upon those scenes where the lighter side appears, slow down and call attention to it.

Those you teach will not only appreciate it, they will also learn that among all His glorious attributes, God has a marvelous sense of humor. And they'll be much more interested in the other things He says that aren't at all funny.

I've noticed that those who are free enough to laugh when something is funny are better equipped not to laugh when nothing is funny.

The Touch of Love

All who now live in simple faith were once rescued from sinking sand. The touch of God's love can reach us anywhere.

The past couple of weeks have been some of the toughest of my life. My emotions have spanned the spectrum: shock, sorrow, horror, intense anger, betrayal, disillusionment, disappointment, and utter bewilderment. I have prayed—without much benefit. I have read the Scriptures from the Psalms and Proverbs to the words of Jesus and various sections of the letters from Paul, Peter, James—without much peace.

When something terrible happens that you can't understand, grief wraps its tentacles around you, squeezing and sucking every little bit of energy and joy you may have been holding in reserve. In the most unexpected moments, tears well up within me. Can't seem to shake it—this deep grief.

I feel like the ancient prophet Habakkuk who, while in the pit, cried out, "How long, O Lord?" and "Why? Why are You silent when the wicked swallow up those more righteous than they?" (Hab. 1:2–3, 13).

Or Job, who admitted, "If I speak, my pain is not lessened and if I hold back, what has left me? . . . He has exhausted me. . . . My spirit is broken . . ." (Job 16:6–7, 17:1).

It occurred to me around 4:20 this morning that perhaps the late, great Spurgeon might have understood my grief better than any other when he wrote over a century ago in his *Lectures to My Students*, in a chapter entitled "The Minister's Fainting Fits":

> Who can bear the weight of souls without sometimes sinking to the dust? . . . To see the hopeful turn aside, the godly grow cold, professors [and pastors] abusing their privileges, and sinners waxing more bold in sin—are not these sights enough to crush us to the earth? . . .
>
> The lesson of wisdom is, be not dismayed by soul-trouble. Count it no strange thing, but a part of ordinary ministerial

experience. . . . Live by the day—ay, by the hour. . . . Be not surprised when men fail you; it is a failing world. . . . Be content to be nothing, for that is what you are.

These are such treacherous times. If nothing else, they intensify our fear of sinning, which is healthy. As Paul warned us all, "Let him who thinks he stands, take heed lest he fall" (1 Cor. 10:12). The secret of our finishing well when the journey is over is being willing to "take heed" along the way.

No longer should we be saying that "perilous times will come." They have arrived, fellow pilgrim; they are *now*. And we must face them head-on, doing whatever is necessary to stand firm.

As Carl Henry wrote so eloquently in *Twilight of a Great Civilization*:

We may even now live in the half generation before all hell breaks loose, and if its fury is contained we will be remembered, if we are remembered at all, as those who used their hands and hearts and minds and very bodies to plug the dikes against impending doom.

A Finishing Touch: The secret of finishing well when the journey is over is being willing to "take heed" along the way.

A Daily Reading: 1 Corinthians 10:11–13

I grew up in the heyday of radio. (Fact is, I didn't even see a television set until I was a teenager.) If we got our homework done, we could listen to various week-night radio shows. Among our favorites were "Fibber McGee and Molly," "Jack Armstrong, the All-American Boy," "The Green Hornet," "Captain Midnight," (remember the code ring you could get in the mail for two Ovaltine labels?), "Amos 'n' Andy," and a couple of scary shows—"Inner Sanctum" (with that frightening squeaky door) and "The Shadow." Remember that spooky line the announcer always gave just before "The Shadow" came on: "Who knows what evil l-l-lurks in the hearts of men? The Shadow knows!" Then there would be a blood-curdling laugh which faded away into the distance. I always liked all the lights on when we listened to that program.

Many years have passed since those simple and innocent days of my childhood, but that single line remains a haunting question to this day: Who, indeed, knows what wickedness lurks in the hearts of men and women?

We think we do. But how wrong we usually are. The heart houses secrets we can never see. People are awfully good at cover-up. Smiling masks often camouflage breaking hearts. About the time we think we've got somebody figured out, we're stunned to discover how much was hidden from view. Lurking in many a life is pain beyond belief.

Stories of hidden heartbreaks are legion. I'm thinking of a minister of the gospel . . . gifted, insightful, well-educated, able to hold vast audiences in rapt attention with his grasp of the biblical text. Yet behind his mask of secure competence and a choice sense of humor he wages a frightening war against alcohol.

Or I remember the man who had virtually everything . . . a master's degree, a good job, a reputation of respect in the community, at his church, among his professional peers, and within his home. He was the epitome of responsibility—a calm, deliberate, quiet, intelligent gentleman. But one rainy evening when his wife returned home from work she punched the garage-door opener and could not believe her eyes as the eerie light automatically clicked on. Her husband had hanged himself in their garage. Not even she knew what foul demons her beloved husband of thirty years had battled silently, secretly, all alone.

In our world of superficial talk and casual relationships, it is easy to forget that a smile doesn't necessarily mean "I'm happy" and the courteous answer "I'm fine" may not be at all truthful. Just because it's Christmas, we can't assume everybody's merry. Even the closest family members can be blindly unaware of each other's pain.

I'm not suggesting that everyone is an emotional time bomb or that masks are worn by all who seem to be enjoying life. But I've lived long enough to know that many a heart hides agony while the face reflects ecstasy.

There is Someone, however, who fully knows what lurks in our hearts. And knowing, He never laughs mockingly and fades away. He never shrugs and walks away. Instead, He understands completely and stays near.

Who, indeed, knows? Our God, alone, knows. He sympathizes with our weaknesses and forgives all our transgressions. To Him there are no secret struggles or silent cries. He hears. He sees. He stays near. He accepts us and loves us unconditionally. He is "the Father of mercies and the God of all comfort."

A Finishing Touch: He who loves us most knows us best. He who knows us best cares the most.

A Daily Reading: Psalm 139

Paul's expose of depravity in Romans 1:18–32 is a chilling account of human wickedness, a vivid pen-portrait of unleashed unrighteousness, unashamed godlessness, and unnatural lust. Paul pulls no punches as he writes of darkened hearts, degrading passions, indecent acts, and reprobate minds. Reaching the final argument of his prosecution, the teacher from Tarsus twists the accusing knife with cruel eloquence: "and, although they know the ordinance of God that those who practice such things are worthy of death, they not only do the same, but also give hearty approval to those who do them" (Rom. 1:32).

It's bad enough that there are those who participate in such a depraved lifestyle . . . but what about those who applaud them for doing so? Rather than being shocked and offended, screaming "No!" there are invariably those who smile and approve, nodding "Go!" When depravity is on display, there is always an audience willing to buy a ticket and applaud the performance.

This came home to me anew when I read about a scam that took place in New York City when some con men decided to make some extra cash by feeding on the depravity of humanity. Naturally, they made a killing.

The got a pile of cardboard boxes, newspapers, stickers that read "Factory Sealed," a roll of bubble plastic, and a stack of stolen shopping bags from Macy's. They stuffed each box with bricks and newspapers until it weighed enough, then wrapped everything in bubble stuff and affixed the stickers.

As the evening rush-hour traffic backed up at the Holland Tunnel, the con artists started wandering the curb, carrying the bogus boxes inside the Macy's shopping bags. When they spotted a potential buyer stranded in traffic, they walked up to the car window and started fast-talking a cash deal.

"Hey, man, I got a Sony Handicam here . . . just got if off a Fed Ex truck."

He lifts the box out of the bag, saying, "Macy's sells 'em for $999."

Then, jerking his head around nervously, he says, "I'll take ninety bucks, cash."

The cars start to edge forward and the other drivers start yelling. The thief delivers his final pitch: "Okay, man, I'll let you have it for forty-five. Take it or leave it."

And the driver takes it, knowing its hot merchandise.

When asked about how it feels to rip people off, selling them empty boxes, one of the men said, "Hey, man, I'm not beating an honest man. No one buys hot unless they've got larceny in their heart."

I must admit . . . the guy's got a point! To paraphrase Paul's wrap-up in Romans 1: the fella who grabbed the box and sped off into the night was just as guilty as the thief on the street, and, along with that, his money gave "hearty approval" to the one who ripped him off.

Happens all the time. The details change, the wrong may bear another name, the consequences will differ, but it's still depravity on display, whether it's the sinner or the sinnee. Furthermore, no one is immune. In fact, the possibilities of appealing to our old nature are endless.

A Finishing Touch: What kind of deals do you make when no one is looking? Are you, right now, aware of wrong and giving hearty approval to another's sin?

A Daily Reading: Romans 1

I had lunch recently with a businessman who runs his own company. As we talked, the subject of wisdom kept popping up in our conversation. We were agreeing on the value of certain qualities that cannot be learned in school—things like intuition, diligence, integrity, perception, consistency, loyalty—when he, again, mentioned wisdom.

So I asked, "How does a person get wisdom? I realize we are to be men of wisdom, but few people ever talk about how it is acquired."

His answer was quick and to the point: "Pain."

I paused and looked deeply into his eyes. Without knowing the specifics, I knew his one-word answer was not theoretical. He and pain had gotten to know each other rather well.

As he told me of the things he has been dealing with in recent months, some professional and some personal, I told him he had spent sufficient hours in the crucible to have earned his Ph.D. in wisdom! It was then I quoted from the first chapter of James:

> When all kinds of trials and temptations crowd into your lives, my brothers, don't resent them as intruders, but welcome them as friends! Realize that they come to test your faith and to produce in you the quality of endurance. But let the process go on until that endurance is fully developed, and you will find you have become men of mature character with the right sort of independence (James 1:2–4 *Phillips*).

Aren't those great words? More importantly, they are absolutely true. By accepting life's tests and temptations as friends, we become "men [and women] of mature character." There is no shortcut, no such thing as instant endurance. The pain brought on by interruptions and disappointments, by loss and failure, by accidents and disease, is the long and arduous road to maturity. There is no other road.

But where does wisdom come in? It comes through the back door of life when we lean out the window and yell "Help!" That's not my idea. James says so in the next verse:

> And if, in the process, any of you does not know how to meet any particular problem he has only to ask God—who gives generously to all men without making them feel foolish or guilty— and he may be quite sure that the necessary wisdom will be given him (1:5).

As I see it, it is a domino effect, One thing bumps up against another, which, in turn, bumps another, and in the long haul, endurance helps us mature. Periodically, however, we will find ourselves at a loss to know what to do or how to respond. It's then we ask for help, and God delivers more than intelligence and ideas and good old common sense. He dips into His well of wisdom and allows us to drink from His bucket, whose refreshment provides abilities and insights that are of another world. Perhaps it might best be stated as having a small portion of "the mind of Christ."

When we have responded as we should to life's blows, enduring them rather than escaping them, we are given more maturity that stays with us and new measures of wisdom which we are able to draw upon for the balance of our lives.

A Finishing Touch: By accepting life's tests and temptations as friends, we become men and women of mature character.

A Daily Reading: James 1

Solomon once wrote: "He who walks in integrity walks securely, but he who perverts his ways will be found out" (Prov. 10:9).

By the time Job had reared his family, established himself in the business world, and gotten up in years, he had become "the greatest of all the men of the east." People respected him because he was "upright, fearing God, and turning away from evil" (Job 1:1–3). Job walked securely.

Similar things were said of Joseph. As a young man he became Potiphar's "personal servant" and eventually was put in charge over all the man owned "in the house and in the field" (Gen. 39:5). Whether managing workers or handling large sums of money or all alone in the home with Mrs. Potiphar, Joseph could be trusted. He walked securely.

Daniel also distinguished himself among his peers because "he possessed an extraordinary spirit," which was observed by his superior, King Darius. The plan to promote him to prime minister so infuriated those who envied him that they "began trying to find a ground of accusation" against him. They struck out. After all their searching and spying, attempting to dig up some dirt, "they could find no ground of accusation or evidence of corruption" anywhere (Dan. 6:1–4). Daniel walked securely.

What did these men have in common?

Perfection? These men were far from perfect.

Easy times? Hardly. All of them experienced heartaches and hardships that would make your head ache.

Well, how about an impressive presence, carefully choreographed by clever public-image makers? Don't make me laugh. That sort of stuff didn't come into vogue until our culture created it in this century.

How about slick rhetoric? Wrong again.

What they had in common was *character*—high moral character. They walked securely; they didn't fear being "found out."

Call me dated or old-fashioned or idealistic if you wish, but my passionate plea is that we unearth and restore the concept of character. It's been buried long enough.

Character belongs first on our list when searching for employees of excellence in the workplace. It must be a nonnegotiable among those we place into leadership positions in our schools, our churches, our cities, our state, and our nation. Character is what wholesome parents strive to cultivate in their children. It is *the* foundational quality all of us expect from the circle of professionals and laborers who serve us up close and personal—our physician, our attorney, our counselor, our pastor, our teacher, our CPA, our banker, our builder, our policeman, our mechanic, our plumber, our repairman . . . you name it.

We may not say it every time, but deep down in our souls we long for and expect character, and when it is lacking, we feel it, we know it, we resent it. It is the "given" in greatness.

Why, then, is character so seldom mentioned? Is it because we have come to believe we have no right to expect it? After all, "nobody's perfect."

Again I am reminded of one of my favorite Greek terms—Hogwash! It is character we require, not perfection.

We have every right to expect of ourselves and others virtue, dignity, self-mastery, resoluteness, determination, strength of will, moral purity, and personal integrity—in public and in private. The fact that many fail to live up to the minimal daily requirement does not change the ideal.

Having just finished reading historian Thomas Reeves' masterful and thorough work on the life of John F. Kennedy, A *Question of Character*, I find myself both angered and saddened by his notorious private life and the absence of true character in JFK's life. As important as intelligence and courage and wit and diplomacy may be, Reeves concludes, "all of these qualities may be connected to an effort to live and lead by those values, known and declared for centuries, that link good character with effective leadership. The United States—and now the world—cannot settle for less."

Solomon was right. Those who walk correctly walk securely . . . with no fear of being "found out." If men like Job and Joseph and

Daniel could demonstrate character in the worst of times, you and I can do so now. And because we can, we must.

A Finishing Touch: Think about the people you admire and respect most. Does character figure into that assessment? What qualities do you look for in a leader . . . in an elected official? Do you need to revise your priorities in light of this?

A Daily Reading: Daniel 6

Unfortunately, we have grown accustomed to shrugging off lapses in moral character, manifested in secretive and deceptive lifestyles.

We are frequently told that trying to find people who value honesty and model responsibility, who promote fairness, accountability, loyalty, respect for others, and who hold to strong, upright convictions is not at all realistic.

"Such people don't exist . . . we need to stop requiring personal purity," we are told. Or, as one air-headed soul said during the last presidential campaign, "We're voting for president, not pope."

To such an analogy, I reply "Nonsense!" That kind of logic (or rather, lack of logic) gives me the jitters. Such reasoning reminds me of a piece of nonsense I learned in elementary school.

> Why Are Fire Engines Red?
> They have four wheels and eight men;
> Four plus eight is twelve;
> Twelve inches makes a ruler;
> A ruler is Queen Elizabeth;
> Queen Elizabeth sails the seven seas;
> The seven seas have fish;
> The fish have fins;
> The Finns hate the Russians;
> The Russians are red;
> Fire engines are always rushin';
> So that's why they're red.

Just think about it.

A New Week
of
Finishing Touches

28

MONDAY

Ever get the feeling that you have a simple answer to a problem, but you're wondering how come nobody else has mentioned it? Maybe you don't understand all the facts, you think. Or maybe your answer is too simple. Sort of like a Band-Aid on a headache. Then again, maybe it is so basic it's being overlooked by those who are focusing so tightly on the problem. Perhaps they've made the thing too complicated.

Well, that's the way I feel about the tragic problem of AIDS.

No, on second thought, AIDS is the result of a deeper problem—promiscuity, which is another word for sexual immorality.

Now, I realize there are exceptions, that some people contract AIDS who were not promiscuous. Because they are innocent victims and in the great minority, I need to make it clear that I do not include them in the thoughts I'm sharing here. My comments are directed toward those who deliberately participate in sexual activities outside the God-ordained bonds of heterosexual marriage.

There is only one, simple, twofold solution to the problem of AIDS. It isn't novel or easy. And it certainly isn't original with me. Nor is it merely a Band-Aid on the problem.

The twofold answer is *marital fidelity* or *sexual abstinence.*

I am always stunned when I hear about more requests for federal funds to promote "AIDS education." How much education is needed to shake your head and say the simplest word in the English language? We don't need to educate folks on how to hop in the sack safely. No big deal. "Just say no."

What really rots my socks is the recent emphasis on condoms. Even schools of higher learning(?) are now distributing these contraceptives, claiming they're not promoting sexual encounters or condoning sexual activity. Sure. You believe that and I've got some great beach sites to sell you in Bakersfield. That's like universities handing out syringes, cocaine spoons, and handbooks on the do's and don'ts of freebasing, yet swearing they're not encouraging dope. Give me a break.

Are morality, chastity, virginity, and decency forgotten words? Have we totally forgotten the fact that centuries ago God established strict codes of moral conduct because He knew that sexual promiscuity spread disease and caused death? Are we so blinded by rationalization that we have blocked out of our minds the calamitous demise of societies that tolerated illicit practices—Sodom and Gomorrah, ancient Greece, debauched Rome?

God's message still speaks with forceful and insightful relevance: "For this is the will of God, your sanctification . . . that you abstain from sexual immorality" (1 Thess. 4:3). "Flee immorality" (1 Cor. 6:18). "Let marriage be held in honor . . . let the marriage bed be undefiled; for fornicators and adulterers God will judge" (Heb. 13:4).

The problem of AIDS is horrible, but understanding the ultimate cause is not complicated. To borrow from the prophet Hosea (who knew the tragic consequences of sexual impurity), our land has sown the wind and we are now reaping the whirlwind. The storm will not subside unless and until we return to marital fidelity and sexual abstinence.

The total cure is repentance.

A Finishing Touch: God's moral codes never go out of fashion.
A Daily Reading: Ephesians 5

The older I get, the less excited I am about theory . . . and the more I care about reality. Who cares if the stuff that flows from my pen stimulates the intellect and gives folks fodder for philosophizing? So what if these words tickle ears and answer questions nobody is asking? Provocative, relevant, issue-related writing with enough creativity and honesty to keep the reader reading is what interests me . . . not much else. And so every once in a while I frown, squint, and peer objectively at a page and ask hard questions: Am I in touch? Does this connect with where people are? Is this worth mentioning? Does it scratch an itch? Will it make any difference? Or am I merely rearranging the deck chairs on the *Titanic*?

I did that after I wrote a column on an "affair." Just decided to face the facts, say it straight, and risk being bold rather than subtle. That's an explosive subject. I realize that. I also realize that a few folks out there might misread me and think the wrong thing. Might as well say it—some will think I'm confessing in a roundabout way . . . that what I am confronting on paper I'm doing on the sly. Or maybe they'll think I'm doing an overkill on extramarital sex because I'm personally frustrated and losing some kind of intimate battle. None of that is true, but that's part of the risk you run when you address gun-powder subjects.

Another risk is being overzealous and offensive. There's a fine line between being necessarily straightforward and needlessly blunt. Jesus, who never once compromised with sins of the flesh, had a remarkable way of keeping the sinner's dignity intact, a la John 8. I love that about Him as much as anything He modeled.

Anyway, the upshot of all this is a letter which I received in response to my "affair" column. The person who wrote it reinforced my hope that my words would indeed connect and communicate. Here are a few excerpts.

> I rarely write letters like this! But I feel so strongly about what you've written. . . . I was the unfaithful partner in a marriage.

Although it was many years ago, it is still a painful memory. It did happen before I knew the Lord, and it has been His grace that has healed and sustained our marriage. My point in writing at all is really to commend and encourage you to continue to address these very difficult subjects. A stand must be taken and too many evade the confrontation. . . . Thank you for your convictions and the courage to speak on them.

So I include this here to ask, again, if this speaks to anyone out there. Perhaps you are still on the fence. Still trying to break off an illicit relationship and come back to your original commitment. Wondering if you dare. If you can. If it's worth it.

It occurred to me that maybe all you need is an extra boost of encouragement . . . like this honest and courageous admission from one who has been there. And owned up to it. And walked away from it, forgiven and free.

You do the same. Walk back into your mate's arms and never walk away again.

As Jesus said, "Go and sin no more."

A Finishing Touch: Telling the truth in love can uncover the lie of sin. Examine your own life with this in mind.

A Daily Reading: John 8:1–11

Instant replays have become old hat. We now expect them in all televised sports. Whether it's an impressive backhand or a slam dunk or a touchdown pass, we never have to worry about missing it the first time around. It'll be back again and again, and probably again. In slow motion at least once. If it's good enough, in super slow motion. Every coordinated movement, every graceful or powerful motion returns to be analyzed by fan and announcer alike.

It occurred to me recently that I'd enjoy (for lack of a better title) *delayed* replays of some of the more significant times in my life. Not photographs—fixed frames on film that can go in an album. But "delayed replays." I'm fantasizing the possibility of going back and being given another chance to relive a particular experience that could have been handled differently. More wisely. With greater tact. In better taste. You know, all those "If-I-had-that-to-do-over-again" thoughts. Wouldn't that be neat? We'd all benefit from that, wouldn't we?

Just think of all the things you'd refrain from saying that you blurted out the first time around. And consider the different attitudes we would have toward unexpected interruptions, unplanned babies, unrealistic expectations, unimportant details. I'll tell you, it would be a whole other story the second time around, wouldn't it?

Even everybody's friend, Erma Bombeck—the gal you'd think would never regret a moment—agrees. Recently, she admitted:

> If I had my life to live over again, I would have waxed less and listened more. Instead of wishing away nine months of pregnancy and complaining about the shadows over my feet, I'd have cherished every minute of it and realized that the wonderment growing inside me was to be my only chance in life to assist God in a miracle. . . . I would have cried and laughed less while watching television . . . and more while watching life. . . . There would have been more I love yous . . . more I'm sorrys . . . more I'm listening . . . but mostly, given another shot at life, I

would seize every minute of it . . . and never give that minute back until there was nothing left of it.

Unfortunately, life doesn't offer "delayed replays." Second times around don't happen.

We cannot rerear our children. I cannot repastor my first church. Initial impressions cannot be remade. Cutting remarks cannot be resaid. Scars can't be completely removed. Tear stains on the delicate fabric of our emotions are, more often than not, permanent. Memories are fixed, not flexible.

"You mean God won't forgive?" You know better than that. "And people can't overlook my failures?" Come on, now. That's not the issue at all. Most people I know are amazingly understanding. Our biggest task is forgiving ourselves.

The main message is clear: Think before you speak. Pause before you act. Make every minute count.

Another chance? No chance. Today is memory in the making, a deposit in the bank of time. Let's make it a good one!

A Finishing Touch: Today is tomorrow's yesterday. How do you want to remember it?

A Daily Reading: Ecclesiastes 12

All of us played follow-the-leader as kids. But even then, when the guide in front was too daring or foolish, we would step aside. There were definite limits on how far we would follow.

Sadly, this is not always true in the spiritual realm, where leaders unworthy of the name sometimes command blind devotion. (Remember Jonestown and Waco and those fallen televangelists?)

No one ever defined that follow-no-matter-what syndrome better than our Lord in Matthew 15:14: "Let them alone; they are blind guides of the blind. And if a blind man guides a blind man, both will fall into a pit."

Remember now, Jesus warned us against blind guides, not *all* guides. God still uses strategic, trustworthy, dedicated leaders. Always has, always will. These visionary guides have 20-20 vision as they continue walking with God. They deserve our respect.

But how can we tell when "blindness "starts to set in? What are the symptoms to look for in strong, natural leaders that tell us trouble is brewing? When should we stop following lest we, too, become blind?

After thinking about this for quite awhile, I am ready to suggest six blind spots we dare not overlook.

Authoritarianism. Take care when a leader begins repressing your freedom. When he or she becomes inflexible, dictatorial, tyrannical, oppressive . . . stop following. If there is the lack of a servant's heart, of a teachable spirit, pride is in control. Be especially wary of one who seems to have all the answers.

Exclusiveness. Watch out for the "we-alone-are-right" and the "us-four-and-no-more" attitudes. When what is being promoted starts making you clannish, closed and cliquish, beware! This reveals itself in an encouragement to break commitments with your mate, family members, and long-standing friends. Paranoia often accompanies such exclusiveness.

Greed. Moneygrubbing is another tell-tale sign. Especially if funds wind up in the leaders pocket and become "nobody's business."

Remember 1 Peter 5:2. Dependable shepherds are not motivated by "sordid gain."

Sensuality. Moral purity is a must if the leader claims God's hand is on his life. Follow no guru, no matter how visionary or charismatic, who promotes and practices sexual looseness, who is too familiar with the opposite sex, who laughs at lust and flirts with infidelity. A holy life is never optional.

Unaccountability. Leaders who refuse to be accountable to anyone forfeit the right to be trusted and followed. Beware of the secretive, irresponsible, untouchable "I am God's anointed" mentality. No matter how eloquent or how competent, every leader needs counsel and occasional confrontation.

Rationalization. When wrong is justified with a defensive spirit, when inappropriate actions are quickly glossed over, when scriptural truth is twisted to fit a sinful life-style, when gray-black facts are whitewashed, stop your support. Remember, "accommodation theology" is a danger signal. Look for these things in the ones you follow: a servant's heart, a vulnerable spirit, a sensitive conscience, and a quick willingness to admit wrong.

The hypnotic, demanding spell of a blind prima donna is exactly as Christ described it: the pits.

Take His advice: "Let them alone!"

A Finishing Touch: If you're going to follow the leader, look where you're going.

A Daily Reading: 1 Timothy 3–4

There are days when the best thing you can do is leave it to God. Don't sweat, don't fret, don't cry, don't curse . . . just smile and leave it to God. Your super-intense brothers and sisters may call it a cop-out. No matter; leave it to God. Your conscience may try to prod you into action. Don't yield; leave it to God.

Philip Melanchthon and Martin Luther were once deciding on the day's agenda. The former was disciplined, intellectually gifted, serious, and goal-driven; the latter was equally intelligent but much more emotional, risky, even playful.

Melanchthon said, "Martin, this day we will discuss the governance of the universe."

To which Luther responded, "Philip, this day you and I will go fishing and leave governance of the universe to God."

What wise counsel!

But, look at all the things yet to be done, you say. Think of those hard-chargers who got up earlier than you did and will skip lunch lest they miss a minute on their Daytimer plan of attack. Think of all those who, while you are "leaving it to God," set new records of achievement. What examples of diligence and determination!

"Good examples" can drive us crazy at times. They make us feel inadequate, they force us to squeeze ourselves into a mold that isn't us, and they leave us with the impression that what we are doing isn't nearly as significant as what they have done. Some days—not always, mind you—but some days you even have to leave "good examples" to God!

I love Jesus' model of balance. He arrived on the planet with a mission more important than any soul who has drawn a breath of earth air. Yet He didn't really get started until He turned thirty. What about all those "wasted" years? He left them to God.

We never read one time that He hurried anywhere. Or that He *worried* about anyone. What did He do with those who heard and shrugged and walked away? He left them to God. And those tight-lipped, nitpicking Pharisees who gave Him grief every time He turned around? You got it! He left them to God, too.

There's a great scene in Luke when a bunch of His disciples returned from their practical-work project. They were all excited about their success, especially that "even the demons are subject to us in Your name." Can't you hear them?

"Wow, Lord . . . you shoulda been there . . . like, *zap*! Out they came! And then a little later another horde of them bowed down in obedience. This is power, Jesus . . . we had power out there. We put 'em in their place. Let's go back and do it again. Hallelujah!"

Ever so graciously He offered this mild rebuke: "Do not rejoice . . . that the spirits are subject to you, but rejoice that your names are recorded in heaven" (Luke 10:20).

He wanted them to realize that they were significant not because of what they had done, but because of who they were. They were dear to the Father! They felt good about themselves because they had done well. Whereas Jesus implied, "Leave all that to God . . . you have nothing to prove, you are approved. Your names are in the Book and that's what really matters."

I can remember as if it were yesterday (though it has been more than twenty-five years) when I felt driven and drained by the never-ending demands of ministry. If folks weren't changing, I felt responsible. If some drifted, somehow I felt at fault. If there wasn't continual growth, I ached as if I needed to make it happen. If a sermon failed to ring with clarity and power, I struggled all of Monday and half of Tuesday. Talk about wasted energy.

Time has helped. So has age. Virtually all of the thieves that once stole my joy and assaulted my motivation I now leave to God.

Don't I care? Of course, I care! But those cares are now placed in the hands of One who can handle them. What once bothered me I have learned to give over to Him who doesn't mind being bothered. Whereas criticism used to cripple me for days, I now do my best to sift and shift and sail; I learn what I can . . . I turn the rest over to God . . . and I get back at it. (Not always, but more often than not.) Leaving such things to God allows me more room down inside to rebuild and roll on.

If I count correctly, there are over 350 "fear nots" in the Bible—think of them as God's one-a-day vitamins.

For, as Barbara Johnson puts it, "Fear is the darkroom where negatives are developed." Get outa there!

A Finishing Touch: Let's declare today the day you and I give ourselves permission to relax without being afraid or feeling guilty . . . and leave the stuff we cannot handle or change to God? Is it a deal? Great! But what shall we do about the person who thinks we are slacking off too much? You guessed it. Just leave it to God!

A Daily Reading: Luke 10

Can't seem to get where you want to go fast enough?
Leave it to God.
Worried about your kids?
Leave it to God.
Living in a place you'd rather not be?
Leave it to God.
Looks like you won't graduate with honors?
Leave it to God.
No matter how hard you try, your life's partner simply is not responding?
Leave it to God.
Found a lump and you see the doctor tomorrow?
Leave it to God.
You've said the right words to that friend who is lost, and you've been all you know to be; still, zip?
Leave it to God.
Haven't got a date for the prom?
Leave it to God.
A mid-career change seems scary?
Leave it to God.
You did the job but someone else got the credit?
Leave it to God.
Getting older, alone?
Leave it to God.

Anyone who loves the sea has a romance with it as well as a respect for it. The romance is difficult to describe—except by poets—for it defies analysis, The mind moves into another gear as the primeval rhythms of the seashore erode tidy resolutions and hectic deadlines. Time tables, appointments, and schedules are blurred by the salt mist. The thundering waves pull us with a powerful magnetism we cannot resist as we toss our cares and responsibilities to the prevailing winds.

Anne Morrow Lindbergh beautifully describes this consuming "deck-chair apathy" in her classic *Gift from the Sea* . . .

> One falls under their spell, relaxes, stretches out prone. One becomes, in fact, like the element on which one lies, flattened by the sea; bare, open, empty as the beach, erased by today's tides of all yesterday's scribblings.
>
> And then, some morning in the second week, the mind wakes, comes to life again. Not in a city sense—no—but beach-wise. It begins to drift, to play, to turn over in gentle careless rolls like those lazy waves on the beach. One never knows what chance treasures these easy unconscious rollers may toss up, on the smooth white sand of the conscious mind; what perfectly rounded stone, what rare shell from the ocean floor. . . .
>
> But it must not be sought for or—heaven forbid!—dug for. No, no dredging of the sea-bottom here. That would defeat one's purpose. The sea does not reward those who are too anxious, too greedy, or too impatient. To dig for treasures shows not only Impatience and greed, but lack of faith. Patience, patience, patience, is what the sea teaches. Patience and faith. One should lie empty, open, choiceless as a beach—waiting for a gift from the sea.

What is hidden in the sea is also hidden in God's wisdom.

> We speak God's wisdom in a mystery, the hidden wisdom, which God predestined before the ages to our glory the wisdom which none of the rulers of this age has understood; for if they had understood, they would not have crucified the Lord of glory; but just as it is written, "THINGS WHICH EYE HAS NOT SEEN AND EAR HAS NOT HEARD, AND WHICH HAVE NOT ENTERED THE HEART OF MAN, ALL THAT GOD HAS PRE-PARED FOR THOSE WHO LOVE HIM." For to us God revealed them through the Spirit; for the Spirit searches all things, even the depths of God (1 Cor. 2:7–10).

The depths! Elsewhere Paul writes, "Oh the depth of the riches both of the wisdom and knowledge of God!" (Rom. 11:33).

Those fathomless truths *about* Him and those profound insights *from* Him produce within us a wisdom that enables us to think *with* Him. Such wisdom comes from His Spirit who, alone, can plumb the depths and reveal His mind.

The hurried, the greedy, the impatient cannot enter into such mysteries. God grants such understanding only to those who wait in silence . . . who respect "the depths of God." It takes time. It calls for solitude.

We live in a loud, volatile world, marked by surface issues, skating relationships, and shallow thoughts. There is more than enough noise, so let's not add to it. Get alone with God and gain a new respect for His wisdom. It won't come in a hurry. Don't be afraid to seek the depths. Ideally, find a beach where you can stroll, a weather-beaten bench where you can sit and think . . . where you can be still and know . . . .

A Finishing Touch: Find your own "seashore" of solitude and reflection.
A Daily Reading: Romans 11:33–36

The thermometer registers in the nineties. The air is still and heavy. The dog is panting, the sun is high, and the birds are silent. It is the middle of summer. Long, hot days . . . uneventful, unguarded, uncomplicated.

How perfectly suited the haunting strains of the "Gaelic Blessing" are for this midsummer-day:

> Deep peace of the running wave to you,
> Deep peace of the flowing air to you,
> Deep peace of the quiet earth to you,
> Deep peace of the shining stars to you.
> Deep peace of the gentle night to you,
> Moon and stars pour their healing light on you,
> Deep peace of Christ, the Light of the world, to you,
> Deep peace of Christ.

The message of that ancient Gaelic blessing is not simply a promise of peace . . . but deep peace. A peace that cancels fear, curbs anxiety, and chases away all those hobgoblins that steal our joy and wilt our zeal.

On this warm summer afternoon, we can be recipients of such a peace. Who cares what surrounds us, who cares how hot it is? His deep peace cools our fevered brow.

Somewhere, miles away, crops push their way toward harvest and waves roar and tumble onto shore. Windswept forests sing their timeless songs, and desert animals scurry in the shadows of cactus and rock.

Within a matter of hours night will fall, the dark sky will glitter with moon and stars, and sleep will force itself upon us. Life will continue on uninterrupted. Appreciated or not, the canvas of nature will go on being painted by the fingers of God.

In the midst of the offensive noise of our modern world—the people, the cars, the sounds, the smog, the heat, the pressures—

there stand those reminders of His deep peace. The running wave, the flowing air, the quiet earth, the shining stars, the gentle night, the healing light . . . and from each, the blessing of the deep peace of Christ to you, to me.

Have you such peace, or is it nothing more than a midsummer-day's dream? If you must confess an absence of such peace, may I suggest a simple change of scenery? Visit the seashore and hear the running wave. Take a drive out to the country, roll the windows down, and feel the air flowing through your hair. Walk out into the night and look up at the stars. Be still and discover anew that He is God. The longing of one's heart for deep peace is somehow recaptured in such settings.

Jim Elliot, the martyred missionary, eloquently expressed his own discovery of such peace in this journal entry:

> I walked out on the hill just now. It is exalting, delicious, to stand embraced by the shadows of a friendly tree with the wind tugging at your coattail and the heavens hailing your heart, to gaze and glory and give oneself again to God—what more could a man ask? Oh, the fullness, pleasure, sheer excitement of knowing God on earth! I care not if I never raise my voice again for Him, if only I may love Him, please Him. . . . if only I may see Him, touch His garments, and smile into His eyes.

A Finishing Touch: May the deep peace of our God cool and quiet our over-heated souls.

A Daily Reading: Isaiah 26:3

While jogging early this morning I found myself humming the tune Bob Hope immortalized during several wars. I can still remember his tailor-made lyrics, fitted to each occasion. He sang them to lonely soldiers, sailors, airmen, and marines from steamy jungles to frozen reservoirs . . . from the decks of aircraft carriers to makeshift platforms on windswept sand dunes. As guys and gals in uniform laughed and cried, screamed and sipped Coke, they always anticipated Hope's finale as he took the mike and crooned, "And thanks for the memories. . . ."

I remember it well: Christmas of '58 on Okinawa. I was homesick, missing my wife, and counting the days. So when the veteran entertainer sang his closing song, I sang along with him in a flood of memories. I recall how grateful I was for that tour of duty: the lessons I had learned, the disciplines I had begun to employ (thanks to the Navigators), the books I had read, the missionaries I had met, the places I had visited, the journal I had kept, the letters I had written, the verses I had memorized, even the things I had witnessed inside a Marine Corps barracks! And, most importantly, the call I had received from God to enter ministry.

Then, all the way through seminary, I pontificated to family and classmates that there were three places I knew I'd never minister: Texas, New England and California . . . especially southern California! But God is God and He knows best, and I ended up going to all three. And, of all things, I'm now back in Texas!

Looking back, all I can do is smile . . . and sing, "Thanks for the memories." I'm doing that a lot these days as I recall the various things God has done in me and through me and for me—and sometimes in spite of me! And I can't help but give Him praise in my heart.

Pastoring a church has to be the highest of all callings. In this position, one has the privilege of touching life at its tenderest points . . . of walking with pain through its darkest valleys . . . of proclaiming truth in its purest form . . . of confronting sin in its ugliest scenes . . . of modeling integrity through its hardest extremes—while everyone is watching as well as when no one is looking. It is no wonder to me why it requires a God-given calling before one enters it or why such a struggle accompanies resignation from it.

And after all these years I say a resounding, "Thanks for the memories!" For the conversions that have occurred, the addictions that have been conquered, the marriages that have been restored, the fractured lives that have been mended. These memories stay with me and revisit me often as I thank Him for His faithfulness.

Who knows what other surprises God has over the horizon? I do not know what lies ahead, but for today I pause and praise Him . . . and thank Him for the memories.

A Finishing Touch: We know who holds the future . . . as we thank Him for the past.

A Daily Reading: Deuteronomy 8

Most noises in church don't bug me. I've heard 'em all.

People snoring. Babies crying. Rain falling. Crickets chirping. Sound systems popping. Toilets flushing. Offering and communion plates dropping. Sirens screaming and cars speeding outside. Kids yelling and phones ringing inside. Hymnals hitting a bunch of piano keys. Organists standing up on a foot full of bass notes. Coughing. Sneezing. Blowing. Laughing. Crying. Shouting. Whispering. Gasping. Yawning. Clapping.

You don't spend most of your life in church without encountering the full spectrum.

I've even witnessed a during-the-sermon, pew-to-pulpit heated argument between parishioner and preacher (the parishioner won!), and I've refereed several fights between husbands and wives both before and after church meetings.

So it's no big deal . . . noises really come with the territory. Even some "joyful noises" are part of the package. I've heard some guys sing so badly they sounded like a bull moose with its hind legs caught in a trap as they bellow the baritone part to "Wonderful Grace of Jesus." And I've heard a few sopranos who really needed to be put out of their misery. (I've often been thankful that stained glass doesn't shatter.) But their motives were right, so they will receive their reward. (I hope it includes heavenly voice lessons or we're all in for an awfully long eternity.)

There is one shrill noise, however, unique to this electronic age, that I find both irritating and irresponsible. It's those plagued digital watches! It's bad enough to have 'em chime and dong and zip and blip and bzzzt and ting every hour on the hour, but since they're not synchronized to go off exactly at the same time, it's fifteen to twenty seconds of every conceivable tone. It's enough to make a hound lift his head and holler.

I'm not alone, believe me. You can't imagine the bulletin stubs, postcards, verbal comments, threats, and letters I've received pleading that somebody say something.

Somehow worship and watches seem to be strange bedfellows. Surely, time and eternity weren't made to mix. Or, as one creative friend wrote:

> In this world of noise and bustle
> Could we not escape this
> High-tech age for one hour
> In Your house?

I think I'll make this suggestion to pastors everywhere: Tell your congregation that if they promise to be more thoughtful with their hourly chimes, you'll be more punctual with your closing time. But warn them that for every weird blip . . . blip . . . blip you hear, you'll add another ten minutes to the sermon.

Won't it be fun watching everybody glare at the guys who turn the meeting into a marathon? Come to think of it, while I've heard lots of sounds and seen lots of sights in churches, I've never seen a Sunday morning congregational mutiny. We could make history!

A Finishing Touch: We cannot watch the clock and at the same time worship the Lord in the beauty of holiness.

A Daily Reading: Psalm 62

Well, it's mid-July. Time to make a mad dash for the pool, or at least a tall, frosty glass of iced tea. But while you're swimming or sipping, think about helping. Yeah, *helping*.

Think about being of assistance . . . your arm around the hunched shoulders of another . . . your smile saying "try again" to someone who's convinced it's curtains . . . your cup of cool water held up to a brother's cracked lips, reassuring and reaffirming.

Every time I pick up my pen, the thought of helping urges me to push ink into words.

There are enough—more than enough—specialists in body blocks, pass defenses, and tackling. There are more than enough causing fumbles, bruises, and injuries. I'd much rather run interference. I'd much rather slap someone on the back and say, "You can do it, now git at it!"

I wholeheartedly agree with Philip Yancey, a man who models his own advice:

> C.S. Lewis once likened his role as a Christian writer to an adjective humbly striving to point others to the Noun of truth. For people to believe that Noun, we Christian writers must improve our adjectives.

Whether in the sweltering heat of summer or the bitter blast of winter, I'd like to think that some carefully selected turn of a phrase, some pointed story, even the choice of a single word I used might reach out with a grip of fresh hope.

It's all part of helping folks. For, as His Word mandates:

> Let us hold fast the confession of our hope without wavering, for He who promised is faithful; and let us consider how to stimulate one another to love and good deeds (Heb. 10:23–24).

The following mid-winter poem may stimulate you to reach

beyond the safe bounds of your private, fenced-off territory. It's called "At the Winter Feeder," a perceptive piece by John Leax, professor of English and poet-in-residence at Houghton College:

> His feather flame doused dull
> by icy cold,
> the cardinal hunched
> into the rough, green feeder
> but ate no seed.
>
> Through binoculars I saw
> festered and useless
> his beak, broken
> at the root.
>
> Then two: one blazing, one gray,
> rode the swirling weather
> into my vision
> and lighted at his side.
>
> Unhurried, as if possessing
> the patience of God,
> they cracked sunflowers
> and fed him
> beak to wounded beak
> choice meats.
>
> Each morning and afternoon
> the winter long,
> that odd triumvirate,
> that trinity of need,
> returned and ate
> their sacrament
> of broken seed.

If birds had souls, I have no doubt that cardinal would, long before springtime, yield to the God of his friends. And that which holds true at the winter feeder also works in mid-July.

A Finishing Touch: Attractive adjectives plus unselfish verbs equal faith in the Noun of truth.
A Daily Reading: Hebrews 10

My own concept of God can never remain static after coming into contact with the fictional output of a man driven by such near-spiritual forces, a writer with such a dynamic view of the God who leads man toward scientific maturity. Bradbury, at his best, is not only a prophet for a depressed people; he is a kind of deliverer, awakening our sensibilities.

—Calvin Miller speaking of the writings of Ray Bradbury

Tolkien set out to entertain with his stories—his own children first, and then others. But in the telling, the stories grew into something far grander than anything he himself imagined when he began. That is always the best way. The writer begins with little more than the thread of an idea and the desire to follow it and see where it will go. But as he works at his creation, his labor becomes a sacrifice, of his time if nothing else (but most often, of much else besides). And if he is faithful to the High Quest, God, I believe, accepts the sacrifice and enters into it in ways unforeseen by even the author himself.

—Stephen R. Lawhead speaking of the works of J. R. R. Tolkien

Think about the truth you have seen through the words of others, in both the written word and the spoken word.

Do your own words speak hope, encouragement, and truth to those around you?

CRICKET PLACES

There was once a cricket on the loose in my former church.

When things were quiet and still, his wings sang at top volume . . . like at weddings. And funerals. And during long prayers. And very early on Sunday morning before the place started jumpin' with cars and microphones and organ preludes.

I looked all around for that critter. About the time I thought I'd found him, I was wrong. So, early one Sunday morning, I decided to let the cricket stay. After all, he'd had plenty of time to leave and chose not to.

Who knows? I thought. Maybe there are times crickets need to be in people places just as there are times people need to be in cricket places.

Like out of doors. Surrounded by the sights and sounds and smells of solitude. And rhythmic running streams. And skies so blue it hurts when you stare. And fragrant, wild blossoms that smell of violet. And awesome, jagged cliffs. And soaring hawks. And field mice playing hide 'n' seek. And funny little lightning bugs. And the shrill screams of whippoorwills on misty mornings. You know, cricket stuff . . . so familiar to them they hardly notice any more.

I've got to hand it to my church-visiting insect friend: he knew the value of variety. The vast majority of his ilk are in a rut. They hang around the familiar, identify with millions of other Jiminys, run with the swarm, and never know what the rest of the world is like. Think of all the things "our" cricket heard and felt that most of the world's crickets won't experience in a lifetime! I tell you, the guy had spunk. He was willing to risk whatever to break with the predictable.

Are you? If you're like most, the answer, unfortunately, is no. Robert Pirsig, insightful author of *Zen and the Art of Motorcycle Maintenance* (don't let the title fool you) writes vividly about this. A real believer in traveling free and relaxed—rather than cooped up in the "compartment" of a car—he talks a lot about the thrill of taking it all in while zipping along five inches above the asphalt blur beneath his feet. The man builds a real case for letting the whole cricket scene envelope you, for tasting and feeling and fully digesting a trip across the country, not just enduring monotonous miles, squinting through a Chevy windshield. He touches the "hot button" inside this Harley-ridin' sermonator!

Unless you plan ahead, life will come and go without your making any break with boredom. Not even for a week. Entire seasons and years will pass without a single significant memory being added to your mental museum . . . unless you determine to split from the swarm.

Isn't it about time you made plans to add some variety to your life? To spend time in a completely different setting? Maybe sneak away for a week to the mountains or the desert or maybe near a lake or alongside the crashing surf . . . you know, cricket stuff!

A Finishing Touch: Sometimes crickets need to be in people places; and sometimes people need to be in cricket places.

A Daily Reading: Psalm 148

A bomb exploded in our nation some years ago. In mid-America, of all places. You know . . . the home of apple pie, hot dogs, and Ford Fairlanes. The fuse was lit first in the mind of Karl Menninger, but its effect was not felt until his pen detonated the blasting cap. Suddenly—without prior warning—BOOM! His book, *Whatever Became of Sin*, stunned and shocked his colleagues.

Most of Menninger's peers had put that hated word to bed decades ago. But now, like another Rip Van Winkle, wrinkled and bearded after a long winter's nap, sin was shaken from its slumber. Not by some frustrated seminary grad who had a bone to pick with "shrinks." This explosion was caused by *the* Karl Menninger, M.D., the Freud of America, whose book *The Human Mind* had introduced that branch of medicine to the American public back in 1930. The founder of a psychiatric center in Topeka, Kansas, known all over the world. And that physician, that respected, competent, pioneer of the profession actually had the gall to reintroduce SIN to the vocabulary!

All had been relatively quiet on the Western front. America was still licking its wounds from the riots, campus rebellions, and political assassinations of the sixties. We were biting the bullet of a prolonged war in Southeast Asia. We were hearing rumblings with strange names back then—ecological concerns, energy crises, and "do your own thing." Most of us sensed trouble was brewing . . . *something* was wrong. But none dared call it SIN.

Maybe our president would admit it. Lincoln did, way back in 1863. Eisenhower did, borrowing his words from Lincoln, when the Day of Prayer rolled around exactly ninety years later.

> It is the duty of nations as well as of men to own their dependence upon the overruling power of God, to confess their sins and transgressions in humble sorrow, yet with assured hope that genuine repentance will lead to mercy and pardon.

But Eisenhower's subsequent calls to prayer never mentioned

that explosive term again. In fact, in 1972, Frederick Fox of Princeton University stated in a compelling article entitled "The National Day of Prayer":

> Since 1953, no President has mentioned sin as a national failing. Neither Kennedy, Johnson, nor Nixon. To be sure, they have skirted the word . . . I cannot imagine a modern President beating his breast on behalf of the Nation and praying, "God, be merciful to us sinners."

"As a nation," admitted one wag at the time, "we officially ceased 'sinning' some twenty years ago."

Then came Menninger, who was gutsy enough to declare the truth. Was what he said new? No, not new. It had been there all the time. It just needed to be declared.

Reminds me of the apocryphal story of two parties of Indians in the desert of New Mexico talking to each other by means of smoke signals. Their conversation was moving along quietly as they released puff after puff into the clear desert sky. Suddenly a huge column of smoke appeared and began to climb rapidly some twenty miles into the air. Neither tribe had seen such a sight—nor had the world. It was exactly 5:30 A.M., July 16, 1945.

One Indian leaned over to another, shook his head, and commented, "Wow! I wish I'd said that!"

May we all have the courage to say that—to call sin SIN.

A Finishing Touch: Some words need to be deleted from our vocabulary; others need to be reinstated.

A Daily Reading: Proverbs 14

Have you ever noticed how uniquely adapted each animal is to its environment and its way of life? On land, a duck waddles along ungainly on its webbed feet. In the water, it glides along smooth as glass. The rabbit runs with ease and great bursts of speed, but I've never seen one swimming laps. The squirrel climbs anything in sight but cannot fly (unless you count great airborne leaps from limb to limb), while the eagle soars to mountaintops.

Each creature has its own set of capabilities with which it will naturally excel . . . unless it is expected or forced to fill a mold it doesn't fit. A duck is a duck—and only a duck. It is built to swim . . . not climb. A squirrel is a squirrel—being expected to swim will drive a squirrel nuts. Eagles are beautiful creatures in the air but not in a foot race. The rabbit will win every time—unless, of course, the eagle gets hungry.

What's true of creatures in the forest is true of Christians in the family. God has not made us all the same. He never intended to. He planned that there be differences, unique capabilities, variations in the Body. So concerned was He that we realize this, He spelled it out several times in His Word. I charge you to take the time to read 1 Corinthians 12 slowly and aloud. Those thirty-one verses tell us about His desires and designs—which are more attractive than any thirty-one flavors!

The subject is commonly called "spiritual gifts," and it is as helpful as any truth the believer can ever know. In a nutshell, here's the scoop.

God has placed you in His family and given you a certain mixture that makes you unique. No mixture is insignificant!

That mix pleases Him completely. Nobody else is exactly like you. That should bring you pleasure, too.

When you operate in your realm of capabilities, you will excel and the whole Body will benefit . . . and you will experience incredible satisfaction.

When others operate in their realm, balance, unity, and health automatically occur in the Body. It's amazing!

But when you compare . . . or force . . . or entertain expectations that reach beyond your or others' God-given capabilities, then you can expect frustration, discouragement, mediocrity, and, in the long run, defeat.

If God made you a duck saint—you're a duck, friend. Swim like mad but don't get bent out of shape because you wobble when you run. Furthermore, if you're an eagle saint, stop expecting squirrel saints to soar . . . or rabbit saints to build the same kind of nests you do.

Accept your spiritual species. Cultivate your capabilities. Stop comparing. Enjoy being you!

A Finishing Touch: No one else is exactly like you. Cultivate your capabilities. Refuse to compare or control.

A Daily Reading: 1 Corinthians 12—slowly and aloud!

"Some things are better felt than telt," say our Scottish friends. And that is so true.

Take insight, for example—that elusive weave of intuition, perception, alertness, and sensitivity,. You just can't teach it. You can, however, nurture it. You can even expand it. But, like matter, you can't create it. There's no one-two-three process that suddenly makes one insightful. Yet insight is essential in things like teaching or counseling or writing. When insight is present, those skills literally come alive. The author's page transports you to a vivid world outside your own. The counselor's comment punches through with an incredible ring of significance. The teacher's communication captures and holds attention. Insight makes the simple profound and the difficult understandable. Those who have it were not taught it; they caught it. From God.

Another example? Touch. We refer to a gifted musician as having the right "touch." We don't mean simply the ability to speed through a chromatic scale on the keyboard in four-and-a-half seconds. That can be learned and perfected through practice. But technique is not touch. Not by a long shot.

Touch is that sixth sense that lifts sterile black notes off white pages and transforms them into the colorful and moving strains of a masterpiece. Give some pianists the score and you get harmony and rhythm played with proper timing. Place the same piece before one with touch—and there is no comparison. One plays music. The other experiences it, feels it, is moved by it, understands, is lost in it . . . and helps us do the same.

When this happens, the audience somehow knows there has been a mysterious, unexplainable visit with the composer during the performance. Just as God gifts some to dream and create, He gifts others to interpret. Touch is somehow caught from God, not taught by man. Either you got it or you ain't!

These two extremes pose a practical problem, however: either we feel deprived . . . or we get stuffy because we got it and they ain't.

What a number the enemy does on us!

Hey, let's once and for all put this frustration to bed. If you've "got it" you caught it. You didn't earn it or learn it or deserve it, nor can you preserve it. God sovereignly marked you out and equipped you with that unique ingredient—be it insight or touch or coordination or whatever—to reflect His glory. That's the reason. Try not to forget that.

"And what do you have that you did not receive? But if you did receive it, why do you boast as if you had not received it?" (1 Cor. 4:7).

And what if you're among the so-called have-nots? You're gifted, but it's not one of those abilities that seem so enviable. Remember, the duck, the squirrel, the rabbit, and the eagle we talked about yesterday? You're unique. Your particular gift or ability or capability—whatever it is—is just as significant, just as deliberately planned by God, as any other. It pleased Him to make you like you are—for His glory.

And on top of the responsibility that's yours to contribute your part, you have the added joy of receiving the benefits from those individuals uniquely gifted with things like insight and touch. Those moments come to us on rare occasions in life, not to frustrate us but to refresh us . . . like the soft rush of wind from the flapping of angels' wings.

I don't know how else to describe it. Some things are better felt than telt.

A Finishing Touch: Have you been envious or jealous of another's gift? Just stop and think of what the world would have missed had you not been in it.

A Daily Reading: 1 Corinthians 4

Lost in the silent solitude of recent days, I have been impressed anew with the vast handiwork of our incomprehensible God.

The psalmist was correct: The heavens *do* indeed tell of the glory of God . . . their expanse *does* indeed declare the work of His hands (Ps. 19:1).

And when you mix that unfathomable fact with the incredible reality that He cares for each one of us right down to the last, tiniest detail, the psalmist is, again, correct: Such knowledge is beyond me . . . I cannot even imagine it (Ps. 139:6).

I find God's incomprehensibility absolutely refreshing, especially in a day when managerial moguls prance like peacocks and deified athletes strut their stuff. At a time when one-upmanship and human intimidation have become an art form, it is delightful to be reminded anew that "Our God is in the heavens" and that "He does whatever He pleases" (Ps. 115:3).

He doesn't ask permission. He doesn't bother to explain. He doesn't feel the need to say, "May I?" or "Please." He just does "whatever He pleases," thank you. After all, He is the Lord, the Maker of heaven and earth, the Alpha and the Omega, the sovereign God of all the universe.

Old Zophar was right on target when he asked, "'Can you discover the depths of God? Can you discover the limits of the Almighty? They are high as the heavens, what can you do? Deeper than Sheol, what can you know? Its measure is longer than the earth and broader than the sea. If He passes by or shuts up, or calls an assembly, who can restrain Him?'" (Job 11:7–10).

We need that reminder, we who are tempted to think we're capable of calling the shots. We need to be brought down to size, we who feel we've got a corner on our own destiny.

How many times does our incomprehensible God need to tell us, "My ways are past finding out," before we begin to believe it? How often must He prove to us that He is the Shepherd and we are the sheep . . . that He is the Vine and we are the branches, before we bow and quietly whisper, "Have Thine own way, Lord"? Seems to me that if the Son of God found it necessary at the crossroad of His earthly existence to pray "not as I will, but as Thou wilt" (Matt. 26:39), we would be wise to use the same words often—like every day.

But we're so smart. Not only do we feel capable of declaring His overall plan for our own lives, we think we have the ability to discern each detail of His panoramic plan across the centuries. What a joke! We're doing well to "trust and obey" on a day-to-day basis.

I'll be honest with you, the more I probe the outer limits of our own universe, be it starry sky or stormy sea, majestic mountains or microscopic minutia, the more I want to be still and let the wonder in.

Author Annie Dillard, in her prize-winning work *Pilgrim at Tinker Creek*, touches some of the same chords as she writes: "In making the thick darkness a swaddling band for the sea, God 'set bars and doors' and said, 'Hitherto shalt thou come, but no further.' But have we come even that far? Have we rowed out to the thick darkness, or are we all playing pinochle in the bottom of the boat?"

Such questions do what they're supposed to do: make us uncomfortable. But in our discomfort an essential change takes place. God becomes what and who He should be to us, namely GOD INCOMPREHENSIBLE.

Holy? Of course. Powerful? Yes, no question. Compassionate? Always. Righteous and just? Gracious, loving, self-sufficient, sovereign? All the above, certainly.

But more, so much more. More than we can grasp. More than we can think. More than the brightest among us can even imagine.

We need to discipline ourselves to think on these things! We need to refocus our minds from the horizontal to the vertical. We need to rise above the nonsense of human viewpoint and tedious worries about non-eternal issues. We need to get on with thoughts that really matter.

It's time we got reacquainted with our Maker. It's time we got closer to His thick darkness. Sure beats playing pinochle in the bottom of the boat.

A Finishing Touch: "Teach us to know that we cannot know, for the things of God knoweth no man. . . . Let faith support us where reason fails, and we shall think because we believe, not in order that we may believe" (A. W. Tozer).

A Daily Reading: Read Job 38:1–40:4 nice and slowly.

What are the benefits of realizing God Incomprehensible? We no longer reduce Him to manageable terms. We are no longer tempted to manipulate Him and His will . . . or defend Him and His ways. Like the grieving prophet, we get new glimpses of Him "lofty and exalted," surrounded by legions of seraphim who witness Him as "the Lord of hosts" as they shout forth His praises in antiphonal voice (Isa. 6:1–2). All this gives new meaning to the psalmist's ancient hymn:

> O Lord, our Lord,
> How majestic is Thy name in all the earth. . . .
> When I consider Thy heavens, the work of Thy fingers,
> The moon and the stars, which Thou has ordained;
> What is man, that Thou dost take thought of him? (Ps. 8:1, 3–4).

"What is man . . . ?" What a great question!

In a world consumed with thoughts of itself, filled with people impressed with each other, having disconnected with the only One worthy of praise, it's time we return to Theology 101 and sit silently in His presence. It's time we catch a fresh glimpse of Him who, alone, is awesome—yea, incomprehensible. He is our infinite, inexhaustible God. Any serious study of Him takes us from an unconscious to conscious awareness of our ignorance.

The One we worship defies human analysis.

With the help of a telescope or a microscope we are ushered into a world of incredible, infinite design. Take your choice: planets or paramecia . . . astronomy or biology . . . "the infinite meadows of heaven" (Longfellow) or the diminutive microbes of earth . . . and sheer, unemotional intelligence will force you to mumble to yourself, "Behind all this was more than chance. This design is the result of a designer!" His name? God, the Creator.

To deny that these worlds beyond the lens are the result of God's design is to defy all mathematical calculations of chance. Let me prove that by borrowing the following illustration from a noted scientist and former president of the New York Academy of Sciences, Dr. A. Cressy Morrison. Suppose I would take ten pennies and mark them 1 to 10 and give them to you to put in your pocket. I'd ask you to give them a good shake then I'd say, "I'm going to reach into your pocket and draw out penny number 1." My chance of doing this would be 1 in 10 . . . and you would be surprised if I accomplished it. Now, let's go further. I would put number 1 back in your pocket, have you shake them again, and I'd say, "I will now draw out number 2." Now my chances are much slimmer—1 in 100. If I were to draw out number 3 in the same way, the chance would be 1 in 1000. If I draw out each number in successive order, following the identical process, the ultimate chance factor would reach the unbelievable figure of 1 chance in 10 billion!

If I performed that act before your eyes you would probably say, "The game is fixed" . . . and you would be correct. That's exactly what I am saying about the galaxies and the germs—and, far more importantly, your life and mine on this earth. The arrangement is fixed . . . there is a Designer—God—and He is not silent. As a matter of fact, He declares His presence twenty-four hours a day. How? Listen to Psalm 19:1–2: "The heavens are telling the glory of God;

they are a marvelous display of His craftsmanship. Day and night they keep on telling about God" (TLB).

Let's remind ourselves of a few fundamental, proven facts of science we learned in high school. It is amazing how they dovetail with the first six verses of Psalm 19.

Temperature. The sun is 12,000 degrees Fahrenheit. All of the earth's heat comes from the sun. We are 93 million miles away—just the right distance. If the earth's temperature were an average of 50 degrees hotter or colder, all life on this planet would cease to exist. Why was the earth fixed at exactly the right distance away? Why not twice as far or twice as close? Was this distance deliberately chosen . . . or did it just happen by chance?

Rotation. This planet rotates 365 times each year as it passes around the sun. Suppose it rotated 36 times instead? Well, our days and nights would be ten times as long—we'd be terribly hot on one side and unbearably cold on the other . . . and life would begin to disappear. By chance?

Air. Let's limit ourselves to just one element of air—oxygen. This constitutes about 21% of our atmosphere. Why not 4% or 10% . . . or 50%? Well, if it were 50%, the first time someone lit a match we'd all be toast. Is it 21% by chance?

This planet was designed by God to support one thing: life. Why life? Because only through life can matter understand God and glorify its Maker! Only through faith in the Lord Jesus Christ can the designed know and glorify the Designer.

If you are making no attempt to know and glorify your Designer, you're taking the greatest chance possible. Correction—that's no chance at all. That kind of life has definite consequences and a fixed destiny: eternity in hell . . . lasting separation from your Designer.

Any possibility that you may be the exception? Not a chance.

A Finishing Touch: Telescopes and microscopes can display the design, but only the eyes of faith can see the Designer.

A Daily Reading: Psalm 19:1–6

Most of us did not learn to pray in church. Nor were we taught at school . . . nor even beside our bed at night. If the truth were known, we've done more praying around the kitchen table than anywhere else on earth. From our earliest years we've been programmed: If you don't pray, you don't eat. It started with Pablum and it continues through porterhouse. A meal is incomplete without it.

Our first impressions of communicating with the Almighty were formed in the highchair . . .with cereal and pudding smeared all over our faces. We peeked and gurgled while everybody else sat silent and still. We then learned to fold our hands and close our eyes. Then one day we gave it a try all alone. We mumbled, looked around, got mixed up . . . then quickly closed with a relieved "Amen!" as we searched mom's and dad's faces for approval.

We then went through three adolescent stages common in most Christian families. Stage one . . . *snickering.* For some strange reason, prayer before the meal became the "comedy hour." In spite of parental frowns, glares, and threats, we simply could not keep from laughing. I remember one time my sister and I giggled so long and so loud that Mother finally joined in. My older brother was praying (he usually remembered every missionary from Alaska to Zurich) and never let up. He finished by praying for the three of us!

Stage two . . . *doubting.* This is a cynical cycle, a tough one to endure. We start questioning the habit. We wrestle with "What does it matter if I don't say grace?" or "This is a ritual—it serves no real purpose—God knows I'm grateful." So we stop for a while.

Stage three . . . *preaching.* This one is difficult to handle because it usually comes from well-meaning lips. Out of sincerity and a desire to prompt obedience, we use the time in prayer as an avenue to rebuke a family member or (very subtly) reinforce our own piety. (Parents occasionally fall into this manipulative technique.)

After passing through these stages, however, we begin to realize how good it is to cultivate this healthy habit. In fact, "asking the blessing" is a sweet, needed, refreshing pause during any hectic day.

But since it occurs so often, the easiest trap to fall into is sameness—meaningless, repetitious cliches that might even be boring to God! (Remember, our Lord Jesus warned against the kind of empty verbosity that characterized the Pharisees.)

I haven't got all the answers, but you might start with these suggestions.

Think before you pray. What's on the table? Call the food and drink by name. What kind of day are you facing . . . or have you faced? Pray with those things in mind. Be specific.

Involve others in prayer. Try sentence prayers involving everyone at the table. Or, ask for their requests.

Sing your blessing. The doxology, a familiar hymn, or a chorus of worship offers a nice change of pace. Holding hands adds a lot.

Keep it brief, please. There's nothing like watching a thick film form over the gravy while you plow through all five stanzas of "And Can It Be?"

Occasionally pray after the meal. An attitude of worship is sometimes easier to maintain when stomachs are full.

In case you wonder if your "grace time" is losing its punch, here's a way to find out. When the meal is over, ask if anyone remembers what was prayed for. If they do, great. If they don't, sit back down and discuss why. You've got a lot more to be concerned about than a stack of dishes.

A Finishing Touch: Prayer is truly the pause that refreshes.
A Daily Reading: Luke 11:1–10

It was one of those days.

Demands. Deadlines. Decisions. Endless interruptions mixed with a nagging headache that Tylenol wouldn't erase and positive thinking wouldn't help.

Right in the middle of the mess, a guy poked his head in the door, smiled, and (among other things) dropped a real gem on me. Pre-occupied as I was, the impact of what he said didn't hit me until I was stacking up the stuff I needed to haul home and work on that night. I stopped stacking and started thinking about his comment. His philosophy was to the point.

"The person who knows *how* will always have a job . . . and he will always work for the person who knows *why*."

Stop your own fretting and stacking long enough to drink that in. It will help you. It will force you, of course, to ask yourself, "Which am I?" Both are absolutely essential. If you question that, try to picture 216 presidents in the outfit you work for . . . or 25 managers in the dugout.

People who *know how* are on the front lines and in the trenches, selling the product, teaching the students, fixing the cars, typing the letters, swinging the bats, getting the job done. They will always be the largest in number among the work force.

But there must also be those who *know why*. Those who can harness the energy and give direction, those who can manage and motivate and generate enthusiasm among those who know how.

The difficulty comes when those who know why spend too much time doing things that ought to be done by those who know how, or when those who know how do not know the why behind what they are doing, and when those who should know why do not know (or care) why! These are three of the most common problems in organizations today. In other words: (1) mismanagement—wrong person doing right job; (2) poor communication—not enough information to incite cooperation; and (3) incompetence—weak leader (Peter principle in action).

Just think about the importance of having and communicating the right philosophy behind what you're trying to accomplish. That's absolutely essential in a local church, for example. Without it we spend our time putting out daily fires, trying to wear too many hats, and wondering what our priorities are.

Jesus Christ—our ultimate Leader—has clearly declared our philosophy: "And He gave some as apostles, and some as prophets, and some as evangelists, and some as pastors and teachers, for the equipping of the saints for the work of service, to the building up of the body of Christ" (Eph. 4:11–12).

Don't just scan those words; study them. They form the philosophy of the local church, but they have been virtually ignored in this day of maddening activity.

Why has the Lord given leadership? To equip saints.

Why are the saints to be equipped? To serve.

Why is it so important to serve? To build up the Body.

These are not pick-and-choose issues. They are our foundation . . . our bottom-line philosophy. Press these matters to the max and it's amazing how simple (and exciting!) our job really is.

Who is the major target of our ministry? The Christian. What is the major need in his/her life? Being equipped to serve . . . in the home, in the community, in the world. Everything we do, everything we promote and finance and endorse, should relate directly to equipping and/or serving.

It's invaluable that people in the church know *why* and *how*. Once they do, it's amazing how involved they become in reaching out to the lost.

A Finishing Touch: Are you equipped to serve? Do you know why and how?

A Daily Reading: Ephesians 4

Okay, folks . . . it's that time again. I'm down to two suits, one sports coat, and only a couple of pants that I can squeeze into. No more excuses. I'm tired of good intentions, secret promises to my-self, groans and grunts as I roll out of bed in the morning, and es-pecially those well-meaning comments from first-time visitors at our church: "You look . . . uh . . . different than I expected." I sup-pose that's better than, "You look . . . uh . . . fat." Erma Bombeck's comment about her weight comes to mind. "I'm not telling you what I weigh, but when I measure my girth and step on the scales, I should be a ninety-foot redwood."

Funny thing about being overweight . . . it's impossible to hide it. So the alternatives are (a) ignore it and lie to yourself by saying nobody notices, (b) make jokes about it, (c) try to solve the problem overnight—which is tempting but dumb, or (d) face the music and get underway with a long-range plan that works.

For me, it's an intelligent diet (ugh!) mixed with a program of regular exercise and do-or-die mind-set that is determined to see it through, followed by a from-now-on game plan that is realistic, workable, and consistent. My problem is not glandular or mysteri-ous, it's merely too much food and not enough exercise. For you, the analysis may be far more complicated, requiring a rather elabo-rate process that you are working through. If so, I commend you and I admire you. Stay at it. With me, I just need to stop with one rea-sonable helping. And I need to make time to jog and/or fast walk, plus mix in a little bicycling and other aerobic exercises. It's that simple. It worked for me in the past and I have no doubt it will again.

Personally, I don't need a shrink to shrink. But what I do need is discipline with a big "D." (It might also help me a lot to think of re-wards other than a strawberry sundae.) You know what I'm getting at, don't you? If I intend to avoid great widths, I need to go to great lengths to make that happen. And if you are put together somewhat like I am, you do too. Of course, if you can eat anything in any amount, yet remain perpetually thin and have never had a battle with the bulge, you don't have a clue about this struggle . . . but maybe you'd be kind enough to pray for the majority of us who are thick and tired of it.

So? So why am I telling you all this? It would be much easier and certainly less embarrassing for me to say nothing, eat little, exercise in obscurity, and start to shrink. I did that once before and it worked. Problem was, when I got down to my desired weight, a rumor spread that I had cancer. Cynthia even got a sympathy card or two. So . . . none of that.

I'm mentioning it because I need to be accountable and we need to be reminded of the importance of our physical appearance. While there is an overemphasis on this in the secular world, for some strange reason, we Christians tend to underestimate its importance. Yet our bodies are indeed the "temple of the Holy Spirit" and we are to "glorify God" in those bodies (1 Cor. 6:19–20).

Since this is true, it seems to me that our appearance ought to enhance rather than detract from His wonderful words of life.

So, let's get serious about something we've ignored or excused or joked about long enough. As for me, I've got about forty pounds to go. How about you?

A Finishing Touch: Have you looked in the mirror lately? Could the Spirit's temple stand a little attention to get it back where it ought to be?

A Daily Reading: 1 Corinthians 6:12–20

Have you counted your blessings lately? If not, allow me to prime the pump.

Start with broad categories like family members, close friends, and fellow Christians who help take the sting out of life. Tell the Lord how thankful you are for each, naming them one by one.

Next, think of significant spots where you often find yourself: home, church, school, car, service stations, stores, restaurants, fitness center . . . you complete the list. Express your gratitude for each.

Don't forget your health, eyesight, hearing, taste, smell, and touch. How easy to take these sensory gifts for granted.

And, yes, clothing to keep you warm, sufficient food to nourish your body, a job that pays the bills, good books that stimulate your mind, laughter and tears, a few comforts not found in many other countries, dreams that keep you going, and memories that bring delight.

We dare not forget the Bible and those who teach it, music and those who help us enjoy it, worship with others of the faith, and a few moments of leisure during each week that enable us to flush out our anxieties and gain fresh perspective.

There is one more blessing we can easily overlook. Let's be thankful for angels—those unseen guardians who work overtime, who never slumber or sleep. Think of all the accidents they have prevented, all the little kids they have protected, all the enemy assaults they have resisted.

The Scriptures speak very clearly of the angels. As the thirteenth chapter of Hebrews opens, we encounter a series of commands, among them: "Do not neglect to show hospitality to strangers, for by this some have entertained angels without knowing it" (Heb. 13:2).

I've said for years that that thought alone, if taken seriously, could revolutionize a church's friendliness. Think of it this way: that new face you greet next Sunday could be one of the cherubim or seraphim . . . one of Gabriel's teammates. They look and sound like us, but they are not human. They exist as supernatural creatures in and about heaven, and they are frequently dispatched to earth in human form to bring encouragement and assistance. If you have ever encountered the sudden appearance and/or departure of an angel after receiving one's help, you are never quite the same. Often they leave telltale signs that they are not of this earth. That always puts a chill down my back.

Several years ago some high school fellas from the church I pastored in Southern California went on a mountain-climbing excursion, along with their youth leader. What began as a fun trip led to a frightening experience. Up at higher elevations the temperature can drop rapidly, covering everything in a blanket of sleet and snow in no time . . . and that's exactly what happened. The white peaks and slopes were beautiful scenes to behold. While taking in the breath-taking sights, however, the leader realized he had lost the trail. The heavy snowfall had completely covered the path, and he didn't have a clue where they were or how they could get back to the main camp. His fears weren't helped by the realization that sundown was not that far away and they were not equipped to spend the night on the craggy, windblown slopes where the temperature would soon drop even lower.

The boys became aware of their plight, which only intensified the leader's worries. In situations like that out in the wilderness, prayer flows freely. A dependence on God to rescue is not merely a convenient option; it's a foundational survival technique.

While trudging through the snow, entertaining thoughts just this side of panic, they suddenly heard someone on the slopes above them yell down: "Hey—the trail is up here!" They glanced up and to their relief saw another climber in the distance. He urged them to climb up to where he was if they wanted to get back on the trail. Without hesitation, they began to make their way up to the large boulder where the man was sitting. The climb was exhausting, but their relief in finding the way gave their adrenaline a rush.

Finally, they arrived . . . but to their surprise the man who had yelled at them was nowhere to be found. Furthermore, there were no traces in the snow that anyone had been sitting on the boulder, nor were there footprints around the rock. The trail, however, stretched out before them, leading them to safety. The boys not only learned a valuable lesson about the wilderness, but also firmed up their belief in encountering "angels without knowing it."

God's special messengers are often invisible but never impotent. As the psalmist has written: "He will give His angels charge concerning you, to guard you in all your ways. They will bear you up in their hands, lest you strike your foot against a stone" (Ps. 91:11–12).

It is amazing how many of us have stories of divine deliverance to tell yet seldom take the time to do so. Take time. It will strengthen your faith. Often, it is not until later, after we've had time to think over what transpired, that we realize how directly God was involved in our experience.

A Finishing Touch: Can you think of occasions in your own life when you had what you would consider "a close call." How about one of your kids or friends? Can you remember a time or two when, through some incredible manner, that they were shielded from harm or delivered from danger?

A Daily Reading: Psalm 91

Many years ago one of my mentors told me a story I have never forgotten. A missionary was home on furlough, traveling by car from church to church. Late one rainy evening, facing a long and lonely all-night journey, he asked the Lord to help him stay awake and make it safely to the next place he would minister.

A few minutes later he came upon a man off to the side, thumbing a ride. Although he rarely picked up hitchhikers, he felt sorry for the man out in the rain and offered him a lift. As the two of them began to visit, the missionary was thrilled to discover that the stranger was a believer and that they also had many mutual friends engaged in the Lord's work.

Time passed rapidly as the two of them laughed and shared stories. The fellowship was so rich that the missionary hated to see the early light of dawn and hear his new-found friend say, "Well, here's where I get off." Before saying goodbye, the missionary invited him to have a cup of coffee at a roadside cafe. As they parted, they promised to pray for each other.

The rain had stopped by now, and a bright sun-drenched sky warmed the missionary's soul. Then, a couple of minutes down the road, he realized that he had failed to get the man's address and phone number, so he quickly returned to the cafe. There was no sign of the man. When he asked the cook if he'd seen which way the other fella had gone, he was shocked to hear him respond, "What other fella? You came in here alone . . . I wondered why you ordered two cups of coffee."

The missionary glanced at the table where the two had sat and noticed that the other cup was still full to the brim . . . and the coffee was cold.

As he returned to his car, another surprising realization came to his mind. He remembered that when he had picked up the hitchhiker in the rain the night before, the man had gotten in the car but he wasn't wet!

383

PREDICTABILITY

Few things interest me less than the routine, the norm, the expected, the status quo. Call it the rebel in me, but I simply cannot bear plain vanilla when life has so many other more interesting and tasty flavors.

John Gardner, a United States cabinet member under President Johnson, once pointed out that by their mid thirties most people have stopped acquiring new skills and new attitudes in any aspect of their lives.

Does that jolt you? Stop and think, you who are over thirty. How long has it been since you acquired a new skill? How many new attitudes have you adopted—personal, political, social, spiritual, financial—since you turned thirty? How bound are you to mechanical performance? Must you always drive the same way to work? Are you compelled to approach a problem the same way every time? Does a maverick (even wild) idea challenge you or make you retreat into your shell? Have you lost that enthusiastic zest for discovery or adventure? Are you becoming addicted to predictability?

I'll let you in on a secret: Living and learning go hand in hand; existing and expiring do too. Every day brings a totally new set of circumstances and experiences. The same hours and minutes that capture the wonder of a child deepen the rut of an adult. The constant curiosity and probing inquisitiveness of the preschooler makes every day completely fresh and exciting. To them learning is natural; to many adults it's a nuisance. I find that amazing.

If you are saying to yourself, "Well, that's just the way I am; you can't change me," then you are limiting God, discounting His power and denying His presence. He's offering you an "abundant life," and you're settling for a bland diet of tasteless existence.

Now I'm not suggesting you go out and do stupid stunts to prove your unpredictability. No need to row to Hawaii in a dinghy or scale Mount Everest. However, why not turn your everyday problems into creative projects? Why not take life by the throat and achieve mastery over a few things that have haunted and harassed you long enough. Or how about taking a course at a nearby school, or doing a serious study of some subject all on your own? Why not broaden yourself in some new way to the greater glory of God?

Remember Caleb? He was eighty-five and still growing when he grabbed the challenge of the future. At a time when the ease and comfort of retirement seemed predictable, he fearlessly faced the invincible giants of the mountain. His story is told in Joshua 14. There was no dust on that fella. Every new sunrise introduced another reminder that his body and a rocking chair weren't made for each other. While his peers were yawning, he was yearning.

If you are determined and work quickly, you can keep the concrete of predictability from setting up around you. But if the risks of sailing your ship in the vast ocean of uncertainty make you seasick, you'd better stay near the shallow shores of security. Concrete sinks fast, you know.

A Finishing Touch: I challenge you: this week do something totally unpredictable, even if it's only taking a different route to work. A change of scenery could change your outlook . . . but you'll never know until you try.

A Daily Reading: Joshua 14

Those words aren't original with me. They came from a shrink living in Marin County, California, Pierre Mornell, who wrote a book that bears that title. It's a good one, written in 1978, but you'd think the ink was still wet. The issue that concerned Dr. Mornell is still as prevalent as it is relevant. And it is found in Christian marriages just as often as in non-Christian ones.

It's the problem of the husband who is "inactive, inarticulate, lethargic, and withdrawn at home. In his relationship to his wife he is passive. And his passivity drives her crazy." He's not necessarily incompetent and dull. At work he may be extremely successful and articulate. And she's not necessarily rebellious and overactive. She may be a good mother, talented, and well-respected by her peers.

At home, however, the husband says, in a dozen different ways, "I'm tired . . . just leave me alone." She makes requests; he ignores them. She gets louder; he retreats further. She adds pressure; he lapses into sullen silence. Ultimately he withdraws; she goes "wild."

What, exactly, is the cause of this husband-wife collision course? Actually, numerous, often complex, reasons lie behind such stand-offs, and it would be impossible to attempt an exhaustive list. But a couple of extremely important factors figure into it.

First, men and women are different, and these differences don't decrease or disappear once people get married. (I've discovered that they gain momentum!)

We have the extreme fringes of the feminist movement to thank for trying to lump us all in one big glob of humanity. Ridiculous. Males are different and distinct from females right down to the physical cells in their bodies, not to mention the unique wiring of emotions in their brains.

The husband who forgets this is asking for trouble, and the wife who ignores this will only add to her frustration.

It helps immensely to try to put oneself in the partner's shoes (albeit an extremely tough thing to do) and to realize the other's needs and viewpoint. If you fail to do that, you wind up on the sofa. (Those who prefer carnal escapes to responsible changes—well, they often wind up in someone else's arms, which solves nothing and only complicates the problems.)

Second, harmonious partnerships are the result of hard work; they never "just happen." I don't know of anything that helps this process more than deep, honest, regular communication. Read those last four words again, please. That's not just talking; it's also listening. And not just listening, but also hearing. Not just hearing, but also responding calmly and kindly. In private. With mutual respect. For extended periods of time.

The "hard work" also includes giving just as much as taking, modeling whatever you're expecting, forgiving as quickly as confronting, putting into the marriage more than you ever expect out of it. Yes, more. In one word that I seldom hear (especially from husbands), it means being *unselfish*.

Few things are better for breaking the passive-wild syndrome than taking off for a couple of days together. Without the kids. Without the briefcase (don't laugh, I know a guy who took his PC along with him). Without plans to stay near anyone you know. Without an agenda, other than time to talk and think and listen. And when you retreat, "Let all bitterness and wrath and clamor and slander be put away from you, along with all malice. And be kind to one another, tender-hearted, forgiving each other, just as God in Christ also has forgiven you" (Eph. 4:31–32).

This will go a long way toward keeping you off a counselor's couch . . . or, for that matter, off your own sofa.

A Finishing Touch: How a scale of 1 to 10, how well are you and your spouse communicating?

A Daily Reading: Ephesians 5:22–33

His face was covered with a full beard. His hair fell almost to his shoulders. When he smiled, his white teeth flashed in contrast to the blanket of brown that concealed his skin. His eyes were blue, clear, and alert. His laughter was strong and familiar to my ears. It reminded me of the times—now but a memory—when we sat together as friends in seminary, wrestling with reason and trying to unscrew the inscrutable.

He's now working at a restaurant, playing bluegrass in a four-piece combo. He also has an exciting ministry in a small church where he works with couples. As we had in the old days, we kicked around all sorts of subjects: his marriage, John Denver, the "Body concept" of the local church, banjos and fiddles . . . and the spiritual hunger on university campuses today. That's what we *talked* about, but we *communicated* more, much more.

Despite the separation of the years and the difference in our current life-styles, we were inseparably linked together as one in the bond of love . . . for, indeed, we were. John Baille's statement hung in my head:

> God meets us on a family, rather than on a forensic basis. His dealings with us are not legal but parental. We are not under the law, but under grace. This means simply that what reigns at the center of the spiritual universe is not overbearing power, nor yet calculating justice, but rather outgoing love.

The bite of legalism spreads a paralyzing venom into the Body. Its poison blinds our eyes, dulls our edge, and arouses pride in our heart. Soon our love is eclipsed by a mental clipboard with a long checklist . . . a thick filter requiring others to measure up before we move in. The joy of friendship is fractured by a judgmental attitude and a critical look.

It seems so stupid to me that fellowship must be limited to the narrow ranks prescribed by a grim-and-narrow mindset. Just because I prefer a certain style or attire doesn't mean that it's best . . . nor that it's for everyone . . . nor that the opposite taste is any less pleasing to God.

This gross intolerance of those who don't fit our mold reveals itself in a stoic stare or a caustic comment. Such legalistic and prejudiced reactions will thin the ranks of the local church faster than fire in the basement or flu in the pew.

If you question that, take a serious look at Paul's letter to the Galatians. His pen flowed with heated ink as he rebuked them for "deserting" Christ (1:6), "nullifying the grace of God" (2:21), becoming "bewitched" by legalism (3:1), and desiring "to be enslaved" by this crippling disease (4:9).

Sure there are limits to our freedom. Grace doesn't condone license. Love has its biblical restrictions. The opposite of legalism is not "do as you please." But listen! The limitations of liberty are far broader than most of us realize.

So, the next time you're in Dallas you might want to look up my friend Larry. He plays great mandolin in a top-notch bluegrass combo. He still loves Christ, but he never forces it on you. If you can get beyond his hairy face, you'll find a humble heart.

A Finishing Touch: The bonds of love that bind us are greater than the boundaries that separate us.

A Daily Reading: Romans 14

Marian Anderson, the great contralto who deserved and won worldwide acclaim, didn't simply grow great; she grew great simply. In spite of her fame, she remained a beautiful model of humility.

A reporter, interviewing Miss Anderson, once asked her to name the greatest moment in her life. She had had so many big moments that to the others in the room that day the choice must have seemed difficult. For example:

There was the night conductor Arturo Toscanini announced, "A voice like hers comes once in a century."

Or the day in 1955 when she became the first Negro to sing with the Metropolitan Opera Company of New York.

Or the following year wher her autobiography, *My Lord, What a Morning*, became a bestseller.

In 1958 she became a United States delegate to the United Nations.

Then there was that memorable time she gave a private concert at the White House for the Roosevelts and the King and Queen of England.

And in 1963 she was awarded the coveted Presidential Medal of Freedom.

To top it all, there was that Easter Sunday in Washington D.C. when she stood beneath the statue of Lincoln and sang for a crowd of 75,000, which included Cabinet members, Supreme Court justices, and members of Congress.

Which of those big moments, among many, did she choose? None of them. Miss Anderson quietly told the reporter that the greatest moment of her life was the day she went home and told her mother she wouldn't have to take in washing any more.

Unlike Marian Anderson, some folks go to great lengths to hide their humble origins. We often think we should mask the truth of our past lest people think less of us—especially if our today is much more respectable than our yesterday. But the truth is, when we peel off our masks, others are usually not repelled; they are drawn closer to us. Frequently, the more painful or embarrassing the past, the greater the appreciation and respect.

The prophet Isaiah mentions this very thing as he reminds us to: "Look to the rock from which you were hewn, and to the quarry from which you were dug" (Isa. 51:1).

That sounds much more noble and respectable than its literal meaning, for in the Hebrew text the word *quarry* actually refers to "a hole." Or, as the old King James Version translates it: "Look unto . . . the hole of the pit whence ye are digged."

What excellent advice! Before we get all enamored with our high-and-mighty importance, it's a good idea to take a backward glance at the "hole of the pit" from which Christ lifted us. In fact, let's not just think about it; let's admit it. And don't kid yourself, even those who are extolled and admired have "holes" from which they were dug.

With Moses it was murder. With Elijah it was deep depression. With Peter it was public denial. With Samson it was recurring lust. With Thomas it was cynical doubting. With Jacob it was deception. With Rahab it was prostitution. With Jephthah it was his illegitimate birth.

Why, some of the greatest saints have crawled out of the deepest, dirtiest, most scandalous "holes" you could imagine. And it was that which kept them humble, honest men and women of God, unwilling to be glorified or idolized.

The next time we're tempted to believe our own stuff, let's just look back to the pit from which we were dug. It has a way of shooting holes in our pride.

A Finishing Touch: Remembering the depths from which we have come has a way of keeping us all on the same level: recipients of grace.

A Daily Reading: Isaiah 51

As our world is getting smaller, our minds seem to be following suit. Our level of selfishness is increasing by the day. Suddenly, nobody wants you to invade his or her "space." Sharing may be the major subject in a kindergarten class, but somewhere on the way to adulthood the lessons get erased.

How easy it is to forget that thinking first of the other person did not originate with Dale Carnegie. It comes straight from the Lord our God, who led Paul to write

> Do nothing from selfishness or empty conceit, but with humility of mind let each of you regard one another as more important than himself; do not *merely* look out for your own personal interests, but also for the interests of others (Phil. 2:3–4).

If you think most people follow that counsel, see what happens the next time you're driving into the mall and you slip into a parking spot, not realizing someone else was waiting to occupy it. We're talking borderline homicide.

I've watched people at the grocery store checkout jockey their carts to get ahead in line—to such extremes at times that it leads to an argument a hair this side of a fist fight. All for the sake of saving sixty, maybe ninety seconds. It's like, "This is my space and nobody is going to squeeze me out of it. I'll sue, if necessary!"

Traffic flow or stop streets are also great places to watch this kind of selfishness on display. Instead of everybody taking turns, there's always some clown who thinks he owns the street. Whenever the game plan calls for letting others in or patiently waiting in turn at the intersection, you can count on this guy to cut in. He's the same one who takes up two parking spaces to keep from getting door dings on his precious paint job. Small world, small mind.

This selfish attitude is also alive and well on airplanes. I remember one in particular: I was sitting on a 727 about halfway back in the coach section (three-plus-three configuration) when a family of three came aboard. Apparently they had purchased their tickets late and were unable to secure reserved seating in the same row. The airline attendant assured them that there were several empty seats . . . surely someone would be willing to swap.

My row on the right side was full, as were several others, but just in front of me were two empty seats, middle and window . . . and on the other side, same row, the middle and aisle seats were open.

The family—all of them friendly and courteous—asked the gentleman on the aisle if he would be willing to move from the right side aisle seat to the left side aisle seat. That's all . . . just stand up, take two steps to the left, then sit back down. Just swap seat 17D for seat 17C.

Do you think he'd do it? No way. He wasn't even courteous enough to answer verbally. Just stared straight ahead as he shook his head firmly. And when a flight attendant tactfully tried again, he unloaded a piece of his mind he couldn't afford to lose. I mean the guy absolutely refused to budge. This was his "space," ladies and gentlemen. He had paid good money for it, and there was no way he was going to let anybody, for any reason, take it away from him. Small world, small mind.

While you're smiling in disbelief, this is a good time to mention "your seat" at church . . . you know, the same one you have occupied since the earth's crust cooled. I know, I know, you realize it's not really your seat exclusively. I'm also aware that it doesn't bother you that much, but . . . .

Oops! I'd better quit while I'm ahead. There's no reason to get fanatical about this business of sharing, is there?

Just remember these thoughts the next time someone cuts in front of you, the next time you are patiently (or impatiently?) waiting your turn in the line or at the light and someone charges ahead of you.

Make it an opportunity to practice Sharing 101.

> Therefore, however you want people to treat you, so treat them,
> for this is the Law and the prophets (Matt. 7:12).

A Finishing Touch: Watch for an opportunity to share "your" space.

A Daily Reading: Philippians 2:1–11

A lady took my seat in church a while back. It's not that important really. She is a very nice lady, kind and considerate. A good friend, in fact. There were several other seats available. I can sit any place. The people in our congregation are as friendly and caring as you will find any place in the world. A person should be comfortable sitting any place. It's no big deal.

My seat is in the seventh row back from the front of the church. I'm sure she didn't intend to take my seat. She just wouldn't do that. Nor would anybody else in our fine church. It doesn't make that much difference.

My seat is on the end of the pew, on the north side by the windows. On your left as you come into the sanctuary. I can rest my left arm on the end of the pew. It's a good seat. But I would never raise a fuss about a seat. . . . She probably didn't intend anything personal by taking my seat. I would never hold a grudge. . . .

Actually, it was about three months ago when she took my seat. I really don't know why she took it. I've never done anything to her. I've never taken her seat. I suppose I'll have to come an hour early now to get my seat. Either that or sit on the south side.

She really took it because it's one of the best seats in the house. That's why she took it. She had no business taking my seat. . . . And I'm not going to go to church two hours early to get what was rightfully mine from the beginning.

This is the way great social injustices begin: abusive people taking other people's seats in church. This is the way the seeds of revolution are sown. A person can only stand so much. Where is it going to end? If somebody doesn't stand up and be counted, nobody's seat will be safe. People will just sit any place they please. And the next thing they'll do is take my parking place, too. World order will be in shambles . . . .

—Zean Carney, Editor, *The Banner-Press*
David City, Nebraska, May 9, 1991

WHOSE TEAM?

With the recent death of Richard Nixon and the twenthieth anniversary of his resignation, strangely juxtaposed only a few months apart, the networks have been overloaded with revisits to and retrospectives on Watergate. Names like Liddy and Dean, Mitchell and Magruder, Ehrlichman and Haldeman are suddenly on lips again. While some seem to find this era in our history endlessly fascinating, others wonder why we can't just leave it behind. Can't we just admit that it happened, wrong occurred, consequences followed, and we'll never know the whole story?

Yes, I suppose. Far be it from me to go snooping around for a few harmless skeleton bones . . . if indeed they are harmless. But if there's a larger lesson to be learned from that national embarrassment, maybe its worth the effort of exhuming and examining the remains yet again.

Part of *my* reason for doing so is prompted by a nagging desire to learn everything possible from previous blunders. In that sense, history alone is a wise pedagogue. But another reason I'm intrigued was brought about by a book by Leo Rangell, M.D., a psychiatrist who explores what he calls "the compromise of integrity" in his careful, articulate analysis of the inner workings within the head and psyche of Richard M. Nixon and several of his closest confidants. It's called, appropriately, *The Mind of Watergate*. Within the book is the transcript of a verbal investigation between Senator Howard Baker and young Herbert L. Porter. Here is just a small portion of it.

Baker: "Did you ever have any qualms about what you were doing? . . . did you ever think of saying, 'I do not think this is quite right.' . . . Did you ever think of that?"

Porter: "Yes, I did."

Baker: "What did you do about it?"

Porter: "I did not do anything."

Baker: "Why didn"t you?"

Porter: "In all honesty, probably because of the fear of the group pressure that would ensue, of not being a team player."

Porter's answer keeps coming back to haunt me these days. How much of that whole, ugly nightmare could have been prevented if only someone had had the courage to stand alone? If only the fear of doing wrong had been greater than "the fear of group pressure?" If only the refusal to compromise one's personal integrity had been stronger than the desire to be loyal to the man at the top?

Easy to say but hard to do? Certainly! It's one thing to write stuff like this years after the fog has cleared and anybody can see the black-and-white issues. Hindsight always has 20-20. But given the pressures, fears, insecurities, uncertainties, and group intimidation at the time everything is caving in, it's terribly hard to stand pat and buck the tide . . . alone.

All this strikes much closer to home than a break-in in D.C. or a break-down in the Oval Office. It's a major motivation behind experimentation with drugs or sexual promiscuity or wholesale commitment to some cult or cooperation with an illegal financial scheme. Group pressure is terribly threatening. The screams and shouts of the majority have a way of intimidating integrity.

So be on guard! When push comes to shove, think independently. Think biblically. If you fail to do this, you'll lose your ethical compass somewhere between your longing to be liked and your desire to do what is right. "Do not be misled," warns the apostle who often stood alone, "Bad company corrupts good character" (1 Cor. 15:33 NIV).

Watergate is a timeless lesson: It is not as hard to know what is right to do as to do what you know is right.

A Finishing Touch: If being a team player requires doing what is wrong, you're on the wrong team.

A Daily Reading: Joshua 24:14–15; 1 Corinthians 6:9–11

Ever get the feeling that life's a little too tight—like an ill-fitting shoe? Commitments are piling up and you're taking things much too seriously? You either can't get to sleep or you wake up at two in the morning and spend the next three hours rehearsing everything you have to do and can't possibly get done? It's enough to make a grown man or woman scream. Or curl up in the fetal position and whimper. Or (perish the thought!) work more hours. A guy considers a lot of dumb solutions when the pressure mounts.

So, instead of blaming others or feeling sorry for myself or planning a jump from the Golden Gate, I'm gonna laugh for awhile. If you don't feel like laughing with me, close the book or turn the page. Far be it from me to force you to smile.

But if you, too, think it seems appropriate to laugh at some of the stuff that drives us nuts, here are a few groaners.

A day without a crisis is a total loss.

The other line always moves faster.

Leakproof seals—will. Interchangeable parts—won't.

Inside every large problem are a bunch of little ones struggling to get out.

Whatever hits the fan will not be evenly distributed.

Friends come and go, but enemies accumulate.

The repairman will never have seen a model quite like yours before.

Any tool dropped while repairing a car will roll underneath to the exact center.

No matter how long or hard you shop for an item, after you've bought it, it will be on sale somewhere cheaper.

There's never time to do it right, but there's always time to do it over.

Once you open a can of worms you are never able to recan them.

You will remember you forgot to put the trash out front when the garbage truck is two doors away and you're in the shower.

If you try to please everybody, nobody will like it.

The chance of the bread falling with the peanut butter and jelly side down is directly proportional to the cost of the carpet.

The light at the end of the tunnel is the headlamp of an oncoming train.

When a broken appliance is demonstrated for the repairman, it will work perfectly.

Not until you get home from the party will you realize you have a string of spinach in your teeth.

There's a committee somewhere right now planning your future, and you were not invited to the meeting.

No one's life, liberty, or property are safe while the legislature is in session.

There are hundreds more, but that's enough for now. I feel better already, don't you?

Truly, laughter is often the best medicine.

A Finishing Touch: Don't sweat the small stuff; in fact, the big stuff isn't worth the sweat either.

A Daily Reading: Psalm 35

Not everybody gets "turned on" over management concepts, but most of us can profit from such information. Obviously we can use them in our business or profession, but they can also be helpful at home or church or school. Even as individuals we may find some of these principles coming in handy.

If organizations are not to become stagnant, they must renew themselves—stay continually fresh. Some years back I found some excellent guidelines for this shared by John W. Gardner in a *Harper's* article entitled "How to Prevent Organizational Dry Rot." I've condensed some of his thoughts here.

1. Have an effective program for the recruitment and development of talent. People are the ultimate source of renewal.

2. Don't kill the spark of individuality.

3. Cultivate a climate where comfortable questions can be asked.

4. Don't carve the internal structure in stone. Most organizations have a structure that was designed to solve problems that no longer exist.

5. Have an adequate system of internal communication.

6. Don't become prisoners of procedures. The rule book grows fatter as the ideas grow fewer.

7. Combat the tendency toward the vested interest of a few. In the long run, everyone's vested interest is in the continuing vitality of the organization.

8. The organization must be more interested in what it is going to become than in what it has been.

9. An organization runs on motivation, conviction, and morale. Each person has to believe that his or her efforts as an individual will mean something for the whole and will be recognized by the whole.

10. The profit-and-loss statement is not a clear measure of present performance.

Any of this sound familiar?

Any of it sound helpful?

Any of this reminiscent of those familiar words of the apostle Paul?

> But let all things be done properly and in an orderly manner (1 Cor. 14:40).

And what about your personal renewal. To paraphrase my earlier statement: If individuals are not to become stagnant, they must renew themselves—stay continually fresh.

You think it over. Go back and look at those ten statements in that light . . . then try them on for size.

A Finishing Touch: We should be more interested in what we are going to become than in what we have been.

A Daily Reading: 2 Corinthians 4

The longer I live the less I know *for sure*.

In my younger years I had a lot more answers than I do now. Things were absolutely black or white, right or wrong, yes or no, in or out—but a lot of that is beginning to change. The more I travel and read and wrestle and think, the less simplistic things seem.

I now find myself uncomfortable with sweeping generalities, neat little categories, and well-defined classifications. Take people, for example. They cannot be squeezed into pigeon holes.

> Not all Episcopalians are liberal.
> Not all athletes are thickheaded.
> Not all Republicans are Christian good guys.
> Not all collegians are rebels.
> Not all artists are kooks.
> Not all movies are questionable.
> Not all questions are answerable.
> Not all verses are clear.
> Not all deaths are explainable.

Maybe that list comes as a jolt. Great! Jolts are fine if they make you think. We evangelicals are good at building rigid walls out of dogmatic stones . . . cemented together by the mortar of tradition.

We erect these walls in systematic circles—then place within each our oversimplified, ultra-inflexible "position." Within each fortress we build human machines that are programmed not to think but to say the "right" things and respond the "right" way at any given moment. Our self-concept remains undisturbed and secure since no challenging force is ever allowed over the walls.

Occasionally, however, a strange thing happens: a little restlessness springs up within the walls. A few ideas are challenged. Questions are entertained. Alternative options are then released. Talk about threat! Suddenly our superprotected, cliche-ridden answers don't cut it. The stones start to shift as the mortar cracks.

We can react in one of two ways. One, we can maintain the status quo "position" and patch the wall by resisting change with rigidity. Two, we can openly admit "I do not know" and let the wall crumble. Then we can do some new thinking by facing the facts as they actually are. The more popular, naturally, is the first. We are masters at rationalizing around our inflexible behavior. We imply that change always represents a departure from the truth of Scripture.

Now some changes do pull us away from Scripture, and these must definitely be avoided. But let's be absolutely certain that we are standing on scriptural rock not traditional sand. We have a changeless message—Jesus Christ—but He must be proclaimed in a changing, challenging era. That calls for a breakdown of stone walls and a breakthrough of fresh, keen thinking based on scriptural insights.

No longer can we offer tired, trite statements that are as stiff and tasteless as last year's gum beneath the pew. The thinking person deserves an intelligent, sensible answer, not an oversimplified bromide mouthed by insensitive robots within the walls.

All I ask is that you examine your life. For, as Socrates said, "The unexamined life is not worth living."

A Finishing Touch: It you've stopped thinking and started going through unexamined motions, you've really stopped living and started existing.

A Daily Reading: Psalm 26

Cynthia and I were enjoying a quiet evening at home. The house was unusually still, and we were sitting there sipping freshly perked coffee and having a quiet conversation. You know, one of those priceless moments you wish you could wrap up and bring out again when you really need it.

For some reason our discussion turned to the subject of Christ's return. Our comments ranged from chuckling over letting the folks in the tribulation worry about cleaning out our garage to contemplating the joys that will be ours as we share eternity with family and friends in the Body of Christ.

Later that evening, however, I found myself returning again and again to the thought, *He is coming back. What a difference it will make!*

It is remarkable, when you stop and get specific about it, how many things we take for granted will suddenly be removed or changed drastically when He returns.

It is also amazing what an overhaul job that does on our scale of values: the stuff we tend to cling to and gloat over and want more of. Christ's return has a way of smashing our idols of materialism and thumping us back to the basics.

Sure, I realize that a lot of heavenly minded nuts have done some dumb things by going to extremes over prophecy. Those who set hard-and-fast dates always make me smile. But that night, God seemed to be saying to me: "Loosen your grip, my son, and try to remember that the bottom line of everything is eternity with Me."

Think about that . . . .

Is it a waste of time to focus on the Lord's return? Quite the contrary. It's *biblical*; it's the very thing Titus 2:13 says we ought to do: "Looking for the blessed hope and the appearing of the glory of our great God and Saviour, Christ Jesus."

When was the last time you—on your own—meditated on that fact?

If you're like me, it's been too long. People who are more practical than mystical, who are realistic rather than idealistic, tend to shove that stuff to times like funerals or near-death experiences. Most of us are more here-and-now than then-and-there people.

But Scripture says we are to "comfort one another" with information about Jesus' return for us (1 Thess. 4:13–18). It says these truths form the very foundation of a "steadfast, immovable, always abounding" life-style (1 Cor. 15:50–58).

Listen, this Bible of ours is full and running over with promises and encouragements directly related to the return of our Lord Jesus Christ. It's not just hinted at; it's *highlighted*. It's an obvious theme of New Testament truth. You can't read very far without stumbling upon it, no matter which book you choose. In the New Testament alone the events related to Christ's coming are mentioned over 300 times. It's like white on rice.

Critics have denied it. Cynics have laughed at it. Scholars have ignored it. Liberal theologians have explained it away (they call that "rethinking" it) and fanatics have perverted it. "Where is the promise of His coming?" many still shout sarcastically (2 Peter 3:4). The return of our Saviour will continue to be attacked and misused and denied. But there it stands, solid as a stone, offering us hope and encouragement amidst despair and unbelief.

"Okay, swell. But what do I do in the meantime?" I can hear all pragmatists asking.

First, it might be best for you to understand what you don't do. You don't sit around, listening for some bugle call or looking for the rapture cloud. You don't quit work. And you don't try to set the date because "the signs of the times" are so obvious!

You do get your act together

You do live every day (as if it's your last) for His glory.

You do work diligently on your job and in your home (as if He isn't coming for another ten years) for His Name's sake.

You do shake salt out every chance you get . . . and you do shine the light . . . and remain balanced, cheerful, winsome, and stable, anticipating His return day by day.

Other than that, I don't know what to tell you.

Except, maybe, if you're not absolutely sure you're ready to fly, you get your ticket fast. As long as they are available, they're free.

405

But don't wait. About the time you finally make up your mind, the whole thing could have happened, leaving you looking back instead of up.

What good is a ticket if the event is over?

A Finishing Touch: He is coming! What a difference it will make!
A Daily Reading: 1 Corinthians 15:50–58

Are you living every day (as if it's your last) for His glory?

Do you work diligently at your job and in your home (as if He isn't coming for another ten years) for His name's sake?

Do you shake salt and shine the light every chance you get?

Do you remain balanced, cheerful, winsome, and stable, anticipating His return?

> But we do not want to be uninformed, brethren, about those who are asleep, that you may not grieve, as do the rest who have no hope.
>
> For if we believe that Jesus died and rose again, even so God will bring with Him those who have fallen asleep in Jesus.
>
> For this we say to you by the word of the Lord, that we who are alive, and remain until the coming of the Lord, shall not precede those who have fallen asleep.
>
> For the Lord Himself will descend from heaven with a shout, with the voice of the archangel, and with the trumpet of God; and the dead in Christ shall rise first.
>
> Then we who are alive and remain shall be caught up together with them in the clouds to meet the Lord in the air; and thus we shall always be with the Lord.
>
> Therefore comfort one another with these words (1 Thess. 4:13–18).

Might be a good idea to commit these six verses to memory. You never know when you're going to need to comfort someone with these words.

How's it going with you and the kids?

Maybe that question doesn't even apply to you. You may be single or you may not have children or you may have already raised your brood. If so, bear with me while I address those of you who are still in the process of training and rearing.

So, how's it going? What word(s) would you check to describe your overall relationship with your offspring?

___ Challenging

___ Strained

___ Pleasant

___ Impossible

___ Angry

___ Threatening

___ Adventurous

___ Heartbreaking

___ Impatient

___ Exciting

___ Fun

___ Busy

If you want to get your eyes opened to the facts, ask your kids this question at the supper table tonight. Ask them to describe their feelings about you and their home. I'd better warn you—it may hurt! But it could be the first step in the right direction . . . the first step toward the restoration of harmony and genuine love under your roof.

Needless to say, having a Christian home is no guarantee against disharmony. The old nature can still flare up, habits set in concrete can lead to broken communication lines, and biblical principles can be ignored. So face the truth, my friend. Stop right now and think about your home.

An evaluation is no good if all it leads to is guilt and hurt. To stop there would be like a surgeon stopping the operation immediately after making his incision. All it would leave is a lot of pain and a nasty scar.

Take time to get next to your children . . . to come to grips with barriers that are blocking the flow of your love and affection (and their's) . . . to face the facts before the fracture leads to a permanent, domestic disease.

Three biblical cases come to my mind:

Rebekah, who favored Jacob over Esau and used him to deceive his father, Isaac, which led to a severe family breakdown (Gen. 27).

Eli, who was judged by God because of his lack of discipline and failure to stand firm when his boys began to run wild (1 Sam. 3:11–14).

David, who committed the same sin against his son, Adonijah, by never disciplining him during his early training (1 Kings 1:5–6).

You see, no one is immune . . . not even you. So move ahead. Refuse to pamper your parental negligence any longer.

A Finishing Touch: Take time to evaluate the present condition of your home. Then take the steps needed to strengthen the weaknesses you uncover.

A Daily Reading: Psalm 127

Tucked away in a quiet corner of Scripture is a verse containing much emotion.

> From the city men groan,
> And the souls of the wounded cry out . . . (Job 24:12).

The scene is a busy metropolis. Speed. Movement. Noise. Rows of buildings. Miles of apartments, houses, restaurants, stores, schools, cars, bikes, kids. All that is obvious, easily seen and heard by the city dweller.

But there is more. Behind and beneath the loud splash of human activity there are invisible aches. Job calls them "groans." That's a good word. The Hebrew term enlarges it as it suggests that this groan comes from one who has been wounded. Perhaps that's the reason Job adds the next line in poetic form, "the souls of the wounded cry out." In that line, *wounded* comes from a term that means "pierced." But he is not referring to a physical stabbing, for it is "the soul" that is crying out.

Job is speaking of those whose hearts have been broken . . . those who suffer from the blows of "soul stabbing," which can be far more bloody and painful than "body stabbing." The city is full of such . . . the wounded, bruised, and broken, crying out in groans from the heart.

That describes some of you, I am certain. You may be "groaning" because you have been misunderstood or treated unfairly. The wound is deep because the blow came from one whom you trusted and respected. It's possible that hurt was brought on by the stabbing of someone's tongue. They are saying things that simply are not true, but to step in and set the record straight would be unwise or inappropriate. So you stay quiet . . . and bleed. Perhaps a comment was made only in passing, but it pierced you deeply.

Others of you are living with the memories of past sins or failures. Although you have confessed and forsaken those ugly, bitter days, the wound stays red and tender. You wonder if it will ever heal. Although it is unknown to others, you live in the fear of being found out . . . and rejected.

Tucked away in a quiet corner of every life are wounds and scars. If they were not there, we would need no Physician. Nor would we need one another.

> Hast thou no wound? . . .
> No wound, no scar?
> Yet, as the Master shall the servant be,
> And, pierced are the feet that follow Me;
> But thine are whole: can he have followed far
> Who has no wound nor scar? (Amy Carmichael).

A Finishing Touch: Only the Great Physician can turn our ugly wound into a scar of beauty.

A Daily Reading: Psalm 147

"Grab here, amigo." I grabbed.

"Hold on tight, por favor." I held on.

"When you come back toward the shore and I blow whistle, you pull cord pronto!"

Within seconds I was airborne. A loud "whoosh," a long strong jerk, and I was three hundred feet or so above the picturesque beach at Puerto Vallarta.

You guessed it . . . my first try at parasailing. Four-and-a-half minutes of indescribable ecstasy sandwiched between a few seconds of sheer panic. Talk about fun!

Above me was the bluest, clearest sky you could imagine. Behind me was a full-blown dazzling red and white parachute. Down in front, attached to my harness and a long yellow rope, was a speed boat at full throttle. Below, the turquoise sea, various sailing vessels, a long row of hotels, sun bathers the size of ants, and one beautiful lady wondering if she would soon be a widow.

The wind whipped through my hair and tore at my swimsuit. But the sensation of flying in silence with nothing surrounding me besides a few nylon straps was absolutely breathtaking. The spectacular view plus the feeling of soaring like a seagull introduced me to an adventurous freedom rarely encountered by earth dwellers.

I must confess, for those few minutes I forgot everything else. Self-consciousness vanished. Worries fled away. Demands and deadlines were erased by the swishing sound of the wind. It was glorious! Never, since childhood, have I felt quite so free, so unencumbered, so completely removed from others' expectations and my own responsibilities.

I like to think that might be the true, authentic, carefree kind of leisure and relaxation Jesus had in mind when He encouraged His twelve to come apart and rest awhile.

How easily we forget the necessity of recreation; how quickly we discount its value! In our neurotic drive for more, more, more, we become all roots and no wings.

Life closes in and takes the shape of a chore instead of a challenge. Fun and laughter, originally designed by God to remove the friction of monotony from the machinery of existence, begin to be viewed as enemies instead of friends. Intensity, that ugly yet persuasive twin of hurry, convinces us we haven't the right to relax . . . we must not take time for leisure . . . we can't afford such rootless, risky luxury. Its message is loud, logical, sensible, strong, and wrong.

We all need roots *and* wings. But most of us are long on the former and short on the latter.

Whether it's a longed-for trip to Europe or a relaxing weekend at a picturesque Bed and Breakfast, a fishing trip to Alaska or an afternoon canoe trip down a nearby river, try some winged adventure. Expand your world, free your mind, and calm your nerves. Don't wait! Quit worrying about the risk or complaining about the cost.

Take time to soar!

A Finishing Touch: "If we don't come apart, we will come apart" (Vance Havner).

A Daily Reading: Mark 6

Who really cared? His was a routine admission to busy Bellevue Hospital. A charity case, one among hundreds. A drunken bum from the Bowery with a slashed throat. The Bowery . . . last stop before the morgue. Synonym of filth, loneliness, cheap booze, drugs, and disease.

The derelict's name was misspelled on the hospital form, but then what good is a name when the guy's a bum. The age was also incorrect. He was 38, not 39, and looked twice that. Somebody might have remarked, "What a shame for one so young," but no one did. Because no one cared.

The details of what had happened in the predawn of that chilly winter morning in New York were fuzzy. The nurses probably shrugged it off. They had seen thousands and were sure to see thousands more.

His health was gone and he was starving. He had been found lying in a heap, bleeding from a deep gash in his throat. His forehead was badly bruised and he was semiconscious. A doctor used black sewing thread to suture the wound. Then the man was dumped in a paddy wagon and dropped off at Bellevue Hospital, where he languished and died. But nobody really cared.

A friend seeking him was directed to the local morgue. There, among dozens of other nameless corpses, he was identified. When they scraped together his belongings, they found a ragged, dirty coat with 38 cents in one pocket and a scrap of paper in the other. All his earthly goods. Enough coins for another night in the Bowery and five words, "Dear friends and gentle hearts." Almost like the words of a song, someone may have thought.

Which would have been a correct, for once upon a time that man had written the songs that literally made the whole world sing. Songs like "Camptown Races," "Oh! Susanna," "Beautiful Dreamer," "Jeanie with the Light Brown Hair," "Old Folks at Home," "My Old Kentucky Home," and two hundred more that have become deeply rooted in our rich American heritage.

Thanks to Stephen Collins Foster.
Makes me think of an old poem preachers once quoted:

> And many a man with life out of tune,
> And battered and scarred with sin,
> Is auctioned cheap to the thoughtless crowd,
> Much like the old violin.
> A "mess of pottage," a glass of wine;
> A game—and he travels on.
> He's "going" once, and "going" twice,
> He's "going" and almost "gone."

Almost. Almost gone. Until someone cares. And steps in. And stoops down. And, in love, restores a soul, rekindles a flame that sin snuffed out, and renews a song that once was there.

Some of these souls are in prison. Some in hospitals. Some in nursing homes. And some silently slip into church on Sunday morning, confused and afraid.

Do you care? Enough "to show hospitality to strangers," as Hebrews 13:2 puts it? It also says that in doing so, we occasionally "entertain angels without knowing it."

Angels who don't look anything like angels. Some might even look like bums from the Bowery, but they may have a song dying in their hearts because nobody knows and nobody cares.

A Finishing Touch: Deep within many a forgotten life is a scrap of hope, a lonely melody trying hard to return.

A Daily Reading: Hebrews 13:1–3

Getting a big job done calls for heart.

Having a high IQ is not essential. Neither is being a certain age. Or possessing a particular temperament. You don't even need the backing of the majority. History books are full of incredible stories of men and women who accomplished remarkable feats in the face of unbelievable odds.

The record books also include the opposite, of course: powerful possibilities that failed to reach full potential due to the loss of "heart."

Napoleon comes to mind. By early 1812, he ruled most of Europe. Every army that opposed him had been defeated. Not only had he provoked the resignation of the last Holy Roman Emperor, he had married the man's daughter. Except for three final "details"—Britain, Spain, and Russia—the French Caesar had everything he wanted. So that year, he decided to invade Russia.

Having mustered his army, Napoleon trounced Russia in a couple of major battles. Even though the Russian army made a gallant last stand, Moscow fell. And by October 1812 Napoleon sat in Moscow, surrounded by his undefeated troops. Nothing on the horizon seemed impossible.

But something happened that changed all that.

Though no one seems to know how it started, a fire broke out in Moscow. It burned much of the city, leaving Napoleon's army without sufficient food, supplies, and protective winter quarters.

Napoleon was forced to abandon the city. He headed west amidst a bitter Russian winter, with the Czar's troops at his heels. All of which proved too much for the once-valiant army of Napoleon.

Within two months of his greatest victory, Napoleon's army had virtually ceased to exist. He struggled on for two more years, but after Moscow he was a beaten man. Interestingly, the reason was not a loss on the battlefield . . . it was a loss of heart. Brilliant and visionary though he was, he was unable to keep his troops alive.

When Moscow went up in flames, Waterloo was inevitable. Why? Because troops without heart can't fight.

While reading through the exciting story of Nehemiah recently, I was reminded again of this principle. You remember Nehemiah, the Jewish leader whose passion for Jerusalem drove him to leave the security of his home and job in Persia to superintend the building of a protective wall around Zion. What a project! And what obstacles stood against him! But the job got done in record time. Why? Because everybody near and far thought the wall project was a neat idea? Because he had thousands of skilled craftsmen who loved masonry work? Get serious. Nehemiah stated the reason in his journal entry: "So we built the wall . . . for the people had a mind to work" (Neh. 4:6).

Check the margin of your Bible. The term translated "mind" is the Hebrew word for *heart*. Another word for it might be *courage*. In fact, they are related.

In an early copy of Webster's dictionary (1828), the author points out that courage comes from *coeur*, the French word for heart: "Courage is the quality that enables one to face difficulty and danger with firmness, without fear or depression." And then, as Webster (a born-again Christian) often did in those days, he concluded his definition with a Scripture reference: Deuteronomy 31. That chapter includes Moses' final speech to the children of Israel, shortly before his death and Joshua's taking up the torch of leadership.

> "Be strong and courageous, do not be afraid or tremble at them, for the Lord your God is the one who goes with you. He will not fail you or forsake you." Then Moses called to Joshua and said to him in the sight of all Israel. "Be strong and courageous, for you shall go with this people into the land which the Lord has sworn to their fathers to give them, and you shall give it to them as an inheritance. And the Lord is the one who goes ahead of you; He will be with you. He will not fail you or forsake you. Do not fear, or be dismayed" (Deut. 31:6–8).

At 120 years of age, Moses tells 'em, "Ya gotta have heart!"

Not being people of great courage (they'd been slaves in Egypt for over four hundred years), Moses knew how easy it would be for Joshua and his troops to lose heart.

I'm not suggesting that all of us must be Nehemiahs or Joshuas. Sometimes that may be necessary. But I have observed over the years that some of the greatest demonstrations of courage occur in private places. At home when dealing with a child's willful defiance or a teenager's rebellion, or facing one's own selfishness, or in a board meeting when you're in the minority. Sometimes just staying with something over the long haul—maintaining the vision year after year—is magnificent proof of a courageous heart. I understand that Westminster Abbey took hundreds of years to complete, under the direction of numerous successive architects. Yet, because each architect stayed with the original design, the structure remained a true representation of the period of its inception. Faithfully, consistently, diligently, each architect showed quiet courage.

You may or may not be a leader. You may or may not be led to accomplish some major wall-building project. You may or may not manage an office of people. You may or may not be engaged in shaping the lives of several children at home. But chances are good that you are influencing others in some measure. Don't just watch things happen. Get in there with both feet. Risk, for a change. Make some waves. Cut a new swath. Quit waiting for the other guy. You get the job done!

One reminder: Ya gotta have heart.

A Finishing Touch: "Great deeds are usually wrought at great risks" (Herodotus).

A Daily Reading: Deuteronomy 31

Leaders must go beyond analysis to action. One cannot lead without energy, motion, risk. Leaders are pathfinders, roadmakers, action-takers.

Cowardice, to put it bluntly, is an ungodly trait. God is not passive in the face of evil, nor is He indecisive.

The Psalms are full of powerful lyrics that give us a clear portrait of the Lord God. Never is He portrayed as a mild-mannered, passive Deity, hoping and waiting for things to happen. Always He is aggressively engaged in an all-out war against injustice and inequity.

Righteousness and truth are causes to be fought for. If left to fend for themselves, they can't withstand the overpowering huns of heathenism.

In every generation, then, conflict is inevitable. And the ammunition for such conflicts? You guessed it. Heart.

Do you have it?

Do you take courageous action in the face of wrong?

Will you stand alone, if necessary, and embrace a principle, even though it means you lose votes or friends or prestige . . . or whatever?

Are you an intellectual analyzer of wrong, a mere advocate of achievement, a person who enjoys discussions of issues to the point of getting bogged down in unproductive semantics . . . or do you translate ideas into action?

I have a close friend who spent a day at San Diego's *Seaworld*. While he and his wife were near the main mall, they saw something unusual in the distance: a bunch of ducks coming toward them . . . on roller skates! They could do it, my friend said, but as they got closer, he could tell that they didn't have their hearts in it.

Some folks are ducks on roller skates; they can do what they do, but they don't have their hearts in it.

A HIGH CALLING

Many professions draw public attention like warm watermelon draws flies. Those who practice them are constantly in the news.

If it isn't the money they make, it's the company they keep or the trends they set or the controversy they spawn. Their notoriety is somewhere between amazing and appalling. In a society like ours, they are significant and often irreplaceable, even though we sometimes wrestle with that. But—as is always the case—the lunatic fringe sells papers, so those with integrity are often forced to practice their profession against the tide of misunderstanding made worse by stormy winds of suspicion.

There is one profession, however, that is neither notorious nor controversial.

Although essential to our future as a nation, being inseparably linked to the home as few other professions are, it has been treated like a stepchild.

Those who make their living in this field press on against overwhelming odds. They live with criticism they usually don't deserve. They invest extra hours for which they are never compensated. They maintain a standard of excellence regardless of resistance. They remain enthusiastic in spite of daily discouragements. They apply creativity and every motivational technique they can muster without applause or thanks from their recipients.

Fueled by hope, these brave men and women shape minds, stretch imaginations, challenge thinking, and model consistency. They have one major enemy they fight with tireless energy: ignorance.

Although he snarls in defiance, clothed in the armor of prejudice and defending himself with the sword of pride, he is ultimately forced to surrender to his skilled opponent. Knowledge will inevitable win out. The truth makes free.

420

And who are those commanding the winning side? Who are the relentless, courageous heroes I'm describing?

By now you know. They are those who teach.

Teachers ply their skills in classrooms large and small all over the globe. The tools of their trade may not seem that impressive—a piece of chalk, a book, an overhead projector, a homework assignment, a smile of encouragement, a nod of affirmation, a strong word of warning, a grade, a project, a question to answer, a problem to solve, a commitment to stubborn facts, tact and timing, a provocative idea—yet they are the very instruments that give keen edges to otherwise dull minds. How powerful are those adept with such tools!

Teachers. Tough-minded, clear-thinking, ever-learning educators who gave me their time and their attention, who early on overlooked my immaturity, who saw raw material behind my boredom, overactivity, and mischievousness, who refused to get sidetracked, who held my feet to the fire and dared me to grab the challenge, who had enough wisdom to drop the bait in just the right places to hook me for life.

So to all of you who teach, hat's off. Yours is an invaluable profession, a calling sure and high and noble, a model we cannot live without if we expect to remain strong and free.

Don't quit. Don't even slack off. If ever we needed you, we need you today.

A Finishing Touch: Think about those who taught you. Thank God for them and the lifelong value of their investment in you.

A Daily Reading: Ephesians 4:11–16

I've never had a strong desire to be a teacher. Obviously as a Christian leader with a pastor's heart, I teach on a regular basis. But the thought of being a professional teacher—standing up before a class of college or high school or grade school students day in and day out—has never given me an adrenaline rush.

Don't get me wrong. I admire tremendously those who teach. Good teachers are invaluable as we make our way along the pathway of life.

I can think of several from my days in school, going all the way back to the elementary school on Evergreen Street in East Houston.

It was a teacher in junior high who taught me to love science.

It was a teacher in high school who got me hooked on history. Another teacher helped me overcome stuttering and learn how to speak in public . . . how to think on my feet . . . how to pace the delivery of words . . . how to use humor.

And it was yet another teacher who passed along the practical techniques I still use in digging pearls out of scriptural oysters.

So, let me firmly establish this fact: I am deeply indebted to several teachers. If you teach, be encouraged! You probably have no idea how great a contribution you are making.

If I *were* to teach, however, I think I would keep a personal journal of the funny things my students said.

I don't mean the jokes they told in class to try to distract the teacher or derail the discussion (anyone ever done that?!). I mean the things they said in all seriousness—the things they said or wrote that were unintentionally funny. Like answers they gave on quizzes, which were seriously written but hilariously wrong.

Actually, Richard Lederer must have had the same brilliant idea. In fact, he even published the mistakes in a book cleverly titled *Anguished English*, in which he sort of pastes together the "history" of the world from genuine student bloopers collected by teachers throughout America, from eighth grade through college level.

Here are a few examples. Hold on tight . . . there's a lot to be learned that you may have missed in your years in school.

For example, did you know that Ancient Egypt was inhabited by mummies who wrote in hydraulics? They lived in the Sarah Dessert and traveled by Camelot. Certain areas of that dessert were cultivated by irritation.

Then we learn that in the first book of the Bible, Guinessis, Adam and Eve were created from an apple tree. One of their children, Cain, asked, "Am I my brother's son?"

After that, Pharaoh forced the Hebrew slaves to make bread without straw, and Moses went up on Mount Cyanide to get the ten commandments. He died before he ever reached Canada.

Later we learn that David was a Hebrew king skilled at playing the liar. He fought with the Finkelsteins. Solomon, one of his sons, had 300 wives and 700 porcupines.

See why I have no compelling desire to be a teacher?

As I said yesterday, hats off to you who do! You deserve a tall statute on the campus in your honor.

A Finishing Touch: "A teacher affects eternity; he can never tell where his influence stops" (Henry Brooks Adams).

A Daily Reading: James 3:1–12

I'm a sports fan. I'm sure that comes as news to no one!

For some strange reason, even when I was growing up I could re-member the most amazing details—okay, maybe *trivia* is a better word—about different ball players: where some all-pro offensive guard went to high school, the average weight of a defensive line, a guy's batting average in 1969, or another's free throw percent-age . . . when some coach changed his strategy (and why), as well as the reason for a little technicality of a rule. You know, stuff no-body really cares to hear, but nevertheless sticks in my head . . . the way it does with most sport fans.

Another characteristic of a fan is an indomitable sense of com-mitment or determination—okay, okay, maybe addiction *is* a better word! Against incredible odds, sound logic, and even medical ad-vice, sports fans will persevere to the dying end! Difficulties are viewed as a challenge . . . a hurdle to be jumped . . . a mountain to be scaled . . . never an excuse to stay away!

I've often wondered what would happen if people were as intense and committed and determined about church as they are about sports—or any number of other pastimes.

This was reinforced some years back in a *Moody Monthly* piece which illustrated twelve excuses a fella might use for "quitting sports." The analogy isn't hard to figure out.

> Every time I went, they asked me for money
> The people with whom I had to sit didn't seem very friendly.
> The seats were too hard and not comfortable.
> The coach never came to call on me.
> The referee made a decision with which I could not agree.
> I was sitting with some hypocrites—they came only to see what others were wearing.
> Some games went into overtime, and I was late getting home.
> The band played numbers that I had never heard before.
> The games are scheduled when I want to do other things.

My parents took me to too many games when I was growing up.
Since I read a book on sports. I feel that I know more than the coaches anyhow.

I don't want to take my children, because I want them to choose for themselves what sport they like best.

I've come up with a few more:

The parking lot was awful . . . I had to walk six blocks to the stadium.

Nobody came up and introduced themselves to me . . . very impersonal, also loud!

The public address and lighting systems don't suit me.

It's always too hot (or cold) in the stadium.

An usher offended me.

They sold out one Sunday . . . and I had to watch the game on T.V.

Enough said. Think it over.

A Finishing Touch: What would happen if we approached church responsibilities with the same enthusiasm we give to our hobbies, sports, and other extracurricular activities?

A Daily Reading: Hebrews 10:23–25

Nobody is a whole chain. Each one is a link. But take away one link and the chain is broken.

Nobody is a whole team. Each one is a player. But take away one player and the game is forfeited.

Nobody is a whole orchestra. Each one is a musician. But take away one musician and the symphony is incomplete.

Nobody is a whole play. Each one is an actor. But take away one actor and the performance suffers.

Nobody is a whole hospital. Each one is part of the staff. But take away one person and it isn't long before the patient can tell.

Cars are comprised of numerous parts. Each one is connected to and dependent upon the other. Even a tiny screw, if it comes loose and falls out of the carburetor, can bring the whole vehicle to a stop.

You guessed it. We need each other. You need someone and someone needs you. Isolated islands, we're not.

To make this thing called life work, we gotta lean and support. And relate and respond. And give and take. And confess and forgive. And reach out and embrace. And release and rely.

Especially in the God family . . . where working together is Plan A for survival. And since we're so different (thanks to the way God built us), love and acceptance are not optional luxuries. Neither is tolerance. Or understanding. Or patience. You know, all those things you need from others when your humanity crowds out your divinity.

In other words:

> Love each other with brotherly affection and take delight in honoring each other. Never be lazy in your work but serve the Lord enthusiastically. Be glad for all God is planning for you. Be patient in trouble, and prayerful always. When God's children are in need, you be the one to help them out. And get into the habit of inviting guests home for dinner, or if they need lodging, for the night (Rom. 12:10–13 TLB).

Why? Because each one of us is worth it. Even when we don't act like it or feel like it or deserve it.

Since none of us is a whole, independent, self-sufficient, super-capable, all-powerful hotshot, let's quit acting like we are. Life's lonely enough without our playing that silly role.

The game's over. Let's link up.

A Finishing Touch: "No man is an island, entire of itself; every man is a piece of the continent . . . " (John Donne).

A Daily Reading: Romans 12

I once ministered in the shadow of Harvard University, and our little church in Waltham, Massachusetts, attracted a few of the Harvard students.

Interesting place, Harvard. If you're ever in Boston you owe it to yourself to drive to nearby Cambridge and visit the campus. When you do, don't miss reading the cornerstone at the old gate giving entrance to the legendary Harvard Yard. In case you never have that opportunity, let me repeat it here. In light of the school's liberal reputation, you may find these words surprising.

> After God had carried us safe to New England and we had builded our houses, provided necessaries for our livelihood, reared convenient places for God's worship and settled the civil government, one of the next things we longed for and looked after was to advance learning and perpetuate it to posterity, dreading to leave an illiterate ministry to the churches when our present ministers lie in the dust.

This, our nation's first institution of higher learning, was founded in 1636 . . . only sixteen years after the pilgrims landed at Plymouth. It was named after John Harvard, a minister of the Gospel, who served as pastor of the Charlestown church after he arrived on American soil. His untimely death a year later resulted in his library of 400 volumes and a gift of 780 pounds sterling being contributed to the fledgling college in Cambridge. Appropriately, those treasures were to help in the training of upcoming generations of Christian ministers.

These facts help explain the original Harvard seal: a shield including three opened books, two facing up, the third facing down, and the Latin words *Veritas Christo et Ecclesiae*—"Truth for Christ and the Church." The university motto was followed by a reference to John 8:32: "And Jesus said, 'If you hold to my teaching . . . then you will know the truth and the truth will make you free.'"

The distinguished seal reminded students that truth and freedom are found only in Jesus Christ, and the display of three books represented the importance of knowledge—yet with one turned down, emphasizing the limits of human reason.

Tragically, with the passing of time, that godly philosophy of education has eroded. Harvard's new seal carries no reference to Christ or the church. The motto that once underscored the end of knowledge as being virtue, service, and love now implies human achievement, power, and arrogance. And to leave no doubt about this humanistic philosophy, the book facing down has now been turned *up*. We can now know it all, this symbol says. There are no divine mysteries. Intellect is everything . . . the *sine qua non* of life.

There is a nasty fly in this humanistic ointment, however. It's the "D" word: Depravity. The sinfulness of the human heart is not altered or eradicated by the pursuit of knowledge. Oh, it may go underground as sophistication and conceit cover it, as fleshly pride and academic accomplishment mask it, but it is there, nevertheless. This explains why the century-one Christian, Saul of Tarsus, warned his friends in Corinth, "Knowledge makes arrogant."

But, wait. Was he suggesting that knowledge has no place among dedicated believers in Christ? Is ignorance bliss?

No, that was not his point at all. His warning had to do with knowledge *alone* . . . knowledge without faith, without love, without respect for God and others, without moral or ethical standards, without standing of right and wrong. *Veritas* minus *Christo*.

Less than ten years ago the Supreme Court ruled that the Ten Commandments could not be posted in schools. Why? Because "students might read them . . . and obey them." In public schools where prayer is banned, where any mention of religious faith is unlawful, and where the teaching of morality is shunned, all that is left is sterile academic knowledge. *Veritas* minus *Christo*.

The result? Students today can analyze exotic computer programs, but they cannot tell right from wrong.

If there is any remaining harbor of hope, it's the family and the church. Moms and dads, stay at it! Pastors and teachers, don't let up! And I should add, seminary profs, stand firm!

Uphold the importance of knowledge, but don't forget to address biblical values, godly character, personal integrity, fear of the Lord, moral absolutes, ethical standards, and the value of virtues like love, faith, discernment, self-control.

As Solomon put it:

> The fear of the Lord is the beginning of wisdom, and the knowledge of the Holy One is understanding (Prov. 9:10).

A Finishing Touch: *Veritas* PLUS *Christo* is the motto to model.
A Daily Reading: Proverbs 9:9–12

Take away the necessary constraints which Christ alone provides, and the raging beast of depravity within the human heart—no matter how intelligent the mind may be—will growl, crouch, claw, and occasionally attack.

Thus, when academic humanity and unrestrained depravity collide, depravity will win the battle.

Sometimes, the scene is shocking, as in the case of the "Honor Roll Murder" of Stuart Tay. Had it happened in some dark alley, it probably wouldn't have made the evening news—at least not in more than a sentence or two. But this occurred among an upscale, financially prosperous, politically conservative, academically gifted group of young men.

Tough thugs did not kill Stuart Tay. He was murdered by youths headed for Princeton, Yale, and Harvard. Valedictorian types. Quick-minded, bright computer whizzes whom anyone would have picked for tomorrow's leaders. These guys had academic knowledge in abundance. What they didn't have was the ability to restrain the raging beast within.

As it was reported in T*Ime*, "the victim was brutally beaten with baseball bats before they poured rubbing alcohol down his throat and forced his mouth shut with duct tape. Tay died within minutes from his own vomit."

Horrible. Yet, to be painfully honest, predictable in a sophisticated, politically correct society that idolizes knowledge while it ignores moral standards.

Veritas minus *Christo*.

A Needed Pit Stop

Is time passing faster or am I just getting older? Can this really be the last hurrah of the summer? School can't actually be starting already, can it? I feel like swapping my calendar for a stopwatch.

It's like watching one of those Formula One car races where a television camera is mounted inside one of the cars and periodically the producer switches to that camera, giving viewers an idea of how life looks as it blows by at 200-plus miles per hour. Virtually everything is a blur. I have no trouble identifying with the driver who has all he can do to stay his course, maneuver the curves, and steer clear of all the other four-wheel missiles only inches away.

Today I have decided to slow down long enough to stop the blur and look. Not just to look, but to see. As Yogi Berra once said, "You can observe a lot just by watching."

Sometimes it helps to open life's door slowly and secretively take a long gaze inside. On other occasions, it's better to jerk it open unannounced, slam on the light, and get a quick read. I've been doing the latter today, and I don't like what I see. My sudden glance has flushed out all sorts of critters.

What have I seen? Which rodents scurried at the flip of the switch? Actually, a whole bunch, but I'll list only a few. I imagine you could find many of the same ones in your own cellar.

— Too many involvements.
— Intensity level much too high.
— Big picture frequently getting blurred.
— Time to pray, to think, to plan, to play is still too rushed.
— Midget worries turning into imaginary monsters.
— Living life too predictable . . . not enough creativity.
— Days off interrupted by needless, low-priority stuff.
— Skating across relationships—need to dig deeper.
— Extra-curricular reading not sufficiently stimulating.

What a pack of rats! They claw and gnaw at our inner peace, leaving it in shreds. What's worse, they multiply.

I know of no better strategy for stopping such an ugly, rat-infested existence than deliberately pulling off the track and taking periodic pit stops to refuel, renew, refresh, and recover in preparation for reentry. Returning to the real world is inevitable and essential, but it need not be irritable. That means our stops during the race of life must be meaningful as well as carefully and thoughtfully managed so as to yield the maximum benefits with minimum hassle.

Let me level with you. Your pace is your problem and my pace is mine. We got ourselves into this maddening race, and each one of us is personally responsible for the speed at which we're driving ourselves. None of us can honestly say, "The devil made me do it!"

Because our traffic jam is of our own making, we are responsible for getting ourselves out. If the brakes should be applied, it will take our foot on the pedal.

If you can say, "I've sinned. The pace I'm keeping is not healthy—spiritually, mentally, or physically. It's not what I want, but it's my own doing," then I urge you to do so—and then do something about changing it.

I can't promise instant and total transformation, but I can assure you of this: It will be the most unusual pit stop you'll ever make. You'll not only get your tank filled, you'll also get your rats killed!

A Finishing Touch: Do you think you should take that needed pit stop to refuel, renew, refresh, and recover so you can reenter the race and run with diligence?

A Daily Reading: Hebrews 12:1–2

Of all the letters Paul wrote, Second Corinthians is the most autobiographical. In it the great apostle lifts the veil on his private life and allows us to catch a glimpse of his human frailties and needs. You need to read that entire letter in one sitting to capture the moving emotion that surged through his soul.

In this letter Paul records the specifics of his anguish, tears, affliction, and satanic opposition. He spells out the details of his persecution, loneliness, imprisonments, beatings, feelings of despair, hunger, shipwrecks, sleepless nights, and that "thorn in the flesh"— his companion of pain. How close it makes us feel to him when we see him as a man with real, honest-to-goodness problems, just like ours!

It is not surprising, then, that he begins the letter with words of *comfort*, especially verses 3 through 11. Ten times in five verses (vv. 5–7) Paul uses the same root word, *Para-kaleo*, meaning literally, "to call alongside."

This word involves more than a shallow pat on the back with the tired expression, "the Lord Bless you." No, this word involves genuine, in-depth understanding . . . deep-down compassion and sympathy. This seems especially appropriate since it says that God, our Father, is the "God of all comfort" who "comforts us in all our affliction." Our loving Father is never pre-occupied and/or removed when we are enduring sadness and affliction!

There is another observation worth noting in 2 Corinthians 1: No less than three reasons are given for suffering, each one introduced with the term "that." Quietly, without a lot of fanfare, the Holy Spirit states reasons we suffer: "That we may be able to comfort those who are in any affliction"; "That we should not trust in ourselves"; "That thanks may be given" {vv. 4, 9, 11}. Admittedly, there may be dozens of other reasons, but here are three specific reasons we suffer.

Reason #1: God allows suffering so that we might have the capacity to enter into others' sorrow and affliction. Isn't that true? If you have suffered a broken leg and been confined to crutches for weeks, you are in complete sympathy with someone else on crutches even years after your affliction. The same is true for the loss of a child, emotional depression, an auto accident, undergoing unfair criticism, financial burdens. God gives His children the capacity to understand by bringing similar sufferings into our lives.

Reason #2: God allows suffering so that we might learn what it means to depend on Him. Doesn't suffering do that? It forces us to lean on Him totally, absolutely. Over and over He reminds us of the danger of pride, but it frequently takes suffering to make the lesson stick. Perhaps that has been your experience recently. Don't resent the affliction as an intruder. Welcome it as God's message to stop trusting in your flesh . . . and start leaning on Him.

Reason #3: God allows suffering so that we might learn to give thanks in everything. Now, honestly, have you said, "Thanks, Lord, for this test"? Have you finally stopped struggling and expressed to Him how much you appreciate His loving sovereignty over your life?

Well, there you have it. How unfinished and rebellious and proud and unconcerned we would be without suffering!

May these things encourage you the next time God heats up the furnace!

A Finishing Touch: Years ago I heard two statements about suffering that I have never forgotten: "Pain plants the flag of reality in the fortress of a rebel heart." And, "When God wants to do an impossible task, He takes an impossible individual—and crushes him."

A Daily Reading: 2 Corinthians 1

Many years ago I broke my left hand. It happened while I was working as an apprentice in a machine shop in Houston. It was a nasty break, a compound fracture that occurred when my hand slipped off a wrench while the lathe chuck was spinning at 2500 rpms. In a split second my hand was covered with blood.

The result was a trip to the hospital, a brief conversation with an orthopedic surgeon, then the surgical procedure, during which the bone was set back in place. The doctor inserted a stainless steel pen from my knuckle to my wrist to hold the bone in place while it healed. He was an excellent physician, not even forty years old, yet he enjoyed a booming practice in a busy, rapidly growing city.

During one of my follow-up visits, after the surgeon examined my hand, he mentioned that he'd not be there when I returned to have the pin removed, but he said his associate was well able to handle everything. Curious, I asked if he was planning to take some well-earned vacation time.

"Yes," he sighed, "I'm feeling a little drained these days, so I think I'll escape for a couple of weeks, play some golf, and relax." Then he added, "Also, I've got this little mole on my belly I need to have re-moved—no big deal, but while I'm away I'll have that taken care of." He even showed it to me, a dark-colored little nodule just beneath his belt line.

When I returned to have the pin removed, I inquired about my physician. The nurse stared blankly as the associate cleared his throat. Without looking up, he said, "Didn't you hear? He died last week." I was absolutely stunned. My mind whirled. Dizzy, I choked out, "He *what*?"

"It was cancer. When his surgeon made the incision to remove a mole, then probed deeper, he discovered that his entire abdomen was laced with malignant tissue. He never had a clue, just a slight yet steady drain in energy. Actually, the only thing on the surface was that innocent-looking little mole. He didn't live a week after they sewed him up."

436

Through the years I've often remembered that incident when I look at the slight scar on my wrist. And I am reminded that sin is a lot like that little mole. It starts "small," but soon it is draining and devouring our spiritual energy, like cancer in a body.

I think particularly of the secret sins of the heart and mind: jealousy, envy, lust, pride . . . .

Because there may be little evidence on the surface to attract anyone else's attention or arouse suspicion, no one bothers to probe and investigate the devastation these sins are causing beneath the surface.

All the while, however, these silent and relentless killers are sucking motivation, draining energy, and blurring vision.

Before such sin eats deeper into our souls, we need to ask the Great Physician to excise it—to cut it away, so that we can become spiritually sound and healthy.

Don't wait. This is one case you don't want to become terminal.

A Finishing Touch: While the mole of sin may appear small, its tentacles reach deep.

A Daily Reading: 1 Corinthians 5

Too good. That's the only way to describe my early childhood. Lots of friends in the neighborhood. Sandlot football down at the end of Quince Street in East Houston or shooting hoops against the garage backboard. Then there was always "Hide 'n' Seek" and "Kick the Can" 'till suppertime. There were family reunions at my grand-daddy's little bay cabin, plus fishing, floundering, crabbing, swimming, and eating. Fresh shrimp, crab gumbo, fried gulf trout, freshly plucked watermelon, homemade biscuits, gravy, handcranked ice cream . . . I gotta stop!

But best of all, we were given room to be kids. Just kids. Listen, I went to school barefoot until the fourth grade, and I was still playing cops and robbers on into junior high. Scouts honor. Nobody pushed me to grow up. I suppose everybody figured it would just happen. Life was allowed to run its own course back then, like a lazy river working its own way to the sea. No big deal, no enormous list of expectations, no adult pressures, just down home, easy livin', fun growin' up stuff.

No longer, it seems. Several decades removed from those laid-back years, there is a new youngster in our city streets. Have you noticed? Perhaps I'm overly sensitive because I've finished reading David Elkind's splendid book, The Hurried Child, with the provocative subtitle, "Growing Up Too Fast Too Soon." On the cover is a little girl, not more than eleven, with earrings, plucked eyebrows, carefully applied cosmetics, teased and feathered hair, and exquisite jewelry. I have looked at her dozens of times, and on each occasion I see more. She bears the look of bewildered innocence, almost like a helpless calf being pushed to slaughter. She's afraid, but she can't say so. It wouldn't be chic. She's being hurried. Too far. Too fast. Too soon.

She reminds me of the seven-year-old whom Susan Ferraro mentioned in her article in American Way magazine entitled "Hotsy Totsy." It was the little girl's birthday party, with ice cream and cake and a pin-the-tail-on-the- donkey poster. But when she opened her presents, they were not toys, books, and the usual childhood fare. There were Calvin Klein jeans, a Gloria Vanderbilt T-shirt, Christian Dior undies from grandma, and mother gave her "a marvelous party outfit from Yves St. Laurent."

It's not the clothes or even those silly brand names that bug me. It's the subtle "hurry-up" message woven through those threads and styles. It's the subliminal strokes and sensations a child in the second grade can wear but isn't equipped to handle.

Music, books, films, and television increasingly portray the young as precocious and seductive. "Such portrayals," writes Elkind, "force children to think they should act grown up before they are ready."

Emotions and feelings are the most complex and intricate part of a child's development. They have their own timing and rhythm which cannot be hurried. Growing up is tough enough with nobody pushing. But it must be absolutely bewildering when children's behavior and appearance are hurried to speak "adult" while their insides cry "child."

Am I overreacting to suggest that the unique traumas among today's children are somehow tied to all this? Younger and younger alcoholics. Increased promiscuity among preteens. Higher crime rate than ever involving the very young. And the all-time high suicide rate among children and adolescents is certainly telling us something . . . if nothing else, at least for those kids, it's telling us we're reacting too late.

Scripture clearly states, "There is an appointed time for everything" (Eccl. 3:1). How about time to be a child? How about time to grow up slowly, carefully—yes, even protected, naive?

Otherwise, it is too far, too fast, too soon.

A Finishing Touch: Allow your children the joys of childhood.
A Daily Reading: 1 Corinthians 13:11

"Be on the alert, stand firm in the faith, act like men, be strong" (1 Cor. 16:13). Those words were written by a man who practiced what he penned. Paul was his name. "Guts" could have been his nickname. With singleminded determination, the rugged apostle hitched in his belt and pressed on.

Through hard labors, imprisonments, beatings, and dangers . . . in spite of a brutal stoning, three frightening shipwrecks, a day and a night in the waters of the Mediterranean, threats on his life, extreme cold and intense heat, sleepless nights, dreadful days when hunger weakened him and thirst tormented him . . . regardless of continued misunderstanding from former companions, hateful treatment and vigorous opposition, ugly letters from the Corinthians, disappointment over the Galatians, mistreatment in Philippi, mocking in Athens, satanic oppression, and sustained isolation in a damp, dark dungeon in Rome before being beheaded, the persecutor-turned-apostle from Tarsus refused to run scared or lick his wounds. Even a cursory review of his life makes most Christians of today look like pantywaists.

Where did Christians get the idea that we'd be appreciated, affirmed, and admired? The Savior himself taught that blessings are reserved for the persecuted, for those who are reviled, for those against whom folks say "all kinds of evil . . . falsely . . ." (Matt. 5:10–11). He is the One who also warned, "Woe to you when all men speak well of you" (Luke 6:26).

It sure is easy to forget those words and get soft, becoming too tender, too sensitive. Fragility is not a virtue extolled in Scripture. Saints with thin skin get distracted and, shortly thereafter, discouraged. There's a long, demanding course to be run, most of which takes place in the trenches and without applause. I suggest we lower our expectations as we intensify our determination and head for the goal.

Endurance is the secret, not popularity. This vile world is no friend of grace to help us on to God. He's looking for troops who are in this thing for the long haul, caring and loving, of course, but not crowd-pleasing cheerleaders who rely on audience reaction to keep going.

Why "be on the alert"? Because we have an adversary who is always ready to pounce. Why "stand firm in the faith"? Because nothing worthwhile was ever accomplished without commitment to truth. Why "act like men"? Because being childish won't cut it when the battle rages. Why "be strong"? Because weakness precedes surrender . . . and quitting is not an option.

There are 1,130 frostbitten miles, mountain ranges, blizzards, hungry beasts, and frozen seas between Anchorage and Nome. This awful trek is the scene of the ultimate endurance test known as the Iditarod Sled Dog Race, where twelve huskies pull a sled and its driver through the most grueling, inhuman conditions one can fathom. The most frequent champion is a woman named Susan Butcher, whose tough-minded fixation on winning has earned her the nickname, Ayatollah Butcher. She holds the record: 11 days, 1 hour, and 53 minutes, but that doesn't satisfy. Her goal is to break the 10-day barrier.

The secret, she will tell you, is her own mindset and the training of those dogs, which gives new meaning to the word "serious." Her 150-dog kennel is a thing to behold. Shortly after each pup's birth, while it is still blind, she holds it in her hands and breathes her breath into its nose. That way, she claims, each one will associate her smell with comfort and encouragement. The rapport begins with that breathing-into-the-nose routine. She personally feeds, trains, massages, and—on a rotation basis—sleeps with each dog. She personally nurses them to health when they are injured. She is infinitely patient with them, talks with them, believes in them, even sings to them (old folk songs by Bob Dylan and Joan Baez, plus a few Irish lullabies). The objective? To bond with them. It pays. They have saved her life on the trail more than once. Back in 1979, she led her dog team to the 20,320-foot summit of Mt. McKinley. It took 44 days.

What a woman! One reporter described her as having "a stiff spine . . . a stubborn mind-set," which is what is needed to endure moose attacks, blizzards so severe that one time for five hours she couldn't see the lead dog, and a sudden plunge into icy water (Granite and Maddie, the mushers, pulled her out). But what is most interesting is that a race you and I would call impossible, she describes as "thrilling . . . especially when you conquer it."

The Christian life isn't an 11-day race. It's a lifetime journey full of more dangers and pitfalls than a hundred Iditarods. So it's foolish to think we can enter it half-heartedly or sustain it easily. More often than not, to borrow from Bunyan, "this miry slough is such a place as cannot be mended." To survive it calls for help from above and toughness from within. If Susan Butcher is willing to give that kind of effort to win a race that is incredible in the eyes of the world, seems to me we should be capable of conquering the marathon from earth to heaven.

A combination of two ingredients is essential: the capacity to accept and the tenacity to endure. It's hard, but what else is new? Sitting around whining and complaining won't cut it. The gutsy apostle didn't, and neither should we. The Christian life is "thrilling . . . especially when you conquer it."

If it's time to vote, I move that we toughen up. All in favor, say "Mush."

A Finishing Touch: "We could never be brave and patient if there were only joy in the world" (Helen Keller).

A Daily Reading: 2 Corinthians 11–13

Take time this weekend to read again, slowly and carefully, through Friday's Scripture reading—2 Corinthians 11–13. List the hardships the apostle Paul endured.

Try putting yourself and your own particular circumstances and trials into Paul's constant affirmations of faith.

Start with . . .

> I have been in labor and hardship, through many sleepless nights, in hunger and thirst, often without food, in cold and exposure.
>
> Apart from such external things, there is the daily pressure upon me of concern for all the churches. . . .
>
> If I have to boast, I will boast of what pertains to my weakness.
>
> The God and Father of the Lord Jesus, He who is blessed forever, knows that I am not lying. . . .

Can you do that . . . honestly?

The word is out. TM is "in."

Ask any number of celebrities or government leaders or public school officials . . . or thousands of college kids who endorse it. All are oohing and aahing over a Hindu monk with a name that looks like a misprint. Maharishi Mahesh Yogi

Transcendental Meditation is his bag and a national craze. With a broad smile and his body wrapped in a bedsheet, he lectured to a standing-room-only crowd at that citadel of sophistication, the Harvard Law School Forum, and received a standing ovation.

That's not all. An issue of *Scholastic Teacher*, national professional journal for public school teachers, openly promoted TM. It gave the location of TM "pushers" and even suggested a special TM scholarship program for teachers. Devotees around this gullible globe have developed a vast network of International Meditation Society centers, declaring them to be the cure for physical and emotional ills and a splendid way to elevate the individual.

Testimonies accompany the propaganda:

"Thanks to TM, my grades are better."

"I now have inner peace. TM works!"

"No longer hooked on drugs . . . I'm addicted to TM. Hallelujah!"

"TM helped me lose 46 pounds."

"I was confused. Jobless. Bitter. But TM changed all that."

"I'm a teacher of high schoolers. TM is rewarding and helpful."

A professional basketball player claims it helps him make his foul shots. Mothers announce it gives them patience with small children. Merchants experience prosperity by practicing it. Scientists gain insight. Politicians enjoy increased public approval. Teens get dates. Prisoners get pardons. Writers get ideas. Salesmen get orders. Habits are conquered. Marriages are saved.

Hold it! Stop the world and let me get on. Beneath TM's surface rests a philosophy that is worse than dangerous. It's demonic. Behind the guru's smile is a set of teeth whose fangs spread the venom of the Vedas, ancient Indian writings linked directly with hard-core Hinduism. Vedic literature includes sacrificial incantations, formulas used by magicians who practice the black arts. TM is witchcraft wrapped in a clean, white bedsheet. It appears attractive, gentle, humble, and innocent. It is not. It is damnable.

How does TM work? A client at a TM center pays the fee and receives instructions. This includes the giving of a "mantra" with simple directions. A "mantra" is a secret, individualized word that is to be used repeatedly during "meditation sessions." Vedism and Hinduism both refer to the mantra. The repeating of the mantra is a signal, asking assistance from the spirit world. Through rigid, disciplined practice, the TM disciple develops the ability to make contact with spirits and thereby gain the so-called assistance he/she desires.

The *Encyclopedia Britannica* defines *mantra* as "a Sanskrit word meaning a sacred utterance considered to possess supernatural power." *Webster* calls it "a mystical formula."

Will you get results if you practice TM? Yes, indeed. Will things happen if you consistently apply the mystical formula? Like you won't believe! Chances are, you'll get more than you bargained for. You'll get much more than assistance. You'll get a glimpse of the guru's guru.

But he won't be smiling . . . and before long, neither will you.

A Finishing Touch: Satan doesn't come to us with horns and pitchfork. He often comes wrapped in attractive and innocent guise.
A Daily Reading: Genesis 3

In September, Terry Shafer was strolling the shops in Moline, Illinois. She knew exactly what she wanted to get her husband, David, for Christmas, but she realized it might be too expensive. A little shop on Fifth attracted her attention, so she popped inside. Her eyes darted toward the corner display. "That's it!" she smiled as she nodded with pleasure. "How much?" she asked the shopkeeper.

"Only $127.50."

Her smile faded into disappointment as she realized David's salary couldn't stand such a jolt. He was feeding and clothing the family on a policeman's wage. It was out of the question. Yet she hated to give up without a try, so she applied a little womanly persistence.

"Uh, what about putting this aside for me? Maybe I could pay a little each week then pick it up a few days before Christmas?"

"No," the merchant said, "I won't do that." Then he smiled. "I'll gift-wrap it right now. You can take it with you and pay me later," he said. Terry was elated. She agreed to pay so much every week, then thanked and thanked the man as she left, explaining how delighted her husband would be.

"Oh, that's nothing at all," the shopkeeper answered, not realizing the significant role his generosity would play in the days ahead.

Then came Saturday, October 1. Patrolman David Shafer, working the night shift, got a call in his squad car. A drug store robbery was in progress. David reacted instantly, arriving on the scene just in time to see the suspect speed away. With siren screaming and lights flashing, he followed in hot pursuit. Three blocks later the getaway vehicle suddenly pulled over and stopped. The driver didn't move. David carefully approached the suspect with his weapon drawn. When he was only three feet from the driver's door, two things happened in a split second. The door flew open as the thief produced a .45-caliber pistol and fired at David's abdomen.

At seven o'clock that morning a patrolman came to the door of the Shafer home. Calmly and with great care, he told Terry what had happened.

Her husband had been pursuing a robbery suspect. There had been gunfire. David was hit. Shot at point-blank range.

Stunned, Terry thought how glad she was that she had not waited until Christmas to give her husband his present. How grateful she was that the shopkeeper had been willing to let her pay for it later. Otherwise, Dave would have surely died. Instead, he was now in the hospital—not with a gunshot wound, but with only a bad bruise.

You see, David was wearing the gift of life Terry could not wait to give—his brand-new bulletproof vest.

There are times that the timing of something is as remarkable as the thing itself. Sometimes more so.

Like a CPA friend of mine who, through a computer mix-up, was bumped off a flight from Baton Rouge to Dallas one Friday evening several years ago. His irritation changed to gratitude when he heard the next morning that the original flight he would have taken had crashed, killing everyone aboard.

Spooky? Weird? Coincidence? Luck?

Well, that's one way to view it. Lots of folks do. They're the same ones who suggest that the mind-boggling planetary motion swirling around us in perfect precision just sorta wound up there on its own. And that things like birth and death, promotions and demotions, early arrivals and late departures, interruptions and delays are little more than the shallow flutter of chance.

I'm persuaded otherwise. Within the movement of events is the Designer, who plans and arranges the times and the seasons, including the minutest detail of life. You question that? Many do.

But unless I miss my guess, David and Terry Shafer don't. Nor does the CPA in Dallas. It's funny . . . people who survive a calamity don't have much struggle with sovereignty.

A Finishing Touch: Behind the maze is the Master.
A Daily Reading: Psalm 31:14–15

Mrs. Bertha Adams, 71 years old, died alone in West Palm Beach, Florida, on Easter Sunday. The coroner's report read: "Cause of death . . . malnutrition." She had wasted away to fifty pounds.

When the state authorities made their preliminary investigation of Mrs. Adam's home, they found a veritable "pigpen . . . the biggest mess you can imagine." One seasoned inspector declared he'd never seen a dwelling in greater disarray. The woman had begged food from neighbors' back doors and gotten what clothing she had from the Salvation Army. From all outward appearances she was a penniless recluse, a pitiful and forgotten widow. But such was not the case.

Amid the jumble of her unclean, disheveled belongings, the officials found two keys to safe-deposit boxes at two different local banks. In the first box were over 700 AT&T stock certificates, plus hundreds of other valuable certificates, bonds, and solid financial securities, not to mention a stack of cash amounting to nearly $200,000. The second box contained $600,000. Adding the net worth of both boxes, they found well over a million dollars.

Charles Osgood, reporting the story on CBS radio, announced that the estate would probably go to a distant niece and nephew, neither of whom dreamed their aunt had a thin dime to her name.

Can you imagine picking up the phone and hearing that you'd just inherited half a million? Why, I wouldn't know whether to shout "Glory," dance the jig, wind my watch, whistle "Dixie," or sing "The Doxology."

You can count on this, friend: those two relatives are awfully glad Aunt Bertha still had their names lying around.

But don't you also wonder about this woman? Why, oh, why would anybody salt away all that bread in two tiny boxes, month after month, year after year, and refuse to spend even enough for food to stay alive? She makes Silas Marner look like a spendthrift.

Fact is, Bertha Adams wasn't saving her money; she was worshiping it . . . hoarding it . . . gaining a twisted satisfaction out of watching the stacks grow higher as she shuffled along the streets wearing the garb of a beggar.

I confess an almost total loss of understanding as I try to imagine pleasure being drawn from simply stacking up one's treasure for the sheer and selfish delight of watching the stack grow higher. Now don't misread me. I'm a firm believer in saving, investing, intelligent spending, and wise money management. But I have trouble finding one word of scriptural support for being a tightwad!

And it isn't hard to spot them. They all start with one main question: How much does it cost? And one main answer: We can't afford it. And one main criticism: We're spending too much money. I have yet to meet a Christian tightwad who knew *by experience* the first principle of enthusiastic faith. Never have I seen one who could dream broad dreams or see vast visions of what God can do *in spite of* man's limitations.

Give me a handful of "greathearts" . . . generous, openhanded, visionary, spiritually minded givers . . . magnanimous giants with God who get excited about abandoning themselves to Him. Now I remind you, they may not need a teller for their fortune when it's over and done with, but who cares? The name of the game is not CAUTION—it's still VISION, isn't it? Seems like I read somewhere that those without it perish.

And speaking of that, when they buried Bertha Adams, she didn't take a penny with her.

A Finishing Touch: Some folks serve the almighty dollar far more faithfully than the Almighty God. They get greater delight out of balancing the budget than watching the Lord multiply the loaves and fishes.

A Daily Reading: Matthew 6:19–21

Thoughts are the thermostat that regulates what we accomplish in life. My body responds and reacts to the input from my mind. If I feed my mind upon doubt, disbelief, and discouragement, that is precisely the kind of day my body will experience. If I adjust my thermostat forward to thoughts filled with vision, vitality, and victory, I can count on that kind of day. Thus, you and I become what we think about.

Neither Dale Carnegie nor Norman Vincent Peale originated such a message. God did. "For as [a man] thinks within himself, so he is" (Prov. 23:7). "Therefore, gird your minds for action" (1 Peter 1:13).

The mind is a "thought factory." It produces thousands, perhaps hundreds of thousands, of thoughts each day. Production in your thought factory is under the charge of two foremen. One we shall call Mr. Triumph, the other Mr. Defeat

Mr. Triumph is in charge of manufacturing positive, wholesome, encouraging, reassuring thoughts. Mr. Defeat is responsible for the manufacturing of negative, depreciating, worrisome thoughts. Mr. Triumph specializes in producing reasons why you can face life victoriously, why you can handle what comes your way, why you're more than able to conquer. Mr. Defeat is an expert in the opposite. He develops reasons why you cannot succeed, why you're inadequate, why you should give up and give in to worry, failure, discouragement, and inferiority.

Both foremen are instantly obedient. They await your signal to snap to attention.

Give a positive signal, and Mr. Triumph will throw the switches as he goes to work. He will see to it that one encouraging, edifying thought after another floods your mind.

But Mr. Defeat is always standing by, awaiting a negative signal (which he would rather you call "reality" or "common sense!"), and when he gets it, he cranks out more discouraging, destructive, demoralizing thoughts than Carters has liver pills. He will soon have you convinced that you can't or won't or shouldn't. Given sufficient time, he will drain your energy, squelch your confidence, and turn you into a frowning, tight-lipped fatalistic victim, strangled by the yellow, clammy fingers of negative thinking.

Thoughts, positive or negative, grow stronger when fertilized with constant repetition. That may explain why so many who are gloomy and gray stay in that mood . . . and why those who are cheery and enthusiastic continue to be so.

Happiness (like winning) is a matter of right thinking, not intelligence, age, or position. Our performance is directly related to the thoughts we deposit in our memory bank. We can only draw on what we deposit.

What kind of performance would your car deliver if every morning before you left for work you scooped up a handful of dirt and put it in your crank case? The engine would soon be coughing and sputtering. Ultimately it would refuse to start. The same is true of your life. Thoughts that are narrow, self-destructive, and abrasive produce needless wear and tear on your mental motor. They send you off the road while others drive past.

You need only one foreman in your mental factory: Mr. Triumph is his name. He is anxious to assist you and available to all the members of God's family.

His real name is the Holy Spirit, the Helper.

A Finishing Touch: If Mr. Defeat is busily engaged as the foreman of your factory, fire yours and hire ours! You will be amazed at how smoothly the plant will run under His leadership.

A Daily Reading: Philippians 4:8

It was one of those backhanded compliments. The kind that make you pause, think, then respond, rather than gush out a quick "Hey, thanks." The guy had listened to me talk during several sessions at a pastors' conference. We had not met before, so all he knew about me was what he'd heard in the past few days: ex-Marine . . . Texan by birth . . . schooled in an independent seminary . . . committed to biblical exposition . . . noncharismatic . . . premil . . . pretrib . . . pro this . . . anti that. You know how all those scary labels go.

I really think he expected your basic, squeaky-clean preacher: dark suit; white shirt (buttoned-down collar); tight-knot tie; scuffed wing-tips; a big study Bible with lots of tiny-print footnotes; deep frown; thunderous shouts; and a rather large fist flailing away in midair.

Since that's not what he got, he was thrown a low curve over the inside corner of the pulpit. Finally, toward the end of the week, he decided to drink a cup of coffee with me and risk saying it straight. It went something like this:

"You don't fit. What's with you? You've got the roots of a fundamentalist, but you don't sound like it. Your theology is narrow, but you're not rigid. You take God seriously, but you laugh like there's no tomorrow. You have definite convictions, but you aren't legalistic and demanding."

Then he added: "Even though you're a firm believer in the Bible, you're still having fun, still enjoying life. You've even got some *compassion!*"

That did it. By then both of us were laughing out loud. A few eyes from other tables flashed us those "Would you two quiet down!" looks. I often encounter such glares, especially when I'm having fun.

Well, what could I say? The man could've been a lot more severe, but he had me pretty well pegged. It was that last statement, however, that really got me thinking. It woke up with me the next morning.

"You've even got some compassion!" As though it was not supposed to be there. Like, if you're committed to the truth of Scripture, you shouldn't get that concerned about people stuff—heartaches, hunger, illness, fractured lives, struggles with insecurities, failures, and grief—because those are only temporal problems. Mere horizontal hassles. Leave that to the liberals. Our main job is to give 'em the Gospel. Get 'em saved! Don't get sidetracked by their pain and problems. It's conversion we're really interested in, not compassion. Once they're born again and get into the Word, all those other things will solve themselves.

Be honest now. Isn't that the way it usually is? Isn't it a fact that the more conservative one becomes, the less compassionate? I know there are some exceptions, but we're talking about the general rule, okay?

I want to know why. Why either-or? Why not both-and?

I'd also like to know when. Not just why can't we be theologically conservative and personally compassionate, but when . . . when did we depart from the biblical model? When did we begin to ignore Christ's care for the needy? When did we stop thinking of how valuable it is to be healing agents, wound wrappers, a la the good Samaritan? When did we opt for placing more emphasis on being proclaimers and defenders and less on becoming repairers and restorers? When did we decide to strengthen our focus on public announcements and weaken our involvement in private assistance?

Maybe when we realized that one is much easier than the other. It's also faster. When you don't concern yourself with being your brother's keeper, you don't have to get dirty or take risks or lose your objectivity or run up against the thorny side of an issue that lacks easy answers.

And what will happen when we traffic in such compassion? *The Living Bible* says, "Then the Lord will be your delight, and I will see to it that you ride high, and get your full share of the blessings I promised to Jacob, your father. The Lord has spoken" (Isa. 58:14).

Yes, He has spoken, but have we heard?

The fact is that He has been talking like this ever since He asked Cain about the welfare of his brother Abel. When did we stop listening?

If you really want to "ride high, and get you full share of the blessings," prefer compassion to information. We need both, but in the right order.

Come on, let's break the mold and surprise 'em. Let's allow compassion to create a hunger for the truth. We'll be in good company. That's exactly what Jesus did with you and me and a whole bunch of other sinners who deserved and expected a full dose of condemnation, but got compassion instead.

A Finishing Touch: Others won't care how much we know until they know how much we care.

A Daily Reading: Colossians 3:12–14; James 5:11

Let's go back to that repairer-restorer comment I made yesterday. It's not an original idea. The prophet Isaiah mentioned it first, way back when. The nation to whom he wrote was going through the empty motions of a hollow religion. All the right words, all the right appearances, but zero results. They even fasted and prayed. I suppose we could say they looked and sounded orthodox, but they missed God's favor. They observed the external Sabbath, but they lacked the internal Shalom. Why? Don't hurry through the answer (Isaiah 58:6–12). It's worth reading aloud, perhaps more than once.

Is this not the fast which I choose, to loosen the bonds of wickedness, to undo the bands of the yoke, and to let the oppressed go free, and break every yoke? Is it not to divide your bread with the hungry, and bring the homeless poor into the house; when you see the naked, to cover him; and not to hide yourself from your own flesh?

Then your light will break out like the dawn, and your recovery will speedily spring forth; and your righteousness will go before you; the glory of the Lord will be your rear guard. Then you will call, and the Lord will answer; you will cry, and He will say, "Here I am."

If you remove the yoke from your midst, the pointing of the finger, and speaking wickedness, and if you give yourself to the hungry, and satisfy the desire of you afflicted, then your light will rise in darkness, and your gloom will become like midday. And the Lord will continually guide you, and satisfy your desire in scorched places, and give strength to your bones; and you will be like a watered garden, and like a spring of water whose waters do not fail. And those from among you will rebuild the ancient ruins; you will raise up the age-old foundations; and you will be called the repairer of the breach, the restorer of the streets in which to dwell.

A New Week
of
Finishing Touches

38

MONDAY

One of the occupational hazards of being a leader is receiving criticism (not all of it constructive, by the way). When that happens, it's easy to go under, throw in the towel, or bail out. Many have faded out of leadership because of intense criticism.

I firmly believe that the leader who does anything that is different or worthwhile or visionary can count on criticism. In this regard, I appreciate the remarks made by Theodore Roosevelt:

> It is not the critic who counts; not the man who points out how the strong man stumbled or where the doer of deeds could have done them better. The credit belongs to the man who is actually in the arena; whose face is marred by dust and sweat and blood; who strives valiantly; who errs, and comes short again and again, because there is no effort without error and shortcoming; who does actually try to do the deed; who knows the great enthusiasm, the great devotion and spends himself in a worthy cause; who, at the worst, if he fails, at least fails while daring greatly.
>
> Far better is it to dare mighty things, to win glorious triumphs even though checkered by failure, than to rank with those poor spirits who neither enjoy nor suffer much because they live in the gray twilight that knows neither victory nor defeat.

To those words I add a resounding AMEN.

And the following advice: A sense of humor is of paramount importance to the leader. Many of God's servants are simply too serious! Leaders must have the ability to take criticism, and they must have the ability to laugh at themselves.

Equally important, of course, is the ability to sift from any criticism that which is true . . . that which is fact. We are foolish if we respond angrily to every criticism. Who knows, God may be using those very words to teach us some essential lessons, painful though they may be.

Isn't this what Proverbs 27:5–6 is saying?

> Better is open rebuke
> Than love that is concealed.
> Faithful are the wounds of a friend,
> But deceitful are the kisses of an enemy.

And let me call to your attention the word *friend* in these verses. Friendship is not threatened by honest criticism. It is strengthened.

Leaders are not the only ones who receive criticism, of course. We all do. So just remember: when you are criticized by someone who hardly knows you, filter out what is fact . . . and ignore the rest!

A Finishing Touch: Read today's Scripture passage and notice how Nehemiah handled criticism. He kept his cool, he considered the source, he refused to get discouraged, he went to God in prayer, and he kept building the wall!

A Daily Reading: Nehemiah 6:1–14

In his fine little volume *In the Name of Jesus*, Henri Nouwen mentions three very real, albeit subtle temptations any servant of Christ faces. They correspond with the three temptations our Lord faced before He began His earthly ministry. They also fit with three observations the apostle Paul mentions in his letter to the Corinthians (2 Cor. 4:1–7).

First Temptation: To be self-sufficient and self-reliant. This attitude works directly *against* depending on the Lord. Instead of being so self-assured, we need to be open, unguarded, and vulnerable.

Second Temptation: To be spectacular . . . a celebrity mentality. Paul says this is to be deliberately renounced, as Jesus renounced it. In Nouwen's words, "Jesus refused to be a stunt man. . . . He did not come to walk on hot coals, swallow fire or put His hand in a lion's mouth to demonstrate He had something worthwhile to say."

Third Temptation: To be powerful . . . in charge. Paul's comment is superb: "We do not preach ourselves but Christ Jesus as Lord, and ourselves as your bond-servants for Jesus' sake" (4:5). To lead is appropriate, necessary, and good. But to push, to manipulate, to be in full control . . . never! To say it simply, one God is sufficient.

Servanthood implies diligence, faithfulness, loyalty, and humility. Servants don't compete . . . or grandstand . . . or polish their image . . . or grab the limelight. They know their job, they admit their limitations, they do what they do quietly and consistently.

Servants cannot control anyone or everything, and they shouldn't try.

Servants cannot change or "fix" people.

Servants cannot explain many of the great things that happen.

Servants cannot meet most folks' expectations.

Servants cannot concern themselves with who gets the credit.

Servants cannot cling to the past.

Servants cannot minister in the flesh or all alone.

In conclusion, let me suggest five practical guidelines for cultivating the right kind of servant habits.

Whatever we do, let's do more with others. Ministry is not a solo, it's a chorus . . . not a one-person performance, but a team effort.

Whenever we do it, let's place the emphasis on quality, not quantity. The numbers game is a no-win racket, bringing guilt or pride . . . shame or arrogance. Excellence is our goal, not expansion.

Whenever we go to do it, let's do it the same as if we were doing it among those who know us the best. Not only will this keep us accountable, it'll guard us from exaggeration.

Whoever may respond, let's keep a level head. If someone criticizes, don't allow it to get you down. If someone idolizes, don't tolerate or fantasize such foolishness. The word is balance. Stay level-headed and realistic.

However long we minister, let's model the Master . . . a servant-hearted attitude and a grace-oriented style.

Let's serve . . . in the name of Jesus.

A Finishing Touch: A servant-hearted attitude keeps us from self-minded altitude.

A Daily Reading: 2 Corinthians 4:1–7

Well, we are nine months into the year. It's funny, but it seems only yesterday when we were nine days into the year! Throughout the past months we've talked about our need to guard against becoming overcommitted, out of balance, and too intense. We've reaffirmed the significance of pacing ourselves and not allowing the tyranny of the urgent to blind us to the value of the important. Maybe you remember.

Those thoughts make sense around the beginning of a new year. Furthermore, everybody nods in agreement. Who could possibly argue against such wise counsel?

Well . . . how's it going? Let's take a brief appraisal. Pause long enough to review and reflect. Try to be painfully honest as you answer these questions.

> Is my pace this year really that different from last year?
>
> Am I enjoying most of my activities or just enduring them?
>
> Have I deliberately taken time on several occasions this year for personal restoration?
>
> Do I give myself permission to relax, to have leisure, to be quiet?
>
> Would other people think I am working too many hours and/or living under too much stress?
>
> Am I becoming boring and preoccupied?
>
> Am I staying physically fit? Do I consider my body important enough to maintain a nourishing diet, to give it regular exercise, to get enough sleep, to shed those excess pounds?
>
> How is my sense of humor?
>
> Is God being glorified by the schedule I keep . . . or is He getting the leftovers of my energy?
>
> Am I getting dangerously close to "burn out"?

Tough stuff, huh? Well, with the fall and winter stretching out in front of us, we can learn a lesson from nature. Periods of rest always follow harvest . . . the land must be allowed time to renew itself. Constant production without restoration depletes resources and, in fact, diminishes the quality of what is produced.

Renewal and restoration are not luxuries; they are essentials. Being alone and resting for a while is not selfish; it is Christlike (see Mark 6:30–32). Taking your day off each week and rewarding yourself with a relaxing, refreshing vacation is not carnal; it's spiritual. Nor is an ultra-busy schedule necessarily the mark of a productive life.

Super-achievers and workaholics, take heed! If the light on your inner dashboard is flashing red, you are carrying too much too far too fast. If you don't pull over, you'll be sorry . . . and so will all those who love you. If you are courageous enough to pull over and make some needed changes, you will show yourself wise. But I should warn you of three barriers you will immediately face.

First, false guilt. By saying "no" to the people to whom you used to say "yes," you'll feel twinges of guilt. Ignore it! Second, hostility and misunderstanding. Most folks won't understand your slower pace, especially those who are in the sinking boat you just stepped out of. Stick to your guns. Third, you'll encounter some personal and painful insights. By not filling every spare moment with activity, you will begin to see the real you, and you'll not like some of the things you observe, things that once contaminated your busy life. But within a relatively brief period of time, you will turn the corner and be well on the road to a happier, healthier, freer, and more fulfilling life.

My desire is that all of us remain "in." In balance. In our right minds. In good health. In the will of God.

Are you?

A Finishing Touch: Don't allow the tyranny of the urgent to blind you to the value of the important.

A Daily Reading: Mark 6:30–32

Fast-lane living in the 1990s does not lend itself to the traits we have traditionally attached to godliness. Remember the old hymn we sang in church years ago? "Take time to be holy, speak oft with Thy Lord; abide in Him always and feed on His Word. . . . Take time to be holy, the world rushes on . . . ."

We read those words, believe them, and would even defend them, but we sigh as we confess that more often than not we are strangers to them. The idea of taking the kind of time "to be holy" that our grandparents once did is rather dated.

Does this mean, then, that we cannot be holy? Does an urban life-style force us to forfeit godliness? Must we return to the "Little House on the Prairie" in order to be godly?

Obviously, the answer is "No." If godliness were linked to a certain culture or a horse-and-buggy era, then most of us would be out of luck! As much as we might enjoy a slower and less pressured life-style, God has not called everyone to such a role or place.

Which brings us to a bottom-line question I seldom hear addressed these days: What exactly does it mean to be holy . . . to be godly? Now be careful. Try hard not to link your answer with a certain geography or culture or traditional mentality. It is easy to let our prejudices seep through and erroneously define the concept on the basis of our bias.

Godliness cannot be confused with how a person looks (hard as it is for us to get beyond that) or what a person drives or owns. As tough as it is for us to be free of envy and critical thoughts, it is imperative that we remind ourselves that "God looks on the heart" (1 Sam. 16:7); therefore, whatever we may say godliness is, it is not *skin* deep.

Godliness is something below the surface of a life, deep down in the realm of attitude . . . an attitude toward God Himself.

The longer I think about this, the more I believe that a person who is godly is one whose heart is sensitive toward God, one who takes God seriously. This evidences itself in one very obvious mannerism:

the godly individual hungers and thirsts after God. In the words of the psalmist, the godly person has a soul that "pants" for the living God (Ps. 42:1–2).

The person who sustains this pursuit may be young or old, rich or poor, urban or rural, leader or follower, of any race or color or culture or any temperament, active or quiet, married or single; none of these things really matter.

What *does* matter is the individual's inner craving to know God, listen to Him, and walk humbly with Him.

Godly people possess an attitude of willing submission to God's will and ways. Whatever He says goes. And whatever it takes to carry it out is the very thing the godly desire to do.

The godly soul "pants" and "thirsts" for God.

A Finishing Touch: The godly take God seriously.
A Daily Reading: Psalm 42

My first direct view of *Titanic* lasted less than two minutes, but the stark sight of her immense black hull towering above the ocean floor will remain forever ingrained in my memory. My lifelong dream was to find this great ship, and during the past thirteen years the quest for her had dominated my life. Now, finally, the quest was over.

So wrote Robert Ballard after discovering the ghostly hulk of the R.M.S. *Titanic* in her lonely berth more than two miles deep in the North Atlantic. For nearly three-quarters of a century, since early April 1912, the great ship had been celebrated in legend, along with the 1,522 souls who had disappeared with her beneath the icy waters hundreds of miles off the coast of Newfoundland.

Not until a stobe light penetrated her eerie, muddy grave on September 1, 1985, did anyone really know her whereabouts. On that eventful day the man whose last thirteen years had been "dominated" by his quest to find her, caught his first glimpse.

How fascinated was he by her? Enough to take 53,000 photos of her. Enough to study every visible foot of her gigantic frame. Enough to respect her privacy and leave her as he found her—undisturbed and unexploited.

As Ballard wrote following his final visit, "The quest for *Titanic* is over. May she now rest in peace."

On several occasions, the explorer used the same word to describe his lifelong dream: "quest." It means a pursuit, a search, or, as Webster colorfully adds, "a chivalrous enterprise in medieval romance usually involving an adventurous journey." That would probably make Robert Ballard smile. For in a strange sort of way, his adventurous journey was indeed a romance with a lady many years his senior.

What is your "quest"? Do you have a "lifelong dream"? Anything "dominating your life" enough to hold your attention for thirteen or more years? Some "adventurous journey" you'd love to participate in . . . some discovery you long to make . . . some enterprise you secretly imagine?

Without a quest, life is quickly reduced to bleak black and wimpy white, a diet too bland to get anybody out of bed in the morning. A quest fuels our fire. It refuses to let us drift downstream, gathering debris. It keeps our mind in gear, makes us press on.

Are you dreaming about writing an article or a book? Write it.

Are you wondering if all that work with the kids is worth it? It's worth it. Keep pursuing!

Want to go back to school and finish that degree? Go back and do it . . . pay the price, even if it takes years!

In the middle of redecorating and getting tired of the mess? Stay at it!

Trying to master a skill that takes time, patience, and energy (not to mention money)? Press on!

Can't get that tune out of your head . . . got some songs that need to get on paper? Stay up later. Work at it. Quit feeling sorry for yourself!

Thinking about going into business for yourself? Why not? Take a chance.

God is forever on a quest, too. Ever thought about that? In fact, His adventurous journey is woven throughout the fabric of the New Testament.

One thread is in Romans 8:29, where He mentions that He is conforming us to His Son's image.

> For whom He foreknew, He also predestined to become conformed to the image of His Son . . . .

Another is in Philippians 1:6 where we're told that He began His "good work" in us and He isn't about to stop.

Elsewhere He even calls us His "workmanship" (Eph. 2:10).

Peter's second letter goes so far as to list some of the things included in this quest:

Now for this very reason also, applying all diligence, in your faith supply moral excellence, and in your moral excellence, knowledge; and in your knowledge, self-control, and in your self-control, perseverance, and in your perseverance, godliness; and in your godliness, brotherly kindness, and in your brotherly kindness, love.

For if these qualities are yours and are increasing, they render you neither useless nor unfruitful in the true knowledge of our Lord Jesus Christ (2 Pet. 1:5–8).

Character *qualities* in His children—that's His quest. That's why His strobe light continues to penetrate our darkness. And He won't quit until He completes His checklist.

When will that be? When we rest in peace . . . and not one day sooner. Thanks, Lord.

A Finishing Touch: If you think you've arrived, you probably haven't even started.

A Daily Reading: Colossians 1

All of us are surrounded by and benefit from the results of someone's quest. Let me name a few.

Above my head is a bright electric light. Thanks, Tom.

On my nose are eyeglasses that enable me to focus. Thanks, Ben.

In my driveway is a car ready to take me wherever I choose to steer it. Thanks, Henry.

Across my shelves are books full of interesting and carefully researched pages. Thanks, authors.

Flashing through my mind are ideas, memories, and creative skills. Thanks, teachers.

Tucked away in the folds of my life are discipline and determination, a refusal to quit when the going gets rough, a love for our country's freedom, a respect for authority. Thanks, Marines.

Coming into my ears is beautiful music—a wonderful mix of melody and rhythm and lyrics that linger. Thanks, composers.

Deep inside me are personality traits, strong convictions, a sense of right and wrong, a love for God, an ethical compass, a commitment to my wife and family. Thanks, parents.

At home is a peaceful surrounding of eye-pleasing design, colorful wallpaper, tasteful and comfortable furnishings, hugs of affirmation—a shelter in a time of storm. Thanks, Cynthia.

My list could go on and on. So could yours.

Because some cared enough to dream, to pursue, to follow through and complete their quest, our lives are more comfortable, more stable.

That is enough to spur me on. How about you?

The ancient prophet Micah isn't exactly a household word. Too bad. Though obscure, the man had his stuff together. Eclipsed by the much more famous Isaiah, who ministered among the elite, Micah took God's message to the streets.

Micah had a deep suspicion of phony religion. He saw greed in the hearts of the leaders of the kingdom of Judah, which prompted him to warn the common folk not to be deceived by religious pretense among nobility. In true prophetic style, Micah comforted the afflicted and afflicted the comfortable. He condemned sin. He exposed performance-based piety. He championed the cause of the oppressed. He predicted the fall of the nation. And he did it all at the risk of his own life.

But Micah didn't just denounce and attack, leaving everyone aware of the things he despised but none of the things he believed. Negative, ultrazealous preaching can lead people to wonder what they should do, since they hear only warnings and tirades of condemnation. Not so with Micah. Like rays of brilliant sunlight piercing charcoal-colored clouds after a storm, the prophet saved his best words for a positive message to the people. Immediately on the heels of the Lord's indictment of His people—about the time many must have begun to wonder what they had to do to make things right—Micah told them, and I am pleased to say that he did it with simplicity.

Using the time-honored method of questions and answers, he asked not one but four questions, each with greater intensity than the previous one:

"With what shall I come to the Lord and bow myself before the God on high? . . . Shall I come to Him with burnt offerings, with yearling calves? . . . Does the Lord take delight in thousands of rams, in ten thousand rivers of oil? . . . Shall I present my first-born for my rebellious acts, the fruit of my body for the sin of my soul?" (Mic. 6:6–7).

Micah's words state exactly what many, to this day, wonder about pleasing God. Teachers and preachers have made it so sacrificial . . . so complicated . . . so extremely difficult. To them, God is virtually impossible to please. Therefore, religion has become a series of long, drawn-out, deeply painful acts designed to appease this peeved Deity in the sky who takes delight in watching us squirm.

Micah erases the things on the entire list, replacing the complicated possibilities with one of the finest definitions of simple faith:

> He has told you, O man, what is good;
> And what does the Lord require of you
> But to do justice, to love kindness,
> And to walk humbly with your God? (Mic. 6:8).

God does not look for big-time, external displays. He does not require slick public performances. He does not expect gigantic acts of self-sacrificial heroism, seventy-hour work weeks of ministry, a calendar of exhausting activities, an endless number of church meetings, massive dedication that proves itself in going to the most primitive tribes hidden away in the densest jungle of the world.

What is required? Slow down and read the list aloud: To do justice . . . to love kindness . . . and to walk humbly with your God. Period.

A Finishing Touch: Faith is not a long series of religious performances or a pile of pious things. All God asks is simple faith.

A Daily Reading: Micah 6:6–8

We salute visionaries of yesteryear. They emerge from the pages of our history books as men and women of gallant faith. We shake our heads in amazement as we imagine the Herculean courage it took to stand so confidently when the majority frowned so sternly. Looking back, we laud those who refused to take "No" for an answer. We quote them with gusto. We even name our children after them. Yesterday's progress earns today's monuments of stone.

But today? What do we do with such creatures today? We brand them as irritating malcontents, reckless idealists who simply won't sit down and be quiet. Today's progressive dreamers are seen as wild-eyed extremists. Since they hate the status quo mold, most of them have a tough time going along with the system. They, in fact, loathe the system. But what they lack in diplomacy they make up for in persistence. Cooperative they're not. Resilient they are.

Give most of them a couple hundred years and they'll be admired, lauded, and knighted. But at the present moment, they just seem nuts.

I can scarcely think of a half dozen churches, for example, that would even consider having Martin Luther candidate for the pulpit. And it's doubtful that any businesses would hire Thomas Edison or Leonardo da Vinci. Which evangelical seminary would chance turning over its students majoring in systematic theology to a firebrand like John Knox? Or tell me, how would an emotionally charged free spirit like Ludwig van Beethoven fit the stuffy chair of any university's department of music? And who, today, would choose to go into battle with a blood-and-guts, straight-shooting commanding officer like George Patton? For that matter, how many votes would a crusty, outspoken, overweight visionary like Winston Churchill or a rugged Andrew Jackson get in our day of slick government and made-for-TV bureaucrats and politicians? Besides, they'd never get past the Senate Judiciary Committee. You think we'd respect their progressiveness and value their vision? Don't bet on it. People didn't in their day, either.

I came across a rather remarkable letter written over 150 years ago by Martin Van Buren, governor of New York, to President Jackson. It contains a strong, critical warning that the "evil" new railroads will disrupt business, boost unemployment, and weaken our nation's defense. Here's his conclusion:

> As you may well know, Mr. President, "railroad" carriages are pulled at the enormous speed of 15 miles per hour by "engines" which, in addition to endangering life and limb of passengers, roar and snort their way through the countryside, setting fire to crops, scaring the livestock and frightening women and children. The Almighty certainly never intended that people should travel at such breakneck speed.

Are you an eagle-type, soaring high beyond your peers? Do you find yourself bored with the maintenance of the machinery . . . yawning through the review of the rules . . . restless to cut a new swath . . . excited rather than intimidated by the risks? If so, don't expect pats on the back or great waves of applause. Chances are you may even lose a few jobs, fail a few courses, ruffle tons of feathers, and be the subject of the town gossip. Mavericks who don't color within the lines are also notorious for not staying within the fences. And that makes folks terribly uncomfortable.

But take heart! You're in good company!

A Finishing Touch: Today's alleged heretic may well be tomorrow's hero .

A Daily Reading: Psalm 103

Paul found himself between a rock and a hard place. He wanted to be in heaven but needed to be on earth. In a temporal sort of way, I share the same frustration.

> But I am hard pressed from both directions, having the desire to depart and watch the Super Bowl . . . yet to remain in the pulpit is more necessary for your sake (Philippians 1:23–24, *Swindoll Paraphrase*).

Now don't get me wrong. I love to preach. It's one of the few things I'd rather do than eat—as my wife can testify. But I also love football. With only minor adjustments, both of these "loves" can be maintained without much difficulty . . . except for one Sunday a year. Super Bowl Sunday. On that particular day I freely admit, I have a conflict.

I've thought of all sorts of alternative plans:

> Have church on Saturday.
> Place a tiny TV on the pulpit shelf and bow in silent prayer several times (to check the score).
> Put a walkman in my suit coat and wear an earphone.
> Ask an usher to signal the score periodically.
> Preach a very short message—then "slip out"
> Call in sick.

Conflicts are common. Unfortunately, they are seldom as light-hearted as this one. Some are, in fact, desperately serious.

What is a conflict? A conflict is an emotional collision. It is stress caused by incompatible desires or demands. It is what occurs when we have two or more impulses in competition with one another. The stronger the impulse, the greater the tension. The greater the tension, the louder the collision.

Conflicts come in many packages.

A mother wants to walk with God, raise her children to love the Lord and honor His name. But her husband wants none of this. He is turned off and tuned out to spiritual things. That woman has a conflict between her "mother impulses" and her "wife impulses." She lives with an emotional collision.

A college student is doing well in his studies, looking forward to medical school. Suddenly he gets word that both his parents have been killed in a car accident. Aside from his personal grief and trauma, he has lost his only source of financial supply. He must go to work, which will cause his grades to suffer, which, in turn, will minimize his chances of being accepted into medical school. The student is under the stress of incompatible desires.

Conflicts lead to frustration . . . the feeling of being "blocked" or restrained from doing what one wants to do because of something one has to do. As tension builds, the burning fuse gets shorter. Tie all this together in one tight knot, multiply it by a dozen daily encounters of a similar nature, and you have raw, naked anxiety.

I have no quick, easy solutions to complex conflicts. But I know this much: our Lord cares for His own. Knowing our limitations, He urges us to "cast all our anxieties on Him" (1 Peter 5:7) and to replace worry with active, specific prayer (Phil. 4:6).

Prayer may not stop the collision, but, like seat belts, it sure can protect us from serious damage.

A Finishing Touch: Subtract the power of Christ, the wisdom of His Word, the calming presence of the Holy Spirit, and you have unbearable collisions that lead to unbelievable tragedies.

A Daily Reading: Ephesians 6:18; Philippians 4:6

I heard a statistic the other day that blew my mind. Anna Sklar, the author of a book called *Runaway Wives*, was a guest on a local talk show. In the course of the discussion, she cited this incredible statistic: Ten years ago, for every wife or mother who walked away from her home and responsibilities, six hundred husbands and fathers did so. Today—only ten years later—for each man who walks away, two women do.

Pause and let that sink in.

Understand, I'm not advocating either, nor am I taking sides. I'm just amazed at the unbelievably rapid rise in the number of women who choose escape as the favorite method of coping.

Once upon a time, when the going got tough, the tough got going.

No longer! Contrary to our great American heritage, many of today's citizens would rather switch than fight . . . or, more honestly, quit than stick. That which was once not even an option is now standard operating procedure. Now, it's "if you start to sink, *jump*, don't bail" . . . or "if it's hard, *quit*, don't bother."

Let's press this philosophy to its ultimate conclusion. How many skyscrapers would sit unfinished? How many patients would die on the operating table? How many churches would be closed? How many athletic records would have been set? How many academic degrees and honors would have been earned? How many cars repaired? Children raised? Books written? Crops grown? Symphonies composed? Teeth straightened?

Every achievement worth remembering is stained with the blood of diligence and scarred by the wounds of disappointment. To quit, to run, to escape, to hide—none of these options solve anything. They only postpone the acceptance of, and reckoning with, reality.

Churchill put it well: "Wars are not won by evacuations."

No, battles are won in the trenches . . . in the grit and grime of courageous determination . . . in the arena of life, day in and day out, amidst the smell of sweat and the cry of anguish.

Must I be carried to the skies
   On flowery beds of ease,
While others fought to win the prize
   And sailed through bloody seas?

The apostle Paul, the man who bore on his body "the brand-marks of Jesus" (Gal. 6:17), was a living example of his own counsel:

> Therefore, my beloved brethren, be steadfast, immovable, always abounding in the work of the Lord, knowing that your toil is not in vain in the Lord. . . . Be on the alert, stand firm in the faith, act like men, be strong (1 Cor. 15:58; 16:13).

Giving thought to giving up?
Considering the possibility of quitting?
Looking for an easy way out?
Entertaining the idea of running away . . . stopping before it's finished . . . escaping from reality?
Don't! The Lord never promised you a Disneyland . . . nor a rose garden. In fact, the only time He ever used the word "easy" was when He referred to a yoke.

A Finishing Touch: Every journey is accomplished one step at a time. Don't stop now.

A Daily Reading: 1 Corinthians 15 and 16

If you question your depravity, check your attitude toward intrusions. Those inevitable, unpredictable interruptions that make us irritable . . . especially when they persist, rudely seizing our attention whether we are ready or not. And usually we're not.

Having a French origin, *intrude* emerges from two terms, meaning "to thrust in." An intrusion, therefore, is someone or something that thrusts itself into our world without permission, without an invitation, and refuses to be ignored.

Like an early-morning knock at your door.

Like a talkative passenger next to you on a packed-out flight.

Like an injury or illness that strikes at the wrong time.

Like the piercing ring of the telephone.

Like the relentless, endless demands of small children.

Like . . . no, let's stop with that one. *The constant needs and demands of a child.* Yes, constant. His or her need to be loved, to be answered, to be listened to, to be helped, held, corrected, trained, always encouraged, and occasionally spanked.

I watched a young mother in a waiting room just last week. She was pregnant and had a toddler plus one in diapers in her arms. Was she busy! Untied shoes, runny noses, twelve questions a minute, dropped rattle (five times), three falls—once on his face, loud crying, a bottle of juice that spilled in her bag. And as she mopped it up with her last clean diaper, the baby barfed right down the back of her neck. Yet with incredible patience, that mother hung in there.

Her whole world is one gigantic intrusion, I thought. *I sure hope she's got a husband who understands . . . and helps her out!*

I also wondered if that young mother realized that she was modeling an unforgettable display of Christ's message. Remember His words?

> At that time the disciples came to Jesus, saying, "Who then is greatest in the kingdom of heaven?"
>
> And He called a child to Himself and stood him in their

midst, and said, "Truly I say to you, unless you are converted and become like children, you shall not enter the kingdom of heaven.

"Whoever then humbles himself as this child, he is the greatest in the kingdom of heaven.

"And whoever receives one such child in My name receives Me; but whoever causes one of these little ones who believe in Me to stumble, it is better for him that a heavy millstone be hung around his neck, and that he be drowned in the depth of the sea" (Matt. 18:1–6).

Yes, children are the finest illustrations Jesus could have used. He flatly declares that receiving them is tantamount to receiving Him. Obviously, He believes they are worth it all, no matter how many intrusions they cause.

Not all agree. Some adults are not only selfish, they're vicious

Bob Greene, syndicated columnist based in Chicago, mentioned one such person in a recent article. This is a true account, but I warn you, it is sickening.

Greene tells of meeting a smartly dressed 27-year-old woman, professionally employed in a prestigious position. She was about to be married to a man who had a 5-year-old son by a previous marriage. Her attitude toward the boy?

"If I had $10,000 I would have the boy killed . . . I've asked around and $10,000 is about what it costs to hire someone to kill someone else."

Thinking she might be trying to shock him with a sick joke, Greene told her that her alleged humor was way off base.

"It's not a joke," she said. "I want him dead."

When Greene asked her why she was saying those things, it boiled down to intrusions. "The boy disrupts my life . . . he's cute, darling to look at. He's a very smart little boy. But he's a very bad little boy. He is overly bright, overly aggressive . . . a very active child." Then, after describing a few rather normal childish ways and demands, she stated, "If he were someone else's kid, I wouldn't mind. But now he is going to be a part of my life, and I consider him an intrusion. I have had a life of total freedom, and now there are going to be restrictions and annoyances . . . because of the kid."

Still stunned, Greene asked the woman directly how she'd feel if she paid someone to kill the boy and she woke up one morning to find the murder actually had been committed. "I'd be secretly relieved. I'd be very happy. Because of this kid I get hassled from seventeen different directions. You should hear the kid's mother after weekends when his father and I have had him. Did I go to church on Sunday? What church did I go to? It drives me crazy . . . I hate this kid."

When the columnist told her that at least this was only a vicious fantasy . . . she really didn't have $10,000 did she? "No," she sighed, "I don't have the $10,000." But as she turned to leave, she added, "But I won't always not have the $10,000!"

Can you imagine the treatment she will give that bright, busy, "very active" 5-year-old boy? Makes us wish we could *intrude* into those marriage plans.

And yet many still think mankind is basically pure and good.

Intrusions prove what the Bible has taught for centuries.

Depravity is a universal disease . . . because sin has "thrust itself in."

A Finishing Touch: Because sin "thrust itself in," God sent His Son into the world.

A Daily Reading: Romans 3

How do you feel about intrusions?

_____
_____

Like an early-morning knock at your door?

_____
_____

Like a talkative passenger next to you on a packed-out flight?

_____
_____

Like an injury or illness that strikes at the wrong time?

_____
_____

Like the piercing ring of the telephone?

_____
_____

Like the relentless, endless demands of small children?

_____
_____

Like . . . ?

_____
_____

Check your attitude.

The
Touch of
the Master

About the time we are ready
to give up, along comes the
Master, who leans over and
whispers, "Don't quit. Keep
going," as He provides His
finishing touch of grace, joy,
and love at just the right
moment. His touch assures
that we will be finishing well.

IT'S MORE THAN A JOB

A young fella rushed into a service station and asked the manager if he had a pay phone. The manager nodded, "Sure, over there." The boy pushed in a couple of dimes, dialed, and waited for an answer. Finally, someone came on the line. "Uh, sir," he said in a deep voice, "could you use an honest, hardworking young man to work for you?" The station manager couldn't help overhearing the question. After a moment or two the boy said, "Oh, you already have an honest, hardworking young man? Well, okay. Thanks just the same." With a broad smile stretched across his face, he hung up the phone and started back to his car, humming and obviously elated. "Hey, just a minute!" the station manager called after him. "I couldn't help but hear your conversation. Why are you so happy? I thought the guy said he already had somebody and didn't need you?" The young man smiled. "Well, you see, I am the honest, hardworking young man. I was just checking up on my job!"

What if you were to call your boss, disguise your voice, and ask if he could use a good employee in the same position you currently occupy. What do you think his answer would be if he didn't know you were listening?

Honest, hardworking employees are tough to find, and when you toss in competence, a positive attitude, teachability, punctuality, proper attire, a team spirit, loyalty, confidentiality, honesty, and an ability to get along well with others, wow! No wonder every boss I talk to answers my question "What is the key ingredient of your organization?" the same way: PERSONNEL.

Products don't make a company; people do. Paper isn't the secret of good communication; people are. Phones can't uphold an organization's image; people must. Projects don't need computers or copiers, slick strategies, or profound objectives nearly so much as they need committed people. Knowledgeable, cooperative, happy, diligent, quality-oriented people who are willing to do their best, regardless of who gets the credit. Servant-hearted souls, whose motives are free of greed and whose eyes are on the task, not the clock. People who think "Why not?" rather than "How come?"

What kind of employee are you? Do a little one-to-ten appraisal (ten being the best) on the following characteristics from the Book of Proverbs: diligent, thoughtful, skillful, sense of humor, loyal, teachable, humble, thorough, fair, cooperative, honest, positive.

Contrary to popular opinion, work is not the result of the curse. Adam was given the task of cultivating and keeping the Garden before sin ever entered (Gen. 2:15).

Then what was the curse? It was the addition of "thorns and thistles" that turned work into a "toil" and made the whole thing a sweaty hassle. But work itself is a privilege, a high calling, a God-appointed assignment to be carried out for His greater glory.

Today, it isn't literal briars and stinging nettles that give us fits; it's thorny people whose thistlelike attitudes add just enough irritation to make the job . . . well, just a job. It's the little things, the small yet persistent stings, that foul up the work and turn a potential thing full of wonder into a sweaty curse.

The difference is people. No, let's get specific. The difference is you.

The place you work will never be better than you make it.

A Finishing Touch: Give your boss an imaginary phone call. Listen to His response with an open mind . . . and start sweating the small stuff.

A Daily Reading: 2 Thessalonians 3

Even though I don't like it, I'm tempted to stand back, shrug, and agree with Virginia Brasier who wrote "Time of the Mad Atom":

> This is the age of the half-read page.
> And the quick hash and the mad dash.
> The bright night with the nerves tight.
> The plane hop and the brief stop.
> The lamp tan in a short span.
> The Big Shot in a good spot.
> And the brain strain and the heart pain.
> And the cat naps till the spring snaps—
> And the fun's done!

It doesn't have to be that way. We're busy, yes. Some of it can't be helped. But since when do we have to stop enjoying life while we're truckin' along at a pretty good clip? Who says that joy must exit whenever the pace picks up? I am determined not to forfeit fun just because my to-do list is so long it could easily take up a whole roll of toilet paper. I refuse to force hilarity into the back seat every time responsibility takes the wheel. If the fun's gone, it's because we didn't want it around, not because it didn't fit.

When my wife turned fifty a few years ago, our younger daughter, Colleen, and I decided it called for a celebration. After all, the half-century mark happens only once in a lifetime. Because Cynthia is so trusting, never suspicious, we knew we'd be able to pull off a classic wingding.

While running together one morning, Cols and I decided on a surprise birthday party boat ride down at the Newport Harbor. We communicated this to the family and several of Cynthia's friends. Anticipation mounted as final plans were laid . . . hors d'oeuvres, lunch on board, helium-filled balloons (all black!), a big cake, plus everyone who came was told to bring "fifty of anything wrapped in black." Cols and Charissa coordinated final plans to meet out-of-town guests at the airport in complete secrecy. The way we synchronized our activities, you'd have thought we were planning the Normandy Invasion.

The strategy was for Cynthia and me to spend the night before her birthday in a hotel on the beach—just the two of us. As we drove to the hotel on a cloudy afternoon, my mind was on "Lord, give us good weather" while she was enjoying the evening rain!

Finally, B-Day arrived—along with the sun. My excuse to get Cynthia to the dock was a boat show that was in progress. Fifteen minutes prior to our arrival, all the gang had slipped on board. Cynthia and I leisurely walked along the dock where I casually asked an individual, who was really in on the plot, if she happened to know where the "Lyn Dee Belle" was docked. "Sure do," she said. "Be happy to show her to you." She offered to climb aboard with us.

"Naw, we'll just jump on board and look around," I said. Then, as Cynthia stepped on deck, fifty family members and friends jumped up and screamed, "SURPRISE!" For the next three hours we motored around the harbor, took pictures, laughed, ate, sang, opened the craziest bunch of gifts you ever saw, celebrated, and had nothing but fun.

Cynthia will never forget her fiftieth birthday. None of us will! "We did it! She was totally surprised!" We're still talking about it.

In this day of demands and deadlines, unrealistic expectations and neurotic imaginations, the fun's often the first thing to go. And we're all tempted to stand back, shrug, and wave it good-bye.

Don't! Not even in this age of the half-read page and the mad dash. Because when the fun's gone, the brain strains and the heart pains. And life itself gets wrapped in black.

A Finishing Touch: Solomon was right: happiness and laughter do us good "like a medicine."

A Daily Reading: Ecclesiastes 3:4

Nothing touches the human heart deeper than music. This is never more true than when a group of Christians sings heartily unto their Lord. Many a cold heart on skid row has melted as the strains of some old hymn lingered in steamy streets and sleazy alleys surrounding a gospel mission. When congregations sing the praises of the King, even the demonic hosts stand at attention. "The powers of darkness fear when this sweet chant they hear, May Jesus Christ be praised!"

Such moving melodies hold out a warm welcome to strangers, comfort to the broken, refreshment to the lonely, and affirmation to the discouraged. Great music from God's people instructs and reproves, blesses and relieves.

Who hasn't nodded in agreement while singing, "Prone to wander, Lord, I feel it, Prone to leave the God I love"? Who hasn't stood taller or felt more confident after all the stanzas of "And Can It Be?" or "Am I a Soldier of the Cross?" or "A Mighty Fortress Is Our God"? And who hasn't found himself lost in wonder, love, and praise while declaring "My Hope Is in the Lord"? Or received fresh strength from "It Is Well with My Soul"?

Charles Wesley, perhaps the most prolific hymnist of all time, realized the value of corporate singing as he wrote "Oh, for a thousand tongues to sing my great Redeemer's praise." There is nothing to compare to that sound. Nothing.

But have you noticed the fly in our melodic ointment? It is not a lack of beauty or harmony, nor is it insufficient volume or intensity. It is, plain and simple, the presence of words with an absence of meaning. We sing well, but we fail to heed the message hidden behind the bars.

Stop and think. There's a line in "Take My Life and Let It Be" that always makes me pause as the words stick in my throat: "Take my silver and my gold, not a mite would I withhold." Imagine! Not even "a mite"! We all sing that with such ease, yet I have known few who wouldn't withhold something. Including me.

And how about this one?

> Have Thine own way Lord! Have Thine own way!
> Thou art the Potter, I am the clay.
> Mold me and make me after Thy will
> While I am waiting, yielded and still.

Really? Truly yielded? Genuinely still? Absolutely willing to be molded and made after His will?

Last Sunday after the service our congregation sang "I Give All My Witness to You" . . . and then we left. We all got into our cars, drove away, and most of us have not seen one another since. What's been happening? Has He had our witness? Have the days that passed been that much different than two weeks earlier? A month? Those thoughts haunt me.

Think of each song or hymn as a promise to God, a binding statement of your commitment. Picture the results of this commitment as you sing it with gusto. Then, after the song has ended, apply it with the same gusto.

God not only loves a cheerful giver, He honors a sincere singer.

A Finishing Touch: This Sunday put yourself into the lyrics of each hymn, considering them your own personal credo. See what a difference it makes.

A Daily Reading: Revelation 5:9–10

There we sat, a cluster of six. A stubby orange candle burned at the center of our table, flickering eerie shadows across our faces. One spoke; five listened. Every question was handled with such grace, such effortless ease. Each answer was drawn from deep wells of wisdom, shaped by tough decisions, and nurtured by time. And pain. Mistakes and mistreatment. Like forty years in the same church. And seasoned by travel. Like having ministered around the world. And honed by tests, risks, heartbreaks, and failures. But, like the best wines, it was those decades in the same crucible that made his counsel invaluable. Had those years been spent in the military, he would have had a chest full of medals.

His age? Seventy-two. His face? Rugged as fifty miles of bad road. His eyes? Ah, those eyes. Piercing. as if they penetrated to the back of your cranium. He had seen it all, weathered it all—all the flack and delights of a flock. Outlasted all the fads and gimmicks of gullible and greedy generations, known the ecstasy of seeing lives revolutionized, the agony of lives ruined, and the monotony of lives unchanged. He had paid his dues—and had the scars to prove it.

This is not to say he was over the hill. Or to suggest that he had lost his zest for living, his ability to articulate his thoughts, or his keen sense of humor. There we sat for well over three hours, hearing his stories, pondering his principles, questioning his conclusions, and responding to his ideas. The evening was punctuated with periodic outbursts of laughter followed by protracted periods of quiet talk.

As I participated, I was suddenly twenty-six years old again. A young seminarian and pastoral intern, existing in a no-man's land between a heart full of desire and a head full of dreams. Long on theological theories but short on practical experience. I had answers to questions no one was asking but a lack of understanding on the things that really mattered. In momentary flashbacks, I saw myself in the same room with this man thirty years earlier, drinking at the same well, soaking up the same spirit. Back then, however, I was merely impressed . . . this time I was deeply moved. Thirty years ago he had been a model; now he had become a mentor. Thoroughly human and absolutely authentic, he had emerged a well-worn vessel of honor fit for the Master's use. And I found myself profoundly grateful that Ray Stedman's shadow had crossed my life.

In a day of tarnished leaders, fallen heroes, busy parents, frantic coaches, arrogant authority figures, and eggheaded geniuses, we need mentors like never before—we need guides, not gods. Approachable, caring souls who help us negotiate our way through life's labyrinth. Invisible partners, whispering hope and reproofs on the journey toward excellence.

As we said good-bye to Ray that evening, I walked a little slower. I thought about the things he had taught me without directly instructing me, about the courage he had given me without deliberately exhorting me. I wondered how it had happened. I wondered why I had been so privileged.

A nostalgic knot formed in my throat as I forced myself to realize that, at age seventy-two, he didn't have many more years left in this world. I found myself wanting to run back to his car and tell him again how much I loved and admired him.

But it was late. And after all, I was a fifty-five-year-old man. A husband. A father. A grandfather. A pastor. To some, a leader.

But as I stood there alone in the cold night air, I suddenly realized what I wanted to be when I grew up

---

A Finishing Touch: A mentor knows how to stretch without insulting, affirm without flattering, release without abandoning us.

A Daily Reading: 1 Thessalonians 5:1–11

Step into the time tunnel with me and let's travel together back to Uz (not the wizard of, but the land of). Wherever it was, Uz had a citizen who was respected by everyone. Why? Because he was blameless, upright, God-fearing, and clean living. He had ten children, thousands of head of livestock, acres and acres of land, a great many servants, and a substantial stack of cash. No one would deny that he was "the greatest of all the men of the East," for he had earned that reputation through years of hard work and honest dealings with others. His name was Job, a synonym for integrity and godliness.

Yet, within a matter of hours, adversity fell upon this fine man like an avalanche of jagged rocks. He lost his livestock, his crops, his land, his servants, and—if you can believe it—all ten children. Soon thereafter he also lost his health.

I plead with you to stop reading right now, close your eyes for sixty seconds, and identify with that good man, crushed beneath the weight of adversity.

The book that bears his name records an entry he made into his journal soon after the rocks stopped falling. With a quivering hand he wrote:

> "Naked I came from my mother's womb,
> And naked I shall return there.
> The Lord gave and the Lord has taken away.
> Blessed be the name of the Lord" (Job 1:21).

Following this incredible statement, God adds: "Through all this Job did not sin nor did he blame God" (1:22).

Right about now, I'm shaking my head and asking myself, "How in the world could he handle such ordeals and such grief so calmly?" Think of the aftermath: bankruptcy, pain, ten fresh graves . . . and the loneliness of those empty rooms. Yet he worshiped God, he did not sin, nor did he blame his Maker.

The logical questions are: Why didn't he? What kept him from bitterness or even thoughts of suicide?

At the risk of oversimplifying the situation, I suggest three basic answers which I have discovered from searching through this book.

First, Job claimed God's loving sovereignty. He believed that the Lord who gave had every right to take away (Job 1:21). In his own words he stated such:

> "Shall we indeed accept good from God and not accept adversity?" (Job 2:10).

Job looked up, claiming his Lord's right to rule over his life.

Who was the fool who said God has no right to add sand to our clay or marks to our vessel or fire to His workmanship? Who dares lift his clay fist heavenward and question the Potter's plan? Not Job! To him, God's sovereignty was interwoven with His love.

Second, he counted on God's promise of resurrection. Do you remember his immortal words?

> "And as for me, I know that my Redeemer lives,
> And at the last He will take His stand on the earth.
> Even after my skin is destroyed, Yet from my flesh I shall see God" (Job 19:25–26).

Job looked ahead, counting on his Lord's promise to make all things bright and beautiful in the life beyond. He knew that at that time all pain, death, sorrow, tears, and adversity would be removed. Knowing that "hope does not disappoint" (Rom. 5:5), Job endured today by envisioning tomorrow.

Third, he confessed his own lack of understanding. What a relief this brings! He didn't feel obligated to explain why. Listen to his admission of this fact:

> "I know that Thou canst do all things,
> And that no purpose of Thine can be thwarted.
> 'Who is this that hides counsel without knowledge?'

"Therefore I have declared that which I did not understand,
Things too wonderful [too deep] for me, which I did not know."
'Hear, now, and I will speak;
I will ask Thee, and do Thou instruct me'" (Job 42:2–4).

Job looked within, confessing his inability to put it all together. He rested his adversity with God, not feeling forced to answer why.

Perhaps you, too, are beginning to get nicked by falling rocks. Or maybe the avalanche has already fallen. Then again, maybe not. Maybe adversity seems ten thousand miles away . . . as remote as the land of Uz. That's the way Job felt a few minutes before it struck.

Review these thoughts as you turn out the lights tonight, my friend, just in case. Some pottery gets pretty fragile sitting in the sun day after day.

A Finishing Touch: When we're looking in all the right directions, we won't take the wrong turn.

A Daily Reading: Job 1–2, 42

Try to make time this weekend to read the entire book of Job, for only then do you really see the true extent of Job's honest dealings with God and his steadfast faith in the face of adversity.

Then, honestly look at your own life and your own dealings with the Lord. Think about your past . . . those times of adversity in your own life. Were you able to look up, look ahead, and look within?

_____

_____

Where are you now in your journey of faith?

_____

_____

If you are climbing over the ragged rocks of adversity, take His hand and let Him lead you through. In the midst of it all, it is His touch which comforts and guides.

If the road ahead is smooth right now, get ready. Watch out for falling rocks!

A MATTER OF OBEDIENCE

Leading can be awfully lonely and terribly frustrating.

I haven't always believed that. Fact is, when I was a starry-eyed seminary student back around '59 and '60, I had this crazy idea that a leader lived a charmed life. Especially a spiritual leader. My fantasy included contented people, smiling and grateful; plenty of time to think, study, and do relaxed research; few interruptions; quick and simple building projects; no financial woes; short counseling sessions with folks who were eager and happy to adjust their lives according to Scripture; untold energy; few committees; sermons that virtually jumped from the text, then into my notes and out of my mouth; unchallenged respect, loud applause, and unending harmony. No conflicts. No confrontations . . . no kidding!

You're smiling. (I told you it was a fantasy.)

It's amazing what three decades can do to a wastebasket full of theories. Today I would tell anyone thinking about becoming a spiritual leader to think again. It's not that they're not needed; goodness knows, this ornery planet of depraved humanity can always use a few more leaders who are Christian to the core. The problem is, it's a lonelier task than it used to be.

Part of that is expected. Nobody who speaks for God can spend all his or her time with people. Furthermore, solitude is a healthy and needed discipline. But there are some things you have to decide on and deal with that take a lot of the fun out of leading. And the frustrations can be downright maddening.

In the midst of all this, it always helps me to return to my "call." Thousands of miles away from home, stationed on a tiny island in the South Pacific, I distinctly remember the inner surge of assurance that I would be neither fulfilled nor happy doing anything other than ministry. It meant changing careers and returning to graduate school. It meant retooling my mental machinery for a lifetime of study. It meant living my life under the always curious and sometimes demanding scrutiny of the public eye, and, if necessary, being willing to go to the wall for the sake of the Gospel. None of this mattered. God had spoken to my heart, and there was no turning back. It was a matter of obedience.

I will spend the rest of my years overwhelmed at His grace in calling me—me, of all unlikely people—to work in His vineyard. The loneliness and the frustrations notwithstanding, I absolutely love it. To tell the truth, I'm having the time of my life!

But that doesn't mean I don't take Him seriously.

We must recognize that the Lord, our God, is responsible for our appointment to any place of leadership.

Over all other suggestions and advice, we must seek to hear the counsel of Almighty God as revealed in Scripture.

We must take refuge in and rely on the Spirit of God rather than our own flesh and skill.

With our whole heart we must fear Jesus Christ, our Lord, and acknowledge Him as the sovereign Head of the church, deserving of our unreserved faithfulness, submission, diligence, and commitment.

For me, there are no other options.

It's a matter of obedience.

How about you?

A Finishing Touch: Take refuge in and rely on the Spirit of God rather than your own flesh and skill.

A Daily Reading: 1 Timothy 2:1–7

When it comes to mistakes, we need a great deal of tolerance. And a sense of humor doesn't hurt, either.

This is certainly true when it comes to mistakes in print. Sometimes these are minor and create no problem for anyone. On other occasions they are embarrassing for the publisher as well as the person being mentioned. Like the one I ran across recently in the sports section of the newspaper.

A volleyball coach was being featured, and the article went on and on about her background, her superb ability, win-loss record, and style of coaching. The next day, tucked away in a much less obvious place, was a one-sentence apology, which said, in the briefest number of words, that the coach was, in fact, a man, not a woman. Ouch! At least they corrected the error!

Occasionally, mistakes are just plain funny . . . not meant to be, you understand, but they are. Who hasn't happened upon one every once in a while in a church bulletin? One of my all-time favorites was the announcement letting people know about a "sing-in" following an evening service. Unfortunately, this is the way it appeared:

> There will be a sin-in at the Johnson home immediately following the pastor's evening message on "Intimate Fellowship."

There are even a few human-error scenes in Scripture that can elicit laughter. Some of them, I freely admit, strike me as nothing short of hilarious.

Among my favorites is the one tucked away in 1 Samuel 15 where King Saul was commanded by Samuel, very clearly, that he should not only destroy the Amalekites, but also every living creature in the region of the Amalekites. He went, he saw, he slew . . . but he failed to complete the task. Instead of total annihilation, he captured the king and also spared a lot of the animals.

When Samuel heard of the king's disobedience, the prophet

showed up and asked why. Saul lied. "I have carried out the command of the Lord," he said.

Samuel's line is classic: "(You obeyed, huh?) What then is this bleating of the sheep in my ears, and the lowing of the oxen which I hear?"

Can't you just picture it? All the time old Saul's mouth was moving, there was this strange mixture of animal sounds in the distance. No, his sin wasn't funny . . . but the way he got caught red-handed was. The animals told on him! "Baa . . . Baa . . . Moo!"

So long as there is humanity on this old earth, there will be mistakes and failures. If you can't tolerate those who make them, I'd suggest you stop making them yourself!

General John Sedgwick did. In fact, his last words were spoken while looking over the parapet at the enemy line during the Battle of Spotsylvania in 1864. With great gusto he sneered, "They couldn't hit an elephant at this dist—"

A Finishing Touch: Remember, when it comes to mistakes, we need a great deal of tolerance. And a sense of humor doesn't hurt, either.

A Daily Reading: 1 Samuel 15

Be honest now, can you keep a secret?

When privileged information passes through one of the gates of your senses, does it remain within the walls of your mind, or is it only a matter of time before a leak occurs? Do you refuse to help the grapevine climb higher, or do you fertilize it with your wagging, unguarded tongue? When someone says, "Now this is confidential," do you respect their trust or ignore it, either instantly or ultimately?

The longer I live, the more I realize the scarcity of people who can be fully trusted with confidential information. And the longer I live, the more I value those rare souls who fall into that category! As a matter of fact, if I were asked to list the essential characteristics that mark a person of integrity and trust, the ability to maintain confidences would rank very near the top.

A portion of the physician's Hippocratic Oath comes to mind:

> And whatsoever I shall see or hear in the course of my profession . . . if it be what should not be published abroad, I will never divulge, holding such things to be holy secrets.

We would be justly offended by a doctor who treated our "holy secrets" lightly. The same applies to a minister or an attorney, a counselor or a parent, a teacher or a secretary, a colleague or a friend. Especially a close friend.

Solomon wrote some strong words concerning this subject in his Proverbs. Listen to his wise counsel and remember it the next time you are tempted to run off at the mouth:

> Wise men store up knowledge, but with the mouth of the foolish ruin is at hand (10:14).

> When there are many words, transgression is unavoidable, But he who restrains his lips is wise (10:19).

He who goes about as a talebearer reveals secrets, But he who is trustworthy conceals a matter (11:13).

The one who guards his mouth preserves his life; The one who opens wide his lips comes to ruin (13:3).

He who goes about as a slanderer reveals secrets, Therefore do not associate with a gossip (20:19).

Like a bad tooth and an unsteady foot is confidence in a faithless man in time of trouble (25:19).

Like a city that is broken into and without walls is a man who has no control over his spirit (25:28).

In light of these scriptural admonitions, I suggest we establish four practical ground rules:
1. Whatever you're told in confidence, do not repeat.
2. Whenever you're tempted to tell a secret, do not yield.
3. Whomever you're talking about, do not gossip.
4. However you're prone to disagree, do not slander.
Be honest now, can you keep a secret? Prove it.

A Finishing Touch: A confidence kept gives others confidence in you.

A Daily Reading: Romans 1:21–32

This thing called life is an awfully long journey. For some, it seems an endless trip, filled with thankless responsibilities and relentless tasks, disappointments and deadlines, and daily demands.

Being imperfect doesn't help. Every so often we make stupid decisions. We don't mean to, but we say things we wish we could retrieve. Selfishly, we look out for number one and later regret it. We act impulsively and realize, after the fact, how foolish we were, how dumb we looked. On top of all that, we hurt the ones we love the most. All this stuff caves in on us at certain times and we wonder how anybody could ever love us . . . especially God.

Ever get the feeling that life is a violin solo and you're wearing boxing gloves? I sure do. Some days it seems like this pilgrimage from earth to heaven is an Indianapolis 500 and I'm driving an obsolete, rusty tank.

That thought hits me when my load seems extra heavy and it appears that the other guy's load is virtually nonexistent. And haven't you noticed, comparison is lethal! When you're down—I mean whale-belly, bottom-of-the-ocean down—and you focus on how easy others seem to have it, self-pity siphons that last drop of motivation you needed to finish the day. Every time we compare (yes, *every* time) we wind up with the short end of the stick. Either we start feeling smug and sassy or we feel even worse because the other person is better looking or makes more money or is thinner or smarter or wears nicer clothes or has gotten the breaks or is better read or . . . or . . . .

When we start thinking like this, we need to turn our mind to the "one anothers" in the New Testament. Here's just a sampling: Love one another, build up one another, live in peace with one another, confess your sins to one another, speak to one another, admonish one another, comfort one another, pray for one another.

I deliberately saved my favorite for last· "Bear one another's burdens . . . " (Gal. 6:2).

Imagine two mountain hikers trudging along, each carrying a

backpack. The one on the left has a tiny, light pack that a kid could carry, while the poor soul on the right is so loaded down we can't even see his head or his body . . . just a couple of spindly legs trying to hold up under the burden he's carrying.

Let's imagine what he might be lugging in that pack down that long road. It could be a long-standing grudge that's poisoning his insides. It might be a broken relationship with his wife or one of his kids. That pack could be loaded with unpaid bills, all of them overdue.

The question is: Where can that fella on the right go to unload so the fella on the left can help "bear the burden?" By sitting in church alongside a few hundred or a couple thousand other folks? Hardly. What he needs most is to be involved in an adult fellowship in a small-group setting, a place where there is the person to person caring and the opportunity for authentic sharing. Where he will feel free, without embarrassment or shame, to tell his secret or state his struggle; where someone will listen, help him unload, and give him fresh strength.

Adult fellowships and small groups are not miniature church services. They are pockets of people who love Christ and believe in helping one another. Their arms are open to those with packs too big for one person. They don't point fingers or preach or compare. They are your brothers and sisters in Christ.

Once you begin unloading that pack, you'll discover how much easier the journey seems.

A Finishing Touch: Are you involved in a small fellowship group? If not, consider doing so—especially if your load is too heavy.

A Daily Reading: Galatians 5 and 6

We don't hear much about *gumption* any more.

Too bad, since we need it more than ever these days. I was raised on gumption (my parents also called it "spizzerinctum")—as were my own children, especially when I was trying to motivate them.

Seems a shame that such a grand old word has dropped through the cracks, especially since quitting is now more popular than finishing.

Can't you just see it as a whole new academic field—"Gumptionology 101"—in some college catalog? That will never happen, however, since gumption is better caught than taught.

As is true of most character traits, it is woven so subtly into the fabric of one's life that few ever stop and identify it. It is hidden—like the thick steel bars set within concrete columns that support 10-lane freeways. And while gumption may be hidden, it's a "most important tool" for getting the job done.

Gumption enables us to save money rather than spend every dime we make. It keeps us at a hard task, like practicing piano or losing weight . . . and keeping it lost . . . or reading the Bible all the way through in a year's time.

Most folks get a little gumption in their initial birth packet, but it's a tool that rusts rather quickly. Here are some pointers that will help you keep it well-oiled:

Gumption begins with a firm commitment. Daniel "made up his mind" long before he was dumped in a Babylonian boot camp (Dan. 1:8). Joshua didn't hesitate to declare his commitment in his famous "as for me and my house" speech (Josh. 24:15). Isaiah "set his face like flint" (Isa. 50:7). You want gumption to continue to the end? Start strong!

Gumption means being disciplined one day at a time. Rather than focusing on the whole enchilada, take it in bite-sized chunks. The whole of any objective can overwhelm even the most courageous.

Writing a book? Do it one page at time. Running a marathon? One step at a time. Trying to master a new language? Try one word at a time. Divide any project into its smallest segment and it doesn't seem all that intimidating, does it? Discipline comes one day at a time.

Gumption requires being alert to subtle temptations. Gumption plans ahead, watching out for associations that weaken us (Prov. 13:20), procrastination that steals from us (24:30–34), and rationalizations that lie to us (23:4, 25:28). People who achieve their goals stay alert.

Our adversary is a master strategist, forever fogging up our minds and senses with smoke screens. Gumption stabs us awake, keeps us wide-eyed and ready.

Gumption requires the encouragement of accountability. People—especially close friends or those with the gift of encouragement—keep our tanks pumped full of enthusiasm. They communicate "You can do it. You can make it!" a dozen different ways.

At David's low-water mark, his friend Jonathan stepped in. When Elijah was ready to cash in everything, along came Elisha. With Paul it was Timothy . . . or Silas or Barnabas or Dr. Luke. People need people, which is why Solomon came on so strong about iron sharpening iron (Prov. 17:17).

Gumption comes easier when we remember that finishing has its own unique rewards. Jesus told the Father He had "accomplished" His assignment (John 17:4). On more than one occasion Paul referred to "finishing the course" (Acts 20:24; 2 Tim. 4:7).

Those who only start projects never know the surge of satisfaction that comes with slapping hands together, wiping away those beads of perspiration, and saying that beautiful four-letter word, "Done!" Desire accomplished is sweet to the soul.

Are you underway? Good for you! If the journey seems extra long today, enjoy a gust of wind at your back from these words out of *The Living Bible*. It's one of those spizzerinctum Scriptures:

> Let us not get tired of doing what is right, for after a while we will reap a harvest of blessing if we don't get discouraged and quit (Gal. 6:9).

A Finishing Touch: Gumption may be hidden, but it always shows.

A Daily Reading: Look up the Scripture references mentioned above.

I ran across the word "gumption" again while reading Robert Pirsig's *Zen and the Art of Motorcycle Maintenance*. Singing the praises of all that gumption represents, he wrote:

> I like the word "gumption" because it's so homely and so forlorn and so out of style it looks as if it needs a friend and isn't likely to reject anyone who comes along. It's an old Scottish word, once used a lot by pioneers, but . . . seems to have all but dropped out of use.
>
> A person filled with gumption doesn't sit around, dissipating and stewing about things. He's at the front of the train of his own awareness, watching to see what's up the track and meeting it when it comes.

A little later Pirsig applies gumption to life, hiding his comments behind the word picture of repairing a motorcycle:

> If you're going to repair a motorcycle, an adequate supply of gumption is the first and most important tool. If you haven't got that you might as well gather up all the other tools and put them away, because they won't do you any good.
>
> Gumption is the psychic gasoline that keeps the whole thing going. If you haven't got it, there's no way the motorcycle can possibly be fixed. But if you have got it and know how to keep it, there's absolutely no way in the whole world that motorcycle can keep from getting fixed. It's bound to happen. Therefore the thing that must be monitored at all times and preserved before anything else is gumption.

Ah, those predicaments . . . life is full of them. Often they are of our own making. Other times they just seem to happen mysteriously to us. Occasionally, predicaments are comical or borderline crazy. Sometimes they can be irritating and troublesome. But one thing is for sure: predicaments are unpredictable. And embarrassing. And confusing. And really weird.

Ever dreamed yourself into a predicament? My wife does so rather regularly. The next morning she has me in stitches as she vividly describes her nocturnal quandary, which usually has all the ingredients of a spine-tingling Robert Ludlum novel. She gets into a jam or she finds herself in a situation which, to borrow from Churchill, is like "a riddle wrapped in a mystery inside an enigma."

The wonderful thing about such dreams, of course, is just that—they're dreams. It's those times when you don't wake up that make predicaments so maddening. How many times have I asked, "Dear Lord, why are you doing this to me?"

Like the time I was leading a Bible study at a church I'd never attended before. Shortly after getting underway, I noticed two people (latecomers) standing at the door, reluctant to join us. The woman was much older than the man, making me think they were mother and son. I paused, looked in their direction, and welcomed them to join our group, saying, "Why don't you and your mother pull up a chair and join us?" Well, you could've heard a pin drop. Too late, I realized my mistake. She was his wife! Throughout the first part of the session (which seemed like an eternity), I felt like dead meat, and they glared at me like a couple of circling buzzards. When we took a coffee break, they were out of there. As Jimmy Durante used to say, "What a revoltin' development!"

At times like this, I find a measure of relief in knowing that Scripture records one predicament after another. Can you imagine how Peter felt immediately after he had deliberately denied the Lord for the third time . . . then heard that ominous cock crowing in the distance? Talk about embarrassing!

And what about Daniel, who refused to obey the injunction of King Darius. Though he did no wrong (in fact, he continued to obey God), he wound up spending the night in a den of lions. Talk about confusing!

And who can forget David's inexplicable actions when he fled from Saul and found himself in enemy territory . . . actually, in the presence of Achish, king of Gath. Instead of realizing that his actions would only complicate his dilemma, "he disguised his sanity . . . and acted insanely in their hands, and scribbled on the doors of the gate, and let his saliva run down into his beard" (1 Sam. 21:13). Talk about weird!

I'm also comforted when I realize that God is in sovereign control of all of life. He not only knows the times and the seasons; He is also Lord of the unexpected and the unpredictable. Our times *and* our trials are in His hands. Even when we feel embarrassed or confused or do something really weird.

Whether we're on Cloud Nine, enjoying His blessings, or caught in the thicket of some tangled predicament, He hasn't let us go. By His grace, He remains "for us" (Rom. 8:31).

A Finishing Touch: Remember, He is the God of your soaring spirits as well as your perplexing predicaments.

A Daily Reading: Romans 8

One of George Bernard Shaw's statements frequently flashes through my mind: "Liberty means responsibility. That is why most men dread it." In a day when most people pass the buck with merely a shrug, those words bite and sting. It's one thing to sing and dance to liberty's tunes, but it's something else entirely to bear the responsibility for paying the band.

There are numerous examples of this. Leadership carries with it a few privileges and perks, but living with the responsibility of that task makes a reserved parking space and your own bathroom pale into insignificance. Conceiving children is a moment of sheer ecstasy, but rearing them as a loving and caring parent represents years of thankless responsibility. Enjoying a great conference is delightful and memorable, but behind the scenes it requires hours of creative thinking, disciplined planning, choosing the right people to lead various activities, and responsible arranging. Running an organization that gets a job done, leaving those involved feeling fulfilled and appreciated, can be exciting, fun, and stretching, but it's a nightmare unless the details of responsibility are clearly set forth and maintained.

Back in the early 1960s Admiral Rickover wrote these lines to those who are at the helm:

> Responsibility is a unique concept. It can only reside and inhere in a single individual. You may share it with others, but your portion is not diminished. You may delegate it, but it is still with you. . . . If responsibility is rightfully yours, no evasion or ignorance or passing the blame can shift the burden to someone else. Unless you can point your finger at the one who is responsible when something goes wrong, then you never had anyone really responsible.

Tough words, but true. Rickover never was one to concern himself with tact. Today, perhaps, his kind of grit is needed more than ever before.

Big projects and meaningful achievements get done not by dreamers but by doers, not by armchair generals who watch and frown from a distance but by brave troops in the trenches, not by fans in the bleachers but by committed coaches and players on the field, not by those who stay neutral and play it safe but by those who get off the fence of indecision, even though their decisions are occasionally unpopular.

All this reminds me of a full-page advertisement I saw in *The Wall Street Journal*:

> DECISIONS, DECISIONS: Sometimes the decision to do nothing is wise. But you can't make a career of doing nothing. Freddie Fulcrum weighed everything too carefully. He would say, "On the one hand . . . but then, on the other," and his arguments weighed out so evenly he never did anything. When Freddie died, they carved a big zero on his tombstone. If you decide to fish—fine. Or, if you decide to cut bait—fine. But if you decide to do nothing, you're not going to have fish for dinner.

The secret of true liberty is responsibility. And that calls for decisions, decisions. Tough decisions. Lonely decisions. Unpleasant decisions. Misunderstood decisions. Courageous decisions.

As I recall, Jesus often had fish for dinner.

A Finishing Touch: "Responsibility is the first step in responsibility" (William Edward Burghardt Du Bois).

A Daily Reading: Joel 3:14

A time-honored, effective method of evangelism is your personal testimony. Just telling about your spiritual pilgrimage. How you found bread as a beggar.

The skeptic may deny your doctrine or attack your church, but he cannot honestly ignore the fact that your life has been cleaned up and revolutionized. He may stop his ears to the presentations of a preacher like me, or the pleadings of an evangelist, but he is somehow attracted to the human-interest story of how you—John Q. Public—found peace within. Believe me, the steps that led to your conversion are far more appealing and appropriate to the lost than a pulpit exposition of John 3 or Romans 5.

On six separate occasions between Paul's third missionary journey and his trip to Rome, he stood before different audiences and presented Christ to them (Acts 22–26). Six times he stood alone, addressing unbelievers, many of them hostile and rude. And each time Paul used the same method: his personal testimony. Each time he simply shared how his own life had been changed by the invasion of Christ and the indwelling of His power. Not once did he argue or debate with them. He didn't try to preach a sermon.

Why? Because one of the most convincing, unanswerable arguments on earth regarding Christianity is one's personal experience with the Lord Jesus Christ along with the exciting results of His presence in your life.

Now I'm not talking about some stale, dragged-out verbal marathon. That kind of testimony never attracted anyone! I'm speaking of an effective, powerful missile launched from your lips to the ears of the unsaved. Consider these five suggestions:

1. *You want to be listened to, so be interesting.* No one, no matter how gracious, enjoys being bored. It's a contradiction to talk about how exciting Christ really is in an uninteresting way. Remember to guard against religious clichés, jargon, and hard-to-understand terminology. Theologians, beware!

2. *You want to be understood, so be logical.* Think of your salvation in

three phases and construct your testimony accordingly: (a) before you were born again—the struggles within, the loneliness, lack of peace, absence of love, unrest, and fears; (b) the decision that revolutionized your life; and (c) the change—the difference it has made since you received Christ.

3. *You want the moment of your new birth to be clear, so be specific.* Don't be vague. Speak of Christ, not the church. Emphasize faith more than feeling. Be simple and direct as you describe what you did or what you prayed or what you said. This is crucial!

4. *You want your testimony to be used, so be practical.* Be human and honest as you talk. Don't promise, "All your problems will end if you will become a Christian," for that isn't true. Try to think as unbelievers think. Theoretical stuff won't attract their attention as much as practical reality. It's helpful if you will admit to some continuing struggles. The secret now is He lives inside.

5. *You want your testimony to produce results, so be warm and genuine.* A smile breaks down more barriers than the hammer blows of cold, hard facts. Let your enthusiasm flow freely. It's hard to convince someone of the sheer joy and excitement of knowing Christ if you're wearing a face like a jail warden. Above all, be positive and courteous. Absolutely refuse to argue. Nobody I ever met was "arm wrestled" into the kingdom. Insults and put-downs turn people off.

Ask God to open your lips and honor your words . . . but be careful! Once your missile hits the target, you'll become totally dissatisfied with your former life as an earthbound, secret-service saint.

A Finishing Touch: No persuasive technique will ever take the place of your personal testimony. If you have not discovered the value of telling others how God rearranged your life, you've missed a vital link in the chain of His plan for reaching the lost.

A Daily Reading: Acts 21:17–21

Average life spans are shorter than most of us realize. Unlike the great redwood trees that can last for a thousand or more years, most other things come and go relatively fast. For instance, a face-lift only lasts six to ten years; a dollar bill only lasts for eighteen months; a painted line on the road only remains for three to four months; and a tornado seldom lasts more than ten minutes.

I purposely omitted human beings. There are differences of opinion, but most agree that our lifespan averages somewhere between seventy-five and eighty years. That may sound encouraging to the young and disturbing to those in their sixties, seventies, and eighties. The simple fact is, however, nobody knows for sure how long he or she may live.

When we read *and believe* the warnings in Scripture, there is little doubt that life is short. James pulls no punches when he writes, "You are just a vapor that appears for a little while and then vanishes away" (4:14).

Life? It's a puff of smoke . . . a cloud of dust. . . .

So? Why are you waiting to do something you've been intending to do? It could be now or never, you know. You don't have forever. Get at it!

> If you're putting off something you've been meaning to do, what are you waiting for? Always wanted to play the banjo? Start taking lessons. Dreamt about visiting the Greek Islands? Call a travel agent. Hate your bathroom wallpaper? Scrape it off and paint. Feel better if you exercised? Start jogging. Love the taste of home-grown tomatoes? Plant your own. Angry about the potholes in your street? Go to your town meetings. Whatever you've been putting off, do it now. Tomorrow may be too late [*Wall Street Journal*].

Go back and read those closing words once again. The average life span may be seventy-five to eighty, but who can say you or I have that long? We may have less than two years or, for that matter, less than two weeks. Vanishing vapors aren't known for longevity.

Since this is true, let's do our best to make the time we have count. Rather than live with reluctance, let's live with exuberance. Instead of fearing what's ahead, let's face it head-on, with enthusiasm. And because life is so terribly short, let's do everything we can to make it sweet.

How? Three thoughts come to mind.

First, *act on your impulse*. Don't wait for the perfect moment. A woman in my former church took these words to heart and contacted a person she hadn't talked to for a long time. The person was surprised and thrilled. "You have no idea how much your call has meant to me," she said. Later the woman who had received the call admitted she had planned to take her life that very afternoon. The call had changed her mind.

Second, *focus on the positive*. Merchants of negativism may be strong and sound convincing, but their message is debilitating. Life's too short for that. Spread germs of cheer. Joy is contagious.

Third, *traffic in the truth*. Refuse to stake your claim on hearsay. Check out the facts. Be discerning. If you are a conduit of communication, speak only the truth. If you're not absolutely sure, keep quiet. Lies can outlive lives, unfortunately.

Short and sweet. That's the only way to go.

A Finishing Touch: Have you been putting off something you really want or need to do? You don't have forever. Get at it!

A Daily Reading: James 4:13–17

Few things turn our crank faster than being around big-minded, enthusiastic, broad-shouldered visionaries. Disinterested in trivial matters and too busy to concern themselves with who might think what about a particular issue, they focus on forests with little worry over a few trees. They are positive, on the move, excited about exploring new vistas, inspired, and inspiring. While others are preoccupied with tiny tasks and nit-picking squabbles, these people see opportunity in every difficulty and helpful lessons in every setback.

Few things turn us off quicker than being around small-minded, pessimistic, narrow-world, tedious frowners. Engrossed in the minutiae of what won't work and remembering a half dozen worst-case scenarios, they can throw more cold water on a creative idea than a team of fire fighters snuffing out a candle.

It's not caution we resent. Caution is necessary and wise. Caution keeps the visionary realistic. No, it's the tiny-focused, squint-eyed, tight-lipped, stingy soul that drives us batty. The best word is petty . . . as in petty cash, petty larceny, petty minded.

"Pettiness," writes George Will, "is the tendency of people without large purposes."

Petty people are worse than stubborn; they are negative and rigidly inflexible. While we work overtime to come up with some soaring idea, they've already thought up eight reasons it won't fly.

And have you noticed? Pettiness is omnipresent. In fact, I have a theory about pettiness: Where two or three are gathered, there it is in the midst, putting a damper on the joy of discovery.

There's a classic example of this in a "Peanuts" cartoon. Snoopy is having the time of his canine life on a frozen pond. On his bare paws he is spinning and twirling with the most satisfied look you can imagine. What fun!

Suddenly Lucy shows up with her famous frown-and-glare stare.

"That's not skating. That's sliding!" she yells, with hands on hips. "You don't have any skates on! You're just sliding on your feet! That's not skating!"

Snoopy glides to a stop in front of her, somewhat startled. He begins to slump as she continues her lecture.

"Skating is when you have skates on! You are not skating at all! You are just sliding!"

By now the poor pup is devastated. Finally he slinks away toward the side of the pond, thinking, "How could I have been so stupid?"

The last scene finds Snoopy off the pond, sitting alone on a bench, saying to himself, "I thought I was having fun."

You've had a similar experience, haven't you? Maybe it came from some authority figure whose commitment to a set of itty-bitsy rules and regulations clipped your creative wings till they bled.

Or maybe your encounter with pettiness came from a perfectionist who locked you behind the bars of his or her own prison.

Perhaps the Lucy in your life was a group of legalists who watched you over the top of their glasses, making sure you colored within the lines as you stayed inside their circle of accepted behavior.

Whatever or wherever or whoever manifests pettiness isn't my concern . . . stopping its effect on us is. Why? Because the church seems to be the breeding ground for this legalistic disease. It's a ruthless killer on the loose, and we have no business nurturing it any longer.

Pettiness takes a terrible toll. It kills our joy!

And when was the last time you heard of any progressive movement for God taking its cues from those who, to quote Mike Yaconelli, spread germs of "discord, disruption, and destruction"?

I have been studying the lives of several of the great visionaries of the church. Each was extremely different, yet they all have one common denominator: not one was petty. I mean *not one*.

Let me remind you of Paul's reaction to those who "sneaked in to spy out our liberty which we have in Christ Jesus." He declares, "We did not yield in subjection to them for even an hour" (Gal. 2:5). Nor should we.

Get back on the pond, my friend. Who cares whether you are a figure skater or whether you do flips or fall flat on your face? The main thing is that you honor God as you move through life.

But count on this: You will encounter the petty Lucy types. So when you do, shrug it off and just keep on sliding.

A Finishing Touch: "Pettiness is the tendency of people without large purposes" (George Will).

A Daily Reading: Galatians 2:4–5

In one of his more serious moments, Mike Yaconelli, editor of *The Wittenburg Door*, addressed the issue of pettiness :

> Petty people are ugly people. They are people who have lost their vision. They are people who have turned their eyes away from what matters and focused, instead, on what doesn't matter. The result is that the rest of us are immobilized by their obsession with the insignificant.
>
> It is time to rid the church of pettiness. It is time the church refused to be victimized by petty people. It is time the church stopped ignoring pettiness. It is time the church quit pretending that pettiness doesn't matter. . . .
>
> Pettiness has become a serious disease in the Church of Jesus Christ—a disease which continues to result in terminal cases of discord, disruption, and destruction. Petty people are dangerous people because they appear to be only a nuisance instead of what they really are—a health hazard.

—*The Wittenburg Door*, December 1984/January 1985

Jesus opened a five-gallon can of worms the day He preached His Sermon on the Mount. There wasn't a Pharisee within gunshot range who wouldn't have given his last denarius to have seen Him strung up by sundown. Did they ever hate Him! They hated Him because He refused to let them get away with their phony religious drool and their super-spiritual ooze.

If there was one thing Jesus despised it was the very thing every Pharisee majored in at seminary: showing off. Another word for it is self-righteousness. They were the Holy Joes of Palestine . . . the first to enlist undiscerning recruits into the Royal Order of Back Stabbers . . . past masters in the practice of put-down prayers. They spent their days working on ways to impress others with their somber look. Above all, they trafficked in criticism and intolerance.

The Messiah unsheathed His sharp sword of truth that day, exposing their pride. Like never before, the smug show-offs were put in their place!

Listen to Matthew 6:1: "Beware of practicing your righteousness before men to be noticed by them. . . ."

In other words, stop showing off! Stop displaying your goodness . . . stop calling attention to your righteousness . . . stop craving to be noticed! Implied in this is the warning to beware of those who do that. And then, to make the warning stick, our Lord gave three specific examples of how people show off their own righteousness so that others might ooh and aah over them.

In Matthew 6:2 Jesus says, "When therefore you give alms, do not sound a trumpet before you. . . ." In other words, when you perform acts of charity or assist someone in need, keep it quiet. Don't scream for attention. Remain anonymous. Don't expect to have your name plastered all over the place. Jesus promises that "your Father who sees in secret will repay you" (6:4).

Modern-day Pharisees love to show off their good deeds; they love to remind others that they were the ones who gave such and such to so and so. Jesus says: Don't show off when you use your money to help somebody out. Give quietly . . . even anonymously.

In Matthew 6:5 Jesus talks about "when you pray. . . . " He warns us against being supplicational show-offs who stand in prominent places and mouth meaningless mush in order to be seen and heard. Show-offs love syrupy words. They've got the technique for sounding high and holy down pat. Their prayers could make listeners believe they are a cross between the angel Gabriel and King James V. You're confident that they haven't had a dirty thought in the past eighteen years . . . but you're also quietly aware that there's a huge chasm between what is coming out of the show-off's mouth and where their head is right then. Jesus says: Don't show off when you talk with the Father.

In Matthew 6:16 Jesus says, "Whenever you fast, do not put on a gloomy face as the hypocrites do. . . . " Fasting is when the show-off really hits his stride! He works overtime trying to appear humble and sad, hoping to look hungry and exhausted like some freak who just finished walking across the Sahara that afternoon. Instead, we ought to look and sound fresh, clean, and completely natural. Why? Because that's real—that's genuine—that's what He promises He will reward. Jesus says: Don't show off when you miss a couple or three meals.

Our Lord reserved His strongest and longest sermon not for struggling sinners or discouraged disciples but for hypocrites . . . for glory hogs. Unfortunately, most of them never change because they don't hear what He says to them. Show-offs, you see, are terribly hard of hearing.

A Finishing Touch: Is your righteousness showing off? Listen to His words!

A Daily Reading: Matthew 6

High-tech times lead to high-stress tension. The never-ending drive for more, mixed with the popular tendency to increase production and intensify involvement, leave most folks in the workplace not only exhausted but dissatisfied.

Instead of Saturday being a change-of-pace day, it has become an opportunity to squeeze in a second job. And Sundays? A time for renewal and refreshment? You're smiling. No, it's the day most type-A high achievers start another to-do list in preparation for the new week. It's become the ideal "let's get a jump on Monday" day. Rest is out of the question.

There is tyranny in all this. Tyranny of the unfinished as well as the urgent. There is discontentment. And ultimately there is disillusionment along with back-burner boredom.

Every time I officiate at a funeral, I'm reminded of the things that really matter . . . things that last. There's nothing quite like a fresh grave to jerk me back to reality. And every quiet conversation I have with the grieving family members only underscores those reminders. Stuff that seemed so all-fired important yesterday loses its steam when you stand on a windswept hill surrounded by weather-beaten grave markers.

At that moment, something within you cries: Simplify!

Jesus mastered the art of maintaining a clear perspective while accomplishing every single one of His objectives. Though we never read of His hurrying anywhere, He managed to fulfill the complete agenda. Just before the agony of the Cross, He told the Father that He had "accomplished the work which Thou hast given Me to do" (John 17:4). And only seconds before He drew His last breath, He made that epochal statement, "It is finished" (19:30). Nothing essential was left undone.

I have thought a lot about that, and I believe that a major reason for His being able to say those things was that He simplified His life.

Jesus followed His own agenda instead of everyone else's. He set predetermined limits: He chose twelve (not twelve hundred) whom

He trained to carry on in His absence. He maintained His priorities without apology. He balanced work and rest, accomplishment and refreshment, never feeling the need to ask permission for spending time in quietness and solitude. He refused to get sidetracked by tempting opportunities that drained energy and time. He was a servant of his Father, not a slave of the people.

Even though misunderstood, maligned, misquoted, and misrepresented by numerous enemies, and even a few friends, His simplicity kept Him balanced: He was firm yet kind and gentle, quick to hear and slow to speak. The complexities that tie us into knots never complicated His life or cramped His style. With deliberate calmness, He persevered.

What's happened to us? When did we buy into all this hectic hassle that steals so much of the joy of just plain living? Who convinced us to feel guilty for taking time to balance work with play?

Get off the treadmill and reorder your life. Go back three spaces and clean out the clutter that led to all this nonsense of busy-ness.

Simplify!

A Finishing Touch: How much longer will we keep adding nonessentials to our agenda? Simplify!

A Daily Reading: John 17

Stories transport us into another world. They hold our attention. They become remarkable vehicles for the communication of truth and meaningful lessons that cannot be easily forgotten. If a picture is better than a thousand words, a story is better than a million!

Some of the best stories are those spun from everyday life or from our past. Family histories are held together and handed down from generation to generation in stories. And these strong cords of memory actually become the ties that bind.

Occasionally, a novel will yield a story that can hardly be surpassed, a plot that cannot be forgotten. Other great stories emerge from lives we read about. Biographies drip with interesting accounts worth passing on. For example, *Human Options*, by the late Norman Cousins, is a treasure-house of his recollections, impressions, and encounters distilled from his dozen or more trips around the world. He calls it an "autobiographical notebook." Of special interest to me were his verbal snapshots of many of the great personalities he had spent time with. Each story—whether about Helen Keller, Douglas MacArthur, John F. Kennedy, Einstein, or Albert Schweitzer—was insightful grist for my mental mill.

Stories, real and imagined, told with care and color, can say much more than a planned speech. It is probably not surprising, then, that the use of story was Jesus' favorite method of preaching: "he did not say anything to them without using a parable" (Matt. 13:34 NIV).

In fact, I've never heard a great preacher who couldn't tell a good story. Woven into the tapestry of the strong message is the ability to communicate solid stuff through an attention-getting story.

Had I lived in Spurgeon's day, I would no doubt have subscribed to his material. He published one sermon per week for every year of his ministry, from 1855 until his death in 1892. So prolific was this prince of the pulpit, that at his death there were still so many unpublished Spurgeon sermons, they continued to be printed at the same rate for twenty-five more years. Many include wonderful, memorable stories.

Are you interested in getting truth to stick in your child's head? Use a story.

Can't seem to penetrate your teenager's skull? Try a story.

Need a tip for making your devotional or Sunday school lesson interesting? Include a story.

Want to add some zest to your letter-writing ministry? A brief story will do the trick.

Want to learn how to tell them so folks will stay interested? Listen to Paul Harvey.

Best of all, read your Bible. His Story is one you won't be able to put down.

A Finishing Touch: Grandparents (and parents, too) need to be reminded that our little ones love to hear about how it was and what it was that brought us to this moment. Tell your stories! Consider recording them or writing them down for future generations.

A Daily Reading: Matthew 13

Maybe it's because I just had another birthday. Maybe it's because I'm a granddad several times over. Or maybe it's because of a struggling young seminarian I met recently who wishes he had been higher on his parents' priority list than, say, fifth or sixth. He was hurried and ignored through childhood, then tolerated and misunderstood through adolescence, and finally expected to "be a man" without having been taught how.

My words are dedicated to all of you who have the opportunity to make an investment in a growing child so that he or she might someday be whole and healthy, secure and mature. Granted, yours is a tough job. Relentless and thankless . . . at least for now. There is every temptation to escape from the responsibilities that are yours and yours alone. But nobody is better qualified to shape the thinking, to answer the questions, to assist during the struggles, to calm the fears, to administer the discipline, to know the innermost heart, or to love and affirm the life of your offspring than you.

When it comes to "training up the child in the way he should go," you've got the inside lane, Mom and Dad. No teacher or coach, neighbor or friend, no grandparent or sibling, counselor or minister will have the influence on your kid that you are having. So—take it easy! Remember (as Anne Ortlund puts it) "children are wet cement." They take the shape of your mold. They're learning even when you don't think they're watching. And those little guys and gals are plenty smart. They hear tone as well as terms. They read looks as well as books. They figure out motives, even those you think you can hide. They are not fooled, not in the long haul.

The two most important tools of parenting are time and touch. Believe me, both are essential. If you and I hope to release from our nest fairly capable and relatively stable people who can soar and make it on their own, we'll need to pay the price of saying no to many of our own wants and needs in order to interact with our young and we'll have to keep breaking down the distance that only naturally forms as our little people grow up.

Time and touch. Nothing new, I realize, yet both remain irreducible minimums when it comes to good parenting. Take it easy! Listen to your boy or girl, look them in the eye, put your arms around them, hug them close, tell them how valuable they are. Don't hold back. Take the time to do it. Reach. Touch.

Don't stand alongside your son or daughter like statues, unable to say what you feel, uncomfortable and distant. Take time to feel, to listen, to hold your child close.

When you are tempted to get involved in some energy-draining, time-consuming opportunity that will only increase the distance between you and yours, stop and think of the unspoken message it will convey. Ask yourself hard questions like, "Could my time be better spent at home?" and "Won't there be similar opportunities in the years to come?" Then turn your attention to your boy or girl. Hold nothing back as you renew acquaintances.

Take it easy!

A Finishing Touch: The two most important tools of parenting are time and touch.

A Daily Reading: Proverbs 22:6

It doesn't take a Rhodes scholar to guess the country, though the towns may be strange sounding: Offenbach, Darmstadt, Mannheim, Coburg, Heidelberg, Worms . . . .

The land of beer steins, sauerkraut, liverwurst, and black bread; cuckoo clocks and overflowing flower boxes; wide, winding rivers and deep-green woods; stone castles on hillsides and quiet, efficient trains; and the greatest music ever written. The beloved homeland of Bach, Mendelssohn, Haydn, Handel, Beethoven, and Wagner.

A plot of land no larger than our state of Oregon, Germany is no dusty relic of the past. Far from it. Modern, efficient, computerized, and an unquestioned leader in the European common market, her cities pulsate with people on the move with that age-old, never-say-die determination. A glance at her skyscrapers reminds you of Dallas or Atlanta or Seattle. Backward, she's not. Nor bankrupt, not by a long shot. Thanks to the fall of the wall, she's unified again and proud of it.

It is not often remembered, however, that this land is also where some of the severest yet most essential battles for the faith were fought.

It was there that the chain that bound the Bible to ornate pulpits of spiritually dead religion was broken. It was there that the Word's truths were liberated from the secret language of a corrupt clergy and placed into the hands of the common people. And it was there those same people were first given a hymnal from which they could sing their faith.

Think of it . . . in place of biblical ignorance and slavery to a system that could never bring light, German believers were provided a Bible in their own tongue with many of its grand themes put to music. Instead of mumbling repetitious prayers, crouching in fear, they could approach the throne of God with confidence and personally praise Him as their shield and their defender.

Ein feste Burg ist unser Gott / "A safe Stronghold our God is still."

Their courage mounted as their doubts faded. And it was all because a sixteenth-century German monk was willing to take his stand against all odds. Yes, never doubt it . . . all odds.

It was in his tiny, stark cell in the Augustinian convent at Erfurt, all alone with a Latin copy of the Word of God, that Martin Luther decided to believe God, to allow Scripture to mean what it says, and then to stand firmly on it, regardless of the consequences. It's that last part we tend to minimize.

Being officially branded a heretic did not hold him back. Being publicly defrocked, rebuked, and excommunicated merely fueled his fire. From those 95 theses he hammered onto the door of the Wittenberg church to the day he stood at Worms before the most impressive array of church prelates and political authorities ever gathered in his lifetime, the man remained the embodiment of authentic courage.

He was only thirty-seven at the time. Not often tactful but always sincere, he hurled himself at religious wrongs like a blazing meteor wrapped in a robe. Not a well man physically, Luther nevertheless maintained a punishing schedule of preaching, publishing, and pouncing for the rest of his days. He summed up his reason in one succinct sentence: "Here I stand; I can do no other." His life, with more turns and tumults than the Rhine, maintained a steadfast course. And the spark he ignited caused the Reformation to burst into full flame.

Last week I walked where he stood. Jeers no longer mark his pilgrimage; instead, one finds monuments and plaques and paintings. Instead of being humiliated as a heretic, he is now honored as a hero. Time has a way of correcting faulty perspective.

I sat in the castle room at Coburg where he once sat and wrote. I saw the same structures and walls and hillsides he once saw in Heidelberg. I imagined some of the feelings he might have had at Worms. I was moved in my soul, and I'm a better man because of it.

I needed that visit to Luther's homeland. I needed to hear those guttural sounds he once spoke and to touch the stones he once touched.

I found myself seeing beyond the temporal stuff like steins and sauerkraut, castles and skyscrapers. I heard Luther's voice in the woodwork, and I felt his fire in the bronze and iron monuments now green with age. It was more powerful than my phrases can possibly describe, making me appreciate again the eloquent words from the sacred text, "He, being dead, yet speaketh."

A Finishing Touch: When we stand on the shoulders of those saints who have gone before, we gain a strategic vantage point.
A Daily Reading: Romans 5

Like silent shadows, the heroes of the faith pass beside us, pointing us toward the upward way, whispering words of courage.

The memory of all those models of righteousness now gone from view puts needed steel in our spirit, prompting us to press forward, always forward.

The legacy of their powerful presence and penetrating pages adds depth to our otherwise superficial existence.

Because their convictions live on in words that challenge today's shallow thinking, we do not—we dare not—remain the same.

I would challenge you to do some further reading about these heroes of the faith. Their lives and their words are there for our edification.

> But as it is, they desire a better country, that is a heavenly one. Therefore God is not ashamed to be called their God; for He has prepared a city for them (Heb. 11:16).

A New Week
of
Finishing Touches

44

MONDAY

I just looked up the definition of "thorough" in my dictionary. Mr. Webster says it means "carried through to completion, careful about detail, complete in all respects."

Somehow, I find that a convicting definition. Few indeed are those who finish what they start—and even fewer do a complete job of it when they do finish a task.

Now I'm not referring to a neurotic fanaticism of extreme, some impractical and unbalanced preoccupation with mundane details. That's the trees-in-the-forest syndrome, and that's not what I'm talking about.

I'm talking about the rare but beautiful experience of carrying out a responsibility to its completion. To name a few:

1. A course at school. Doing the very best you can to the peak of your performance for the sheer joy of total fulfillment.

2. A project at home. Mapping out a plan and then tackling the task with abandoned energy, dedicated to the goal of "doing the job right."

3. An occupation. The fine art of working is the lost art of today—really getting in there and studying the job, reading and expanding your knowledge. Modeling diligence. Serving with a positive attitude. Becoming an expert in your field—for the simple delight of accomplishment!

4. Everyday duties. Is the telltale sign "unfinished" written across your housework? Is your trademark "Mañana," or, "Someday, I'll have to get that done"?

There is a verse in Proverbs that is commonly quoted around the Swindoll house when we really finish a job the way it should be done: "Desire accomplished is sweet to the soul" (Proverbs 13:19).

When you have accomplished or thoroughly fulfilled a task, you experience a feeling of satisfaction that cannot be expressed in words.

Listen to another proverb: "The soul of the sluggard craves and gets nothing, but the soul of the diligent is made fat (13:4).

The sluggard longingly craves, but because he is "allergic to work," he gets nothing in return! Proverbs 20:4 makes this clear.

So, what are you waiting for? Does it need painting? Paint it—and do a thorough job! Does it need cleaning? Clean it—thoroughly! Does it need ironing? Iron it—wrinkle free, with gusto! Does it need attention? Give it your thorough, unrestrained attention!

Stop being satisfied with a half-hearted, incomplete job! Stun those around you with a thorough, finished product! AND STOP PUTTING IT OFF! As an oboe teacher of mine used to say when I would stare in disbelief at the difficulty of a piece of music, "Attack it, boy!"

The difference between something good and something great is attention to detail. That is true of a delicious meal, a musical presentation, a play, a clean automobile, a well-kept home, a church, our attire, a business, a lovely garden, a sermon, a teacher, a well-disciplined family.

Let's make a long-term commitment to quality control. Let's move out of the thick ranks of the mediocre and join the thin ranks of excellence.

I'm ready if you are.

A Finishing Touch: Does something need doing? Dig right in and refuse to give up until that task is done. Tighten your belt a notch and wade into that unpleasant job with renewed determination to write "finished" over it.

A Daily Reading: Proverbs 13:4, 9; 20:4

My younger daughter and I sat and stared in silence. We were looking at the same thing, thinking similar thoughts. Both of us shed a few tears of gratitude, said little, then drove on. It had been well over forty years since I'd seen the sight. For her, it was a first. It was a tiny, plain, unimpressive garage apartment, leaning and peeling with age. It was the place of my birth.

As the little south Texas town of El Campo faded in the rear-view mirror, scenes of the history of my roots passed in review. The contrast between my life in the mid 1930s and my life today stood out in bold relief. When I could restrain myself no longer, I blurted out, "I feel like a turtle on a fence post." Startled, my daughter asked for an explanation.

I first heard this imagery used by Dr. Robert Lamont, a Presbyterian pastor who felt incredibly blessed by God, yet obviously humbled and unworthy. "When I was a schoolboy," he said, "we would occasionally see a turtle on a fence post, and when we did, we knew someone had put him there. He didn't get there by himself. That is how I see my own life. I'm a turtle on a fence post."

The Bible is chock-full of turtles: one person after another who knew that his or her position of power, authority, or promotion was given by Another.

Joseph was a turtle. How often, on his Egyptian chariot or in his opulent surroundings, he must have sat back, closed his eyes, and reflected on his humble beginnings. His jealous brothers. The pit. Slavery. Prison. Now this! What an incredible fence post! How faithful of God . . . how gracious!

Moses was a turtle. As leader of the Israelites, he surely awoke many a morning in the wilderness shaking his head in disbelief, remembering his murderous and monotonous past. How good of God to have put him on the fence post!

Gideon was a turtle. Remember his response to the angel when he was informed that he was to be commander of the Israeli troops? "Sir, how can I save Israel? My family is the poorest in the whole tribe of Manasseh, and I am the least thought of in the entire family!" (Judges 6:15 TLB). That's turtle talk, spoken in due humility atop a fence post.

David was a turtle. Imagine how often his thoughts must have returned to the Judean slopes where he had tended his father's sheep. The awesome throne in Jerusalem, the resplendent beauty of his own personal residence, the ear-splitting applause of his admiring public could not eclipse the realization that he was merely a turtle on a fence post.

What a healthy perspective for each of us to maintain! The next time we are tempted to think we're self-appointed fence-post sitters, I recommend the prophet's counsel: "Listen to me, you who pursue righteousness, who seek the Lord: Look to the rock from which you were hewn, and to the quarry from which you were dug. Look to Abraham your Father, and to Sarah who gave birth to you in pain . . . " (Isa. 51:1–2).

There's nothing better for a turtle temporarily elevated on a fence post than to return to those humble roots, the quarry from which you were dug, and remember the strong determination of a mother who bore you and the quiet commitment of a father who cradled you through poverty, hardship, and pain. It's enough to make you sit and stare in silence.

A Finishing Touch: Think about your own fence post and then call to mind the quarry from which you were dug.

A Daily Reading: Isaiah 51

It's easy to get confused these days. "Out of control" isn't what we want to be. People who drink too much are said to be "out of control." The same goes for those who go too far with anything: prescription drugs, food, fitness, sex, work—you name it. A home that lacks direction and leadership, affirmation and love, fair and consistent discipline represents a family that is "out of control." Someone who talks too much is verbally "out of control." Those who worry too much become emotionally "out of control."

But wait. Does this mean we're supposed to be "in control?" Is that our goal? Before you answer, consider. I know a boss (in fact I know several) who is definitely "in control." Folks who work for him either grin and bear it or jump ship as soon as another job surfaces. Some fathers are, without question, "in control." They intimidate, dominate, moderate, and manipulate. Mothers-in-law are notoriously known for this—not all, but many. They are usually the same ones who control their husbands. He finally gets so weary that he resorts to long golf games and, when home, hours and hours in front of the TV. Interestingly, he has become an out-of-control couch potato, married to an in-control Mother Superior . . . and no one resents it more than their kids.

Webster defines control: "to exercise restraining or directing influence over: REGULATE; to have power over: RULE." Perhaps one of the synonyms for being "in control" would be "controlling." That helps relieve some of the confusion. Being "in control" doesn't necessarily mean "controlling." A healthy, happy life requires being in control of ourselves. To be punctual, we must control the use of our time. To be prepared and ready, we must be in control of our schedule. To be a good listener, our minds and tongue must be controlled. To get a project completed, our tendency to procrastinate must be under the firm control of our determination.

This means, then, that we need to be in firm control of ourselves . . . but not controlling of others. Our example? Christ, of course. He got the job done. Without wasted effort, personal panic, or extreme demands, He accomplished the objective. Right on schedule, He went to that cross. When He sighed, "It is finished," it was. Absolutely and completely.

Did most believe? Are you kidding? The vast majority back then, as now, didn't give Him the time of day. Could He have grabbed the controls and forced them to sit up and take notice? I hope to shout! Remember what He said? ". . . do you think that I cannot appeal to My Father, and He will at once put at My disposal more than twelve legions of angels?" (Matt. 26:53). I'd call 72,000 angels, being in charge, wouldn't you? It was His own control that restrained Him from controlling others.

The Christian life boils down to a battle of the wills: Christ's vs. our own. Every day we live we must answer, "Who's in charge here?"

Recently I received a letter from a fine Christian couple, and I smiled understandingly at one line: "Although the Lord has taken good care of my wife and me for the past 38 years, He has taken control of us for the past 2 1/2."

Tell me, how long has the Lord taken care of you? Be honest now . . . has He also taken control of you? It's easy to get confused these days. It's even easier to take control.

A Finishing Touch: Don't get "out of control" because you're so determined to stay "in control."

A Daily Reading: Galatians 3

For the next few minutes, imagine this scene:

> But the day of the Lord will come like a thief, in which the heavens will pass away with a roar and the elements will be destroyed with intense heat, and the earth and its works will be burned up. Since all these things are to be destroyed in this way, what sort of people ought you to be in holy conduct and godliness, looking for . . . the coming of the day of God, on account of which the heavens will be destroyed by burning, and the elements will melt with intense heat! (2 Peter 3:10–12).

Scary stuff, that business about the heavens passing away and the astronomical destruction and the twice-mentioned "intense heat" that will result in a total wipeout of Planet Earth. Makes me wonder *how*. Oh, I've heard the same things you have about super-atomic warheads and World War III. But somehow that never explained how "the heavens will pass away" or how the surrounding atmosphere and stratosphere could be "destroyed by burning."

Since that would usher in "the day of God," I've always questioned whether He would use manmade, adult fireworks to announce His arrival. These verses describe a phenomenal destructive force that makes our demolition devices look like two-bit firecrackers under a tin can. It's impossible to imagine!

But in my reading recently I stumbled across a possible hint of how the Lord might be planning to pull off this final blast.

On March 9, 1979, nine satellites stationed at various points in the solar system simultaneously recorded a bizarre event deep in space. It was, in fact, the most powerful burst of energy ever recorded. Astronomers who studied the readings were in awe.

The burst of gamma radiation lasted for only one-tenth of a second . . . but in that instant it emitted as much energy as the sun does in 3000 years. If the gamma-ray burst had occurred in the Milky Way Galaxy, said one astrophysicist, it would have set our entire atmosphere aglow. If the sun had suddenly emitted the same amount of energy, our earth would have vaporized. Instantly.

There's more. The satellites were able to pinpoint the location of the burst to a spot in a galaxy known as N-49, which is associated with the remnants of a supernova believed to have exploded about ten thousand years ago.

When a star explodes into a supernova, the outer shell is blown away and the inner core condenses from its own gravity to create a neutron star. That core becomes a single, huge nucleus, shrinking from a size larger than the sun (860,000 miles in diameter) to a compact ball no more than five miles across. Those neutrons are so incredibly dense that one cubic inch weighs 20 *million, million pounds*. Go figure!

As untrained and ignorant as we may be about the technical side of all this, I suggest it might cast some light on the validity of Peter's remark. At least, in my estimation, it makes a lot more sense than atomic wars.

It's probably going to be more like star wars. The good news is this: I have no plans to be around at the premier showing.

How about you?

A Finishing Touch: We may not understand all His ways, but we can know Him whose ways are "unfathomable."

A Daily Reading: Romans 11:33–36; 2 Peter 3

The law of supply-and-demand is something we face every day. Because there are those who need, there must also be those who provide. It's really not that complicated.

There are employers and employees.

There are counselors and counselees.

There are teachers and teachees (I couldn't resist).

But it breaks down when it comes to refugees. There aren't enough "refugers" to meet the demand.

Now, when I mention refugees, I don't necessarily have in mind those who cross oceans to America to find relief, freedom, and protection from governments gone wild. I mean someone already here who needs a refuge. A place of shelter. I'm talking about a person who is broken or guilty or bleeding with a heartache or exploding with anxiety . . . or all the above.

Back in the days when the Hebrews settled in Canaan, they set up cities of refuge. People who were in danger—even those guilty of wrongdoing—could escape to one of these seven cities and find personal relief and refreshment.

Don't misunderstand. These weren't sleazy dumping grounds for hardened criminals. These were territories dedicated to the restoration of those who had made mistakes. People who had blown it could flee to one of these places of refuge and not have those inside throw rocks at them. Rather, they could admit their faults and not be threatened by pious looks or caustic sermons from prejudiced lips.

Which reminds me of an old Marine buddy of mine who came to know Christ after he was discharged from the Corps. I was pleasantly surprised when I heard about this because, you see, he wasn't your basic, clean-cut, Little Lord Fauntleroy type. Back when we were in the same outfit, he cussed loudly, he drank heavily, he fought hard, he chased women, he loved weapons and war, and he hated chapel services. (He made a great Marine.) But back then he and God weren't on speaking terms. Then—miracle of miracles—through a chain of events too lengthy to describe, the guy was converted. Christ came into his life.

I'll never forget the day we ran into each other. He put his hand on my shoulder, sighed, and said, "Chuck, I'll be honest. The only thing I really miss is that old fellowship all the guys in our outfit used to have down at the slop shoot (Greek for "tavern on the base"). All the guys would sit around, laugh, tell stories, drink a pitcher of beer, and really let our hair down. Man, it was great! I just haven't found anything to take the place of those times . . . and I still need it! I ain't got nobody to tell my troubles to, to admit my faults to . . . to have 'em listen when I need to say, 'I'm sunk. I'm beat. I've had it!' There isn't anybody who will put his arm around me and tell me I'm still okay . . . somebody who will keep my secrets and help me get back up."

That man is a refugee in search of a refuger. But the supply-and-demand has broken down.

Too bad. No, tragic is a better word. We have lots of places to meet and sing. To pray. To hear talks from big wooden pulpits. To watch fine things happen. Yes, even to participate occasionally in the action. Or buy and read good books that help us do better.

But where do the escapees go? To whom do the wounded turn?

We have a place for the healthy and productive. We love and use the gifted, the leader types, the strong and the confident. But where is our compassion? Where is the place of refuge for those whose lives have gotten soiled in the streets. Rather than being committed to restoration, we bypass the dirty with a shrug. Sometimes even thinking, "I'm not surprised."

More often than we want to admit, we're bad Samaritans. In our outfit we're notorious for not knowing what to do with our wounded. Getting in there and cleaning up those ugly wounds and changing bloody bandages and taking the time to listen and encourage, well . . . let's be practical, we're not running a hospital around here. That makes good sense until you or I need emergency care.

Like when you discover your husband is a practicing homosexual. Or your unmarried daughter is pregnant and isn't listening to you. Or your parent is an alcoholic. Or you get dumped in jail for shoplifting. Or you blew it financially. Or you lost your job and it's your own fault. Or your wife is having an affair. Or your dad or mom or mate or child is dying of cancer.

Thankfully, in the church today, there are a few lights to help the hurting find their way back. In my opinion they are the brightest hope on our horizon.

Like the group that meets weekly to help people who struggle to conquer alcohol and drug addiction . . . brave souls who admit by their presence, "We don't have it all together." Or the group of single parents who are attempting to believe in themselves again . . . as much as they believe in Jesus. Besides these, there are dozens and dozens of small groups in churches across our land comprised of caring, authentic, but very human Christians who are committed to growing friendships and deepening relationships. Good Samaritans who have compassion. May their tribe increase!

These are our modern-day cities of refuge.

A Finishing Touch: Genuine, New Testament Christianity doesn't hang out at headquarters; it gets into the trenches with the wounded and weary.

A Daily Reading: Joshua 20

"A certain man was going down from Jerusalem to Jericho; and he fell among robbers, and they stripped him and beat him, and went off leaving him half dead. . . .

"But a certain Samaritan, who was on a journey, came upon him; and when he saw him, he felt compassion, and came to him, and bandaged up his wounds, pouring oil and wine on them; and he put him on his own beast, and brought him to an inn, and took care of him.

"And on the next day he took out two denarii and gave them to the innkeeper and said, 'Take care of him; and whatever more you spend, when I return, I will repay you.'

"Which of these three do you think proved to be a neighbor to the man who fell into the robbers' hands?"

And he said, "The one who showed mercy toward him." And Jesus said to him, "Go and do the same" (Luke 10:30–37).

People don't want to listen to a cassette of some sermon when the bottom drops out. They want a place to cry . . . a person to care . . . someone to bind up their wounds . . . someone to listen . . . the security of a few close, intimate friends who won't blab their story all over the church . . . who will do more than say, "I'll pray for you." They want refuge.

Stop and think. Who and where is your refuge for bruised believers?

Solomon's life reminds me of the swing of a pendulum. Smooth and graceful . . . silent and elegant . . . yet periodically given to extremes.

Born with a silver spoon in his mouth, blessed with blue blood and an abundance of brains, he was a natural for the throne. As the heir-apparent, he was tutored at the feet of godly Nathan, groomed by the beautiful Bath-sheba, shaped under the watchful eye of David, and polished by the hand of God. The stamp of excellence was upon young Solomon.

Wisdom, loyalty, diplomacy, and efficiency marked his attitude and acts during the early years of his reign. Best of all, "Solomon loved the Lord" (1 Kings 3:3). His achievements could not be listed on ten pages this size. When visited by surrounding magistrates, he was viewed with awe. And rich? Multiplied millions annually. And creative? He was an architect, songwriter, artist, author, and inventor of unparalleled ability.

Things slowly began to change, however, as the pendulum began its tragic swing. Farther and farther . . . and farther.

Solomon seized the reins of wrong and drove his glistening chariot of gold onto the misty flats of licentiousness, pride, lust, profanity, and paganism. Silently, gradually, like eroding soil near the banks of a deep, angry river, he began to believe the lie that has captured many a top executive . . . or super salesperson . . . or successful physician . . . or athletic prima donna . . . or film star . . . or TV celebrity.

In the eloquent words of one biographer: "Solomon . . . drove too fast and traveled too far . . . the monarch became debauched and effeminate; an egotist and cynic, so satiated with the sensual and material affairs of life that he became skeptical of all good."

Materialism, polygamy, brutality, and idolatry now crippled his steps. Revolts fractured his nation and irrational decisions characterized his rule. All to him became "vanity and striving after wind"

(Eccl. 2:26). Nothing satisfied him any longer. The normal, God-given drives lost their appeal as deterioration took its final toll. And when death finally came, Solomon left in his wake a confused following and a broken, rebellious family.

Deterioration is never loud. Never obvious. Seldom even noticed. Like tiny cracks in a stucco wall, it hardly seems worth our time and attention. Never sudden.

Character threads don't "suddenly" snap. No building "suddenly" crumbles. No church "suddenly" splits. No professional "suddenly" compromises. No husband or wife "suddenly" cheats. No nation "suddenly" dissolves. No business "suddenly" becomes mediocre. As the British expositor of yesteryear, F.B. Meyer, once put it, "No man suddenly becomes base."

Slowly, silently, subtly, things are tolerated that once were rejected. At the outset everything appears harmless, maybe even a bit exciting. But with it comes an "insignificant" wedge, a gap that grows wider as moral erosion joins hands with spiritual decay.

Be on guard! Those of us who stand must take heed lest we fall.

The pitfalls are still present. Still real.

The stones that make us stumble are still there: silver, sex, sloth, and self.

They wait in silence. As unobtrusive as the ticking of a clock. As attractive as the swinging of a pendulum . . . until. . . .

A Finishing Touch: "There is a way which seems right to a man, but its end is the way of death" (*Solomon*, Prov. 14:12).

A Daily Reading: 1 Kings 3, 11

"How much does it cost?"

"What's it worth?"

These two questions may sound alike, but they are different. Very different.

When you shop, you can ask either question and invariably be given the price of the item. But the "cost" of something is its actual price. The "worth" of something is its personal value. There's a world of difference between the two. Any salesperson can quote the cost . . . but only you can determine the worth.

"Cost" is the amount of money it takes to complete a purchase . . . the bill, the tab, the monetary expense required to accomplish a financial transaction. After paying the cost, we receive a receipt that declares we have paid in full what was marked on the price tag . . . and we are legally free to call it our own possession. It may be a bicycle or a box of candy, a new lawnmower or a college education, a painting for the living room or a sleek sailboat.

"Worth" is the usefulness of the object . . . the benefit, value, and importance of the thing purchased. It is the long-lasting return we derive from the item. Justification for paying a certain cost is usually determined on the basis of the personal worth that accompanies the purchase.

One other distinction must be emphasized. "Cost" is cold, objective, and even painful. Nor is it necessarily easy to accept. That's where "worth" plays a vital role. In our minds we juggle the unemotional, hard facts of cost along with the subjective, magnetic appeals of worth. When the current price tag is high, worth steps up and introduces the future. It challenges you to consider the benefits, to focus on the enduring dividends that soften the abrasive, brutal blow of the actual price. Worth, when it does its job, convinces the buyer that either the cost is acceptable . . . or it says, "Don't do it . . . it isn't worth that kind of money."

The difference between handling our money wisely or foolishly is largely determined by the interplay between these two forces.

Obviously, we have spent wisely when the cost is eclipsed by the worth. Again, that must be determined individually. That is why, in the long run, we can usually determine a person's scale of values by the things he or she purchases.

Or, to use the words of Jesus: "For where your treasure is, there will your heart be also" (Matt. 6:21).

Now, anyone who knows me knows that I never speak against having nice things. In fact, I encourage quality purchases, for in the long run, they actually cost less.

So next time you ask, "How much does it cost?" think also about "What's it worth?" This is especially true when we are deciding how to spend the money God's people have given for the upkeep and ministry of the church. While our stewardship should guard against extravagance, we certainly do not want to clothe the riches of Christ in rags.

Think about Sundays—your church life and the motivation you receive. Think about your children and their future. And their children's future. Think about your neighborhood—unreached individuals by the hundreds. Think about the possibilities of radio or television outreach, perhaps a Christian school, enlarged missionary outreaches, room to grow, room to park! What's it worth?

Deciding whether something is worth the cost requires intense, effective, prevailing prayer, as well as the hard work of objective thinking. And then it requires courage to act on God's clear direction.

A Finishing Touch: Ministries that stay alive are forever moving forward—walking along the ridge called "faith" overlooking that chasm called "impossibility."

A Daily Reading: Matthew 6

Billy Wilder, the great movie producer, openly admitted: "I have a vast and terrible desire never to bore an audience."

With tacit agreement, Jack Parr once declared: "The greatest sin is to be dull."

Those two statements ought to haunt anyone who regularly practices the fine art of communication.

Boredom is a gross violation! Being dull is a grave offense! Unfortunately, however, both are crimes that go unpunished . . . and the chronic offender is seldom even made aware of his or her habit, much less reprimanded.

Communication is a competitive field. Like it or not, the teacher, writer, speaker, or preacher contends with ABC, NBC, CBS, CNN, Rush Limbaugh, magazines, paperbacks, CDs, the theater, the cinema, the thrilling excitement of sporting events, and a zillion other attractions. Pity the missionary whose mimeographed letter arrives in the same mail with *Sports Illustrated* or *Newsweek*. God help the Sunday evening services across America that do battle with "60 Minutes, " "Murder She Wrote," and "Masterpiece Theater."

Today's communicator faces a stiffer challenge than ever before. This means that we who communicate Christ must work especially hard at *winning* and then *maintaining* a hearing.

This doesn't mean we need to put on a better show or shout louder or attack our competition. What it does mean is that we must meet at least three demands.

We must be prepared. This includes being accurate, logical, and knowledgeable, yet well aware of opposing positions or opinions. Basically, it necessitates doing our homework. But it also means we must determine what ought to remain behind the counter, held in reserve, and what ought to be placed on display. It's the art of verbal economy .

We must be interesting. With a careful choice of words and methods of approach, we must paint verbal pictures for the uninitiated, preoccupied mind to see. To do this we need energy (a natural flow of enthusiasm, force, or intensity); subtlety (communicating without overdrawing the conclusions); relevance (in touch with today); changes of pace (understanding the listener and being sensitive to his or her reactions).

We must be practical. We are communicating with people who have needs, people who are asking, "So what? . . . Why bring this up? . . . How does this relate to me, personally?" Communicating the Scriptures is more than dumping out a truckload of biblical facts; it means using those facts to meet practical, everyday needs.

Communicating is like fishing. We need to provide the right lures and bait to attract our listeners.

"But," say some, "the fish are there and waiting . . . just let down the line, wait awhile, and reel 'em in."

Well, friend, even hungry fish know a naked, dull, rusty hook when they see one. They aren't going to be attracted when dozens of more-appealing prospects are dangling nearby.

Check out Paul's address on Mars Hill (Acts 17) or Stephen's defense before the Council (Acts 7) or Jesus' great sermon on the mountain (Matt. 5–7) or His conversation with Nicodemus (John 3). Not a rusty hook in the bunch!

Funny thing about fish: they keep their eyes open even when they're bored and sound asleep. Myopic communicators tend to forget that.

A Finishing Touch: When we communicate Christ we are like GE: we bring good things to light.

A Daily Reading: Acts 7, 17

There's a new virus going around. It's called P.E.B.—Post Election Blues. The symptoms? Oh, stuff like moping around, whining, and feeling a mixture of self-pity, resentment, smoldering anger, and even entertaining thoughts of moving to Tahiti or Australia because your candidate didn't win.

Well, I've got news for you. That won't help. The best antibiotic is to buck up, stand firmer than ever on the solid rock of God's sovereignty, and face the future with renewed confidence—no matter who's in office. Tough as it is to say that at times, nothing that happens in this old world—even in the election booth—surprises or frustrates our Lord. These words are still in the Book:

> For not from the east, nor from the west,
> Nor from the desert comes exaltation;
> But God is the Judge;
> He puts down one, and exalts another (Ps. 75:6–7).

Somehow those words are easier to read when my candidates get elected; they stick in my throat when the other folks get in! Ever noticed that?

And then I happen across Solomon's proverb: "The king's heart is like channels of water in the hand of the Lord; He turns it wherever He wishes" (Prov. 21:1).

And I find fresh perspective and hope, especially when I substitute "The president's heart" or "The senator's heart" or "The mayor's heart" for "The king's heart."

Remember' Daniel? He lived victoriously through strong and weak national leaders, yet he didn't hesitate to declare that "Heaven rules" and that it is the living God who "changes the times and seasons; he sets up kings and deposes them" (Dan. 2:21; 4:26 NIV).

So, then, I suggest we start thinking theologically and acting responsibly. Both are hard, hard work. That's right! Recovering from a bad case of P.E.B. requires being *hardy*.

Ever used that word? Somehow it has kind of an old-fashioned ring in this day and age. Look at it again.

Obviously, "hard" is at its root. Webster states that it means "bold, brave" and even suggests that to be hardy can mean being "audacious, brazen . . . inured to fatigue or harsh: ROBUST." (Ah, that's *another* great old word!)

The man or woman who is hardy can withstand adverse conditions, is firm in purpose, and has a vigorous outlook on life. We might say that many missionaries and most mountain climbers are hardy folks.

The hardy person remains productive under difficult situations, all the while maintaining emotional, physical, and spiritual health.

It should be remembered, however, that hardiness is not an inherent attitude, temperament, or gift. It is a quality that must be consciously developed. And it's the best treatment for the P.E.B. virus (and a number of others!).

Let's work on cultivating them. It's a project we can undertake together—with God's help.

A Finishing Touch: Measure your own "hardy" quotient. Do you measure up?

A Daily Reading: Psalm 75:6–7; Daniel 2:21; 4:26

This actually happened years ago.

It was in 1968 on an airplane headed for New York—a routine and normally very boring flight. But this time it proved to be otherwise.

As they were on their descent pattern, the pilot realized that the landing gear was not engaging. He messed around with the controls, trying again and again to get the gear to lock into place . . . without success. He then asked ground control for instruction. As the plane circled the landing field, the emergency crew coated the runway with foam and fire trucks and other emergency vehicles moved into position.

Meanwhile, the passengers were told of each maneuver in that calm, unemotional voice pilots do so well. Flight attendants glided about the cabin with an air of cool reserve. Passengers were told to place their heads between their knees and grab their ankles just before impact. There were tears and a few cries of despair. It was one of those "I can't believe this is happening to me" experiences.

Then, with the landing only minutes away, the pilot suddenly announced over the intercom: "We are beginning our final descent. At this moment, in accordance with International Aviation Codes established at Geneva, it is my obligation to inform you that if you believe in God you should commence prayer." Scout's honor . . . that's exactly what he said!

I'm happy to report that the belly landing occurred without a hitch. No one was injured and, aside from some rather extensive damage to the plane, the airline hardly remembered the incident. In fact, a relative of one of the passengers called the airline the very next day and asked about that prayer rule the pilot had quoted. The answer was a cool, reserved "No comment."

Amazing. The only thing that brought out into the open a deep-down "secret rule" was crisis. Pushed to the brink, back to the wall, right up to the wire, all escape routes closed . . . only then does our society crack open a hint of recognition that God may be there and—"if you believe . . . you should commence prayer."

Reminds me of a dialogue I heard on the tube shortly after Mount St. Helens erupted. The guy being interviewed was a reporter who had "come back alive" from the volcano with pictures and sound track of his own personal nightmare. He was up near the mouth of that mama when she blew her top, and he literally ran for his life . . . with camera rolling and the mike on. The pictures were blurred and dark, but his voice was something else.

It was eerie, almost too personal to be disclosed. He breathed deeply, sobbed, panted, and spoke directly to God. No formality, no clichés—just the despairing cry of a creature in crisis.

Things like, "Oh, God, oh, my God . . . help! Help!" More sobbing, more rapid breathing, spitting, gagging, coughing, panting. "It's so hot, so dark . . . help me, God! Please, please, please, please. . . ."

There's nothing like crisis to expose the otherwise hidden truth of the soul. Any soul.

We may mask it, ignore it, pass it off with cool sophistication and intellectual denial . . . but take away the cushion of comfort, remove the shield of safety, interject the threat of death without the presence of people to take the panic out of the moment, and it's fairly certain most in the ranks of humanity "commence prayer."

Crisis crushes. And in crushing, it often refines and purifies. I've stood beside too many of the dying, ministered to too many of the victims of calamity, listened to too many of the broken and bruised to believe otherwise.

Unfortunately, it usually takes such brutal blows of affliction to soften and penetrate hard hearts.

Remember Alexander Solzhenitzyn's admission?

"It was only when I lay there on rotting prison straw that I sensed within myself the first stirrings of good. . . . So bless you, prison, for having been in my life."

Those words provide a perfect illustration of the psalmist's instruction:

> Before I was afflicted I went astray, but now I obey your word. . . .
> It was good for me to be afflicted so that I might learn your decrees (Ps. 119:67, 71 NIV).

After crisis crushes, God steps in to comfort and teach. This actually happens somewhere in our world every day.

A Finishing Touch: There's nothing like crisis to expose the hidden truth of the soul.

A Daily Reading: Malachi 3

God's Word is filled with examples of those who believed God and "commenced prayer." David certainly did.

> I waited patiently for the Lord; And He inclined to me, and heard my cry. He brought me up out of the pit of destruction, out of the miry clay; And He set my feet upon a rock making my footsteps firm (Ps. 40:1–2).

Paul and Silas experienced the same thing in that ancient Philippian prison when all seemed hopeless (Acts 16:25–26). And it was from "the deep" that Jonah cried for help. Choking on salt water and engulfed by the Mediterranean currents, the prodigal prophet called out his distress:

> Then Jonah prayed to the Lord his God from the stomach of the fish, and he said, "I called out of my distress to the Lord, and He answered me. I cried for help from the depth of Sheol; Thou didst hear my voice. . . . All Thy breakers and billows passed over me. . . . But Thou hast brought up my life from the pit, O Lord my God" (Jonah 2:1–6).

Often it is the crucible of crisis that energizes our faith. Think it over.

Laurence J. Peter and I are close friends. No, actually, we've never met, but we've visited together numerous times. We've never even shaken hands, but we've been in agreement ever since we crossed paths. Although I've never laid eyes on him, I've smiled at his comments and nodded at his conclusions . . . amazed with his remarkable insight into my own life and those around me.

The simple and obvious answer to the riddle is this: I own a copy of his book *The Peter Prescription*, and you should too! It's an insignificant looking paperback filled with significant, sound principles. He says it talks about "How to be Creative, Confident, and Competent," but I think he's overlooked a better word: How to be *Content*.

Isn't it strange that we need a book to help us experience what ought to come naturally? No, not really . . . not when its major theme is contentment . . . not when we've been programmed to compete, achieve, increase, fight, and worry our way up the so-called "ladder of success" (which few can even define).

Contentment is the unknown "X" in life's equation. It is as strange to most of us as living in an igloo or eating fried worms or raising a live gorilla in our backyard.

Face it. You and I are afraid that if we open the door of contentment, two uninvited guests will rush in: loss of prestige and laziness. We really believe that "getting to the top" is worth any sacrifice. To proud Americans, contentment is something to be enjoyed between birth and kindergarten . . . retirement and the rest home . . . or (and this will hurt) among those who have no ambition.

Stop and think. A young man with keen mechanical skills is often counseled against being contented to "settle" for a trade right out of high school. A teacher who is competent, contented, and fulfilled in the classroom is frowned upon if she turns down an offer to become a principal. The owner of Super-Duper Hamburgers on the corner has a packed-out joint everyday and is content. But chances are selfish ambition won't let him rest until he opens ten other joints and gets rich—leaving contentment behind. A man or woman who serves as an assistant or in any kind of support position in a ministry, company, or the military frequently wrestles with feelings of discontentment until he/she is promoted to the so-called "top rung." This applies to homemakers and nuclear scientists . . . plumbers and cops . . . engineers and seminary students . . . caretakers and carpet layers . . . artists and waitresses.

It's a curious fact that when people are free to do as they please, they usually imitate each other. As a result, we are rapidly becoming a nation of discontented, incompetent marionettes, dangling from strings manipulated by the same, stupid puppeteer.

Now, listen to Jesus: "Be content with your wages" (Luke 3:14). Hear Paul: "I am well content with weaknesses," and, "If we have food and covering . . . be content!" (2 Cor. 12:10; 1 Tim. 6:8). And hear another apostle: "Let your character be free from the love of money, being content with what you have" (Heb. 13:5).

I warn you: this isn't easy to implement. You'll be outnumbered and outvoted. You'll have to fight the urge to conform. Even the greatest of all the apostles admitted, "I have *learned* to be content" (Phil. 4:11). It's a learning process . . . and it isn't very enjoyable marching out of step until you are convinced you're listening to the right drummer.

When you're fully convinced, however, two things will happen: Your strings will be cut and you'll be free, indeed!

A Finishing Touch: "Striving to better, oft we mar what's well" (William Shakespeare).

A Daily Reading: Philippians 4

The heart of the term "cordial" is the word "heart." And the heart of "heart" is *kardia*, a Greek term that most often refers to the center of our inner life—the source or seat of all the forces and functions of our inner being. So when we are cordial, we are acting on something that comes from and affects the very center of life itself. Maybe that's why Webster defines "cordial" as "of or relating to the heart: vital, tending to revive, cheer or invigorate, heartfelt, gracious."

Being cordial literally starts from the heart, as I see it. It begins with the deep-seated belief that the other person is important, genuinely significant, deserving of my undivided attention, my unrivaled interest, if only for a few seconds. Encouraged by such a belief, I am prompted to be sensitive to that person's feelings. If he is uneasy and self-conscious, cordiality alerts me to put him at ease. If she is shy, cordiality provides a relief. If he is bored, cordiality stimulates and invigorates him. If she is sad, cordiality brings cheer. What a needed and necessary virtue it is!

How do we project cordiality? Try these four basic ingredients:

1. A warm smile.

Lest you try, let me warn you right now against faking this. You don't learn to smile by practicing in front of the mirror. A smile needs to become a natural part of your whole person, reflecting genuine friendliness. Nothing is more magnetic or attractive than your smile, and it will communicate volumes to the other person.

Unfortunately, I'm afraid some long-faced saints would crack their concrete masks if they smiled—I really do! Nothing repels like a frown . . . or attracts like a smile.

2. A solid handshake.

Now I'm something of a specialist when it comes to handshakes. I've experienced about every kind. Some are bone crushers—like a cross between the Terminator and Goliath (sometimes even from little, elderly ladies!). Others are completely boneless—like a handful of cool seaweed or a glove full of warm pudding. Some handshakes leave you exhausted, some cling like a crab, others turn into a small curious wrestling match—you can't pull free! There are those, however, that are solid, sure, filled with such thoughts as, "Oh, how I appreciate you!" and, "My, it's good to be in your presence!" and, "Let me assure you of my love and interest!"

Never underestimate the value of this cordial expression, my friend. The handshake is a rare remaining species in the family of touch, and it is threatened with extinction.

3. Direct eye contact.

Accompanying every handshake and conversation, no matter how brief, ought to be an eyeball-to-eyeball encounter. The eyes reflect deep feelings enclosed in the secret chamber of your soul . . . feelings which have no other means of release. Eye contact allows others to read these feelings.

Cordiality cannot be expressed indirectly.

4. A word of encouragement.

Keep this fresh, free from cliches, and to the point. Call the person by name and use it as you talk. If time permits, mention something you honestly appreciate about him or her. Be specific and natural, and deliberately refuse to flatter the person. Let your heart be freely felt as your words flow.

"Oil and perfume make the heart glad, so a man's counsel is sweet to his friend" (Prov. 27:9).

Spread some sweetness . . . have a heart . . . convey cordiality!

A Finishing Touch: How are you doing in the cordiality department? Try to be conscious of it this week, without being self-conscious.

A Daily Reading: Proverbs 15

We must have resembled a family of Gypsies or a scene from *The Grapes of Wrath* as we rambled along the highway. Several layers of redwood forest dust mixed with pine tree sap covered our car. The car-top carrier was loaded with miscellaneous stuff, including a bike wrapped in a blanket flapping in the air, piled on top of several boxes of "family fun stuff." We were homeward bound and glad of it.

As most of the family dozed, I hummed a tune from John Denver's best album, the main line of which says, "Hey, it's good to be back home again. . . ." Truer words were never sung!

Lake Tahoe had been crystal clear and beautifully therapeutic. Ten days out under the stars beside an open fire is good for what ails ya . . . but coming home is better!

Mount Hermon was crispy cool and memorable with its giant Sequoias and rippling streams. A week up in the Santa Cruz area can hardly be beat . . . but coming home is better!

Coleman lanterns, coffee pot black from the campfire, sleeping bags, a low-burning, snapping campfire, the smell of smoke, the infinite silence of solitude, the awesome majesty of the mountains, the soft crunch of the foot trails, the outburst of laughter from a happy family—ah, such nostalgic memories will never be erased . . . but coming home is better!

Why? Why would anyone prefer the maddening pace, the freeways, the smog, the crowds, loads of laundry, stacks of mail (especially unpaid bills), a desk piled with a backlog of office details? What is so magnetic about coming home to all that? Why is the appeal of the familiar so powerful that we're always anxious to return?

I really have no profound answer. But consider this . . .

Home represents our point of identity, our base of operations, our primary realm of responsibility. Home gives life its roots, its sense of purpose and direction. Even with the hammer blows of pressure, stress, and struggles, home is the anvil used of God to forge out character in the furnace of schedule and demand. We count on it over the long haul and thereby develop security, stability, and consistency.

For me, coming home has an added benefit. It means returning to ministry. It means accepting the most exciting challenge life offers . . . one with eternal dimensions and incredible proportions. It means facing every new dawn with total dependence, living literally on the raw edge of reality. To me, that's not an optional existence . . . that's the only way to live.

I received the following "welcome home" letter today that seems to put this into proper, if humorous, perspective.

> This chain letter is meant to bring relief and happiness to you.
>
> Unlike other chain letters this does not cost money. Simply send a copy of this letter to six other churches who are tired of their ministers. Then bundle up your pastor and send him to the church at the bottom of the list.
>
> In one week you will receive 16,436 ministers—and one of them should be a dandy!
>
> One man broke the chain and got his old minister back.

I'm back.

A Finishing Touch: We are invariably drawn to come back home not because of where it is but because of what it represents.

A Daily Reading: Ruth 1

The children worked long and hard on their little cardboard shack. It was to be a special spot—a clubhouse, where they could meet together, play, and have fun. Since a clubhouse has to have rules, they came up with three:

> Nobody act big.
> Nobody act small.
> Everybody act medium.

Not bad theology!

In different words, God says the very same thing:

"Give preference to one another in honor" (Rom. 12:10).

"Let each of you regard one another as more important than himself" (Phil. 2:3).

"Through love serve one another" (Gal. 5:13).

"Whoever wishes to become great among you shall be your servant, and whoever wishes to be first among you shall be your slave" (Matt. 20:26–27).

"Let another praise you, and not your own mouth; a stranger, and not your own lips" (Prov. 27:2).

Just "act medium." Believable. Honest, human, thoughtful, and down to earth. Regardless of your elevated position or high pile of honors or row of degrees or endless list of achievements, just stay real. Junk any idea that you deserve some kind of super recognition for a job well done. Who did you do it for anyway? If you did it for God, He has an infinite number of unseen ways to reward you. If you did it for human glory, no wonder you're seeking the credit! So easy to draw out that praise for yourself, isn't it? Ye olde ego is a wily one.

Just "act medium."

Again, what is it Solomon said? "Let another praise you . . . a stranger, and not your own lips."

Meaning what? Meaning no self-reference to some enviable accomplishment. Meaning refusal to scratch a back when yours itches. Meaning no desire to manipulate and manufacture praise. Meaning authentic surprise when applauded.

Like the inimitable Principal Cairns, headmaster of an English school, who was walking onto the platform along with other dignitaries. As he stepped up, a burst of spontaneous applause arose from the audience. In characteristic modesty, Cairns stepped back to let the man behind pass by . . . as he began to applaud his colleague. He genuinely assumed the applause was for another.

Just "act medium."

But one final warning: Don't try to fake it. False humility stinks worse than raw conceit.

The answer is not in trying to appear worthless or "wormy." The answer lies in consistently taking notice of others' achievements, recognizing others' skills and contributions . . . and saying so. That's called serving others in love. And that's what Christ did.

Got the rules memorized?

"Nobody act big. Nobody act small. Everybody act medium."

Such good advice from a clubhouse full of kids who, by the way, are pretty good at practicing what they preach.

A Finishing Touch: Make yourself a little plaque with this rule on it and put it in a place where you will see it every day.

A Daily Reading: Matthew 20

"Now a new king arose over Egypt, who did not know Joseph" (Exod. 1:8).

Too bad. Tragic, in fact. The new monarch would've been a much better man if he had known Joseph. Seems a shame Joseph had to die at the young age of 110(!) before he had a chance to impact the new king. What a difference that encounter might have made in the lives of the Hebrews, who were now reduced to the monotony of mixing mortar and making bricks.

If only the Pharaoh could have met Joseph.

Sounds cruel, but some people seem to live too long. Sadly, the converse is also true: Seems like some people die too soon. About the time you realize just how valuable their contribution is, it's too late. They're gone.

As a preacher, I think about this a lot. I think about how helpful it would be if some of the men who preached and wrote so well could have lived another twenty, maybe thirty years.

G. Campbell Morgan left us in 1945. Had he lived fifteen to twenty more years, I could have studied under him.

Spurgeon was only fifty-eight when he died. That was the same year my dad was born.

Oh, that he—or F. B. Meyer or Alexander MacLaren or Joseph Parker or Dwight L. Moody or Martyn Lloyd-Jones or Donald Grey Barnhouse or Peter Marshall—could have stayed longer! Or A. W. Tozer.

Aiden Wilson Tozer died the year I began studying for the ministry (1959). He had spent thirty-one years pastoring the unobtrusivve Southside Alliance Church in Chicago. During his ministry , which included both the spoken and the written word, that intense, provocative little man functioned as the conscience of evangelicalism. Yet I never once heard him in person. Nor did most of my contemporary ministerial colleagues.

A. W. Tozer knew God and proclaimed Him fervently.

"To listen to Tozer preach was as safe as opening the door of a blast furnace!" says Warren Wiersbe, aptly describing the man's style.

No, I never heard him preach, Yet, in a very real sense, this great man of God lives on, for his pen continues to punch holes in our pseudo-sophistication. It prods us awake when we would otherwise nod off into dreamland.

I haven't counted them recently, but I suppose I have ten or more of Tozer's tough-minded volumes that dare me to drift off course. I don't always agree with him, but he never fails to stimulate my thinking and challenge my way. Mystical and picky though he may have been, the man asked the right questions:

> Is God *real* to you?
> Is your Christianity a set of definitions?
> Is it a list of orthodox doctrines?
> Or is it a vital relationship with Christ?
> Is your Christianity firsthand and fresh or secondhand?
> Do you genuinely hunger after God?

With daring dogmatism, the man didn't stop with casual investigation. He assaulted with insightful and relentless determination.

What he lacked in humor, he made up for in zeal.

And it didn't take him a hundred pages to get to the point— something most of us would do well to remember.

He pounced like a hen on a June bug. And woe betide the thing within his claws! Those who respect his prophet-like call do not remain the same. His *Pursuit of God* and *Divine Conquest* and *Root of the Righteous* and *God Tells the Man Who Cares* continue to be some of my most treasured works.

Now a new generation of pastors has arisen over the church who did not know Tozer . . . or Moody . . . or Meyer . . . or. . . . Seems such a shame.

We need to read and heed these great pastors and teachers and prophets of recent generations. Although dead, they still speak.

The truth of the matter is, God shares His prophets briefly. Often, only when it is too late, do we realize how much more we wish we had invested.

A Finishing Touch: There's nothing like the old to help us see all things new.

A Daily Reading: Deuteronomy 18

"There are two kinds of ground: fallow ground and ground that has been broken up by the plow.

"The fallow field is smug, contented, protected from the shock of the plow and the agitation of the harrow. Such a field, as it lies year after year, becomes a familiar landmark to the crow and the blue-jay. . . . Safe and undisturbed, it sprawls lazily in the sunshine, the picture of sleepy contentment. . . . Fruit it can never know because it is afraid of the plow and the harrow.

"In direct opposite to this, the cultivated field has yielded itself to the adventure of living. The protecting fence has opened to admit the plow, and the plow has come as plows always come, practical, cruel, business-like, and in a hurry. Peace has been shattered by the shouting farmer and the rattle of machinery. The field . . . has been upset, turned over, bruised, and broken, but its rewards come hard upon its labors. The seed shoots up into the daylight, its miracle of life, curious, exploring the new world above it. Nature's wonders follow the plow.

"There are two kinds of lives also: the fallow and the plowed.

"The man of fallow life is contented with himself and the fruit he once bore. He does not want to be disturbed. He smiles in silent superiority at revivals, fastings, self-searchings, and all the travail of fruit bearing and the anguish of advance. The spirit of adventure is dead within him. . . . he has fenced himself in, and by the same act he has fenced out God and the miracle.

"The plowed life is the life that has . . . thrown down the protecting fences and sent the plow of confession into the soul. . . . Such a life has put away defense and has forsaken the safety of death for the peril of life. Discontent, yearning, contrition, courageous obedience to the will of God: these have bruised and broken the soil till it is ready again for the seed. And as always fruit follows the plow."

—A. W. Tozer, *Paths to Power*

Frank Gifford and his team turn the Swindoll family room into a stadium on Monday nights. That's one part of my week when all pressures shift into neutral and my thoughts are concerned only with play-action fakes, complicated zone defenses, halfback options, post patterns, safety blitzes, and screen passes. To me, that's fun. Even though I may shout and scream and jump and jeer, it's a relaxing and rewarding experience I thoroughly enjoy. What's more, it's the same for Gifford and those players and the refs and those nutty fans surrounding the gridiron. They're all having a ball!

In fact, I remember when Don Meredith was doing commentary and was interviewed, he stated that one of the reasons he retired from the Cowboys was he stopped "having fun." He caught himself getting so all-fired serious about the game that he was no longer able to hang loose, laugh off a mistake, and look forward to that next set of downs. His job became a demanding tyrant that slapped him across the mouth rather than across the back. When the fun stopped, so did the desire, the delight, and the determination. So what did he do? He got into another phase of his specialty that allowed him to bring back the fun that had departed. He exchanged the uniform for the microphone . . . and started smiling again. Good for him! May his tribe increase!

Now, some frowning, neurotic soul is reading this and saying, "Well, somebody's got to do the job. Life is more than fun 'n' games, Swindoll. Grow up and get down to business! Laughter is all right for kids, but adults, especially Christian adults, have a job to do that's serious."

Okay, pal, so it's serious. So it isn't all a joke. Nobody's going to argue that life has its demands and that being mature involves discipline and responsibility. But who says we have to get an ulcer and drive ourselves (and others!) to distraction in the process of fulfilling our God-given role? No one is less efficient or more incompetent than the person on the brink of a breakdown. The person who has become a pawn in the brutal hands of his responsibilities, who has lost the ability to relax and laugh and "blow it" without guilt. Our hospitals are full of victims of the let's-cut-the-fun philosophy of life. And today they really aren't much of an asset to society—or to the cause of Christ. And that's not a criticism; it's reality.

Old Solomon knew that. Remember his words of wisdom? "A joyful heart is good medicine, but a broken spirit dries up the bones" (Prov. 17:22).

There is no more effective safety valve in all of life than balancing the serious, somber side with frequent flashes of fun, fun, fun!

I don't care if you're white collar or blue . . . teacher or student . . . old or young . . . busy or bored . . . wealthy or poor . . . married or single . . . childless or the old woman in a shoe . . . retired or just getting started in business . . . brilliant or dull—if you're not enjoying most of your day, if you've stopped having fun, you're missing more than you are contributing.

One final word, especially for my super-serious friend. You may be a fundamentalist at heart, and that's fine. Welcome to the club. But remember, you don't have to look like one or sound like one!

Oops, gotta go. The stadium is almost full and it's kick-off time.

A Finishing Touch: When was the last time you laughed till you cried? Did you know that a good belly laugh is a proven stress reliever?

A Daily Reading: Ecclesiastes 3:4; Proverbs 17:22

I will never forget that Thanksgiving.

I will never forget standing erect in my classroom, my hand over my heart, as I repeated the Pledge of Allegiance to our flag.

Our nation was at war and times were hard.

My teacher had lost her husband on the bloodwashed shores of Normandy. After we had saluted the flag, we bowed our heads for prayer. As we did, she began to weep. I did too. All the class joined in. Then she stumbled through one of the most moving expressions of gratitude and praise that I have ever heard emerge from a soul plunged in pain.

At that moment in my young life I fell in love with Thanksgiving.

Lost in sympathy and a boy's pity for his teacher, I walked home very slowly that afternoon. Although only a child, I had profound feelings of gratitude for my country . . . my friends . . . my school . . . my church . . . my family. I swore before God that I would fight to the end to keep this land free from foes who would want to take away America's distinctives and the joys of living in this good land.

I have never forgotten that childhood promise. I never shall.

Thanksgiving puts steel into our patriotic veins. It reminds us of our great heritage. It carries us back with humbling nostalgia to that first dreadful winter at Plymouth where less than half the handful of people survived.

Thanksgiving speaks in clear, crisp tones of forgotten terms like integrity . . . bravery . . . respect . . . faith . . . vigilance . . . dignity . . . honor . . . freedom . . . discipline . . . sacrifice . . . godliness. Its historic halls echo with the voices of Washington, Franklin, Jefferson, Adams, Henry, Lincoln, Lee, and Jackson, who challenge us to trim off the fat of indolence, compromise, passivity, and the stigma of strife.

Thanksgiving gives a depth of relevance and meaning to the nineteenth-century words of Katharine Lee Bates:

> O beautiful for spacious skies,
> For amber waves of grain,

For purple mountain majesties
Above the fruited plain!

O beautiful for patriot dream
That sees beyond the years
Thine alabaster cities gleam
Undimmed by human tears!

America! America!
God shed His grace on thee
And crown thy good with brotherhood
From sea to shining sea!

Thanksgiving . . . mark it well. It is a day of eminence, a day of memories, a day of commitment. May it not be eclipsed behind the shadows of our national aches nor beneath the passing pain of personal hardship.

May it arrive with forceful and throbbing impact upon our lives . . . and the lives of our children.

May we all, indeed, give thanks.

A Finishing Touch: Thankful living is thanks giving.
A Daily Reading: Psalm 100

I keep meeting these wonderful people whose lives belie their age. Their enthusiasm is contagious, their zest for life captivating. They're still thinking and dreaming, determined not to miss out on the fun, and they're definitely not interested in planting themselves in a rocking chair and watching sunsets.

Last Turkey Day, as we wrapped up our Thanksgiving celebration at the church, I spotted a visiting gentleman who was shaking hands with a half dozen folks he'd never met before. Then he looked at me, and with a grin and a twinkle, he whipped out his hand. It was a hand you could strike a match on, toughened by decades of rugged toil.

"You look like a man who enjoys life. What do you do for a living," I asked.

"Me? Well, I'm a farmer from back in the Midwest."

"Really? I guess I'm not surprised, since you've got hands like a tractor tire."

He laughed . . . asked me a couple of insightful questions, then told me about his plans for traveling on his own through California.

"What did you do last week?" I asked. His answer stunned me. "Last week I finished harvesting 90,000 bushels of corn," he said with a smile.

I then blurted out, "Ninety thousand! How old are you, my friend?"

He didn't seem at all hesitant or embarrassed by my question. "I'm just a couple months shy o' ninety." He laughed again as I shook my head.

He had lived through four wars, the Great Depression, sixteen presidents, ninety Midwest winters, who knows how many personal hardships, and he was still taking life by the throat. I had to ask him the secret of his long and productive life. "Hard work and integrity" was his quick reply.

As we parted company, he looked back over his shoulder and added, "Don't take it easy, young feller. Stay at it!"

His final comment reminded me of a physician's words to me

several years ago. As he was completing my physical checkup, we got on the subject of staying fit, and he told me a story I often recall. Some months earlier he had examined a lady in her eighties. She was still in fairly good physical condition, which prompted him to ask her if she stayed pretty active. With a wink she bragged, "I jog about four to five miles a day . . . every day." Surprised, he told her she didn't need to overdo it. "Take it easy," he suggested. She took his words to heart and decided to slow down. She reduced her jog to a much slower walk and cut back to three or four days a week. I'll never forget the doctor's sad sigh as he finished the story. "She died a month ago. Never again will I tell a patient doing as well as she was doing to take it easy."

The Bible is filled with folks who refused to take it easy. Remember our friend Caleb, who, at age 85, attacked the Anakim in the hill country and successfully drove them out (Josh. 14)? Or Abraham, who had a baby (well, actually Sarah did) when he was "in his old age" . . . he was 100, she was 90 (Gen. 21)? Or Noah or Moses or Samuel or Anna, the 84-year-old prophetess . . . significant people, all.

Age means zilch. Wrinkles, gray hair, and spots on your hands, *less than zilch.* If God chooses to leave you on this old earth, great. If He makes it possible for you to step aside from your work and move on to new vistas with fresh challenges, that's also great. And whatever else you do, don't take it easy!

Few things will get you in a rut quicker than sittin' around watching hummingbirds suck red juice out of a jar!

A Finishing Touch: "No disease is more lethal than the boredom that follows retirement" (Norman Cousins).
A Daily Reading: Psalm 90

"Time to reflect." That would be my answer to the question: "What do you like most about the year-end holidays?"

Oh, the food is good—those delectable, fattening morsels that make Thanksgiving, Christmas, and New Year's so special. So are the parties and the people. The songs, the smiles, the smells. We live in the warmth of them for days. Sometimes months.

But the best those traditional holidays can offer, in my opinion, is time to reflect. To stand in front of the full-length mirror of memory and study the scene. Thoughtfully. Silently. Alone. At length. To trace the outline of the past without the rude interruption of routine tasks. Taking time to stop and listen. And think. To sit by a crackling fireplace with all the lights out, staring into the flames, and letting thoughts emerge, drift, and linger. To remember the line of a poem. To listen to some grand music, submerging all petty noises and worries beneath the waves of its stimulating sound.

Maybe it's part of what Charles Wesley meant by being "lost in wonder, love, and praise." A kind of solitary worship. An extended leisure, yielding rich benefits and deep insights. Invariably, those occasions leave me feeling grateful to God. Often I end up thanking Him for something or someone specifically that He provided in the yesterday of my life that makes my today much more meaningful.

It happened again last week. As one by one the rest of the family drifted off to bed, I put a couple more logs on the fire, slid into my favorite chair, and read for well over an hour. I came across a few thoughts put together by Ed Dayton, a long-time leader in the World Vision ministry. His words sent me back many, many years when he mentioned watching a short film called *The Giving Tree*, a simple, fanciful piece about a tree that loved a boy.

When the boy was young, he swung from the tree's branches, climbed all over her, ate her apples, slept in her shade. Such happy, carefree days. The tree loved those years.

But as the boy grew, he spent less and less time with the tree. "Come on, let's play," invited the tree on one occasion, but the young man was interested only in money. "Take my apples and sell them," said the tree. He did, and the tree was happy.

He didn't return for a long time, but the tree smiled when he passed by one day. "Come on, let's play!" But the man was older and tired of his world. He wanted to get away from it all. "Cut me down. Take my large trunk and make yourself a boat. Then you can sail away," said the tree. The man did, and the tree was happy.

Many seasons passed—summers and winters, windy days and lonely nights—and the tree waited. Finally, the old man returned, too old and tired to play, to pursue riches, or to sail the seas. "I have a pretty good stump left, my friend. Why don't you just sit down here and rest?" said the tree. He did, and the tree was happy.

I stared into the fire, watching my life pass in review as I grew older with the tree and the boy. I identified with both—and it hurt.

How many Giving Trees have there been in my life? How many have released part of themselves so I might grow, accomplish my goals, find wholeness and satisfaction? So, so many. Thank you, Lord, for each one. Their names could fill this page.

The fire died into glowing embers. It was late as I crawled into bed. I had wept, but now I was smiling. "Good night, Lord," I said. I was a thankful man.

Thankful I had taken time to reflect.

A Finishing Touch: Reflect upon the Giving Trees in your own life. Thank God for them. Is it your turn to do the same for another?

A Daily Reading: Psalm 104

It's coming!

That quiet, unheralded day that refuses to be glamorized is just around the corner. If you're not careful, you'll let it slip right on by with only a plate full of turkey and a passing nod. It's the only national holiday that frustrates merchants since they can't make an extra buck off it.

And it always falls on a Thursday, of all things!

That's right, it's Thanksgiving . . . my favorite.

Why?

I prefer it because it's so healthy, so encouraging . . . and so understated. No jingles to sing, no commercials to endure, no gifts to buy—just a day to be thankful. To look up and around and within and say, "Thank you, Lord."

Maybe these few thoughts will stimulate you to give God your own thanks in greater abundance.

> **LOOKING UP . . .** thank You, Lord:
>> for Your sovereign control over our circumstances
>> for Your holy character in spite of our sinfulness
>> for Your commitment to us even when we wander
>>>> astray
>> for Your Word that gives us direction
>> for Your love that holds us close
>> for Your gentle compassion in our sorrows
>> for Your consistent faithfulness through our highs
>>>> and lows
>> for Your strong "no" when we need to hear it
>> for Your surprising "yes" when we lack the faith to
>>>> believe it
>> for Your wise "wait" when we are impatient and rash
>> for Your understanding when we are confused
>> for Your Spirit that enlightens our eyes
>> for Your grace that removes our guilt

Thank You, Lord, for all You are, all You do, all You say. If we were unable to look up into Your face, Thanksgiving would be just another day.

LOOKING AROUND . . . thank You, Lord:
for our wonderful country, so blessed, so unique
for close family ties, so affirming, so enjoyable
for teachers, mentors, and personal heroes who
    spur us on
for an opportunity to be of help and encouragement
    to others
for the embrace of a friend who really cares
for the joy of seeing our children and grandchildren
    grow and learn
for an occupation that enables us to make a living
for a place to live, clothes to wear, and food to eat

Thank You, Lord, for such incredible abundance. By just looking around, we are made aware of how rich we really are.

LOOKING WITHIN . . . thank You, Lord:
for the gift of good health, a hidden treasure easily
    overlooked
for eyes that see the beauty of Your creation
for minds that are curious, creative, and competent
for memories of past pleasures and recent
    accomplishments
for ears that receive the world of sounds
    surrounding us
for the special stimulation of taste and touch
for hands to work with and legs to walk with
for heartaches that force us to rearrange our
    priorities
for broken dreams and lingering afflictions that
    humble us

for the courage to tell the truth, though it hurts
for the determination to finish a demanding task
for a sense of humor that brings healing and hope

This is Thanksgiving, O Lord, not Thankskeeping. And so we pause to declare to You these expressions of gratitude. They are merely an overview of the thousands of things for which we are thankful. You are indeed worthy of our highest praise. To You goes all the glory! Amen.

A Finishing Touch: On the next page, make your own personalized list of thanksgiving: look up, look around, look within.
A Daily Reading: Psalm 95

LOOKING UP . . . thank You, Lord, for:

_____
_____
_____
_____
_____

LOOKING AROUND . . . thank You, Lord, for:

_____
_____
_____
_____
_____

LOOKING WITHIN . . . thank You, Lord, for:

_____
_____
_____
_____
_____

A severe case of ingrown eyeballs strikes all of us every once in a while. In both dramatic and subtle ways, the stubborn enemy of our souls whispers sweet little nothings in our ears. He reminds us of how unappreciated and ill-treated we are . . . how important yet over-looked . . . how gifted yet ignored . . . how capable yet unrecognized . . . how bright yet eclipsed . . . how valuable yet unrewarded.

He visits the mother of small children and the wife of a wretch-of-a-husband and tells her, "How terrible is your plight . . . how un-fair, how unbearable!"

He slips into the office of the faithful worker who has been by-passed . . . swamping his mind with the slimy green silt of self-pity.

He frequents the sick room of the sufferer and announces: "You've been forgotten. No one really cares about you. Folks don't drop by as often. You're out of sight and out of mind."

He plagues the bench warmer with, "Face it, man, you'll never make first string!" To the unemployed he says, "No chance!"

To the divorced he says, "No place!" To the bereaved he says, "No hope!" To the struggling he says, "No way!"

The most damaging impact of self-pity is its ultimate end. Cuddle and nurse it as an infant and you'll soon have a full-grown beast . . . a monster . . . a raging, coarse brute that will spread the poison of bitterness and paranoia throughout your system.

A frown will replace your smile. A pungent criticism will replace a pleasant, "I understand." Suspicion and resentment will sub-merge your selfish island like a tidal wave, and you will soon dis-cover that this sea of self-pity has brought with it urchins of doubt, despair . . . and even the desire to die.

An exaggeration? A wild imagination? If you think so, sit with me awhile beneath the shade of a juniper tree located at 19 First Kings, the current address of a prophet named Elijah.

Elijah had just won a great victory over Ahab and his Baal-worshiping pawns. In fact, God stamped His approval upon Elijah in such a way that all Israel knew that he was God's mouthpiece. As a result, Jezebel, Ahab's spouse (he was her mouse) declared and predicted Elijah's death within twenty-four hours.

Now, the seasoned prophet had surely been criticized before. He lived with threats—all prophets do. But this threat somehow found the chink in his armor.

So Elijah ran for his life. Then, beneath the tree, overwhelmed with self-pity, he said. "'I've had enough . . . take away my life. I've got to die sometime, and it might as well be now. . . . I've worked very hard for the Lord God of the heavens; but the people of Israel have broken their covenant with You and torn down Your altars and killed Your prophets, and only I am left; and now they are trying to kill me, too'" (1 Kings 19:4, 10 TLB).

There you have it. Self-pity in the raw. His eyeballs were so ingrown he saw two of everything—except God. Self-pity is like smog. The more you're out in it, the worse you feel.

Yet God didn't rebuke His man, nor strike him dead. He encouraged him to take a rest, enjoy a catered meal or two . . . and get his eyes off himself and his situation so that they might get back on the Lord. God even gave him a close friend, a fella named Elisha, with whom he might share his life and his load.

Feeling sorry for yourself today? Why not try God's remedy: take a break, stop trying to work things out yourself. And take a long, loving look at your Savior in His Word . . . and then spend some time with a friend. You'll be amazed at the outcome . . . you may even discover the solution to the smog problem.

A Finishing Touch: Self-pity is the smog that pollutes and obscures the light of the Son.

A Daily Reading: 1 Kings 19

As an ex-Marine I am often the brunt of jokes told by ex-dog faces and ex-swabbies. Since my outfit is viewed as the guys with more muscles than brains, the jokes usually portray leathernecks as disciplined yet dull, brawny oxen with IQs about six points above a plant. I heard another hilarious one last weekend at a men's conference I attended.

In America they say, "It's 10:00. Do you know where your children are?"

In France they say, "It's 10:00. Do you know where your wife is?"

In Italy they say, "It's 10:00. Do you know where your car is?"

In the Marines they say, "It's 10:00. Do you know what time it is?"

Marines aren't the only ones notorious for being thick and tired of life. Evangelical Christians run a close second!

We get our theological ducks in a row, we make sure our eternal destination is sealed in a fireproof safe, we surround ourselves with a predictable schedule that protects us from contamination with the lost world, and then, like a 600-pound grizzly, we settle down for a long winter's snooze.

Our hope? Do not disturb 'til the Rapture. And we're content to spend the balance of our lives as unconcerned and uninvolved in our world as a silverfish crawling over a pile of discarded *Time* magazines.

Only one problem. The battle continues to rage, no matter what the season. From spring to summer. In relaxed autumn and icy winter. Whether we choose to believe it or not.

It is so easy to forget that our adversary, like our Advocate, neither slumbers nor sleeps. With relentless, unslacking energy . . . as sure as this morning's dawn, he's on the prowl, "seeking someone to devour" (1 Peter 5:8).

He's been at it for centuries. By means of a brilliant strategy, an insidious scheme, he takes advantage of our mental dullness. Surprise attacks are his specialty.

Small wonder Jesus kept urging His followers to "be on the alert," to "watch," to "resist," to keep a clean crop, free of stuff that "chokes the word, making it unfruitful."

Why? Because you never know when you are in the cross-hairs of the scope of the enemy's high-powered rifle. It could be today that you will be the target. When you least expect it . . . in the lazy days of summer, in the cool days of autumn, in the fog of false security, under the frost of a laid-back lifestyle.

He's looking for you. He's primed and ready to fire. And he doesn't wait for hunting season. In fact, as far as Satan is concerned, it's always open season on Christians.

Are you alert to the danger?

A Finishing Touch: If you're going to stand firm in the faith, you can't be lying down.

A Daily Reading: 1 Peter 5

To rally: "to muster for a common purpose . . . to arouse for ac-tion . . . to come together again to renew an effort." That's the way Webster defines the meaning of the verb. He says the noun means: "a mustering of scattered forces to renew an effort; a summoning up of strength or courage."

Throughout Scripture, we encounter God's rallying points: places where His people assembled for a common purpose, for recovery and refreshment, to muster forces and get recharged for battle.

For Abraham it was Bethel, the place of the altar. For Moses it was the bush in the desert. For the Hebrews en route to Canaan? Well, they had several. During the day, a massive cloud overhead. At night, an enormous column of fire. Along the way, the tabernacle, that portable sanctuary where the Lord met with His chosen ones. Later, it was the temple. Then, following the terrible years of Baby-lonian captivity, Nehemiah envisioned a plan for "mustering scat-tered forces to renew an effort" as he led a rag-tag group of dejected Hebrews back to Jerusalem to rebuild the city walls.

Jesus Himself became a rallying point for a handful of men whose lives were otherwise destined for mediocrity. And after His depar-ture His Spirit came at Pentecost and ignited a spark as the church universal came into existence, offering perpetual hope for fractured, lost humanity.

What a history followed the church's birth! Giantlike men and women of faith stood in the gap, aroused people to action, and led movements that swept continents back to God. And with each one, there was an anointed rallying point where embers burst into flame, where hearts were broken, lives were healed, songs were born, souls were saved.

Finally, today, you and I can look back and recall a specific place—our own Bethel or desert bush—where God became real to us again.

Perhaps it was on a majestic mountain, high above the noise and worries of life below. Or maybe beside the pounding surf, where you were forced to come to terms with an issue that required a painful decision. Many would say their spot was at a Christian conference, where, alone with God, they finally said "Yes." For some, it occurred behind iron bars or on a sprawling university campus or in a place of worship packed with people, when "heaven came down and glory filled [their] soul."

Where would we be without rallying points? Places that catapult us into new dimensions we would otherwise never inhabit.

Today, rallying points are often provided by evangelistic crusades. Critics, of course, want us to believe these are nothing more than some old-fashioned revivals where church folks gather, sing a few songs, listen to Bible preaching, then promptly go back to business as usual. You and I know, however, that these meetings can be some of the most significant events ever held in America, for they may provide a fresh spiritual awakening that will be nothing short of revolutionary.

So, thank God for your own Bethel. And pray that He will provide the same for others.

Pray that He will arouse us for action and muster us for a common purpose in these days when our forces often seem scattered and when we need a summoning up of strength and courage.

A Finishing Touch: Rallying points replace flabby faith with the grit and gristle of godliness.

A Daily Reading: Exodus 40

Ours is a hell-bound, degenerate world and you know it. Political corruption abounds. International peace, a splendid ideal, continues to blow up in our faces. The crime rate escalates as domestic violence and gang wars and drug traffic and overcrowded jails continue to plague society. Pending legal cases choke the courts of our land with an endless litany of litigation. And even when cases are finally brought to trial, no courtroom or prison cell can remove madness from minds or hatred from hearts.

The world is a war zone. If it were not for the reliable promises God has given in the pages of His Book, a spirit of fatalism would reign supreme. The battle would already be lost.

Too bleak? An exaggeration?

Satan, our relentless enemy, has a game plan, and it's on the board. Knowing that his days are numbered, knowing that he has an appointed amount of time before the scoreboard counts him out, he holds the world in his lap and gives it directions, implementing his strategy day after day. On the surface, his plays are impressive and appealing and even very satisfying . . . for a while. So long as the adversary can keep earth's inhabitants believing his lies and blinded to his schemes, he will continue his subtle strategy. But the truth is, his ploys work against everything that is holy and just and good.

If our message is a mirror image of the message of the world, the world yawns and goes on its way, saying, "What else is new? I've heard all that since I was born." But if the Christian lifestyle and motivation and answers are different, the world cannot help but sit up and take notice, thinking: *How come they live in the same place I live, but they are able to live a different kind of life? Why is their love so deep and lasting and ours so shallow and fickle? How is it that she can forgive and never hold a grudge? Why do these people have so much more compassion, kindness, integrity, and patience than anyone else I know?*

Do you get the message? It's the difference that makes the difference!

Think about it: Do people feel more alive when they're around you? Do you create within them a thirst for God? Does anyone ever wonder why you are so unselfish, so thoughtful, so caring? Do the neighborhood children want to be in your home because of the way you treat your children?

People who live in the darkness have no ray of light; that's the way it is for the majority in the world. Some folks are born, raised, and die without ever seeing their first flashlight of hope. Imagine it!

When the truth of that hits me, I find myself a little impatient with Christians who do nothing but shine lights for themselves. Jesus says to shine for the world.

Jesus never said to His disciples, "You know, fellas, we have to work on gathering a better crowd. They're getting pretty thin, especially on Sunday night." No, it was never like that. He turned on the light, and they came. He was so different, they flocked to hear Him. In the wilderness. In the city. On a hillside. At the lakeside.

What do people see when they look at you? Do they see your good works? Do they hear your courtesy? Do they detect your smile? Do they notice that you stop to thank them? Do they hear you apologize when you are wrong? Do they see every visible manifestation of Christ's life being normally lived out through you? When they see all that, Jesus said, they "will glorify your Father who is in heaven" (Matt. 5:16).

Isn't it a pleasure when someone says to you, "Why are you like that?" And isn't it a natural thing to respond, "I'm glad you asked. Let me tell you what's happened"? And then you light their way home.

A Finishing Touch: "When the Church is absolutely different from the world, she invariably attracts it. It is then that the world is made to listen to her message, though it may hate it at first" (D. Martyn Lloyd-Jones).

A Daily Reading: Matthew 5:13–16

It's baa-aack!

That ol' yuletide season has slipped in the door once again, and the malls will be playing "Jingle Bells" at least a thousand times between now and the 25th. If you're not careful, you'll resent the crowds and merchandising hoopla so much you'll resist the spirit of the season. And there's nothing worse than a jaded attitude for twenty-five days before Christmas. So let's do something to keep that from happening.

It occurred to me last week that there is a practical reason Thanksgiving always precedes Christmas: It sets in motion the ideal mental attitude to carry us through the weeks in between. In other words, a sustained spirit of gratitude makes the weeks before Christmas a celebration rather than a marathon. Matter of fact, since there are four weeks, our sustained thankfulness could be tied into the four seasons of the year.

Here's what I'm getting at. Four weeks before Christmas, let's carry within us hearts of gratitude for the spring of the year. During the third week, be thankful for the summer months, in the second week, the autumn season, and the final week before Christmas Day, the winter. Instead of fretting about how many shopping days are left, reflect on the many wonderful memories each season of the year brought your way. As you do, I think you'll find that the traffic and the crowds aren't nearly so irritating and the music in the malls may even be downright enjoyable.

Here are some suggestions to get you started. Later you can personalize each season for yourself.

Four Weeks Before Christmas: Spring
Newly planted flowers
The smell of fresh earth
Gentle falling rain
Easter: Christ's resurrection
Spring-season baseball

Young colts frolicking in a meadow
Rainbows and wind chimes
A small, warm child, right after a bath
A hug from a friend
A clean house with clear windows
A letter from someone you love
Church bells in the distance
Geese flying north

Three Weeks Before Christmas: Summer
Longer days, warm nights
Water skiing, fishing, swimming
A night under the stars at the Hollywood Bowl
Sunset over the ocean
Graduation
Walking barefoot over fresh-cut grass
A bride and groom at the altar
Hot doughnuts on Saturday morning
Bible study and prayer with your closest friends
That long-awaited vacation
Hot-air balloons
A double-header at the stadium
Leading someone to Christ

Two Weeks Before Christmas: Fall
Crisp mornings, turning leaves
Pumpkin pie
Great worship, grand music, glorious pipe organ
Gathering at home for Thanksgiving
Hugs and kisses from grandkids
Football season
Staying up late to watch a movie
Sense of God's nearness
Meeting a new friend at school
The freedom to vote
Trying to lose weight . . . and doing it

A sermon that met a particular need
Being preserved from a terrible accident

One Week Before Christmas: Winter
Reconciling a conflict with someone
Remembering something your parents taught you
Skiing on fresh snow
Listening to Handel's *Messiah*
Reading the Christmas story
The smell of a Christmas tree in your home
Memories from a photo album
Curling up with a good book
Realizing the Savior came for you
A mother's smile, a father's embrace
Snowcapped mountains in the distance
Going to sleep beside a crackling fire
Hot apple cider with a cinnamon stick
Children singing, bells ringing

Well, there you have it. Thoughts of gratitude that will chase away those jaded goblins who would otherwise steal your joy.

Remember, this is a time for rejoicing.

A Finishing Touch: Enjoy Thanksgiving throughout the yuletide season.

A Daily Reading: 1 Thessalonians 5:12–28

Personalize each season by remembering and recording things that have made that particular season meaningful to you.

Spring

_____

_____

_____

_____

_____

Summer

_____

_____

_____

_____

Fall

_____

_____

_____

_____

_____

Winter

_____

_____

_____

_____

_____

DOING THE UNEXPECTED

There are various ways to describe it: turning the other cheek . . . going the extra mile . . . doing good to those who hate us . . . loving our enemies . . . pouring coals of fire on another's head. We may say it in different ways, but the action amounts to the same thing. By doing the unexpected, we accomplish a twofold objective: (1) we put an end to bitterness, and (2) we prove the truth of the age-old axiom, love conquers all. I've seen it happen over and over again. I've also seen occasions when it could have worked, but neither side was willing to give it a whirl.

Why are we so hesitant? What keeps us from doing the unexpected for the undeserving so that we might watch God accomplish the unbelievable? Why? Because it goes against our human nature. Furthermore, it's a major risk. Of course, that is where faith comes in: to believe the Lord against all odds and to obey Him even if the action backfires. But some of you are frowning, thinking, *Yeah, that sounds good, but nobody could pull it off.*

Joseph did. After suffering years of consequences brought on by his hateful brothers' mistreatment, he lived to see the day that the tables were turned. Joseph was powerful, wealthy, respected, and surrounded by bodyguards. His brothers were weak, broke, unprotected, guilty to the core. It was his moment to unleash his rage and retribution, and they had it coming . . . in spades! Instead, he did the unexpected, which shocked them down to their worn-out sandals. No get-even attack. Not even a tongue lashing. Those who deserved hatred received love and forgiveness . . . and the rest is beautiful history.

I can sense some cynic's shrug: *Well, that was then, this is now. No one would ever do that today.* How wrong you are.

Rabbi Michael Weisser did. It happened in Lincoln, Nebraska, where for more than three years, Larry Trapp, a self-proclaimed Nazi and Ku Klux Klansman, spread hatred through mailings and ugly phone calls. He promoted white supremacy, anti-Semitism, and other messages of prejudice, declaring his apartment the KKK state headquarters and himself the grand dragon. Weisser became one of Trapp's targets, receiving numerous pieces of hate mail and offensive phone calls. At first, the Weissers were so afraid they locked their doors and worried themselves sick over the safety of their family. Trapp, a 42-year-old clinically blind, double amputee, continued to spew out his hate-ridden racial slurs and obscene remarks.

One day Rabbi Weisser decided to do the unexpected. He left a message on Trapp's answering machine, telling the man of another side of life . . . a life free of hatred and racism. "I probably called ten times and left messages before he finally picked up the phone and asked me why I was harassing him. I said I'd like to help him. I offered him a ride to the grocery store."

Trapp was stunned. Disarmed by the kindness and courtesy, he started thinking. He later admitted, through tears, that he heard in the rabbi's voice, "something I hadn't experienced. It was love."

Slowly the bitter man began to soften. One night he called the Weissers and said he wanted out but didn't know how. They grabbed a bucket of fried chicken and took him dinner. Before long they made a trade: in return for their love he gave them his swastika rings, hate tracts, and Klan robes. That same day Trapp gave up his recruiting job and dumped the rest of his propaganda in the trash. "They showed me so much love that I couldn't help but love them back," he finally confessed.

Christmas is right around the corner. How about giving the gift of forgiveness, a cup full of kindness, a sincere phone call of grace to someone who would never expect it and might not deserve it . . . with no strings attached? It's risky . . . but you wouldn't be the first to try it.

A Finishing Touch: God's gift to us came wrapped in swaddling clothes, lying in a manger. Talk about doing the unexpected for the undeserving!

A Daily Reading: John 1

Americans like things to be logical and fair. We operate our lives on that basis. Meaning this: If I do what is right, good will come to me; and if I do what is wrong, bad things will happen to me. Right brings rewards and wrong brings consequences.

That's a logical and fair axiom of life, but there's one problem with it. *It isn't always true.* Life doesn't work out quite that well. There isn't a person reading these words who hasn't had the tables turned. All of us have had the unhappy and unfortunate experience of doing what is right, yet suffering for it. And we have also done what is wrong on a few occasions without being punished. The latter we can handle, but the former is a tough pill to swallow.

We hate being ripped off. Consequences belong to wrong actions. When they attach themselves to right actions, we struggle with resentment and anger.

This can even happen in a life of servanthood. You will give, forgive, forget, release your own will, obey God to the maximum, and even wash dirty feet with an attitude of gentleness and humility. And after all those beautiful things, you will get ripped off occasionally.

Believe me, if you serve others long enough, you will suffer wrong treatment for doing right things. The Bible doesn't hide this painful reality from us. In 1 Peter 2:20–24 (addressed to servants, by the way—see v. 18), we read:

> For what credit is there if, when you sin and are harshly treated, you endure it with patience? But if when you do what is right and suffer for it you patiently endure it, this finds favor with God.
>
> For you have been called for this purpose, since Christ also suffered for you, leaving you an example for you to follow in His steps, who committed no sin, nor was any deceit found in His mouth; and while being reviled, He did not revile in return; while suffering, He uttered no threats, but kept entrusting Himself to

Him who judges righteously; and He Himself bore our sins in His body on the cross, that we might die to sin and live to righteousness; for by His wounds you were healed.

Part of this makes sense, according to our logical and fair standard. Part of it doesn't. If a person does wrong and then suffers the consequences, even though he or she patiently endures the punishment, nobody applauds. But—now get this clearly fixed in your mind—when you do what is *right* and suffer for it with grace and patience, God applauds!

I have found great help from two truths God gave me at a time in my life when I was bombarded with a series of unexpected and unfair blows (from my perspective). In my darkest hours these principles became my anchor of stability, my only means of survival.

First, *nothing touches me that has not passed through the hands of my heavenly Father.* Whatever occurs, God has sovereignly surveyed and approved. We may not know why, but we do know our pain is no accident to Him. He is not surprised by it.

Two, *everything I endure is designed to prepare me for serving others more effectively.* Since my heavenly Father is committed to shaping me into the image of His Son, He knows the ultimate value of this painful experience. It is a necessary part of the preparation process.

Looking back I can clearly see that the process required that I be emptied of my own strength so I could discover that His was more than sufficient.

A Finishing Touch: When you feel as if God is taking things away, maybe He's just trying to make room in your life for better things that He wants to give you.

A Daily Reading: 2 Corinthians 4:10–11, 16–18

I love memories. Today I've been remembering a perfect Monday evening from years back. . . .

The smell of homemade clam chowder greeted me as I walked through the front door. After kissing the kids and hugging the cook, I settled into my favorite chair, loosened my tie, and kicked off my shoes—just in time to watch the beginning of the game .

Our two youngest were upstairs fiddling around with a rabbit, two hamsters, and a guinea pig. Our older daughter was on the phone with her best friend, whom she hadn't seen for at least two hours. Curt was sitting on the floor in his room strumming his guitar and singing "Raindrops Keep Fallin' on My Head." In between chopped onions and diced potatoes, Cynthia was doubled over with laughter in the kitchen as she tried to finish a chapter of Erma Bombeck's latest book.

Although my "to do" list was, again, incomplete, the day was done. Tomorrow would bring its own set of needs and responsibilities, but that was tomorrow. We all enjoyed supper (at half-time, of course) then knocked out the cleanup in exactly five minutes as we moved faster than six speeding bullets, laughing like mad the whole time. . . .

No amount of money can buy that feeling of incredible contentment, that inner sense of fulfillment, that surge of release and relief as the noise and pace of the world are muffled by the sounds and smells and sights of a happy, relaxed evening at home.

What therapy! How essential! And yet how seldom we really relax. It's almost as though we are afraid to slow down, shift into neutral, and let the motor idle.

With a drive that borders near the neurotic, we Americans hit the floor running at 6 A.M., then drop, exhausted, at midnight . . . scarcely able to remember what transpired during that 18-hour interim. If God is going to get our attention, He better plan on (1) making an appointment, (2) taking a number, or (3) driving at least 55 miles per hour—otherwise, forget it!

Strange, isn't it? We place such a high priority on achievement that we actually feel guilty when we accomplish nothing over a period of several hours. When others ask, "What did you do last night?" we actually feel guilty if we can't justify every moment. This is underscored by the number of churches who literally brag about "something for everybody every night of the week"!

I visited a small town in central Oregon during a recent trip, one of those places that was so relaxed I found myself getting antsy. You know, the kind of place where people gather to watch hub caps rust. I asked my friend: "How do you stand it? Doesn't the slow pace drive you crazy?"

He responded with a smile, "Well, it took us about eight months to unwind. You gotta learn how to relax, you know. It isn't something that you do automatically. Now, we love it."

Relaxing isn't automatic, is it? It's a skill that must be learned. Here are a couple suggestions to help you cultivate that skill:

Block out several evenings each month on your calendar. Make special plans to do nothing—except something you (or your family) would enjoy.

Each day, look for times when something humorous or unusual makes laughter appropriate . . . then laugh out loud! That helps flush out the nervous system.

And when you relax, really relax .

A Finishing Touch: A relaxed, easy-going Christian is far more attractive and effective than the rigid, uptight brother who squeaks when he walks and whines when he talks.

A Daily Reading: Psalm 27

Contentment is something we must learn. It isn't a trait we're born with. But the question is *how*? In 1 Timothy 6 we find a couple of very practical answers to that question:

A *current perspective on eternity*: "For we have brought nothing into the world, so we cannot take anything out of it either" (v. 7).

A *simple acceptance of essentials*: "And if we have food and covering, with these we shall be content" (v. 8).

Both attitudes work beautifully.

First, it really helps us to quit striving for more if we read the eternal dimension into today's situation. We entered life empty-handed; we leave it the same way. I never saw a hearse pulling a U-Haul trailer!

The truth of all this was brought home forcefully to me when a minister friend of mine told of an experience he had several years ago. He was in need of a dark suit to wear at a funeral he had been asked to conduct. He had very little money, so he went to a local pawn shop in search of a good buy. To his surprise, they had just the right size, solid black, and very inexpensive. It seemed too good to be true. As he forked over the money, he asked how they could afford to sell the suit so cheaply. With a wry grin the pawnbroker admitted that all their suits had once been owned by a local mortuary, which they used on the deceased, then removed before burial.

My friend felt a little strange wearing a suit that had once been on a dead man, but since no one else would know, why not? Everything was fine until he was in the middle of his sermon and casually started to stick his hand into the pocket of the pants . . . only to find there were no pockets!

Talk about an unforgettable object lesson! There he stood, preaching to all those people about the importance of living in light of eternity today, as he himself wore a pair of trousers without pockets that had been on a corpse.

Second, it helps us model contentment if we'll boil life down to its essentials and try to simplify our lifestyle. Verse 8 spells out those essentials: something to eat, something to wear, and a roof over our heads. Everything beyond that we'd do well to consider as extra.

You see, society's plan of attack is to create dissatisfaction, to convince us that we must be in a constant pursuit for something "out there" that is sure to bring us happiness. When you reduce that lie to its lowest level, it is saying that contentment is impossible without striving for more.

God's Word offers the exact opposite advice: Contentment is possible when we *stop* striving for more. Contentment never comes from externals. Never!

As a Greek sage once put it: "To whom little is not enough, nothing is enough."

But I'll be frank with you. My bottom-line interest is not the words of some Greek sage. It's *you*. It's helping you see the true values in life, the exceedingly significant importance of being contented with what you have rather than perpetually dissatisfied, always striving for more and more.

I recall hearing some pretty good counsel one time on how to overrule those television commercials that are so good at attempting to convince us that we need more. The guy suggested that every time we begin to feel that persuasive tug, we ought to shout back at the tube at the top of our voices: "WHO ARE YOU KIDDING!"

It really works. Our whole family tried it one afternoon during a televised football game. Not once did I feel dissatisfied with my present lot or sense the urge to jump up and go buy something. Our dog almost had a canine coronary, but other than that, the results were great.

A Finishing Touch: Great wealth is not related to money. We are being enriched by our investment in eternity.

A Daily Reading: I Timothy 6:6–20

When it came to clear communication, Jesus was a master. Children and adults alike had no difficulty understanding His words or following His reasoning.

This is remarkable, because while He was on earth He lived in a society that had become accustomed to religious double-talk. The scribes, priests, and Pharisees who dominated the synagogue scene in Palestine saw to that. They unintentionally made Jesus' simple style and straightforward approach seem all the more refreshing.

When Jesus spoke, people listened. Unlike the pious professionals of His day, Jesus' words made sense.

This was never truer than when He sat down on a hillside with a group of His followers and talked about what really mattered. His words were authoritative but not officious; insightful but not sermonic. His hillside chat was an informal, reasonable, thoughtful, and unpretentious presentation. Those who had endured a lifetime of boring and irrelevant sermons sat spellbound to the end.

People were fed up with the manipulation, the pride, and especially the hypocrisy of their religious leaders. Years of legalism, mixed with the pharisaic power plays designed to intimidate and control, held the general public in bondage. Man-made systems of complicated requirements and backbreaking demands shut the people behind invisible bars, shackled in chains of guilt. They could not measure up. Many were losing heart. But who dared say so?

Then out of the blue came Jesus with His message of liberating grace, encouragement to the weary, hope for the sinful. Best of all, everything He said was based on pristine truth—God's truth—instead of rigid religious regulations. He talked of faith in terms anyone could understand. His teaching released them from guilt and shame, fear and confusion. His authenticity caught them off guard, disarmed their suspicions, and blew away the fog that had surrounded organized religion for decades. No wonder the people found Him amazing! No wonder the scribes and Pharisees found

Him unbearable! Hypocrisy despises authenticity. When truth un-masks wrong, those who are exposed get very nervous.

The boldness of authenticity is beautiful to behold, unless you happen to be a hypocrite.

Hypocrisy permits us to travel both sides of the path—to look righteous but be unholy, to sound pious but be secretly profane. In-variably, those who get trapped in the hypocrisy syndrome find ways to mask their hollow core. The easiest approach is to add more activity, run faster, emphasize an intense, ever-enlarging agenda. The Pharisees were masters at such things. Not content with the Mosaic Law that included the Ten Commandments, they tacked on 365 prohibitions and 250 additional commandments. But did that make them righteous? Hardly.

How easy it is to fake Christianity . . . to polish a superpious im-age that looks good but is phony. Far too many Christians are sim-ply trying too hard. They are busy, to be sure. But righteous? Sincere? Many of them. Intense? Most. Busy? Yes . . . but far from spiritual.

So what does Jesus want? What was He getting at?

He was simply saying that He wanted His followers to be people of simple faith, modeled in grace, based on truth. Nothing more. Nothing less. Nothing else.

Jesus put it straight: "Beware of practicing your righteousness be-fore men to be noticed by them" (Matt. 6:1). In other words, stop acting one way before others when you are really not that way at all. He applied this admonition to three specific areas: giving, praying, and fasting. When we live by faith, big-time performances that bring us the glory are out of place.

Following His passionate reproach against hypocrisy Jesus also warned the people against judging each other. "How can you say to your brother, 'Let me take the speck out of your eye,' and behold, the log is in your own eye?"

The tendency to judge others was not a trait that belonged exclusively to Jesus' first-century audience. Christians today are "speck specialists." We look for specks and detect specks and criticize specks, all the while ignoring the much larger and uglier and more offensive logs in our own lives that need immediate attention.

Jesus was encouraging tolerance. Be tolerant of those who live different lifestyles. Be tolerant of those who don't look like you, who don't dress like you, who don't care about the things you care about, who don't vote like you. Furthermore, be tolerant of those whose fine points of theology differ from yours, whose worship style is different. Be tolerant of the young if you are older . . . and be tolerant of the aging if you are young.

Jesus' words that day on the hillside were powerful. When He finished speaking, nobody moved. Small wonder. His words were like spikes nailing them in place.

A Finishing Touch: People of faith mean what they say and do what they hear. They do not substitute words for action or pious discussion for personal involvement.

A Daily Reading: Matthew 7

Some years ago I was given a book of Puritan prayers called *The Valley of Vision*. I have worn out one copy and had to purchase another. I recommend this volume to you. Read the following prayer from the Puritan's pen slowly (preferably aloud).

O LORD,
I am a shell full of dust,
but animated with an invisible rational soul
and made anew by an unseen power of grace;
Yet I am no rare object of valuable price,
but one that has nothing and is nothing,
although chosen of thee from eternity,
given to Christ, and born again;
I am deeply convinced of the evil and misery of a sinful state,
    of the vanity of creatures,
but also of the sufficiency of Christ.
When thou wouldst guide me I control myself,
When thou wouldst be sovereign I rule myself.
When thou wouldst take care of me I suffice myself.
When I should depend on thy providings I supply myself,
When I should submit to thy providence I follow my will,
When I should study, love, honour, trust thee, I serve myself;
I fault and correct thy laws to suit myself,
Instead of thee I look to man's approbation,
and am by nature an idolater.
Lord, it is my chief design to bring my heart back to thee.
Convince me that I cannot be my own god, or make myself happy,
nor my own Christ to restore my joy,
nor my own Spirit to teach, guide, and rule me. . . .
Then take me to the cross and leave me there.

Dr. Seuss wasn't thinking of me when he wrote *The Grinch That Stole Christmas.* Charles Dickens would not have asked me to play Scrooge. In spite of what you may read later, remember that! Our family has a tree every year, we exchange presents, play Christmas records, sing carols, enjoy the festivities, and even wish folks "Merry Christmas." Believe me, I have no bone to pick with the yuletide season, unless it's off the turkey.

But you'll have to agree, it's not without its unique problems and temptations. Our lovely land of plenty drifts dangerously near insanity three or four weeks every year. If you doubt that, consider these statistics: Americans spend 8.5 billion dollars during the Christmas season; 150 million dollars will go for wrappings alone, most of which will be immediately discarded; 100 million dollars will be spent on trees; 200 million dollars will be spent on postage; 2 million telegrams will be sent between the 23rd and 25th of December. (My figures are slightly out of date, but if anything, each could be increased this year.)

Along with all this, emotions, unpredictable and undisciplined, begin to run wild. Nostalgia mixed with eleven months of guilt can prompt illogical and extravagant purchases. Neighborhood pressure can cause perfectly normal people to mount extravagant displays and string hundreds of lights on their houses. Television advertising, Christmas bank accounts, and special "wish books" only increase the pull of the magnet that inevitably ends with the sound of cash register or the hollow snap of the credit card.

While we think we may be immune to all this, we Christians need to be especially alert to the dangers and think through a strategy that allows us to combat each one. I'll mention only four.

Doctrinal Danger . . . substituting the temporal for the eternal. A couple of Scriptures give needed counsel here: ". . . keep seeking the things above, where Christ is . . . . Set your mind on the things above, not on the things that are on earth. . . . And do not be conformed to this world, but be transformed . . . (Col. 3:1–2; Rom. 12:2).

It's important that we understand exactly what we're celebrating. It is our Savior's arrival, not Santa's. The significance of giving presents is to be directly related to God's presenting us the Gift of His Son.

Personal Danger . . . impressing but not imparting. We represent the King. We are His chosen ambassadors, doing His business "in season and out of season." So let's do it this season! People are wide open to the Gospel these days.

Economical Danger . . . spending more than you have. Before every purchase, think: Is this within my budget? Is it appropriate? Is it really saying what I want it to say? And remember, homemade gifts are often more appreciated and much less expensive.

A safe rule to follow is this: If you don't have the cash, don't buy it.

Psychological Danger . . . getting built up for a letdown. One of the most effective maneuvers of the world system is to create a false sense of excitement. The Christian can get "high" very easily on the crest of Christmas, and the afterglow can be a dangerous, depressing experience.

Guard yourself. Keep a firm hand on the controls. Don't be deceived. Enjoy the 25th . . . but not at the expense of the 26th.

If you stay occupied with the Person, you'll seldom have to fight off the plague. Make Hebrews 12:3 your aim: "Consider Him . . . so that you may not grow weary and lose heart."

A Finishing Touch: This Christmas, let's forget about trying to impress others by what we buy and spend more time imparting what we already possess.

A Daily Reading: Luke 1

Christmas comes each year to draw people in from the cold.

Like tiny frightened sparrows, shivering in the winter cold, many live their lives on the barren branches of heartbreak, disappointment, and loneliness, lost in thoughts of shame, self-pity, guilt, or failure. One blustery day follows another, and the only company they keep is with fellow-strugglers who land on the same branches, confused and unprotected.

We try so hard to attract them into the warmth. Week after week church bells ring. Choirs sing. Preachers preach. Lighted churches send out their beacon. But nothing seems to bring in those who need warmth the most.

Then, as the year draws to a close, Christmas offers its wonderful message. Immanuel. God with us. He who resided in Heaven, co-equal and co-eternal with the Father and the Spirit, willingly descended into our world. He breathed our air, felt our pain, knew our sorrows, and died for our sins. He didn't come to frighten us, but to show us the way to warmth and safety.

In spite of this, however, some—in fact, most—still keep their distance. It happened when He first came; it happens to this day.

Nevertheless, Christmas comes again. And again. And again. The story of Bethlehem's babe is told another time. We sing the same carols, return to the same manger, watch the same bewildered couple, Mary and Joseph, as they caress their firstborn, and we stand in awe for the umpteenth time . . . and it never grows old!

Why? Because we all know what it feels like to shiver on the frozen branches of our world, rejected, wounded, and scared . . . because each one of us can remember when we finally flew into the warmth of His love . . . and because we keep hoping that maybe, just maybe, this Christmas will be the one for some sparrow we love to come in from the cold.

For many, Christmas is the loneliest or most depressing time of the year. Families of those in prison—and the prisoners themselves. Single parents. The aged. The hospitalized. The dying and those ministering to them. Men and women in the military. Adults still haunted by frightening memories of their childhood. Recently widowed men and women. Students who can't go home for Christmas.

For most, Christmas can become little more than a selfish, greedy, unsatisfying experience. When gift-buying gets out of control, the season turns into a financial, frustrating frenzy. Instead of slowing our pace, enjoying the lights, drinking in the music, and sitting quietly with those we love, we fall in with the hectic hurry to find this and mail that, allowing it to eclipse the meaning.

For a few, Christmas is the only time they ever hear or think seriously about the Lord Jesus Christ. The carols include some of the finest theology in all of hymnody. The message of the Incarnation is portrayed clearly in dramatic pageants, readings, and special services. Christmas cards are opened and read by those who would never otherwise entertain the Gospel story.

So, this Christmas season I pray that the warmth of the Savior's love will spread itself over you as never before. And that whenever and however possible, you will keep reminding yourself that there are still tiny, shivering sparrows who are too terrified to come in from the cold Maybe, just maybe, this Christmas, because of something you do or say . . . they will.

A Finishing Touch: Pray for those who are lonely or depressed. Whenever possible, reach out to include them. Ask our Lord to touch many hearts through you this season.

A Daily Reading: Luke 2

It's not too early to give some things away this Christmas. Not just on Christmas Day, but during all the days leading up to December 25. We could call these daily gifts "our Christmas projects." Maybe one per day from now 'til then. Here are a few suggestions.

Mend a quarrel.

Seek out a forgotten friend.

Dismiss suspicion.

Write a long overdue love note.

Hug someone tightly and whisper, "I love you so."

Forgive an enemy.

Be gentle and patient with an angry person.

Express appreciation.

Gladden the heart of a child.

Find the time to keep a promise.

Make or bake something for someone else. Anonymously.

Release a grudge.

Listen.

Speak kindly to a stranger.

Enter into another's sorrow.

Smile. Laugh a little. Laugh a little more.

Take a walk with a friend.

Kneel down and pat a dog.

Read a poem or two to your mate or friend.

Lessen your demands on others.

Play some beautiful music during the evening meal.

Apologize if you were wrong.

Turn off the television and talk.

Treat someone to an ice-cream cone (yogurt would be fine).

Do the dishes for the family.

Pray for someone who helped you when you hurt.

Fix breakfast on Saturday morning.

Give a soft answer even though you feel strongly.

Encourage an older person.

Point out one thing you appreciate most about someone you work with or live near.

Offer to baby-sit for a weary mother.

Give your teacher a break: be especially cooperative.

Let's make Christmas one long, extended gift of ourselves to others. Unselfishly. Without announcement. Or obligation. Or reservation. Or hypocrisy.

This is Christianity, isn't it?

A Finishing Touch: When you give yourself, the gift never has to be returned.

A Daily Reading: Matthew 1 and 2

In his album *The Eagle*, country-western singer Waylon Jennings tugs at my heartstrings. One of his tunes, "Old Church Hymns and Nursery Rhymes," takes me back to the simple days of yesteryear and swamps me with nostalgia: "With a child's wisdom, passin' time, / Singin' old church hymns and nursery rhymes."

As another Christmas rolls around, seems to me the nudge of a little "child's wisdom" might help put things in perspective. So this year I've decided to look at everything through the eyes of a child: the holidays, the tree, the lights, the songs, the smells, the brightly colored presents, the decorated houses—everything. Lost in the wonder of it all, I believe a little child would whisper these five simple requests.

Slow down. It's so easy to crank up the car, dash from one store to the next, become frustrated because the thing you had your eye on got sold fifteen minutes ago. A child would say, "So what? Take your time, Mom. There's lots of other stuff. What I want are a few extra minutes with you—just you and me." The special joy of Christmas is spending extra hours with folks you love. That takes time. Rather than talking about how much we'd like to make it happen, why not slow down and do it?

Stay home. Commercial schemes abound during the yuletide season to get you to go somewhere, and it seems everyone is giving a party. A little of that is fine, but I can hear that little child whisper, "Tonight, let's stay home. Let's make popcorn and eat it in front of the fireplace and watch the lights on the tree." Some of the finest music the ear can hear celebrates the holiday season—and the best place to hear it? Even if all you've got is a little apartment and an inexpensive tape player, home is the spot. Children love the security and the solitude of that protected retreat. Guard your time at home this Christmas season.

Tell stories. Storytelling has almost faded from our modern scene. Nevertheless, the child in all of us urges, "Tell me a story." Stories transport us into other worlds with new faces and different streets and exciting surprises. This season, spend at least one evening a week (with the television off) telling stories—and don't forget the original Christmas story.

Have fun. Joy becomes the season. It can be traced back to the fields near the little town of Bethlehem where the angel startled a cluster of shepherds with the happy words, "I bring you good news of a great joy!" Every child loves to play . . . so, play! Let's take our cues from the young and do things that will bring back the joy. Cook a meal together, or make cookies and take them to someone who's stopped smiling, or have an old-fashioned songfest where everybody joins in nice 'n' loud. Go Christmas caroling. Whatever . . . don't forget to have fun.

Give yourself. Sure is easy to substitute store-bought things for the gen-u-ine thing—YOU. Your touch of appreciation. Your listening ear. Your phone call of love. Something you make with your own hands. That's what makes God's gift to us so valuable. On that first Christmas morn, He wrapped himself in human flesh and smiled at us from a manger. His tiny outstretched arms would one day embrace the bruised and brokenhearted. His tears would again stain His face as He wept over us. He didn't hold back. Let your mind run free—like a child—and think of ways to extend expressions of yourself to folks who could use a boost of encouragement.

These suggestions are neither sophisticated nor expensive, but since when do kids care about either? This year, for a change, slow down . . . stay home . . . tell stories . . . have fun . . . give yourself.

Just a little "child's wisdom" to bring us back to the basics. You'll be glad you made this Christmas a child's Christmas!

A Finishing Touch: Christmas strips away the veneer of stacked-up years and brings us back to where we started.

A Daily Reading: Mark 1

Last year a large section of a tree fell not far from where we have lived for over twenty-two years. During those years it became one of the grand landmarks that gave our neighborhood its character as well as a touch of charm.

Nobody saw it happen . . . but within minutes several of us had gathered to grieve the loss. It was a sad sight to see those once-sturdy branches full of leaves now spread awkwardly across the sidewalk and out into a neighbor's lawn.

As I stood there staring in disbelief with the others, the thought struck me, *This happened only minutes ago . . . but it's been in the process of happening for a long, long time.* No tree just suddenly breaks apart.

We tree-lovers had no way of knowing, of course. Not being experts, we just kept driving by. In fact, only a few hours earlier my youngest grandchild and I had strolled by, enjoying the shade and listening to the busy chirping of birds up there among all the leaves.

And then, without announcement, CLUNK! A giant section collapsed and landed like a hundred bags of cement.

Once we were able to see beneath the thick bark inside the break, it was obvious that some kind of killer disease had been at work. Though nobody knew ahead of time, that fall was inevitable. Slowly, silently, secretly, deep within the core of that tall and handsome timber, an erosion was taking place; a "destruction of substance" (Webster) was underway, which could not stay hidden forever. By and by, everyone would see that what looked healthy was only external. The unseen truth was not obvious, but internal decay had been present for years.

The good news is that no one was near when the moment of reckoning arrived. I'm sure a few birds squawked and fluttered to safety, but thankfully, nobody was on the sidewalk or parked under the shade of the old tree.

The city was notified, and within an hour or two they came in their orange trucks with heavy equipment, chain saws, rakes and brooms, and had everything whisked away in no time. I suppose the clean-up crew does that sort of thing every day. They've got it down to a science. Passersby would not even know anything unusual had happened if they weren't familiar with how things had been before. Cleaning up after a fallen tree is a rather quick and efficient matter.

Not so with a fallen life.

Unlike trees, people don't grow up all alone or exist in a world of stoic and hard independence. We mingle and we merge into one another's lives. Sometimes we even bleed together. Neither our laughter nor our tears remain aloof. We lean on each other, our roots get intertwined, the fruit we bear gets mutually enjoyed, and because we care for one another, we don't hold back. Within a matter of time, we become so interwoven, we can hardly imagine life without one another.

All the while there is a healthy and appropriate respect for each other. This includes respect for one another's privacy. After all, there is a limit to how close friendships ought to get. Outside of marriage, nobody expects to be inseparably linked to someone else . . . and so we back off, trusting one another in realms too personal and intimate to share. We appreciate each other, which includes allowing one another space.

But herein lies "the rub," for it is in this unmentionable realm, this altogether personal region of intimacy, that trouble begins. A core disease in the thought-life goes unnoticed and untreated. A tragic inner erosion begins its downward path toward destruction. No one knows that the pulp behind our wholesome, healthy looking bark is neither wholesome nor healthy.

Furthermore, no one feels the freedom to come close to warn us that, as F. B. Meyer writes, "sin is dark, dangerous, damnable," for there is no sign of disease. No one realizes that the vulture feeding on the vitals is a nestling of our own rearing. And so the erosion continues its slow, silent, secret process.

Years pass.

And then one day—like that leafy giant at the end of our block— there is a sudden collapse, a terrible break, that allows everyone to see what no one expected. But because fallen people are not like fallen trees, many around the fallen one are always injured. A family, a circle of friends, a body of fellow believers, a group of distant admirers, a watching world . . . like concentric ripples following a rock dropped into a placid lake, the list of those injured goes on and on.

And the clean-up is never efficient. In fact, there is no crew to remove the evidence and sweep away the debris, so the damage lingers . . . sometimes for years.

I think we can learn several things from this analogy between our lives and the tree that fell in Fullerton.

First: A good start doesn't necessarily assure us of a strong finish. Not even if we stand tall and handsome. Not even if we still produce fruit.

Second: Erosion could be at work, even though the bark looks healthy and the fruit tastes good. Don't be fooled by attractive bark, branches, and leaves.

Third: Strength comes from deep within. Attend to what's not seen. Invite a few to keep watch over your pulp. Welcome their questions. Be grateful for their concern. Hide nothing . . . not even the uglies inside your head.

Fourth: Never try to convince yourself that a fall—your fall—won't hurt anyone all that much. More people than you will ever know admire you and trust you from a distance. If you collapse, they *will* be injured.

And just in case you may be feeling a bit smug, thinking, "I'm sure glad you wrote about this, Chuck. So and so needs to read it," hear and heed this warning: "Let him who thinks he stands take heed lest he fall!"

A Finishing Touch: Truly, "man looks at the outward appearance, but the Lord looks at the heart" (1 Sam. 16:7).
A Daily Reading: 1 Corinthians 10:11–13

When I think of fallen people, my mind returns to an ancient example: King Saul, the tall, dark, handsome monarch of the Hebrews. What an impressive specimen of humanity! He was the one of whom the Lord had said to Samuel, "Behold the man of whom I spoke to you! This one shall rule over My people" (1 Sam. 9:17).

With humility and genuine reluctance Saul accepted the appointment, acknowledged God's anointing, and graciously stood before the cheering masses as Samuel announced:

> "Do you see him whom the Lord has chosen? Surely there is no one like him among all the people." So all the people shouted and said, "Long live the king!" (1 Sam. 10:24).

To save you pages of reading and a long, depressing list of facts, let me hurry to the dismal end of Saul's story where the man takes his own life. Observing the scene, David wrote a song of grievous lyrics as he lamented:

> "How have the might fallen in the midst of the battle! . . . How have the mighty fallen!" (2 Sam. 1:25–27).

Like the sickening sound of an enormous tree plunging to the ground, Saul fell, and anyone caring enough to look inside his life can analyze why. He became diseased to the core. An erosion of character went on, unchecked, a "destruction of substance," which took a dreadful toll on the man who once stood tall.

Someday, when you die, someone will speak for you and sing of you. Think about what you'd like them to say and sing on that day in the future. Then live like it today.

THE SECRET PLACE

The psalmist said, "He who dwells in the shelter of the Most High will abide in the shadow of the Almighty" (Ps. 91:1).

Do you have a place of shelter where you seek only His face? Do you spend time in that secret place?

Have you given prayer the priority it deserves? And when you pray, do you remember that it is the Lord's face you seek?

It is possible to be engaged in the work of ministry, in the work of the church, yet be in secret very, very seldom. There is this great tendency to think our best work is done at our desk or on our feet . . . but it's really done on our knees.

It is easy to become so caught up in people's needs (which are endless and usually urgent) and to be so preoccupied with meeting those needs that we miss "the shelter of the Most High."

It is so easy to emphasize all the involvements of being with people, rather than being alone in a secret place with Him. And I do mean *alone* with God, as though there is not another care, another need, another person . . . only "the Almighty."

In the last year and a half, maybe two, I have begun to realize the value of this. As a result of time invested in the secret place we gain an invincible sense of God's direction and the reassurance of His hand on our lives, along with an increased sensitivity regarding iniquity in our lives.

Being alone with God is not complicated, but it is tough to maintain. Nevertheless, we need secrecy, especially in this hyperactive, noisy, busy world of ours.

Consider the beauty, the wonder, the magnificence, the awe-inspiring times of praise in the secret place! There is nothing to be compared to it. As great as corporate worship may be, with a magnificent pipe organ and full orchestra and a congregation singing at full volume, it cannot compare to the secret place where our best work is done and where God's best work is accomplished in us.

I am fully convinced that doing justice and loving kindness and walking humbling with our God simply cannot happen without sufficient time in the secret place.

When Jesus was instructing His disciples regarding prayer, He said, "Pray to your Father who is in secret, and your Father who sees in secret will repay you" (Matt. 6:6).

A Finishing Touch: Our best work is done on our knees.
A Daily Reading: Psalm 27:8; Psalm 91:1

Back in 1958 when I was a young Marine stationed on the island of Okinawa, I became closely associated with a man I deeply admired. His name was Bob Newkirk.

I didn't know what it was exactly that first drew me to Bob. More than anything else, I guess, there was something refreshingly unpretentious about him. He was devoted to the things of the Lord, no question, but it was never on parade, never for the purpose of public display. And I loved that.

Perhaps it was his balanced Christian life that I admired most. He was serving back then with The Navigators, an international Christian organization committed to ministering to military personnel. However, he never tried to squeeze me into some Navigator mold. I liked that especially.

When we worked, we worked hard. But when we played, we had a first-class blast.

I never got the idea that Bob was interested in making big impressions on me or other people. He was what he was, plain and simple—far from perfect, but authentic. Real.

I remember dropping by his home late one rainy afternoon to pay an unexpected visit. His wife met me at the door and informed me that he was not home.

She added, "You've probably noticed lately that he has been under some stress. I think he may be down at his office. I'm not really sure. But he told me he just wanted to get alone."

I decided to try Bob's office, a little spot down in Naha. I caught the three-wheel jitney that took me from the village where the Newkirks lived down to the capital city of the island. It was still raining lightly, so I stepped around and over the puddles as I made my way down a street, across an alley, then another alley until I came upon his unassuming, modest office.

Before I arrived, however, I could hear singing in the distance . . . "Come, Thou Fount of every blessing, tune my heart to sing Thy grace."

It was Bob's voice! I'd know it anywhere.

I stood outside in the rain for a few moments, listening, as my friend continued singing the simple hymn. Then, I confess, I peeked in the window and saw a candle on a table, my friend on his knees, and not another soul around. He was spending time with the Lord . . . all alone.

As I stood outside, the soft-falling rain dripping off my nose and ears, my eyes filled with tears of gratitude. Bob never knew I came by that evening, but without his knowing it, I got a glimpse of authentic Christianity that night. Not piety on parade . . . not spiritual showtime, but a man "in the shelter of the Most High."

In the back streets of Naha I learned more about simple faith than I would later learn in four years of seminary.

A Finishing Touch: When it comes to faith, there is no substitute for the real thing.

A Daily Reading: Galatians 2:20

Several years ago my family and I were invited to spend Thanksgiving weekend at a picturesque ski resort in Colorado with about five hundred single young adults, most of whom were staff personnel with Campus Crusade. I spoke all week on the subject of servanthood, emphasizing the importance of believers being those who help, encourage, affirm, and care for others.

By Friday of that week I decided to take a break and hit the slopes (emphasis on *hit*, since it was the first time I had ever attempted to ski). It had snowed all day Thanksgiving, so the ski areas were absolutely beautiful and in perfect condition. I struck out on my virgin voyage with a positive mental attitude, thinking, "I'm going to be the first person who learns to ski without falling down. *Guinness Book of World Records* will hear of this and write me up!"

Don't bother to check. I'm not in the book.

It was unbelievable! It is doubtful that anyone else on planet earth has ever come down any ski slope more ways than I did. Or landed in more positions. Or did more creative things in the air before landing.

Working with me that humiliating day was the world's most encouraging ski instructor (yes, I had an instructor!) who set the new world record in patience. She is the one Guinness needs to interview.

Never once did she lose her cool.

Never once did she laugh at me.

Never once did she yell, scream, threaten, or swear.

Never once did she call me "dummy."

Never once did she say, "You are absolutely impossible. I quit!"

That dear, gracious lady helped me up more times than I can number. She repeated the same basics time and again—like she had never said them before. Even though I was colder than an explorer in the Antarctic, irritable, impatient, and under the snow more than I was on it, she kept offering words of reassurance. On top of all that, she didn't even charge me for those hours on the baby slope when she could have been enjoying the day with all her friends on the fabulous, long slope up above.

That day God gave me a living, never-to-be-forgotten illustration of the value of encouragement. Had it not been for her spirit and her words, believe me, I would have been back in the condo, warming my feet by the fire, in less than an hour.

What is true for a novice on the snow once a year is all the more true for the people we meet every day. Harassed by demands and deadlines; bruised by worry, adversity, and failure; broken by disillusionment; and defeated by sin, they live somewhere between dull discouragement and sheer panic.

Even Christians are not immune! We may give off this "I've got it all together" air of confidence, much like I did when I first snapped on the skis. But realistically, we also struggle, lose our balance, slip and slide, tumble, and fall flat on our faces.

All of us need encouragement. All of us need somebody to believe in us. To reassure and reinforce us. To help us pick up the pieces and go on. To provide us with increased determination in spite of the odds.

We all need encouragement . . . and we all need to be encouragers.

A Finishing Touch: The beautiful thing about encouragement is that anybody can do it.

A Daily Reading: Hebrews 10:19–25

Ours is a tough, rugged, wicked world. Aggression, rebellion, violence, cutthroat competition, and retaliation abound. Not just internationally, but personally. What is true in the secret council chambers of nations is also true behind closed doors of homes. We are stubborn, warring people. Outside of riots and war, studies have concluded, the most dangerous place to be is in the American home! With domestic violence and child abuse on the rise in our hard, hostile society, one might wonder what possible influence the servants of Christ can be.

What impact—how much clout—do the poor in spirit, the gentle, the merciful, the pure in heart, or the peacemakers actually have? Such feeble-sounding virtues seem about as effective as pillow fighting in a nuclear war.

Especially with the odds stacked against us. Servants of Jesus Christ will always be in the minority . . . a small remnant surrounded by a strong-minded majority with their fists clenched.

Can our presence do much good? Isn't it pretty much a wasted effort?

Jesus, the One who first painted the servant's portrait, both in words and with His own life, did not share this skepticism. But neither did He deny the battle. Don't forget the final touches He put on that inspired canvas. Remember these words! They make it clear that society is a combat zone not a vacation spot.

> Blessed are those who have been persecuted for the sake of righteousness, for theirs is the kingdom of heaven.
>
> Blessed are you when men revile you, and persecute you, and say all kinds of evil against you falsely, on account of Me.
>
> Rejoice, and be glad, for your reward in heaven is great, for so they persecuted the prophets who were before you (Matt. 5:10–12).

No. Our Lord never promised us a rose garden. He came right up front with us and admitted that the arena of this world is not a friend of grace to help us on to God.

Nevertheless, strange as it may seem, He went on to tell that handful of Palestinian peasants (and *all* godly servants in every generation) that their influence would be nothing short of remarkable. They would be "the salt of the earth" and they would be "the light of the world." And so shall we!

So far-reaching would be the influence of His servants in society that their presence would be as significant as salt on food and as light on darkness. Neither is loud or externally impressive, but both are essential.

Without our influence this old world would soon begin to realize our absence. Even though it may not admit it, society needs both salt and light.

A Finishing Touch: God has called us to be light-and-salt servants in a dark-and-bland society.

A Daily Reading: Matthew 6:1–16

During my growing-up years in East Houston, I didn't entertain many fantasies. Life was simple for the three Swindoll kids, especially for me, the baby in the family. Chores were clearly defined: I was to empty the wastepaper baskets every day, mop the kitchen and bathroom floors twice a week, mow and trim the yard once a week, and of course keep my side of the room I shared with my older brother picked up, my bed made, and my clothes hung up. Things were not fancy at our place, but they were tidy. My sister and I took turns doing the dishes, and when it came time to wax the hardwood floors, the whole tribe pitched in. That was only a couple of times a year . . . usually before the Fourth of July and between Thanksgiving and Christmas

My mother liked to have folks over for the holidays, during which time she would whip up a few pies to go along with a table full of food she served. We'd end those times standing around the piano harmonizing, laughing, and generally having a ton of fun.

One particular Christmas season I began to drop hints on how great it would be to get a new rubber basketball. That was the time I was in about the eighth grade and the world of athletics was opening up before my eyes. I played basketball on the "B" team at my junior high school, and I was improving rapidly.

My dad, who worked in a machine shop, had made me an iron hoop which we screwed onto the garage out back. Actually, the diameter was smaller than regular basketball hoops in the gym, but my dad convinced me mine was better. "Son, if you can put the ball through this hoop, you won't have any trouble shooting it through the ones at school." Clever salesmanship to cover his mistake, but I bought it. It got to where I could sink nine out of ten free throws, plus I had a hummer of a two-hand set shot that led me to believe every college in the country would be hunting me down in a few years. We're talking major fantasy here, but that's the kind of stuff boys imagine when they play ball out back until dark.

Suddenly, one raw November evening, my old tattered basketball, which a neighbor had given me, burst. I had already patched the thing twice, which made it bounce funny, making one more patch out of the question. That's when the hints began. And during the next six weeks I made sure that I got in my comment, especially at suppertime.

Now, you need to understand something. My mother didn't know zip about sports. She was the type who would ask in the middle of a crucial football game being broadcast over the radio, "What inning is it?" or "Why are all those people screaming?" She was a classy, cultured lady whose idea of a well-rounded education included an appreciation of the arts and a good grip on social skills, but a fifteen-foot jump shot? Get serious. So I knew if I would ever see a new round ball under our Christmas tree, I would have to turn it on thick. If ol' Santa was gonna come through, I was committed to all nice and no naughty until the big day arrived.

The bathroom and kitchen got a daily mopping. The lawn began to resemble the greens at Augusta. I was borderline neurotic about every wastepaper basket in the house, and the trash cans got put out front a day early. The dishes? You would have thought we were getting ready to pass a White House inspection. I even set the table every evening. It was shades of the Ritz-Carlton on Quince Street in Houston. I mean, how many junior highers do you know who have dishpan hands? I even volunteered to wax the floor alone.

And then it happened. One evening when my folks had a living room full of company, what should my wandering eye observe beneath a thousand icicles but a BOX. A brightly wrapped, correctly shaped BOX . . . with guess whose name on it? You are exactly right, young CRS. It was exciting enough to make me applaud my brother's performance at the piano, clearly a first.

Christmas Day never arrived so slowly, but finally it dawned. While no one was looking, I had shaken the BOX enough to know that it had to contain what I had been wanting so badly—right size, right weight, everything. When my turn came, I lunged for it like a hungry bear grabbing a salmon. I tore at the wrapping and ribbon, pulled open the top, and to my disbelieving eyes there it was . . . *a world globe.*

Looking up at me was Italy. No, I thought, *not a chance*. But it was. The exact size, shape, and weight of a basketball, but a WORLD GLOBE! Have you ever tried to dribble a world globe? Trust me, not even the time-honored, two-hand set shot will drop.

What a thrill! All Christmas afternoon I had the joy of locating geographical spots my mom would call out . . . Singapore, Latvia, Montreal, New Zealand, the Amazon, Moscow, Delhi. I kept thinking I'd wake up the next morning and the Rand McNally logo would read Voit or Rawlings, but it never happened. That was as much a fantasy as my playing hotshot ball one day for some big-time school.

Many, many Christmases have slipped past since those simple days on Quince Street. As I drove by the old place some time ago, now an older, run-down part of the city, I realized how much has changed. The old hoop, now rusty, still hangs from a mildew-covered garage. The lawn, once thick and green and manicured, is now choked with weeds. The beautiful notes from an upright piano no longer drift across the neighborhood. And the laughter that filled those rooms? It, too, is silenced, at least in that little house. My mother and dad have gone home, leaving only the legacy of strong faith and sweet memories, which Christmas always revives.

And today, while I still enjoy watching basketball, what really excites me is not a hoop and a ball but hope on a globe . . . where people in places like Singapore and Moscow, Delhi and Montreal will hear the story of a Savior who came into the world to save people of every tongue and tribe and nation from their sins.

Could she have known? I do wonder. Little did I realize that my mother's vision would one day eclipse a boy's Christmas fantasy and become his personal reality.

A Finishing Touch: We never know when our disappointment will be His appointment.

A Daily Reading: Isaiah 9:1–7

This season, beneath many a tree are brightly wrapped surprises, some of which will seem momentarily disappointing to a little boy or girl. There will be a book instead of a game, a dress instead of a doll, a globe instead of a ball.

But time will put it all in perspective . . . and many a mother's vision for her child will one day replace his fantasy. I know. It happened to me.

Think about your own Christmas memories. Any disappointments among the bunch? How do they look to you now?

"A word fitly spoken," wrote the wise Solomon, "is like apples of gold in settings of silver" (Prov. 25:11 KJV).

Like Jell-O, concepts assume the mold of the words into which they are poured. Who has not been stabbed awake by the use of a particular word . . . or combination of words? Who has not found relief from a well-timed word spoken at the precise moment of need? Who has not been crushed beneath the weight of an ill-chosen word? And who has not gathered fresh courage because a word of hope penetrated the fog of self-doubt? The word *word* remains the most powerful of all four-letter words.

Colors fade. Shorelines erode. Temples crumble. Empires fall. But "a word fitly spoken" endures.

Fitly spoken words are *right* words . . . the precise words needed for the occasion.

Mark Twain, a unique wordsmith himself, once wrote: "The difference between the right word and almost the right word is the difference between lightning and a lightning bug."

And what power those "right words" contain! Some punch like a jab to the jaw, others comfort like a down pillow, still others threaten like the cold, steel barrel of a .38 Smith and Wesson.

One set of words purifies our thoughts, transplanting us, at least for an instant, to the throne room of God; another set of words ignites lust, tempting us to visit the house of a harlot. Some words bring tears to our eyes in a matter of seconds; others bring fear that makes the hair on the back of our necks stand on end.

Now, let's return again to more choice words from the pen of Solomon.

> In addition to being a wise man, the Preacher also taught the people knowledge; and he pondered, searched out and arranged

many proverbs. The Preacher sought to find delightful words and to write words of truth correctly.

The words of wise men are like goads, and masters of these collections are like well-driven nails; they are given by one Shepherd (Eccl. 12:9–11).

I love that! The man deliberately sought out "delightful" words (the Hebrew here is colorful: words that find favor, are easily grasped, readily digested), knowing that they are like "goads" (prodding, pushing us on) and "well-driven nails." Beautiful . . . and so true.

J. B. Phillips correctly assessed the impact of such words when he wrote: "If . . . words are to enter men's hearts and bear fruit, they must be the right words shaped cunningly to pass men's defenses and explode silently and effectually within their minds."

The finest examples of that are the words and phrases of Jesus Christ. His choice of words. His placement of words. His economy of words. Even His eloquent turn of a phrase. The life-changing message of Jesus

Being the ultimate wordsmith, Jesus wrapped up some of His most significant words in a brief statement we commonly call the Golden Rule: "Therefore, however you want people to treat you, so treat them, for this is the Law and the Prophets" (Matt. 7:12).

What a classic example of "apples of gold in settings of silver."

A Finishing Touch: Are your words fitly spoken?
A Daily Reading: Ecclesiastes 12:9–14

> Therefore, however you want people to treat you, so treat them,
> for this is the Law and the Prophets (Matt. 7:12).

That single sentence is perhaps the most universally famous statement Jesus ever made. It is "the Everest of Ethics," as one man put it.

In some ways it is the cornerstone of true Christianity, certainly the capstone of Jesus' Sermon on the Mount.

I appreciate the positive emphasis. Instead of saying, "Don't do this," He says, "Do this."

If you have wondered about how to get started in a lifetime of simple faith, here it is.

The principle? *Modeling must accompany our message.*

You want to be forgiven. Forgive.

You need affirmation? Affirm.

You feel hurt, wounded, broken, and could stand a gentle touch? Be gentle with others.

You have discovered the value of tact when something sensitive needed to be addressed? Be tactful.

The examples are endless. Unfortunately, models of such great-hearted behavior are rare. Is it any wonder the non-Christian world looks with suspicion in our direction?

The best part of the whole principle? It is so simple. Living by the Golden Rule prevents the need for laying down an endless list of little rules and regulations to govern conduct. Just put yourself in the other person's place and think, *What is it I would need if I were him or her?* And then? Do it. When you do, you will fulfill the essence of "the Law and the Prophets."

Do you know the greatest message we can deliver? It is the message of Christlike character. No message on earth is more needed or more powerful.

You want to impact your family, your church, your community, your place of employment? You want to make a difference in the life of your mate, a family member, a friend (Christian or not), some person in the workplace? Demonstrate the characteristics of Christ.

It has been said that the only Bible most folks ever read is the daily life of the Christian. If that is true, I believe the world needs a *revised version*. Our problem is not that too many of us are being ignored, it's that we are all being observed!

A Finishing Touch: Words fitly spoken are powerful, but they are nothing compared to the power of a life fitly lived.

A Daily Reading: Matthew 5

Yourself. Yourself. Yourself. We're up to here with self!

Do something either *for* yourself or *with* yourself or *to* yourself.

How very different from Jesus' model and message! Instead of a "philosophy" to turn out eyes inward, He offers a fresh and much-needed invitation to our "me-first" generation. There is a better way, Jesus says. "Be a servant. Give to others!" Now that's a philosophy that anybody can understand. And, without question, it is attainable. Just listen:

> Do nothing from selfishness or empty conceit, but with humil-ity of mind let each of you regard one another as more impor-tant than himself; do not merely look out for your own personal interests, but also for the interests of others (Phil. 2:3–4).

Know what all that means? Well, for starters, "nothing" means just that. Stop permitting two strong tendencies—selfishness and conceit—to control you! Let nothing either of them suggests win a hearing. Replace them with "humility of mind."

But how?

By regarding others as more important than yourself.

Look for ways to support, encourage, build up, and stimulate the other person. And that requires an attitude that would rather give than receive.

"Humility of mind" is really an attitude, isn't it? It's a preset men-tality that determines ahead of time thoughts like this:

I care about those around me.

Why do I always have to be first? I'm going to help someone else win for a change.

Today, it's my sincere desire to curb my own fierce competitive tendencies and turn that energy into encouraging at least one other person.

I willingly release my way this day. Lord, show me how You would respond to others, then make it happen to me.

To get started in this unselfish lifestyle, let me suggest three basic ingredients: giving, forgiving, and forgetting.

Once we make up our minds to implement the truth of Philippians 2:3–4 (taking a special interest in others) or Galatians 5:13 (serving others in love), those three basics will begin to emerge.

Instead of always thinking about receiving, we'll start looking for ways to give.

Instead of holding grudges against those who have offended us, we'll be anxious to forgive.

And instead of keeping a record of what we've done or who we've helped, we'll take delight in forgetting the deed(s) and being virtually unnoticed.

A Finishing Touch: It is impossible to give yourself at arm's length.

A Daily Reading: Romans 12:10–13

Do you know which sin is the subtle enemy of simple faith?

Materialism and greed? Anger? Lust? Hypocrisy? No. All of these sins are certainly our enemies, but none of them qualify as *subtle* enemies.

Stop and think. Once you decide to trust God in simple faith and allow Him complete freedom to carry out His plan and purpose in you, as well as through you, you need only to relax and count on Him to take care of things you once tried to keep under control.

From now on you won't step in and take charge. "God is well able to handle this," you tell yourself. Then, in a weak moment, the adversary of your soul whispers a doubt or two in your ear, like, "Hey, what if—?" If that doesn't make you churn, he returns in the middle of the night and fertilizes your imagination with several quasi-extreme possibilities, leaving you mildly disturbed if not altogether panicked. No one can tell by looking (and you certainly wouldn't think of *telling* anyone), but in place of your inward peace and simple faith, you are now immobilized by . . . what?

You guessed it, the most notorious faith killer in all of life: *worry*.

> For this reason I say to you, do not be anxious for your life, as to what you shall eat, or what you shall drink; nor for your body, as to what you shall put on. Is not life more than food, and the body than clothing? (Matt. 6:25).

Being something of a wordsmith, I find the term "worry" fascinating, though the reality of this in our lives can be downright maddening. To begin with, the word used by Matthew (translated here as "anxiety" and "anxious") is the Greek term *merimnao*. it is a combination of two smaller words, *merizo*, meaning "to divide," and *nous*, meaning "the mind." In other words, a person who is anxious suffers from a divided mind, leaving him or her disquieted and distracted.

Of all the biblical stories illustrating *worry*, none is more practical or clear than the one recorded in the last five verses of Luke 10. Let's briefly relive it.

Jesus dropped by His friends' home in Bethany. He was, no doubt, tired after a full day, so nothing meant more to Him than having a quiet place to relax with friends who would understand. However, Martha, one of those friends, turned the occasion into a mild frenzy. To make matters worse, Martha's sister, Mary, was so pleased to have the Lord visit their home that she sat with Him and evidenced little concern over her sister's anxiety attack.

As Luke tells us, "Martha was distracted with all her preparations" (Luke 10:40). We can imagine her scurrying around the kitchen, kneading dough, basting the lamb, boiling the vegetables, trying to locate her best dishes, hoping to match tablecloth and napkins, ultimately needing help to get it all ready at the proper time. But Martha didn't have help, and that was the final straw. Irritated, exasperated, and angry, she reached her boiling point; and her boiling point led to blame. "Lord, do You not care that my sister has left me to do all the serving alone? Then tell her to help me" (10:40).

But Jesus was neither impressed by her busyness nor intimidated by her command. Graciously, yet firmly, He said, "Martha, Martha, you are worried and bothered about so many things; but only a few things are necessary, really only one, for Mary has chosen the good part, which shall not be taken away from her" (10:41-42).

Worry occurs when we assume responsibility for things that are outside our control. And I love the Lord's solution: "only a few things are necessary, really only one." What a classic example of simple faith!

Martha had complicated things by turning the meal into a holiday feast. Not Mary. All Mary wanted was time with Jesus . . . and He commended her for that. Mary's simple faith, in contrast to her sister's panic, won the Savior's affirmation.

A Finishing Touch: Worry and faith just don't mix.
A Daily Reading: Matthew 6:25, 33–34; Luke 10:38–41

One of the great doctrines of Christianity is our belief in a heavenly home. Ultimately, we shall spend eternity with God in the place He has prepared for us. And part of that exciting anticipation is His promise to reward His servants for a job well done. Scripture not only supports the idea of eternal rewards, it spells out the specifics. I find three primary facts about rewards in 1 Corinthians 3:10–14.

Most rewards are received in heaven, not on earth. Now don't misunderstand. There are earthly rewards. But when it comes to servanthood, God reserves special honor for that day when "each man's work will become evident" and "he shall receive a reward" (3:13–14).

All rewards are based on quality, not quantity. We humans are impressed with size and volume and noise and numbers. It is easy to forget that God's eye is always on motive. When He rewards servants, it will be based on *quality*—which means everybody has an equal opportunity to receive a reward. The elderly woman who prays before an audience of one will be rewarded as much as the evangelist who preaches before an audience of thousands.

No reward that is postponed will be forgotten. God doesn't settle His accounts at the end of every day. Nor does He close out His books toward the end of everyone's life. But when that day in eternity dawns, when time shall be no more on this earth, no act of serving others— be it well-known or unknown to others—will be forgotten. Unlike many people today, God keeps His promises.

Someone once counted all the promises in the Bible and came up with an amazing figure of almost 7500. Among that large number are some specific promises servants can claim today. Believe me, there are times when the only thing that will keep you going is a promise from God that your work is not in vain.

When we have done what was needed, but were ignored, misunderstood, or forgotten . . . we can be sure it was not in vain.

When we did what was right, with the right motive, but received no credit, no acknowledgment, not even a "thank you" . . . we have God's promise that "we shall reap."

When any servant has served and given and sacrificed and then willingly stepped aside for God to receive the glory, our heavenly Father promises he will receive back.

Among the temporal rewards we will receive is the *quiet awareness that the life of Christ is being modeled.* I know of few more satisfying and encouraging rewards than the realization that our actions are visible expressions of Christ to others.

Another temporal reward is the *joyful realization that a thankful spirit is being stimulated.* "All this is for your benefit, so that the grace that is reaching more and more people may cause thanksgiving to overflow to the glory of God" (2 Cor. 4:15 NIV).

And then there are the eternal rewards. Some of them are referred to as "crowns" that are being set aside for God's servants. The Bible speaks of at least five crowns.

The imperishable crown (1 Cor. 9:24–27). This reward will be awarded to those believers who consistently bring the flesh under the Holy Spirit's control and refuse to be enslaved by their sinful nature.

The crown of exultation (Phil 4:1; 1 Thess. 2:19–20). Our Lord will distribute this crown to those servants who are faithful to declare the gospel, lead souls to Christ, and built them up in Him.

The crown of righteousness (2 Tim. 4:7–8). The crown of righteousness will be awarded to those who live each day with eternity's values in view, anticipating Christ's imminent return.

The crown of life (James 1:12). This crown is promised not to those who simply endure suffering and trials, but to those who endure their trials, loving the Savior all the way.

The crown of glory (1 Pet. 5:1–4). This reward is promised to those who faithfully "shepherd the flock" in keeping with the requirements spelled out in verses 2 and 3.

What a scene! All God's servants before His throne.

Are they strutting around heaven displaying their crowns?

No.

The servants are bowing in worship, having cast all crowns before their Lord in adoration and praise, ascribing worth and honor to the only One deserving of praise—the Lord God!

A Finishing Touch: God alone is perfectly and consistently just. We forget; God remembers. We see an action; God sees a motive. This qualifies Him as the best record keeper and judge.

A Daily Reading: 2 Corinthians 3:10–14

We have reached the end of another year and now face a new one. When we stood in this same spot 364 days ago, we looked ahead to what the Lord was going to teach us in the coming year and we anticipated the many ways we were going to see Him at work in our lives.

We said, "By the end of this year we will discover that God had wondrous things for us which we would never have known or experienced had we not accepted the challenge changes inevitably bring."

Today, as you look back over the past weeks and months, what do you see? How have His grace, joy, and love touched your life?

When we began the year, we also talked about finishing well. The reality is, of course, we are not finished. The race is not over. Our lives are still being perfected. We still need much more of the Master's touch.

> Wherefore seeing we also are compassed about with so great a cloud of witnesses, let us lay aside every weight, and the sin which doth so easily beset us, and let us run with patience the race that is set before us, looking unto Jesus the author and finisher of our faith . . . (Heb. 12:1–2 KJV).

ACKNOWLEDGMENTS

Grateful acknowledgment is made to the following authors, publishers, and other copyright holders for permission to reprint copyrighted material:

Christopher Bacorn, "Dear Dads, Save Your Sons," from "My Turn" column, *Newsweek*, December 7, 1992, © 1992 by Newsweek, Inc. All rights reserved. Reprinted by permission.

"Gaelic Blessing," words adapted by John Rutter from an old Gaelic rune, © 1978 by the Royal School of Church Music. All rights reserved. Reprinted by permission.

John Leax, "At the Winter Feeder," from *The Task of Adam*, © 1984 by John Leax. Used by permission.

Virginia Brasier, "Time of the Mad Atom," from *Of Quarks, Quasars, and Other Quirks*, collected by Sara and John E. Brewton and John Brewton Blackburn, © 1977 by John E. Brewton and John Brewton Blackburn, published by Thomas Y. Crowell Company. Used by permission.

Anne Morrow Lindbergh, *Gift from the Sea*, © 1978 by Anne Morrow Lindbergh, published by Random House, Inc. Used by permission.

Todd Phiphers, *The Denver Post*. Used by permission.

Daniel E. Weiss, *One Hundred Percent American*, © 1988 by Daniel E. Weiss, published by Poseidon Press. Used by permission.

John Powell, S.J., *Fully Human, Fully Alive*, © 1976 by Tabor Publishing, Allen, Texas 75002. Used by permission.

Calvin Miller and Stephen R. Lawhead from *Reality and the Vision*, Philip Yancey, Editor, © 1990 by The Chrysostom Society, published by Word Publishing.

Zean Carney, *The Banner-Press*, David City, Nebraska. Used by permission.

Robert Pirsig, *Zen and the Art of Motorcycle Maintenance*, © 1984 by Robert Pirsig, published by Bantam. Used by permission.

United Technologies, "Decisions, Decisions" and "Do It Now," advertisements in *The Wall Street Journal*, © United Technologies. Used by permission.